Creators of the
Jewish Experience
in the Modern World

The B'nai B'rith History of the Jewish People
was first published during the years 1959–1964
as the B'nai B'rith Great Book Series.
The present edition, in five volumes,
has been selected to be part of the B'nai B'rith Judaica Library.
The Library is sponsored by the
B'nai B'rith International Commission on Adult Jewish Education
in an effort to promote a greater popular understanding
of Judaism and the Jewish tradition.
The volumes in the series are:

Creators of the Jewish Experience in Ancient and Medieval Times
Creators of the Jewish Experience in the Modern World
Concepts that Distinguish Judaism
Great Jewish Thinkers of the Twentieth Century
Contemporary Jewish Thought

The B'nai B'rith History of the Jewish People

CREATORS OF THE JEWISH EXPERIENCE
IN THE MODERN WORLD

Edited with introductory notes by
Simon Noveck

Annotated bibliographies by
Michael Neiditch

B'nai B'rith Books
Washington, D.C.

Jerusalem • London • Paris • Buenos Aires • East Sydney

Library of Congress Cataloging in Publication Data

Creators of the Jewish experience in the modern world.

Bibliography: p.   Includes index.
1. Jews—Biography. 2. Rabbis—Biography. 3. Zionists—Biography
I. Noveck, Simon
DS115.C74 1985   920′.0092924   85-72298
ISBN 0-910250-04-9   ISBN 0-910250-05-7 (pbk.)

Contents

Introduction

The towering achievement in publishing by the B'nai B'rith International Commission on Adult Jewish Education has been, to this date, the B'nai B'rith Great Book Series edited for four volumes by Simon Noveck and for the fifth by Abraham Ezra Millgram. These books, as Rabbi Noveck described, presented "the inner-content of Jewish tradition, the great personalities and thinkers, the ideas, beliefs and religious movements of Judaism." In short, they are a *History of the Jewish People*. The nearly fifty scholars, teachers, and rabbis who contributed original essays to these volumes were a preponderant majority of the great interpreters of Jewish civilization at mid-century. Twenty-five years after they began to appear, the freshness and vigor of each essay is undiminished.

The continuing demand for each of the volumes by colleges and universities, synagogues and day schools, is being met by this revised edition. The essays are presented as they originally appeared, though for greater clarity the volumes themselves have been retitled and the series renamed. It was my belief that this new edition would enjoy a greater utility if each of the essays were supplemented by annotated bibliographies that reviewed the literature relevant to the subjects of the essays. Three distinguished scholars and teachers have joined me in the preparation of these bibliographies: Steven T. Katz of Cornell University, Reuven Kimelman of Brandeis University and Arthur Kurzweil, the noted author and lecturer. Each of us benefitted as students from this series, and the opportunity to enhance its value has brought us much satisfaction.

The American journalist George Will recently wrote of the growing rootlessness of our lives, our failure to connect to our past and our neglect of our legacy of a shared and valuable civilization. He was addressing himself to the inadequacies of the American educational system as it teaches the essence of Western civilization, but his point applies with a special urgency to the demands of a sound Jewish education. He chose, quite fortuitously, a Biblical example to illustrate his argument:

> In 1940, a British officer on Dunkirk beach flashed to London a three-word message, "But if not. . . ." It was instantly recognized as a quotation from the Book of Daniel, where Nebuchadnezzar commands Shadrach, Meshach and Abednego to worship the golden image or be thrust into the fiery furnace. They reply defiantly; "If our God whom we serve is able to deliver us, he will deliver us from the fiery furnace, and out of thy hand, O king. But if not, be it known unto thee, O king, that we will not serve thy gods, nor worship the golden image which thou hast set up."

The message from Dunkirk is stirring evidence of a community deriving cohesion, inspiration and courage from a shared history. The question this story raises is how many of us today could either receive or transmit such a message from the rich legacy of Jewish civilization?

B'nai B'rith International through its Commission on Adult Jewish Education is sponsoring the republication of these volumes in the belief that they can play a large role in stimulating a desire to learn about Judaism, Jewish history and Jewish civilization, and that of themselves they are superb examples of the living Jewish tradition.

The joy of being a Jew is not derived from books. It is a product of a rich family life wherein Judaism radiates a happiness and contentment that passes beyond the ability of language to describe. It is the product of partaking of the company of other Jews. Yet for the connectedness of one Jew to his religion and peoplehood there is a need for the passion to be grounded in understanding and knowledge. These essays can play an important part in awakening and satisfying a desire to learn and comprehend.

There is nothing obscure in these volumes. They have been written with an enviable clarity, and they will inform the non-Jewish reader as fully as the Jewish reader. In presenting these volumes to the public, B'nai B'rith looks forward to a full engagement of the ideas presented therein with the wisdom and curiosity of men and women everywhere.

The B'nai B'rith Commission on Adult Jewish Education continues to enjoy the support, advice and commitment of its founder Maurice A. Weinstein, and the then B'nai B'rith International President who worked diligently to establish the Commission's work at the center of the B'nai B'rith—Philip M. Klutznick.

This new edition has benefitted from the encouragement of B'nai B'rith International President Gerald Kraft and key members of the Board of Governors. Mr. Abe Kaplan, the immediate past chairman of the Commission, and Dr. A.J. Kravtin, the current chairman have been effectively energetic in promoting this work. Executive Vice President Dr. Daniel Thursz and Associate Director Rabbi Joel H. Meyers provide the leadership and environment necessary for a Jewish educational program of quality to flourish, and within the Commission my patient secretary Mrs. Edith Levine does the same. My collaborator on this project has been Mr. Robert Teitler, a devoted B'nai B'rith member and a creative publisher.

> Michael Neiditch, Director
> B'nai B'rith International Commission
> on Adult Jewish Education

Washington, D.C.
July 24, 1985
5 Av 5785

Foreword

In the long history of the Jewish people no era has presented the Jew with greater challenges to his traditional beliefs and way of life than the modern period, which began some two centuries ago. The impact of enlightenment, emancipation, and the industrial revolution has changed the whole character of Jewish existence and made inevitable a series of fundamental adjustments.

During the Middle Ages life for the Jew in Christian Europe was often insecure and oppressive. He had to endure economic and social discrimination, the constant threat of persecution and expulsion. But though he lived in a ghetto community, isolated from many of the intellectual and social developments in the outside world, he had the benefit of the warmth and security of a stable community and of a religious orientation which gave meaning to his life. The round of Sabbath and holiday observance added beauty and dignity to an otherwise bare existence, while a universal system of education for adults as well as children gave scope to his intellectual capacities.

These cohesive forces, however, began to break down as the Jew entered the modern world at the end of the eighteenth century. Emancipation, while it brought greater political freedom and new economic opportunities, deprived him of the values of the stable medieval community. As he came in closer contact with the non-Jewish world and as his intellectual horizons widened, he began to question some of the basic doctrines of Judaism, and his traditional patterns of religious observance were weakened. Jewish learning lost ground; even the will to live as a Jew was often lost.

The ability of the Jew to meet these challenges and to adapt himself to the modern world, therefore, represents an important chapter in the history of Judaism. The gradual achievement of political equality by the Jews of Western Europe, the emergence of modern religious movements, each with its own unique approach to Judaism, the dramatic revival of Hebrew as a spoken tongue, the renaissance of Hebrew as well as of Yiddish literature, and, finally, the emergence of the Zionist movement and the rebirth of the State of Israel in our time—each is a creative achievement of great significance.

These achievements are the result of many factors, not the least of which is the contribution of a group of outstanding Jewish personalities who have lived during the past two centuries. It is the purpose of this volume to present the life story and contributions of eleven such personalities—ten men and one woman—who have become Jewish heroes of the modern era. Though full-length biographies of many of these individuals are available, to our knowledge no book exists, both authentic in scholarship and popular in approach, which contains the biographies of outstanding Jews drawn from this entire period.

The present book begins with two fascinating and colorful personalities, key figures in the long, arduous struggle of the Jew for emancipation—Moses Mendelssohn, symbol of the cultural emancipation of the Jew in eighteenth-century Germany, and Moses Montefiore, spokesman for Jewish rights during most of the nineteenth century. We then turn to three religious leaders who have become founding fathers of the three dominant religious movements in modern Judaism—Samson Raphael Hirsch, learned spokesman of neo-Orthodoxy in Germany, Isaac Mayer Wise, founder of the major institutions of Reform Judaism in America, and Solomon Schechter, president of the Jewish Theological Seminary and one of the founders of Conservative Judaism. In the third section we describe two well-known Jewish literary figures—Hayyim Nahman Bialik, poet laureate of the Jewish people and its greatest Hebrew poet since Judah Halevi, and Sholom Aleichem, whose humorous Yiddish stories have made him a favorite all over the Jewish world. These men represent high points in the renaissance of Hebrew and Yiddish literatures in modern times. The volume concludes with accounts of four great personalities in the Zionist movement— Theodor Herzl, modern-day Jewish statesman who awakened the world to the Jewish problem, Justice Louis D. Brandeis, American leader, Chaim Wiezmann, for many years the leading figure in world Zionism and the first president of the State of Israel, and Henrietta Szold, whose work for Hadassah and Youth Aliyah have won her immortal fame.

Why have these particular figures been selected for inclusion in this volume? In our judgment, each of the personalities who appears here has made a distinctive contribution to the development of the Jewish tradition or to the advancement of Jewish rights. An attempt has also been made to have as many different countries represented as possible—Germany, England, Russia, and America. Where several outstanding personalities existed in the same country, we have chosen the one who seemed to us the most universal symbol. Thus in America we have chosen Brandeis as the symbol of the compatibility of Judaism and Americanism, though Stephen S. Wise would have been an almost equally good choice. In Eastern Europe we have picked Sholom Aleichem as the outstanding symbol of the renaissance of Yiddish literature, though cogent reasons could be advanced on behalf of Isaac Leib Peretz or Mendele Mocher Sephorim. It was also felt that at least one outstanding woman ought to be included among the twenty-three great personalities in the two volumes. While names like Donna Gracia and Glückel of Hameln were suggested, it seemed to us that Henrietta Szold had already emerged as the outstanding Jewish woman of modern times. Finally, it should be pointed out that several of the great names in modern Judaism, such as Ahad Ha-am, Rabbi Abraham Kook, Aaron David Gordon, Hermann Cohen, and Franz Rosenzweig, are included in the third volume of this series which deals with modern Jewish thinkers.

The personalities in this book differ in many ways from the Jewish heroes of ancient and medieval times. They were not all religious in the traditional sense as was true in the past. Some were secularists who, though deeply spiritual, did not accept all the basic theological principles of Judaism. Nor were they all men of thought concerned primarily with the problems of the mind as was characteristic of medieval Jewish heroes. More often than not, modern leaders have been men of action, devoted to the task of defending Jewish rights or to the movement for the upbuilding of Palestine. Even religious personalities like Hirsch or Wise, who represented definite ideological viewpoints, or outstanding scholars like Schechter, made their mark because of the institutions they built and the impact of their personalities on their generation. Modern Jewish heroes have not usually been prophets, sages, or mystics; they are more frequently philanthropists, literary men, or statesmen. Nevertheless, these men shared at least some of the characteristics of Jewish heroes of the past—the same passion for justice, the same concern for the underprivileged, for the laborer, the stranger, and the homeless. We see this in the diplomatic missions of Montefiore, the legal decisions of Brandeis and his concern with the Jewish problem, and the humanitarian activities of Henrietta Szold. They demonstrated the same love for their people and the same willingness to sacrifice on its behalf. No more dramatic example need be cited than Herzl's devotion to the Zionist cause at the expense of his life.

Because of these traits a study of the personalities in this book can be helpful to those in search of a set of values or a philosophy of Jewish life, or those who must face conflicting loyalties in our complex society, or who want guidance and perspective for their activities in the contemporary Jewish community.

The book can also serve as an introduction to the study of Jewish history since the French Revolution. While we do not accept Carlyle's thesis that history is "at bottom the history of the great men who have worked here," it is true that biography often simplifies the past, reducing the complexities to the events, forces and facts witnessed by one person. The life stories of these eminent people can help us understand the major areas of Jewish adjustment during the past two centuries—the struggle for emancipation, the development of modern religious movements, renewed literary creativity, and the resurgence of Jewish nationalism. They give us a glimpse of modern Jewish history in Germany, Eastern Europe, and America during the modern era and some insight into modern Jewish thought.

To make this volume useful as a text in Jewish history and thought, detailed introductions appear before each chapter or collection of chapters. These essays aim to help the reader see each personality in proper historical perspective and to cover the gap between one era and the next. The contributions of many of these figures to their respective areas of interest represent the culmination of a long period of previous development. Thus, to understand the significance of Samson Raphael Hirsch, one should be familiar with the development of Reform and Historical Judaism in Germany during the first half of the nineteenth century. To appreciate Bialik and Sholom Aleichem, one should know something of the earlier growth, of modern Hebrew and Yiddish literature during the *Haskalah* (Enlightenment) period. Similarly Herzl should be seen against the background of the early advocates of Jewish nationalism and the experiences of the *Hovevei Zion* (Lovers of Zion) movement organized fifteen years before the first World Zionist Congress. Nevertheless, each chapter is designed to stand on its own and may be read by itself without the introduction.

Every effort has been made to make this book as useful a learning tool as possible. Though written by ten contributors, all the essays have a common frame of reference. Most of the authors indicate at the very outset the significance and lasting contribution of the personality discussed, and make some reference to the character of the era in which he lived. The life story of each figure is then presented in some detail so the reader can feel a sense of identification with him. Each essay concludes with a summary of the thought or the most significant work or achievements of the future, and an evaluation of his legacy for the modern world.

It is our hope that the reader will become sufficiently interested in some of the personalities treated in this volume to pursue further reading. For that purpose bibliographic guides have been provided at the end of each chapter. Those desiring to delve more deeply into the historical background will find references in the footnotes to the editor's introductions.

A project of this scope cannot succeed without the cooperation of many persons in various capacities in the Jewish community. First and foremost go our thanks to the individual contributors who have graciously revised and in many instances rewritten their essays to fit into the frame of reference of this volume. Professor Oscar I. Janowsky of the College of the City of New York, Chairman of the Publications Committee of the B'nai B'rith Department of Adult Jewish Education, has read the essays and the editor's introductions from the point of view of an historian. It is a pleasant duty to express my gratitude to him for his continuing interest and many helpful suggestions. Dr. Harry Essrig of Grand Rapids, Michigan read the entire manuscript from the adult education point of view, and I am greatly indebted to him for many suggestions both as to content and style.

Individual chapters were read by Dr. Max Arzt, Dr. Henry Brann, Rabbi Mordecai Chertoff, Isaac Franck, Rabbi Marvin Goldfine, Dr. Isaac Fein, Dr. Lloyd Garner, Edward Grusd, Dr. Louis Kaplan, Rabbi Abraham Karp, Rabbi Aaron Seidman, Milton and Zelda Taylor, Sefton Temkin, and Rabbi Arthur Zuckerman. I am grateful to them for their valuable and constructive suggestions.

I have benefited greatly from stimulating conversations with several colleagues and friends who have generously made available their time and shared their specialized knowledge with me: Rabbi Myron Berman in nineteenth-century Jewish history, Dr. Jacob Agus and Rabbi Ludwig Nadelmann in modern Jewish philosophy and thought, Rabbis Simeha Kling and Emanuel Green in Hebrew literature, and Dr. Judah Stampfer in comparative literature. Rabbis Berman and Nadelmann have also read the editor's introductions and given me the benefit of their critical suggestions. These introductions have also been carefully read by the following members of the Publications committee of the B'nai B'rith Department of Adult Jewish Education: Rabbi Norman Frimer, Dr. Ira Eisenstein, Rabbi Arthur Lelyveld, Professor Sol Liptzin, and Professor Harry Orlinsky. I welcome this opportunity to thank these scholars for their valuable suggestions both as to content and style. None of these colleagues, however, should be held responsible for the point of view of the editor nor for any inadequacies that may be found in the conception or execution of the present volume.

I want to thank Bea Shere, Gertrude Greisman, and Mary Helen Persh for their clerical assistance. Thanks go also to Dr. Alfred Jospe, Rabbi Mordecai Waxman, Dr. Samuel Grand, Yale Goldberg, and Michael Arnon for various acts of personal helpfulness.

For their general encouragement and support of the Great Books Series and for granting the editor complete freedom to plan and carry out this project, I wish to thank the officers and leaders of B'nai B'rith, in particular Label Katz, President of the Order, Maurice Bisgyer, Executive Vice President, Maurice Weinstein, Chairman of the Commission on Adult Jewish Education, and Philip Klutznick, who during his term as president gave these books the highest priority.

Finally, it is only fitting that a word of tribute be paid to the late Isadore Bennett of Charlotte, North Carolina, whose generous bequest to B'nai B'rith and to the Department of Adult Jewish Education has made possible the preparation of the first three volumes of this series.

SIMON NOVECK

Washington, D.C.

HERALDS
OF JEWISH
EMANCIPATION

The beginning of the modern period in Jewish history is usually associated with the rise of Jewish enlightenment in the middle of the eighteenth century, and the subsequent movement for political emancipation which was signalized by the granting of political rights to the Jews of France in September 1791. This political enfranchisement of the Jew, however, followed a period of Jewish economic expansion and cultural development, and was a formal recognition of the social and economic progress which Jews had already achieved. The personality who best symbolized that early cultural emancipation is Moses Mendelssohn. In his life and activities he demonstrated the possibility of ending the isolation which had characterized European Jewry for several centuries. Mendelssohn was not, however, the creator of a new era in Jewish history but rather one of its outstanding products, who gave it strength and stimulation.[1] Long before his time an intellectual unrest had taken hold of some individuals in Germany and Western Europe, who began to break loose from the confines of the ghetto and of traditional Jewish study and to go in search of secular knowledge.

What were the factors which brought about this entrance of the Jew into Western society? What led him to overcome his isolation and to accept the surrounding non-Jewish culture? The answers lie in the fundamental transformations which were taking place in Europe during the sixteenth and seventeenth centuries and in the new winds of doctrine which were gradually changing the prevailing political and religious outlook. This period was marked by fundamental changes in human life and thought. These included the development of national states, the growth of trade and commerce, the decreasing authority of the church, and greater reliance on science both to understand the universe and to control nature. The rise of capitalism with its emphasis on private profit, the development of banking and modern finance, the increase of wealth and higher standards of living brought into being an altogether different type of economy. Land, no longer the most important economic element, was replaced by money in the form of cash or credit. Consequently, the Jew, who had been excluded in the later

Middle Ages from agriculture, many forms of commerce and from the religiously oriented guild system, now found new fields of economic endeavor open to him. The expansion of commerce offered him innumerable new opportunities. Jews lived in the towns and were part of the rising middle class. They were industrious, thrifty, and full of initiative. Thus they soon became active as exporters, importers, and brokers, engaging in these areas as equals and often as leaders.

Mercantilism, the dominant economic theory of the seventeenth and eighteenth centuries, stressed the importance of a favorable balance of trade. In what was an age of political absolutism, each king, feeling he was in competition with other sovereigns, made every effort to increase his country's trade and to make his state as strong and prosperous as possible.

Consequently Jews became welcome allies to these mercantilist statesmen. They could serve as entrepreneurs and help in developing native industries. As a people with ties in many lands, they could help build up foreign trade and commerce. At a time when communication was little developed, Jews were "like pegs and nails in a great building" serving to keep the state strong.

Because of this potential strength, Jews were readmitted unofficially to Cromwell's England in the middle of the seventeenth century.[2] They were also welcomed to the Netherlands, which soon became one of Europe's most prosperous countries. It was in the German states, however, that the Jew really became indispensable. After the devastation of the Thirty Years' War (1618-1648) each of the states and principalities of Germany was striving to build up its army and strengthen its financial structure. Since Germany's middle class was greatly weakened, Jews began to play an increasing role in the economic life of the country.

A series of colorful and adventurous personalities emerged, known as court Jews, who played an important part during this period in the financial and business affairs of many of the German states. Serving as purveyors or agents to provide supplies for the armies or the general population, they organized the financial structure of the state, helped the princes to develop the economy, and served as bankers, particularly for the Hapsburg emperors.

One of these court Jews was Samuel Oppenheimer (1635-1703), banker for Leopold I of Austria, who supplied provisions to the Austrian and German armies. Another was Joseph Oppenheimer (1698-1738), better known as the Jew Süss, hero of Leon Feuchtwanger's novel *Power*, who obtained virtual control of the financial administration of Württemberg and was a major influence in

Europe until the premature death of Prince Karl Alexander left him without a protector.

These court Jews were often able to intercede with the authorities on behalf of their coreligionists, or to whittle down some of the restrictions from which the Jewish masses suffered throughout this period. They gained admittance for Jews to Brandenburg and Saxony in the north and Württemberg in the south. It was through them that Dresden, Leipzig, Brunswick, and Breslau were opened to Jews. Though local German artisans, merchants, and church people might have petitioned against the admission of Jews, the mercantilist princes found it to their interests to turn a deaf ear to their plea. When Jews were expelled from Vienna in 1670, Frederick William admitted them to Prussia.

Court Jews were often given permission to live outside the ghetto. They frequently dressed ostentatiously and entertained Christian princes and noblemen in their luxurious homes. While they themselves were not accepted into Christian homes, it became the fashion for courtiers to attend weddings of rich Jews, thus allowing the court Jews to move at least on the outskirts of Christian society. Though outwardly assimilated, they remained Jews, supporting the Jewish community, founding synagogues, building libraries, and serving as links with the outside world. By familiarizing the German aristocracy with Jewish manners and by introducing whatever culture existed at the beginning of the eighteenth century into ghetto homes, they served as forerunners of the social emancipation of Mendelssohn's day. While their influence should not be exaggerated, it is possible that without the court Jew in Dessau there might not have been a Moses Mendelssohn; if there had been no court Jew in the Palatinate, perhaps no Heine would have arisen.[3]

Another factor which contributed to the breakdown of Jewish isolation was the new liberal climate of opinion which began to prevail in Western Europe at this time. The end of the seventeenth century ushered in the Age of Reason and the liberalizing pattern of thought known as the Enlightenment.

Influenced by Newton's concept of a harmonious universe ruled by natural law, the philosophy of Enlightenment asserted man's ability to understand the world about him without supernatural revelation. Knowledge, according to John Locke, does not come from "innate ideas" but is rather the product of experience and reflection. Doctrines were to be tested by reason and accepted only if found to be in accord with the great rational design of the universe. Natural law rather than revelation also became the basis of political theory. The state was an artificial creation to insure for the individual his natural rights to life, liberty, property, and the pursuit of happiness.

The study of comparative religions which developed at this time and the writings of rationalists furthered these liberal attitudes. While most people remained faithful to traditional religious tenets, some thinkers now found the teachings of Christianity incompatible with this more rationalistic view of the world. They generally adopted the deistic outlook which had developed in England during the seventeenth century and which stressed that religion should be simple and natural, without priests, churches, dogmas, and miracles. According to Deism, revelation and prophecy were not possible in a world governed by natural law.

The Age of Reason also saw the rise of the humanitarian ideal which stressed the importance of helping the unfortunate members of society. It condemned human slavery and the Negro slave trade. It urged the adoption of legal and prison reforms. The leaders of Enlightenment were also advocates of toleration, condemning censorship and defending freedom of conscience and speech. There were a few who were willing to go beyond toleration and drew no line at all among peoples and religions. Here and there men also began to question why the ancient restrictions against Jews should be maintained.

While the majority of Jews in Germany and France were unaffected, the new currents which swirled through western society did reach some individuals who began to take an interest in secular studies. Actually contact with the general secular culture had taken place at the time of the Renaissance, in the fourteenth and fifteenth centuries. While remaining loyal to their ancestral tradition, Jews had served as musicians and playwrights, attended universities, read Petrarch and Dante, and in many other ways had reflected their secular environment. Five centuries before Mendelssohn pleaded with German Jews to use the German tongue, Emanuel ha-Romi (c. 1270-1330) had written sonnets in Italian, often on frivolous themes, and throughout the following centuries Italian Jews spoke the vernacular and mingled with the non-Jewish population.[4] In the sixteenth century, Azariah de Rossi (1514-1578), in his *Meor Enayim* (The Light of the Eyes), challenged many assumptions of the Bible and became the father of Jewish historical science. Leon de Modena (1571-1648), who had an excellent knowledge of the classics, wrote an interesting defense of Judaism for Christians. In the early eighteenth century, Moses Hayyim Luzzatto of Padua (1707-1747) wrote plays and poems on philosophical and secular themes in a beautiful Hebrew style, thus helping to pave the way for the rebirth of modern Hebrew.

In seventeenth-century Holland there were also manifestations of modernism among Jews. Some of the leading medical men of the age were Amsterdam Sephardim. Secular studies were given an important place in the famous Ets Haim *yeshiva,* and Amsterdam schools were orderly and scientific in comparison with Polish schools.[5] The culture of this unique Jewish community, many of whose members had been Marranos, was Spanish-Portuguese. Because of their background and origins their general intellectual interests extended far beyond traditional Jewish studies. Rabbi Menasseh ben Israel (1604-1657) had a classical background and published books in Spanish, Portuguese, Dutch, and Latin, as well as Hebrew. His friends included leading Christians of his time, thus indicating the close relationship of Dutch Jewry with the general culture and political life of the country.[6] Amsterdam Jewry also produced the rationalistic thinking of Uriel Acosta (c. 1585-1640), who denied such Jewish tenets as belief in the immortality of the soul and resurrection of the dead, and also Spinoza (1634-1677), one of the noblest of the great philosophers, who advocated the separation of church and state and who because of his views on the Bible is sometimes spoken of as the father of modern Biblical criticism.[7]

But in neither Italy nor Holland did these individual expressions develop into any kind of organized effort for the adjustment of Jews to the new conditions of the modern world. In Italy, the Catholic counter-reformation and the establishment of ghettos throughout the peninsula in the middle of the seventeenth century prevented any widespread and lasting influence of Italian Jewish culture on Jewish life. In Holland, though they remained steadfast in their devotion to Judaism, Jews of the eighteenth century felt no need to reconcile Judaism to the new forces of the environment.

It is Germany that must be credited with being the birthplace of modern Judaism. It was there, at the end of the eighteenth century, that the influence of the general enlightenment and of the new economic conditions led to the *Haskalah* movement and to the first concerted efforts to adjust Judaism to the times. Individuals here and there had broken loose from the ghetto and taken an interest in secular studies. From the end of the seventeenth century on, an occasional Jewish youth was admitted to the University of Frankfurt on the Oder; by the time of the French Revolution, several hundred Jews had managed to attend German universities as well as a variety of secondary schools. A few Polish Jewish students found their way to Germany, where they studied the sciences and learned to write German. Some of the rabbis in Germany interested themselves in secular studies. Jonathan Eybeschütz, Chief Rabbi of Altona and Hamburg, and one of the foremost preachers of his day, declared that the study of mathematics, physics and other sciences, as well as music, drawing, and painting was legitimate from the Jewish point of view. Rabbi Jacob Emden, another well-known German rabbi, boasted of his interest in all the sciences and "affairs of the world." He knew Dutch, could read and understand a great deal of Latin, and was also interested in astronomy and the sciences. Other rabbis, aware of intellectual shortcomings, began to read books on philosophy or science. These early tendencies among the rabbis of Germany, however, were primarily of an intellectual character. Though they admired the new secular learning, they did not delve into its philosophical implications.[8] The tensions which a later generation felt in reconciling Judaism and general culture did not exist among these precursors of Jewish enlightenment.

Interest among Jews in secular culture began to increase around the middle of the eighteenth century in Eastern Germany, in the Prussian cities of Königsberg, Breslau, and above all in Berlin. In Königsberg, several families gave their children a secular education and assembled in their homes libraries of secular books and collections of art. During the 1770's the philosopher of Königsberg, Immanuel Kant, was working out theories which were to revolutionize modern thinking. Kant had many Jewish admirers, including Marcus Herz (1747-1803), a medical student, who attended his lectures and was treated as a favorite disciple. When Kant, in order to receive his professorship, had to argue publicly upon a philosophical subject, as was the custom, Herz acted as his assistant. Though not himself an original thinker, Herz later moved to Berlin, joined Mendelssohn's circle and gave lectures on Kant's philosophy. Other disciples of Kant included Lazarus ben David (1762-1832), who later lectured in Vienna, and Isaac Euchel (1756-1804), one of the founders of the Hebrew periodical *Ha-Measseph* (The Gatherer), which was devoted to *Haskalah*.

The person most influenced by Kant was himself undoubtedly the most original thinker produced by Jewry in the eighteenth century—the vagabond Solomon Maimon. When Marcus Herz saw the manuscript of Maimon's *Transcendental Philosophy* (1790), he sent it to Kant, who replied; "A mere glance at it enabled me to recognize its merits, and showed me that not only had none of my opponents understood me and the main problem so well, but very few could claim so much penetration as Herr Maimon in profound inquiries of this sort." [9]

Maimon spent some time in Breslau, which boasted of several wealthy Jews in the last half of the eighteenth century who were assimilated in dress, language, and ideas. He instructed sons of these enlightened Jews in "physics and belles lettres, and also gave them lessons in arithmetic," as well as in algebra and the rudiments of German and Latin.[10]

But it was among the Jews of Berlin that secular interests made their greatest progress. Here existed the largest Jewish community in Germany, totaling around four thousand Jewish inhabitants even before Mendelssohn's death. It was in Berlin that the organized *Haskalah* movement, representing the first systematic attempt of Jews to meet the challenges of the modern world, grew up. The leader of that movement, around whom the enlightened gathered and to whom all looked for inspiration, was Moses Mendelssohn.

1 . Moses Mendelssohn
[1729–1786]

ALFRED JOSPE

ONE day in 1743, a weak and deformed boy of fourteen knocked at one of the gates leading into the city of Berlin, the capital of the Kingdom of Prussia. A Jewish watchman, whose special task it was to screen every Jew seeking admission and to turn away all arriving without means of support, harshly questioned the pale and crippled boy, who managed to tell him stammeringly that he was from Dessau and that he had come to enroll in the Talmudic Academy of the renowned rabbi of Berlin, David Fränkel.

Eventually the boy was admitted. He was Moses Mendelssohn. That knock at the Rosenthaler Gate, the only gate through which Jews could enter Berlin, was one of the dramatic turning points in Jewish history. It signaled the entry of Judaism into the modern world. Today the train trip from Dessau to Berlin takes two hours. In Mendelssohn's time, the trip required several days on foot. But in Jewish history, it represented a journey across several centuries—from the Jewish Middle Ages to modernity. Mendelssohn was the bridge that led from the ghetto to Europe.

Mendelssohn's greatness lies in the perception and boldness with which he set two tasks for himself. He wanted to end the cultural isolation and backwardness of the medieval ghetto and make the culture of the world acceptable to the Jew. And he wanted to make Jews acceptable to Christians as their fellow citizens. He wanted to bring about nothing less than the inner liberation of Jews through cultural enlightenment and their outer liberation through civil emancipation.

Mendelssohn was a fascinating and colorful man. Small, homely, humpbacked, afflicted with a slight stammer, he managed to gain acclaim for the charm of his language, the elegance of his style, the clarity of his thought. A timid and retiring person, he found himself in the forefront of numerous controversies and battles to win respect and recognition for Jews and Judaism. Though not a brilliant philosopher, he became one of the fashionable thinkers of his time. He was no profound theologian yet was the first to define the crucial question which has confronted the modern Jew ever since the Emancipation: how to harmonize Jewish tradition with contemporary thought? How to reconcile the supernaturalism of an ancient faith with the demands of reason and modern science?

Nor was he the first to advocate enlightenment for Jews. Long before Mendelssohn's time there had been Jewish physicians, scientists, writers, musicians who had played distinguished roles in the general European culture. Jewish diplomats and financiers had enjoyed great prestige and influence. Moses Luzzatto, a sensitive intellect in Italy, wrote poems and plays on secular themes in masterful Hebrew. Azariah de Rossi first applied the principles of modern historiography to the study of the traditional texts of Judaism. Individual Jews had achieved prominence in the culture of the world long before Mendelssohn's time. But Mendelssohn was the first to make a deliberate effort not to acquire European culture solely for himself but also to bring enlightenment and modern culture to his fellow Jews. Though the emancipation of the German Jews was not the achievement of any single man, Mendelssohn became the key figure in the struggle to tear down the intellectual, social, and cultural barriers separating Jews from the outside world and to prepare the way toward their civic and cultural equality.

Early Years in Dessau

Mendelssohn was born in Dessau, capital of the German state of Anhalt, on September 6, 1729. Throughout his life, he was known to his fellow Jews as Moses Dessau. He himself preferred the name of Mendelssohn, which was derived from the name of his father, Menachem Mendel, who earned a precarious living as a *sofer*, a scribe of Torah scrolls and other Hebrew documents. Before his sixth year, Moses was enrolled in the *heder*, the traditional Jewish elementary school of the time. The story is told that his father, anxious not to have his son miss a single lesson, wrapped the boy in an old coat on winter mornings and carried him through the darkness and cold to the *heder*. Moses soon showed such brilliance in his study of the traditional Hebrew texts that he attracted the attention of the rabbi of Dessau, David Fränkel, the author of a well-known commentary on the Jerusalem Talmud. Under Rabbi Fränkel's guidance, the boy continued his studies of Bible and Talmud; he became an accomplished Hebraist and by the age of thirteen was working in material far beyond his years. He had discovered the world of medieval Jewish philosophy and was entranced by it, especially by Maimonides' *Moreh Nevukhim* (*Guide for the Perplexed*).*

The World of German Jewry

In 1743, when Fränkel accepted a call to become rabbi of the Jewish community of Berlin, Mendelssohn, then fourteen years old, followed his teacher. In Berlin Mendelssohn entered a different world, a world of strange contrasts. The capital of Prussia was a different place from the small provincial ghetto in which he had been born. Jews had lived in the province of Brandenburg since 1247, and in Berlin, its largest city, since 1295. Since then, Jewish life had been a tragic seesaw of flight and return. Expelled from Brandenburg in 1446, Jews were readmitted in 1509, driven out again in 1573, this time "for eternity." But soon they reappeared, and in 1650 the Great Elector legalized their residence in a decree permitting Jews to engage in trade and commerce for seven years. Twenty years later, another edict brought additional Jewish settlers; fifty of the wealthiest families of Austrian Jewry, who had been expelled by the Austrian empress, received permission to settle in Berlin provided they brought their wealth along and invested it in the country's commerce.

But the number of these privileged Jews was small. The

* See *Great Jewish Personalities*, I, Chapter 8.

Jewish masses were still subject to medieval limitations and restrictions. Some of them were self-imposed. The ghetto knew no modern language. People spoke a dialect akin to the Yiddish of Eastern Europe. The standards of Jewish learning had declined sharply. There was no native rabbinical leadership; spiritual leaders and teachers had to be imported from the Talmudic academies of the East. The rabbis, fearful that knowledge of even the superficial aspects of German culture would weaken the loyalty of their congregants, discouraged the use of the German language. It was a serious offense to read a German book. Mendelssohn himself tells how the Jewish communal authorities made short shrift with a boy whom he had asked to get a German book for him; when caught carrying (not reading!) it, the boy was expelled from Berlin.

Other restrictions were imposed from without. The walls of the ghetto were still standing, and few Jews could escape. Freedom of movement was severely restricted since many localities excluded or expelled Jews altogether. Where they were allowed to live, their rights of residence were sharply circumscribed. A few wealthy Jews were able to attain the status of *"Schutzjuden"* (privileged Jews); they had the right of domicile in the cities of Prussia. But this right was transferable only to the eldest son in each family. Other children were merely "tolerated" and had to seek new homes as they came of age. People often were desperately poor, restricted in their occupations, burdened with heavy taxes, packed together in overcrowded quarters, and not even allowed to marry except by permission of the government.

There was little Jews themselves could do to find release from their legal disabilities. But many, rebellious against the burdens of the ghetto, were anxious to improve their condition. Their hopes for freedom were encouraged by the changing patterns of German society and thought.

A wealthy upper class was beginning to emerge within German Jewry, especially in Berlin. The status of the Jew improved in direct relationship to his wealth (money has always been the great equalizer). In spite of the economic restrictions to which Jews were subjected, a handful of Jews succeeded in rising to positions of wealth and influence in commerce and industry—as contractors, purveyors, bankers, court agents. Their prosperity opened doors heretofore barred by bigotry. They had attractive, often luxurious homes. They spoke German, not Yiddish; they had social contact with Gentiles, sent their children to German schools, read the fashionable novels, became patrons of art and literature, went to concerts, frequented the theater. In 1779, a visitor to Berlin reported that on Saturday nights most orchestra seats in the theaters were occupied by Jews.

As the wealthy Jew moved from the ghetto into the world, however, he became more and more attracted by the host culture. He discovered that Jewish life had little of that beauty, art, and worldly sophistication that made Gentile civilization graceful and attractive. The Jewish religion involved a body of beliefs which seemed outmoded or contrary to reason; and Jewish religious law expected the individual to practice a daily regimen of rituals and customs which were inconvenient and set him apart from his fellow citizens.

It was inevitable that the Jew should begin to ask questions. If the world refused to complete the process of liberation, could it be that the fault was with the Jew himself? The Jew had to earn his self-emancipation through his enlightenment. As long as he insisted on being different, on maintaining certain habits which were strange and inexplicable to the Gentile world, had he a right to expect full acceptance?

The temptation to break with the past was therefore great. In order to win the approval of the Gentile world and clear the way for securing equal rights, some Jews began to feel that they had to "modernize" Judaism—or even forsake it altogether so that they could no longer be distinguished from their Gentile neighbors.

A second factor which nourished the rebellion of many sensitive young Jews against the limitations of the ghetto was the spirit of rationalism permeating the thought and literature of the time. Kant had defined rationalism by admonishing his contemporaries, *"Sapere aude"*—"dare to use your reason." Reason was the supreme judge and arbiter of all human affairs. The churches and their doctrines were boldly criticized, and French critics like Voltaire and d'Holbach went so far as to assert that religion was ignorance and illogical stupidity; that worship was weakness and self-delusion; and that the earth would come into its own only when heaven was destroyed. These were extreme views. Other thinkers retained a belief in a universal God but they, too, maintained that man's reason was the ultimate test of what was true and good; that the laws governing man had not been made by God but by man himself; that the essential purpose of human institutions and social arrangements was to promote the welfare and happiness of all men regardless of nationality and creed; and that only ignorance, which would soon be overcome, barred mankind from achieving utopia on earth.

These new ideas penetrated even the walls of the ghetto. The insistence of the Enlightenment on the use of reason, its demand for freedom and the equality of all people, its rejection of dogma, and its belief in progress found a ready response. Jews could not anticipate that this rationalism would eventually threaten to undermine the very foundations of their existence as they had known it. The keystone of Jewish tradition had been faith in God as the creator of the universe, the source of all life, the giver of all law, the center of authority and meaning. How could this faith be reconciled with the demands of reason? What would happen if the keystone were removed? Was there anything else that could take its place?

Study in Berlin

These were the ideas and problems that agitated the world which Mendelssohn entered on his arrival in Berlin. Without funds or the right of domicile, he found a place to live in the garret of a Jewish merchant and managed to earn a meager living by copying letters for his landlord. He enrolled in Rabbi Fränkel's academy, but his thirst for knowledge was no longer satisfied with study of the Talmud. There were other fields he wanted to explore. He studied the German language and mastered it in a short time. He read voraciously. He was aware that it was a break with tradition and a violation of his religious duties when he, who had been brought up solely on the Hebrew language and its literature, read a German book.

But Mendelssohn would not turn back. One of the first German books which fell into his hand was a volume on the early history of Protestantism—which opened a new world for him. Until then, he had not had the slightest notion of the existence of a Christian theology or of a philosophy which went beyond Maimonides. He was even more impressed by Locke's famous essay "Concerning Human Understanding," which he read in Latin. Its common sense and insistence on reasonableness in all things influenced him deeply.

Mendelssohn sought more knowledge, extending his studies into other fields. A brilliant Polish Jew, Israel Zamoscz, taught him the fundamentals of mathematics and introduced him to Euclidean geometry. Abraham Kisch, a Jewish physician who had come to Berlin from Prague, taught him Latin and encouraged him to take up French and English on his own. Another doctor, Aaron Gumpertz, member of a prominent Berlin family who had received a medical degree from the University of Königsberg (an unprecedented achievement for a Jew at that time), introduced Mendelssohn to the world of the great contemporary philosophers, especially Leibnitz and Christian Wolff.

Mendelssohn's poverty was great; often he could not afford the books he wanted to read. At times, his only food for days was bread. But he did not allow hardships to deter him from his studies, and he made rapid progress.

When he was about twenty, Mendelssohn left Fränkel's academy. In order to support himself he accepted a position in the home of a silk manufacturer, Isaac Bernhard, a "privileged" Jew, whose children he tutored in Hebrew and mathematics. A few years later he became head bookkeeper and finally a partner in Bernhard's firm. This association gave Mendelssohn security and some of the leisure which he needed for his studies. During the day he was a businessman; in the evening he dwelled in the world of ideas.

Mendelssohn and Lessing

Mendelssohn's first impulse to write came from the brilliant German critic and dramatist, Gotthold Ephraim Lessing. The two men met during the course of a chess game at the home of a friend one afternoon in 1754. Lessing was immensely impressed by the young Jew. Though only a few months older than Mendelssohn, he himself was already well known in the German literary world. A few years earlier, he had written a drama *Die*

Juden (The Jews), in which he had pilloried the bigotry and ignorance of the Christian world vis-à-vis the Jew, whom he had idealized as a man of integrity, selflessness, and nobility of character. Lessing was delighted to discover in Mendelssohn a Jew who personified the virtues with which he had endowed the hero of his play—his brilliant intellect, his moral integrity and questing for truth, his modesty and gentleness, his love for people. In a letter to the friend who had brought them together Lessing wrote that he saw in Mendelssohn "a second Spinoza lacking only his errors to be his equal," and he described his excitement about having met "a real Jew . . . who will bring great honor to his people provided his fellow Jews, who have always liked to persecute people of his kind, will allow him to develop his talents and personality fully."

Mendelssohn, on his part, found in Lessing a kindred spirit, a man whom he could admire as much for his brilliant style of writing and mastery of German literature as for his liberal convictions and courageous defense of freedom of thought and of a persecuted people. The two men became close friends; Mendelssohn inspired Lessing's portrait of the Jew in his most important play, *Nathan the Wise*, a powerful plea for religious tolerance. Their friendship ended only with Lessing's death in 1781.

Literary Success

Under Lessing's influence, Mendelssohn turned to the study of German literature and literary criticism. He worked hard to improve his mastery of the German language, and rapidly learned to use the vernacular with a facility which made him a leading figure on the German literary scene. His first German essay was a vigorous defense of Lessing's drama *The Jews* against an attack by a professor of theology, Johann David Michaelis, who had asserted that Lessing's hero, who combined integrity with nobility of spirit, could not be true to life. Passionately, Mendelssohn expressed his anguish. "Is it not enough that we must suffer the cruel hatred of the Christian world in countless ways? Must calumny and slander be added and our character be defamed in order to justify the injustices committed against us?"

Other writings followed in rapid succession. Mendelssohn's

interests covered many fields. He wrote a philosophic essay, *Philosophische Gespräche* (Philosophic Discourses), which Lessing arranged to have printed without Mendelssohn's knowledge as a surprise for his friend. Collaborating with Lessing, he also published a study on the English poet Alexander Pope.

His works impressed the literary world even more by the gracefulness of his style than by the lucidity of his arguments. It was something extraordinary that a Jew should be able to master the German language as completely and write as beautifully as Mendelssohn did. His literary contributions were eagerly sought. When the scholarly publisher Friedrich Nicolai founded a journal for studies in literature and the arts, Mendelssohn became a contributor and published numerous essays on the philosophy of beauty and principles of esthetics. He again collaborated with Lessing in the publication of the *Literatur Briefe,* devoted chiefly to literary criticism. Nor did he neglect his first love, philosophy; in 1767 he won the prize of the Prussian Academy for an essay on the *Evidenz der metaphysischen Wissenschaften,* in which he attempted to show that metaphysical truths (i.e., truths proclaimed by religion) were not contrary to reason and could be proved as logically as the tenets of science. His thesis has long been outdated but his achievement was spectacular in view of the fact that one of the other contestants was the future "king" of German philosophy, Immanuel Kant.

Mendelssohn's essay was published by the Academy and translated into Latin and French. He thus became a figure of national fame and stature and was ranked as one of the leading minds and writers of Germany. About that time, he married Fromet Guggenheim of Hamburg, and their home soon became a meeting place for writers, artists, and thinkers.

Mendelssohn's success, however, did not protect him against the indignities to which Jews were exposed at that time. On a trip to Dresden, he could not enter the city until he had paid a head tax levied upon Jews and cattle. When he took an evening walk with his wife and children in Berlin, Gentile boys would yell "Jew" and even throw stones at them. As an "immigrant" from Dessau, he was permitted to live in Berlin only because he was employed by a *"Schutzjude,"* and could be expelled at any time. The uncertainty of his residence status was finally ended through the effort of the Marquis d'Argens, one of his admirers at the court of Frederick the Great. The Marquis supported Mendelssohn's application for the privilege of permanent residence with the laconic comment, "A philosopher who is a bad Catholic begs a philosopher who is a bad Protestant to grant the privilege to a philosopher who is a bad Jew. There is too much philosophy in all this for justice not to be on the side of this application." Though Mendelssohn was anything but a "bad" Jew, the adroit phrase was effective. Mendelssohn received his permit as "*Schutzjude*" though only for himself; it could not be transferred to his children. Later, when his name was proposed for membership in the Berlin Academy of Sciences, the king vetoed the proposal; Queen Catherine of Russia also was a candidate and Frederick did not want to offend her by having her name on a membership list which included the name of a Jew.

For the indignities which he had to sustain, Mendelssohn found compensation in his work and in the recognition he won among the intellectual elite. He reached the height of his fame and popularity with the publication of his *Phädon*, which, modeled on Plato's famous dialogue *Phaedo*, defended the belief in the immortality of the soul against the skeptics of the time.

Mendelssohn felt there were compelling proofs for the immortality of the soul. Like Leibnitz before him, he thought that existing things which perish do not pass into nothingness but are only dissolved into their elements. The soul, according to Mendelssohn, is a perfectly simple substance. It has no elements into which it can dissolve. Hence it must be imperishable. But there was another, even more forceful reason. God had implanted in man the idea that his soul was immortal. How could it be compatible with the goodness and justice of God to suppose that such an idea was deceptive? "I feel I cannot reject the notion of the immortality of the soul without destroying my faith in everything I have always believed to be true and good. If our souls were mortal, then reason would be a dream . . . we would be like animals destined only to seek food and perish."

The book seemed to meet a need of the time and was immediately successful. Reprinted a number of times and translated into several languages, it was widely read throughout Europe. Its author was called the "Jewish Plato," whose home was a mecca for many visitors to the Prussian capital.

Yet in spite of the success of his works, Mendelssohn influenced his time far more by the impact of his personality than by his contributions to German philosophy and literature. His *Phädon* was outdated a mere twenty years after it had appeared. Though Mendelssohn has a place in the history of philosophy, he was overshadowed by Kant, Fichte, Hegel, and other thinkers who followed him. Nevertheless, the influence of the "Jewish philosopher" was exceptional. The world was intrigued by this man who was a loyal and strictly observant Jew and yet at the same time a leading citizen of the world of European culture. The public admired his personality which combined in a unique way a capacity to think clearly with a keen sensitivity to beauty and a deep-grained integrity in personal conduct.

Controversy with Lavater

Mendelssohn had always carried his Jewishness with dignity and had openly associated himself with the life of his people. He felt keenly about the continuing indignities of Jewish life. But he still felt that his own experiences and success showed the best way to improve the condition of the Jews: not by pleading with the mighty but by winning their respect through distinguished acts and the acquisition of German culture and refinement. In a letter to Herz Homberg he wrote, "There must arise among us more and more men who without noise should come to the front and perform valuable services to humanity. Recognition to our people will then follow."

Mendelssohn might not have changed his thinking and might have made no contribution to Judaism had he not been challenged by a Christian admirer, who regretted that Mendelssohn was not a Christian and was eager to convert him. Johann Kasper Lavater, a Swiss preacher, had visited Mendelssohn several times to discuss religious questions with him. In 1769, he translated a French book by Charles Bonnet of Geneva into German and published it under the title, *An Examination of the Proofs for Christianity*. Lavater dedicated the translation to Mendelssohn and in his preface challenged him either to refute

Bonnet's arguments or to do "what truth and honesty demanded and what a Socrates would have done had he read the book and found it irrefutable"—abandon his religion and accept Christianity.

Mendelssohn hated controversy of any kind and was reluctant to be drawn into a public dispute about the comparative merits of Judaism and Christianity. He did not want to give offense to Christians but felt he would be accused of fear or evasiveness if he let this challenge to his religion and personal faith go unanswered. He responded in a letter in which he defended his loyalty to Judaism tactfully but forcefully. "I cannot see what could possibly have kept me tied to so severe and generally despised a religion if in my heart I had not been convinced of its truth. If I ever became convinced that my religion was not the true one I would feel compelled to leave it. . . . And if I were indifferent to my religion, what could have prevented me from changing it in order to better myself? Fear of my fellow Jews? Certainly not. Their power is nil. Stubbornness? Inertia? A blind clinging to tradition? I have spent part of my life in the study of my religion and hope no one expects that such personal foibles would make me surrender the results of my studies."

Mendelssohn frankly conceded that his religion was not free of certain human additions and abuses. But he was firmly convinced of the irrefutable truth and superiority of Judaism as a religion. Rebuking Lavater for his ill-considered zeal, he pointed out that Judaism was tolerant of the convictions of others; it had never sent out missionaries to make converts; and, unlike Christianity, Judaism maintained that even the unbeliever was in God's care and could attain salvation if he was a man of moral stature.

In Defense of Jewish Rights

Mendelssohn's answer was effective and brought a letter of apology from Lavater. But the incident convinced him of the need to devote more time and energy to the welfare of his people. Having become the leading Jewish personality in Europe, he was looked upon as the man to whom other Jews in need or danger could turn for aid. Opportunities for action were not lacking. The first appeal came from the Swiss villages of Endingen and Lenglau, where the authorities had denied Jews the right to marry; Mendelssohn was urged to persuade Lavater to intervene on their behalf. Distasteful as it was to resume his contact with Lavater, Mendelssohn complied with the request, and the ban was eventually rescinded. Through his friendship with Von Ferber, the privy councillor of Saxony, he was also able to secure the withdrawal of an order directing the expulsion of hundreds of Jews from Dresden. Upon the request of the Chief Rabbi of Berlin, he compiled a compendium of all Jewish laws concerning marriage, wills, and inheritance for the use of the Royal Ministry of Justice; and he drafted a new oath for use in the courts which replaced a medieval Yiddish oath whose language and content he found degrading to his coreligionists.

Mendelssohn was soon drawn into other battles for Jewish rights. In 1779, the Jews of Alsace were viciously attacked in a pamphlet written by a French judge. The leaders of the Jewish communities, wanting to appeal to the French government for relief from their intolerable conditions, turned to Mendelssohn to draft an appropriate petition. Not wanting to undertake the task himself, he persuaded Christian Wilhelm Dohm, a young publicist and liberal spirit, to undertake the defense of Alsatian Jewry. In response to Mendelssohn's request Dohm wrote the first systematic argument by a non-Jew in favor of Jewish emancipation, *Über die bürgerliche Verbesserung der Juden* (Concerning the Civil Amelioration of the Jews, 1781). Dealing with the position of Jews not only in Alsace but throughout Germany, Dohm pointed out that they possessed all the necessary qualifications for citizenship. His recommendation was that Jews should be granted civic rights (*"bürgerliche Rechte"*) rather than citizenship rights (*"Bürgerrechte"*). They were not to hold public office or engage in political affairs, but to retain their own communal autonomy under government supervision, including the right to discipline recalcitrant members of the community and to maintain their own rabbinical courts for the disposal of civil cases in which both litigants were Jews.

Dohm's plea did not have immediate practical results but it placed the question of Jewish rights into the center of public discussion. Numerous statements were published in the press, some supporting Dohm, and others opposing and attacking his views. It was clear that a centuries-old tradition of prejudice could not be silenced by a single courageous voice. Additional efforts were needed, and Mendelssohn induced another friend, the physician Marcus Herz, to publish a German translation of *Vindiciae Judaeorum*, by Menasseh ben Israel, a seventeenth-century Amsterdam rabbi, whose defense of the Jews addressed to Oliver Cromwell in 1656 had helped to persuade that ruler to readmit Jews to England.

This time Mendelssohn did not hesitate to become personally involved. He wrote an extensive introduction to the translation. He wanted to add his voice to that of Dohm and press home the attack against bigotry. But he also wanted to correct certain views of Dohm which, while well-intentioned, had been misconceived. His impression was that Dohm himself was not wholly free from prejudice as revealed, for example, in his expressed view that Jews were not yet ready to receive the full rights of citizenship. Mendelssohn was also critical of Dohm's proposal that the Jewish community should have the right to punish members for religious infractions or dissent. This proposal was incompatible with Mendelssohn's concept of religious freedom. In his view, pure religion should not be coercive. Jews should be as free to believe and act as Christians were. Nothing less than complete freedom of conscience and equality was acceptable to Mendelssohn.

Mendelssohn, in a passionate dissent, put the responsibility where he felt it belonged: upon the prejudices and cruelty of the world. He showed how bigotry changed its face in every century. In the Middle Ages the Jews had been accused of using blood, desecrating the host, or poisoning wells. In Mendelssohn's time, Jews were accused of having an aversion to manual labor, an antipathy to science and culture, a preference for trade, a concern for money. "People continue to keep us away from all contacts with the arts and sciences or with trades and occupations which are useful and have dignity. They bar all roads leading to increased usefulness and then use our lack of culture to justify our continued oppression. They tie our hands and then reproach us that we do not use them. . . ."

Quest for Inner Renewal

Mendelssohn's plea was a moving appeal to the conscience of the world for Jewish dignity and human rights. But he knew that more than the liberation of the Jew from the political and civic restrictions of ghetto life was needed if the barriers which separated him from the non-Jew were to be demolished. The acquisition of external freedom had to be accompanied by renewal from within; political emancipation had to be accompanied by cultural emancipation. The world had to revise its attitude toward the Jew; but the Jew, too, had to change his attitude toward the world. For centuries, he had cut himself off deliberately, had isolated himself from the world not only in speech and dress, habits and manners, but also in cultural affairs. When he read, he confined himself to stories of rabbinic lore, pious legends designed to instruct or edify, or tales springing from the fertile imagination of the *Kabbalists*. When he studied, he concentrated his intellectual energies on the clarification of some intricate and often obscure Talmudic passage and neglected the Bible. The thought and culture of the world were rejected. Mendelssohn felt that intellectually the Jew still lived in the Middle Ages while the world had progressed. But he was confident that the cultural and spiritual level of German Jews would be raised if the treasures of German thought and literature could be opened to them. The first step was to teach them German. And the best way to teach them German was through a German translation of the Bible.

Mendelssohn had already started a translation in order to prepare a textbook for the instruction of his son. The boy was not sufficiently fluent in Hebrew, and Mendelssohn taught him the Bible in German in order to make it easier for him to understand the text and the nuances of the Hebrew language. Solomon Dubno, a Polish Hebraist whom he had engaged to teach Hebrew grammar to his son, urged Mendelssohn to have that translation published so that other children could also profit from his efforts. Dubno's suggestion coincided with Mendelssohn's own thinking. He disliked intensely Yiddish, which was still the vernacular in the ghettos of Germany. He knew the doors to German culture would never open to the Jewish masses unless the barrier of language was torn down. And he hoped that the introduction of Jews to German language and culture would secure for them as a group the same welcome and acceptance which he had received as an individual.

Translation of the Bible

In 1778 he issued a prospectus in order to solicit subscriptions for the Bible translation which he called *Alim li Terufah* (Healing Leaves), a title which referred to the need for healing the cultural ills of German Jewry. The first volume, Genesis, came off the press in 1780, the others following rapidly. The translation, in beautiful German prose, was printed in Hebrew letters, with which Jewish readers were more familiar; each volume contained not only the German text but also a commentary called *Biur*, designed to provide a better understanding of the text. This translation was entirely Mendelssohn's work as were the Hebrew introduction and commentaries on the first part of Genesis and the entire Book of Exodus. Dubno completed the commentary on Genesis, supplied extensive notes on the rules and use of Biblical Hebrew, and supervised, at least initially, the publication of the work as a whole. Other friends and associates also helped. Naftali Herz Wessely wrote the commentary on Leviticus, and Aaron Friedenthal and Herz Homberg composed those on Numbers and Deuteronomy, while Mendelssohn himself prepared the comments on the poetic portions of Deuteronomy.

The impact of the translation was enormous. Orders were received from all parts of Europe. Well-known rabbis welcomed and endorsed the work, among them the famous Gaon of Vilna.* Herschel Levin, Chief Rabbi of Berlin, expressed the hope that the translation would achieve what Mendelssohn had set out to do—namely, put an end to the ignorance of German Jewry. Some outstanding spokesmen of traditional Judaism, however, objected to the translation precisely because they were fearful that Mendelssohn's plan would succeed and that a knowledge of German would tempt Jewish youth to neglect

* See *Great Jewish Personalities*, I, Chapter 12.

their Jewish studies for the pursuit of secular interests. Three leading rabbis issued a ban against the book and threatened to excommunicate those who read it. In some communities, the book was burned publicly as a gesture of protest and warning. But Mendelssohn was able to silence the opposition, especially that of its leading member, Rabbi Raphael Kohn of Altona, by a subtle strategy. Through the intervention of his friend, Councillor von Henning of Copenhagen, he obtained subscriptions for the translation from the King and the Crown Prince of Denmark and other leading personalities. Since Altona belonged to Denmark at that time, Rabbi Kohn's hands were tied: he could take no action against a book that had found the approval of the rulers of the country.

The work, completed in 1783, caused a cultural revolution among German Jews. It provided the bridge on which they could pass from the ghetto to Europe; it ended their use of Yiddish, introduced them to the German language, and gave them the key to the world of literature, science, and philosophy from which they had been cut off until then. The commentary gave them new understanding and appreciation of the grammatical structure of the Hebrew language.

Gradually, the entire structure and control of Jewish education were changed under the impact of the translation. Mendelssohn persuaded some friends to establish a school for Jewish children in Berlin which soon became a model for others. German replaced Yiddish as the language of instruction, and secular subjects supplemented the traditional Jewish studies. Religious instruction included not only the reading of Hebrew texts but also study of the principles of Judaism. In addition, boys received vocational guidance and training, especially in manual occupations.

The influence of Mendelssohn's translation went beyond the borders of German. It gave Russian and Polish Jews who read German a new insight into the literary and linguistic structure of the Bible, and the graceful Hebrew of the *Biur* was one of the forces that contributed to the renaissance of Hebrew, the language in which Jews of Eastern Europe pursued enlightenment and sought to acquire the culture of the world. Mendelssohn also encouraged Wessely and other scholars to found a

Hebrew journal, *Ha-Measseph* (The Gatherer), which published articles on religious and secular subjects in order to bring the best fruits of contemporary thought and culture to its readers.

Jerusalem

While Mendelssohn was still occupied with his translation, he could not withdraw completely from the discussions and controversies which his preface to Herz's translation of the *Vindiciae Judaeorum* had started. His views were harshly questioned in numerous handbills and pamphlets. Some opponents flatly rejected his appeal for civic freedom on behalf of Jews. Germany was a Christian state; the state and the church were coextensive; Christianity was the established religion, and only those who were church members were eligible for citizenship in the Christian state. Others attacked Mendelssohn's view that a man's religion was his personal affair and that no religious authority should be permitted to punish or exclude dissenters. But neither the Christian nor the Jewish authorities were prepared to accept Mendelssohn's reasoning and give up their disciplinary powers, especially the weapon of excommunication. Mendelssohn's views were challenged by a number of writers, one of whom published an anonymous letter under the title *"Das Forschen nach Licht und Recht"* (The Search for Light and Right), in which he argued that Mendelssohn either was a hypocrite or had discarded Judaism. He pointed out that the Jewish religion as laid down in the Torah possessed an elaborate system of rewards and punishments to compel obedience to its laws. How then could Mendelssohn seriously advocate that a man's religion should be his private concern and that the use of religious compulsion be banished? Either his proposal was untenable or he was no longer a real Jew.

Mendelssohn realized that he could not remain silent in the face of these public challenges. He presented his views in a small work which he published in 1783 under the title *Jerusalem, or Religious Power and Judaism.*

Jerusalem consisted of two parts. The first was a powerful restatement of his convictions on freedom of conscience and a fervent plea for religious tolerance. Mendelssohn knew that

Jews could not hope to be admitted to citizenship in a "Christian" state and that genuine freedom of conscience was impossible. Therefore, nearly a hundred years ahead of his time in Europe, he pleaded for the separation of state and church. In broad philosophical terms, he defined and delineated their respective spheres of competence. In sharp contrast to the theories underlying the concept of the Christian state, he showed that their functions and rights were not identical but essentially different. The state governs the relationships between man and man, and therefore has the right to control or regulate the actions of its citizens. It can compel them to obey the law and punish them for infractions even though they may disagree with the wisdom or fairness of the law itself. But the state cannot control or regulate the ideas or convictions of its citizens, and must not be allowed to favor one religion over another or to require its citizens to hold particular beliefs as a condition of citizenship.

The church, on the other hand, is concerned with man's relationship with his God, his faith and thoughts, his beliefs and convictions. But a man's thoughts are free. This was Mendelssohn's personal credo and the heart of his argument. A man's beliefs are his personal affair; he has a right to defy any attempt on the part of state or church to control his thoughts or convictions. The state may force a person to act in a certain way, but not even the church can force him to think or believe in a certain way. The church has the right and, in fact, the duty to seek to influence his ideas by instruction and persuasion. But this is where its power ends. It can neither control his actions, impose its beliefs upon him, nor punish him if he disbelieves. The only judge of man's convictions is reason, and the only yardstick of a man's worth is his actions. "Observe what men do or fail to do, and judge them by their actions. . . . Don't reward or punish them in accordance with their thoughts! Let every man who does not disturb the public welfare, who obeys the law, who acts righteously toward his fellow men, be allowed to speak as he thinks, to pray to God after his own fashion or after the fashion of his fathers, and to seek his eternal salvation where he thinks he can find it."

But were these views of Mendelssohn compatible with the teachings of Judaism? Did not Judaism reject the freedom of conscience which the German philosopher advocated? Were his critics right when they implied that he had broken away from the faith of his fathers?

Mendelssohn used the second part of *Jerusalem* to defend himself against the charge of insincerity and to counter the challenge to his Jewishness by presenting his concept and philosophy of Judaism. First he defined what he meant by religion. Like the rationalists of his time he held that no belief was valid if it was contrary to reason. Reason was the medium through which man could discover what he needed to know in order to achieve happiness on earth. Mendelssohn did not recognize any truth or eternal verities except those which could be comprehended by man's intellect and verified by it.

For Mendelssohn, Judaism was the ideal religion precisely because its basic principles were in harmony with the demands of reason. Unlike Christianity, Judaism had no dogmas which were contrary to reason, no doctrines in which the faithful had to believe in order to attain salvation, no mysteries which men had to accept on faith but could not understand. Judaism offered complete freedom of thought. There were no binding articles of faith choking independent thought. No one was asked to believe what his reason was compelled to reject. Judaism was not concerned with what a man believed; its stress was on what he did and how he acted. According to Mendelssohn's definition, Judaism was not revealed religion; it was revealed law. "Among all the laws and commandments of Moses, there is none saying, 'Thou shalt believe' or 'thou shalt not believe.' They all say, 'Thou shalt do' or 'thou shalt not do.' " Judaism did not address itself to a man's mind and tax his credulity. It addressed itself to his will. It sought to influence and guide his daily actions but did not seek to control his thoughts.

Distinction between Religion and Law

Mendelssohn's distinction between "religion" and "law" is crucial to the understanding of his philosophy. To him, Judaism actually was not a religion in the strict sense of the word at all. What were considered its religious tenets—its belief in the existence and unity of God, His providence, and the immortality of the soul—were not specifically Jewish notions. These teachings were the principles of Deism, the general religion of reason. They were self-evident to reason and required no proof, no mysterious supernatural act of revelation in order to be intelligible to men of reason everywhere. Judaism had not discovered them. Reason had. Judaism merely reaffirmed them.

What was specifically Jewish and distinguished the Jew from the non-Jew was not his religion, those general teachings which were the common property of all men of reason, but rather the unique "laws" and commandments which had been revealed at Sinai. These were valid only for the Jewish people. Their purpose was to distinguish the Jew from the non-Jew, to guide his moral and spiritual conduct, to teach him the acts which were conducive to human happiness, to stimulate his imagination and make him ponder man's nature and destiny in God's world. Above all, the commandments enabled Jews to maintain their identity and integrity as a distinct group that was the carrier of the pure religion of reason.

Mendelssohn hoped to prove the permanent validity and truth of Judaism by defining it as revealed "law" rather than as revealed "religion." What he did not realize was that he had merely discovered that the nature of Judaism had become a problem in his time but that he had not solved it. If reason is the only criterion of what is true, how can God's revelation on Sinai be "true" since it can neither be explained logically nor verified by reason? What Mendelssohn did was simply to take the religion of reason of his time and graft upon it an emasculated Judaism which had been deprived of its rational elements and which consisted solely of customs, rituals, and ceremonial laws. The paradox was that he, the rationalist and man of enlightenment, the thinker for whom no belief was valid if it was contrary to reason, declared that all those concepts and ideas which were rational were not Judaism, and that Judaism consisted solely of elements which were not rational, which reason could neither prove nor understand, which had to be accepted on faith, and which God, therefore, had to disclose to Jews in a mysterious and non-rational act of revelation.

Mendelssohn was not conscious of the paradox of his position. He saw no contradiction. The God of reason and the God of Israel were one and the same God. God was both the benevolent creator and sustainer of the world whom his reason could affirm, and the king and guardian of Israel who had spoken on Sinai and ordained the laws which governed Jewish life. This was the only way in which Mendelssohn could harmonize his deepest feelings and convictions: his insistence on reason and on man's freedom of conscience and thought, and his determination to observe and preserve Jewish law and thus maintain his membership in the congregation of Israel. He was able to bring together in his personal life what his theory of Judaism failed to reconcile philosophically.

Mendelssohn's thinking can be understood only against the background of the causes which commanded his deepest loyalties. His faith in the power of reason was linked with his passion for human equality and his uncompromising attachment to traditional Judaism. If, as he firmly believed, a knowledge of truth was indispensable to the achievement of man's happiness, truth had to be accessible to all people alike without distinction of race, creed, or social status. It was inconceivable to him to believe that God, in His goodness, could capriciously have revealed the truth only to a part of mankind and left the rest of mankind without revelation and therefore without access to happiness. No religion, not even his own Judaism, could be the sole instrument through which God revealed His truth. Truth was indivisible and reason was its source; it belonged to all men.

But it was equally impossible for Mendelssohn to surrender his deep attachment to Jewish life. He found great emotional and intellectual satisfaction in the observance of Jewish law. It was the instrument by which he could translate his convictions into action. It was his great means of self-discipline; it enabled him to perform the acts (*mitzvot*) that bound him to God and united him with his people. Above all, such acts safeguarded the continued existence of the Jewish people. Therefore Mendelssohn insisted time and again on the crucial importance of Law for the Jew. He even proclaimed boldly that if a choice had to be made it would be better that the Jew surrender the benefits of emancipation than his loyalty to Law.

Jerusalem had a powerful impact on the general reading public. Many non-Jews were impressed by its author's compelling analysis of the relationship of state and church, and his courageous defense of man's inalienable right to freedom of thought. Mirabeau, who was soon to become one of the leading spirits of the French Revolution, declared that the book ought to be translated into every European language, while Kant wrote to Mendelssohn that he considered the little volume a masterful statement which would spur a reform from which not only Jews but countless non-Jews would benefit.

The impact of the work upon Mendelssohn's coreligionists, however, was negligible. Mendelssohn's arguments for the preservation of Jewish law, persuasive as they were to individuals like himself, who had been brought up in a completely Jewish environment, had little influence on most of his contemporaries, who preferred the actual or presumed benefits of civic emancipation even if they had to be acquired at the expense of surrendering their distinctive Jewish observances and identity. Mendelssohn's own children were an example. Only one of them, Joseph, remained a Jew, while the others defected shortly after their father's death. One daughter, Dorothea, after leaving her first husband, the Jewish banker Simon Veit, was married to the famous romantic poet Schlegel and turned first Protestant and then, together with her husband, converted to Catholicism. Another daughter, Henriette, who had been trained as a teacher, turned Catholic. Abraham Mendelssohn, father of the famous musician Felix Mendelssohn-Bartholdy, became a Protestant.

Final Years

The completion of *Jerusalem* had left Mendelssohn physically and mentally exhausted. He had never been strong, and the intellectual battles and efforts over the years had drained his limited reservoir of energy. He was aware that a new philosophical literature of vast importance was being published in Germany and that its theses challenged some of his deepest convictions. But he felt too exhausted to read the new works and either challenge their claims or revise his own thinking. He devoted his remaining strength to the religious and philosophical instruction of his son Joseph, and gave a daily lecture on the philosophical proofs for the existence of God to a circle of young people that included his own children and a group of their friends. He did not propound any new ideas; his main argument was the so-called cosmological proof of God which proceeds from the assumption that everything that exists must have a cause. The world exists; hence it must be caused by a power other than itself, and itself "uncaused." This final original cause is God.

The lectures were published in 1784 in a small volume called *Morgenstunden* (Morning Lessons) because they had been given in the morning when he still felt strong enough for the task. The book added little to Mendelssohn's stature. His assumptions and views in philosophy had long been known and had, in the meantime, been effectively refuted by Kant and others.

His final work was an essay addressed to Lessing's friends, in which he attempted to vindicate the memory of his beloved friend by proving that, contrary to an assertion of the philosopher Jacoby, Lessing had never been a follower of Spinoza. Mendelssohn caught a cold while delivering the manuscript of his reply to the publisher. He died a few days later on January 4, 1786, and was mourned by Jews and Christians alike.

Contribution to Jewish Life

The nature and extent of Mendelssohn's contribution to Jewish life have been the subject of a great deal of controversy. Peretz Smolenskin, a Hebrew writer and ardent proponent of Jewish nationalism, denounced him as the father of the German Reform movement which, in his view, had weakened the Jewish people by proclaiming it to be merely a religious group and not a nation. The attack was pointless since, contrary to Reform's repudiation of the divine origin and validity of the Law, Mendelssohn himself strictly observed it and persistently upheld its immutability. Orthodox leaders also continued to denounce him long after his death as a destructive influence, drawing young Jews away from their Talmudic studies and turning their interest to mundane matters and the study of general European culture.

This of course was what Mendelssohn had hoped to achieve. His significance for Jewish life lies in the fact that he was the bridge between the Jewish world and that of Europe. A citizen of both worlds, he had managed to bridge them in his own personality. In his thinking, he was a European; in sentiment and

conduct, he was anchored in the Jewish community and identified with its traditions.

Mendelssohn also enabled other Jews through his work and
personal example to bridge the same two worlds. His translation of the Pentateuch prepared the way for the cultural emancipation of Jews by placing the treasures of European culture
within their reach. His writings and the example of his personality helped to pave the road for civic emancipation as well. As
he gained the friendship and admiration of influential Christians,
he won allies who associated themselves with the Jewish battle
for human rights and created the moral and intellectual climate
for the ultimate emergence of Jewish emancipation.

However, Mendelssohn's attempt to bridge the two worlds
philosophically as well as culturally and socially did not succeed.
He wanted to harmonize the traditional teachings of Judaism
with the rational spirit of the age. But how could faith and reason be reconciled? How is it possible to believe in a God whose
existence reason cannot prove? To these questions, Mendelssohn
had answered that Judaism was compatible with reason because
it was not a religion. It was merely revealed law which required
certain actions and not an act of faith on the part of the Jew. But
Mendelssohn's contemporaries and successors were unable to
accept this definition of Judaism. They agreed that Law—customs and ceremonials—was one of Judaism's vital ingredients.
Obviously, however, Judaism is more than a mere system of
legal prescriptions. The law itself presupposes a belief in God
who has given it, who requires its observance, who is the master
of man's destiny and the source of all life. This God cannot be
"proved" by reason, and therefore the question still remains as
to how the faith of Biblical Judaism can be harmonized with the
demands of reason and the findings of science.

What makes Mendelssohn important to the modern Jew is not
his definition of Judaism but the questions which he raised.
Standing at the threshold of Jewish modernity in Central
Europe, he was the first to recognize and formulate the central
problems which had begun to trouble his generation and to
which, since then, each new Jewish generation has had to find
a meaningful answer: how to live as a Jew without surrendering
the values of Judaism to the values of the modern world, or the
wisdom of the world to the claims of Judaism.

FOR FURTHER READING

Books by Moses Mendelssohn:

Jerusalem, Or On Religious Power and Judaism translated by Allan Arkush with an introduction and commentary by Alexander Altmann (Hanover, NH: Brandeis University Press, 1983). This classic statement of the compatibility of Judaism with the ideas of the Enlightenment reviews a wide body of issues as relevant to the present as they were to the turbulence in Europe at the end of the 18th century. Altmann's commentary is very helpful for placing the work in the context of Mendelssohn's life work and in the evolution of modern Jewish thought.

Selections From His Writings edited and translated by Eva Jospe with an introduction by Alfred Jospe (New York: Viking, 1975). Quite simply the best one volume introduction to Mendelssohn's work. The editing is careful and the translation is clear and fluent. Alfred Jospe's introduction expands upon the themes of his essay in this volume.

Books about Moses Mendelssohn:

ALTMANN, Alexander, *Moses Mendelssohn: A Biographical Study* (University, AL: University of Alabama Press, 1973). This monumental work by the acknowledged dean of Mendelssohn scholars has been called the "definitive work on the subject."

WALTER, Hermann, *Moses Mendelssohn: Critic and Philosopher* (New York: Bloch Publishing Co., 1930). An older study still fresh and helpful.

PATTERSON, David, "Moses Mendelssohn's Concept of Tolerance," in *Between East and West*, Alexander Altmann editor (London: East-West Library, 1956) pp. 149–163.

Sir Moses Montefiore

The half century from the death of Moses Mendelssohn to Moses Montefiore's humanitarian missions in the 1840's marked the beginning of the movement for Jewish emancipation. Political equality, however, was not achieved by the Jew overnight but only after a long hard struggle. Great progress was made in France and Holland and to a large degree in England during this period, but full political equality was not achieved in Central and West European countries such as Germany and Italy until the beginning of the 1870's, and in Eastern Europe until the twentieth century.

While leaders of the Enlightenment such as Voltaire and Diderot were hostile to Jews, there were several advocates of Jewish emancipation during the last decades of the eighteenth century. Christian Wilhelm Dohm, as we have seen, wrote a plea at the request of Mendelssohn, urging that civic rights be granted to the Jews. In 1787 Count de Mirabeau (1749-1791), an admirer of Mendelssohn, published a tract entitled *Moses Mendelssohn and the Political Reform of the Jews* (1787) in which he showed the absurdity of the objections to the Jews by their enemies and suggested that the best way to make Jews "better men and useful citizens" was to "banish every humiliating distinction, open to them every avenue of gaining a livelihood." Mirabeau's views were supported by the liberal cleric Abbé Henri Grégoire, who in his essay *On the Physical, Moral and Political Regeneration of the Jews* blamed Christian society for whatever faults Jews may have. "In their place would we not be worse?" he asked.[1]

The first country to emancipate its Jews was France. In 1789 King Louis XVI convened the States General, which transformed itself into a revolutionary National Assembly. This body destroyed the foundations of feudalism and serfdom, issued a declaration of the Rights of Man, and proclaimed religious toleration. It was inevitable that the question of Jewish rights should come up for discussion at this time.

There were forty thousand Jews in France in 1789—thirty thousand Ashkenazim living in ghettos in Alsace Lorraine, a few thousand Sephardim in Bordeaux, Bayonne, and Avignon, the former Papal possessions, and several hundred in Paris.

In January 1790, the wealthy Sephardi Jews of Bordeaux, having dissociated themselves from the German-speaking Jews of Alsace by claiming they were the élite of their people, were granted citizenship. And in September 1791 the much larger group of Ashkenazi Jews was given similar rights.

The news of their changed status was received with enthusiasm by most of France's Jews, who began to enlist in the National Guard and to participate in the life about them. For a brief period during the reign of terror synagogues as well as Catholic churches were closed, but they were reopened after the death of Robespierre (1758-1794), one of the leaders of the radical faction.[2] Though the peasants in Alsace, particularly those in debt to Jewish moneylenders, retained their hatred of the Jew, and royalists accused the Jews of being a nation within a nation, Jews managed to integrate themselves rapidly into French society.

The principles of the Revolution spread to other lands in the wake of the French armies. As the ghetto walls were torn down, emancipation came to fifty thousand Jews of the Netherlands (1796), the thirty thousand Jews in Italy (1798), and to parts of western Germany. Not all the Jews in these countries, particularly in Holland, were enthusiastic over their newly gained freedom. They sensed that a price might have to be paid—the loss of communal authority, the increased danger of assimilation, and the loss of their distinctive way of life. But the more enterprising elements were determined to achieve civic rights.

How high the price was to be became apparent when Napoleon became Emperor. Acting on complaints against the Jews by the Alsatian peasants and wanting to hasten the process of Jewish integration, Napoleon convened an assembly of Jewish notables, a gathering of 112 businessmen, financiers, and rabbis, to whom he put twelve basic questions. Did the Jews consider themselves Frenchmen? Can Jews and Christians marry? Does Jewish law encourage usury? Most of the questions could be answered without difficulty except for the one on intermarriage. To this the assembly replied that the Bible forbade intermarriage with heathens, but since French Christians were not heathens, the prohibition did not apply to them. Napoleon seemed satisfied with the answers, and, to the amazement of the entire Jewish world, called into being a Sanhedrin of Jewish leaders (1807), as in ancient times, to invest the answers with the authority of Jewish law. The eighty delegates, forty-six of whom were rabbis, reaffirmed the fact that Jews consider themselves Frenchmen, that they can participate in all professions, and that Jewish law condemns usury. They also explained that while rabbis cannot officiate at mixed marriages, the decision of the civil courts had priority over religious courts.

This dramatic gesture of convening a Sanhedrin made Napoleon seem like a Messiah to the Jews of Eastern Europe; but the Jews of France saw it in a different light. In March 1808 he issued a series of regulations which the Jews called the "Infamous Decree," restricting Jewish rights for ten years and creating a consistorial system which insured the quota of Jewish draftees to the army and brought the Jewish communities under state supervision. Perhaps even more disturbing in the long run was the fact that the members of the Sanhedrin, by renouncing separate Jewish nationhood and by rejecting the wider cultural and ethnic aspects of Judaism, set the tone for a century to come that Judaism was only a faith in a very restricted sense.

In the course of the Napoleonic wars, measures for the emancipation of the Jews were taken in several German states. Napoleon appointed his brother Jerome king of Westphalia, and the latter granted Jews complete equality, including the right to hold office and enter the professions (1808). Equality was also given in the Grand Duchy of Frankfurt, Mecklenburg and other parts of the Confederation of the Rhine, which Napoleon established in 1811.

In Prussia prejudice and hatred of the Jew persisted. After the disasters at the hands of Napoleon, however, Prussia reformed her political system, and in 1812 Jews were declared citizens. They no longer had to pay special taxes nor were they required to live in slum areas, but they were still not allowed to hold public office.

With the downfall of Napoleon in 1814, many of the gains of the previous quarter of a century were lost. The statesmen who gathered in Vienna wanted as far as possible to re-establish the old order, and this led to the withdrawal of the rights granted Jews. Except in France, where the basic gains of the Revolution were kept intact, and the Netherlands, which continued unwaveringly the provisions for emancipation, privileges conferred during the struggle were withdrawn.

Though Prince Hardenberg (1750-1822) and Baron Wilhelm von Humboldt (1767-1835), leaders in the political and social regeneration of Prussia, made every effort at the Congress of Vienna on behalf of Jewish rights, there was strenuous resistance by the states forming the Germanic Confederation. A compromise clause proposed that "rights already granted 'in' the confederated states were to remain in force." A shrewd delegate, however, replaced the word "in" with the word "by." Since in most instances these rights had been imposed by the French occupation armies and not by the states themselves, the Jews in those states were cheated out of their freedom. In Prussia, where citizenship had been granted by the state itself, the edict of 1812 was soon limited and the Jews lost many of the rights they had gained. In several places there were anti-Jewish riots like those common in the Middle Ages.

These retrogressions shocked and embittered the Jews. Many young men, despairing of any possibility for improving their lot, emigrated to the United States; others sought in baptism the pass-port to personal advancement.

A reaction also took place in the Italian states. In Sardinia reli-gious toleration was withdrawn and the whole anti-Jewish code was enforced once again. In Piedmont Jews were once more confined to ghettos. Worst of all were conditions in the Papal States, where Jews were again herded into ghettos and the Inquisition restored to power. Out of desperation many Italian Jews emigrated to France.[3]

In the Hapsburg Empire, where no reform had taken place dur-ing the Napoleonic period, Jews continued to bear the whole array of medieval disabilities. Count Metternich (1773-1859), the domi-nant personality in Austria as well as in Europe at this time, refused to alleviate even the worst injustices.

In spite of this political retreat, the three decades following the defeat of Napoleon saw progress in the struggle for Jewish rights. In 1818, the restrictions imposed by Napoleon on French Jewry expired. In 1831, after the July revolution, state support was granted the consistories, and Judaism was put on terms of equality with other religious bodies. The special Jewish oath was done away with through the efforts of Adolph Crémieux (1796-1880), the most brilliant representative of the first generation of Jews born in France after the Emancipation.[4]

Progress was also made in England. The law did not treat Jews as a class apart from the rest of society, but not being members of the established church they were subject to individual disabilities. The prejudices of the mob could easily be aroused, as during the furore which caused the hasty repeal of Prime Minister Pelham's "Jews Bill" of 1753, which sought to establish almost full equality of rights for the Jews of England. Nevertheless, Jews rose in British society during the ensuing decades. They participated in the war effort against Napoleon, entered into finance, banking, large-scale commerce and the professions, and by the end of the war had won acceptance on all levels of English society. But no Jew could sit in Parliament or hold any office under the crown, for loyalty had to be sworn "on the faith of a Christian."

With typical British gradualism, however, the remaining restrictions were eliminated one by one. In 1831 English universities opened their doors to Jews, and an act was passed permitting them to hold the local office of sheriff. In 1835 David Salomons was elected Sheriff of the city of London, and Parliament changed the wording of the oath for that particular office. Years later, when Salomons was elected Alderman, a similar change was extended to municipal offices. Though elected to the House of Commons he was unable to take his seat on account of the Christological oath. It was not until 1858 that the Lords agreed to a compromise which allowed each House of Parliament to modify the oath as it desired. In that year Lionel de Rothschild took his place as the first Jewish member of Parliament, and two years later the Parliamentary oath was changed for all members and for both the House of Commons and the House of Lords.

In the struggle for Jewish rights, whether or not successful, the cause was usually taken up by the liberal parties. In Germany the anti-Semitic outbreaks aroused many Jews, who began for the first time to stand up and fight for their rights. Outstanding among such German Jewish liberals was Gabriel Riesser (1810-1863), for many years the leading protagonist in the struggle for Jewish emancipation, who in a series of pamphlets and in his periodical *Der Jude* argued for Jewish rights as part of human rights. Another spokesman for emancipation was Ludwig Börne (born Loeb Baruch) of Frankfurt, gifted publicist and apostle of freedom who helped to found the "young Germany" movement and who though himself a convert to Protestantism refused to dissociate himself from his Jewish forebears. Similarly, Heinrich Heine, greatest of German poets after Goethe, though he had accepted baptism as the "admission ticket to European civilization," continued like Börne to concern himself with the quest of Jews for freedom and security.[5]

During the revolution of 1848 it seemed as if emancipation had arrived for German Jewry. The new Prussian constitution granted complete equality before the law to all citizens, including the Polish Jews in Eastern Prussia. But in the ensuing reaction, Jewish emancipation, like German liberalism as a whole, lost out, and thousands of German Jews left their native land for the New World.

In Italy also Jews participated in large numbers in the general movement for freedom. For a brief period during the revolution of 1848 a republic arose in Venice, led by Daniele Manin, a converted Jew, which proclaimed complete civil and political equality for all inhabitants regardless of race or creed. Jews also supported the movement for unity under King Charles Albert of Sardinia. But Austrian intervention put an end to these democratic experiments, and everywhere Jews were returned to the old humiliating disabilities.

Thus a survey of Jewish rights at the beginning of the 1840's, when Moses Montefiore began his missions, indicates there were areas of freedom and areas of continuing suppression, in spite of the long struggle by liberals. In the Middle East, at that time a part of the Ottoman Empire, Jews theoretically enjoyed equality before the law. But they were affected by the poverty, economic stagnation, and corruption which beset Ottoman society as a whole. How insecure the situation of the Jew could be was brought to the attention of the world by the Damascus Blood Libel (1840), the sensational cause célèbre in the resolution of which Montefiore played such an important role.

Far more serious was the position of the Jew in the Russian empire. Liberal notions of government and personal equality made little headway against the autocracy of Nicholas I, who reigned from 1825 to 1855. Nicholas regarded the Jews as an alien people and tried to force their assimilation into Greek Orthodox culture. Jewish boys were drafted into the army often at the age of twelve for a preliminary period of six years prior to the regular conscription of twenty-five years. Most of these "cantonists," as they were called, either died before the end of their service or were converted to Christianity. Among the other restrictions from which Jews suffered were the laws making it extremely difficult for them to live outside of certain specific provinces known as the Pale of Settlement. In 1835 they were driven from the countryside of the province of Kiev and out of the capital city itself. In the 1840's another edict threatened the eviction of Jews from the border zones near Germany and Austria. The plight of the Jew in Russia was thus more precarious than in any of the West European countries.[6]

It is against this background of continuing suppression in spite of the gains that had been made that we must view the various humanitarian missions of Moses Montefiore. For the next few decades he was to be the principal spokesman for world Jewry.

2 . *Moses Montefiore*
[1784–1885]

CECIL ROTH

M O S E S Montefiore was in his day and long after considered to
be the most notable Jew, and indeed one of the most notable
Englishmen, of the nineteenth century by virtue of his outstanding philanthropic work extending over a period of three quarters of a century, into his venerable old age. Today he remains
the symbol of the emancipated Western Jew at his finest—an
honored son of Britain, and fully accepted in his environment,
and at the same time unfaltering in his Jewish allegiance—in his
meticulous religious observances and support of the synagogue,
in his agonized care for the well-being of his persecuted coreligionists in every land, and in his perpetual devotion to the idea
of the regeneration of a Jewish settlement in the Holy Land,
and the regeneration of the Holy Land through a Jewish settlement. Proudly and intensely English, he belonged in a unique
sense to the entire Jewish world.

Ancestry and Background

The Montefiore family derived from the little town of
Montefiore in the region of Ancona, and belonged to the native
element in Italian Jewry—the oldest Jewish colony in Europe,
neither Sephardi nor Ashkenazi. They had settled later in the
free port of Liborno (Leghorn) in Tuscany, and had become
absorbed in the vibrant Sephardi community which had helped
to create that city's remarkable prosperity. It was thus natural
for the Montefiores, when they moved to London in the early

eighteenth century, to become attached to the Spanish and Portuguese community, which had been established in the English capital under Cromwell, and to intermarry with one of its leading families, the Mocattas, to which Montefiore's mother belonged.

As though to emphasize his Italian ancestry, Moses was, as it happens, born during a visit of his parents back to Leghorn, in 1784. He received, mainly from private tutors, the usual inadequate education of the well-to-do eighteenth-century English Jew, who (along with Catholics and Protestant nonconformists) was not admitted at that time to the universities and higher seats of learning. At the age of twenty-eight he married—exceptionally for a patrician English Sephardi in those days—a member of the Ashkenazi community, Judith Cohen—the daughter of a family which later was to provide English Jewry with many outstanding leaders, and English law with some of its most distinguished exponents. These genealogical details are necessary for understanding Montefiore's position in the world—an English Jew through and through, but with Italian background; a member of the Sephardi community, but closely allied with the Ashkenazim; a northerner, but with his roots in the Mediterranean lands.

His upbringing was insular, in an England in which Jews (Anglicized Jews at least) were to a great extent, as they had been almost from the beginning of their resettlement in the seventeenth century, emancipated socially and were subjected to no galling restrictions. But they were still excluded from political rights, as were Dissenters and Catholics. As one of the twelve authorized "Jew brokers" (a term which reflected something of the inferiority of the Jewish status), Montefiore's first business ventures were unsuccessful, not to say disastrous. But he recovered honorably, and became the close associate of his remarkable brother-in-law Nathan Meyer Rothschild, the founder of the English banking house and, it is said, the most amazing financial genius of his age. Largely but not entirely as a result of this connection, Montefiore made a comfortable though by no means enormous fortune, and from middle age found himself financially independent.

Religious Orientation

Montefiore was tall, strikingly handsome, and of remarkably good address—factors of great importance in his subsequent career. In his personal life he remained a pious and zealous Jew, meticulously observant (later in life, at least), attending services frequently on weekdays as well as on the Sabbath, and serving devotedly as a matter of course in all the lay offices of the Spanish and Portuguese community. When the Reform movement in Judaism began to establish itself in England, Montefiore was therefore one of its most uncompromising opponents—a reflection of his general attitude in religious matters. His opposition was perhaps responsible in part, together with the traditionalist tendencies of the country as a whole, for the fact that Reform Judaism had such scant success in England in the nineteenth century, if not indeed down to the present.

In 1827 and again in 1838 (as well as on various subsequent occasions) Montefiore and his wife (always his faithful companion and assistant in all he did) visited Palestine, which was then still a somewhat perilous adventure. He did this not in the spirit of the nineteenth-century English tourist but rather of the eighteenth-century Italian Jewish pilgrim, who went to pray at the Temple site in Jerusalem and at the graves of the patriarchs. This was a determining episode in his career: it extended his purview outside the bounds of Europe and into areas of which not many Westernized European Jews had personal knowledge at that time.

Montefiore Enters Public Life

Shortly after Montefiore's first Palestine visit, in 1828 and 1829, Catholic emancipation and the removal of nonconformist disability changed the position of Jews in England. Previously, they had shared, as we have seen, the disabilities of other religious dissenters in that country; now they found themselves the only substantial religious minority excluded from full (or nearly full) political rights. A movement therefore began for the emancipation of the Jews; though approved in 1833 by a majority of the reformed House of Commons, the bill granting

Jews full political rights was held up by the reactionary House of Lords for a generation. So far as civic affairs were concerned, however, the opposition was anemic—as indeed was inevitable in the age of the Industrial Revolution, when the successful merchant-financier was the beau-ideal of enlightened society. Already one Jew, David Salomons, had managed through his pertinacity to become Sheriff of the city of London (1835); in due course, he was to become also Alderman (1845) in the teeth of some opposition, and in 1855 Lord Mayor.

In 1837, Montefiore, whose political ambitions were not over-whelming—in contrast to Salomons—was prevailed upon to accept nomination also as Sheriff. He was knighted almost as a matter of routine, therefore, when young Queen Victoria paid her first official visit to the Guildhall, immediately after her accession. The entire Anglo-Jewish community rightly regarded this honor to him as a symbol of its own improved status. But there was more to it than a picturesque dignity, almost unprecedented though it was for an English Jew at that time. (It had been well over a century since the financier Solomon de Medina had received the same status at the hand of William III as a personal favor, in 1701, and there had been no other instance since then.) Sir Moses Montefiore had a status in the world, in the nineteenth century, which plain Mr. Montefiore would not have commanded, and this was to be of great importance in the years to come.

The Damascus Mission

In February 1840, in consequence of the disappearance of the superior of the Franciscan convent in Damascus, who happened to be a French subject, a charge of ritual murder was brought against the Jews of that ancient community; many of the Damascus Jews were thrown into prison and barbarously tortured, some actually dying. In that age of improved communications, the news spread rapidly throughout Europe and America, and aroused some anti-Jewish feeling in France, where it was widely believed that the "blood libel," so often disproved by scholars and condemned even by the Popes, was based on fact. The accusation obviously constituted an indictment of Judaism as well as of the persons immediately involved.

Sir Moses was serving at that time as president of the Board of Deputies of British Jews, an inter-synagogal Jewish organization that had come into existence in the mid-eighteenth century and, though hitherto inactive, had achieved some importance during recent years as a result of the movement for Jewish emancipation. As an experienced Mediterranean traveler, Montefiore offered to proceed to the Levant and see whether it would be possible to intervene with the Muslim authorities there on behalf of the accused persons; with him went Adolphe Crémieux, the lay leader of French Jewry. Montefiore was helped by the sympathy and support of the British representatives throughout the Eastern Mediterranean area acting under the instructions of the home government. As the result of representations to the Viceroy of Egypt, the two Jewish envoys secured the release of the imprisoned Jews. They then went on to Constantinople, where they procured from the Sultan, true to the ancient tradition of Turkish tolerance, a firman (royal decree) condemning the blood accusation in the most uncompromising terms and reaffirming that Jews of the Ottoman Empire were under imperial protection.

This mission—wholly successful in its outcome—was an epochal event in European Jewish history. It was the first occasion in which Western Jewry was able to exert itself effectively on behalf of its persecuted coreligionists elsewhere. This had been achieved through its constituted organizations and—an especially important detail—with governmental support. Montefiore's work thus provided the precedent and model for the activities of the American Jewish Committee and similar European institutions a century later which pursued comparable activities.

Montefiore's Levant mission initiated the "philanthropic" era of Jewish history which lasted unchallenged until the rise of Zionism, and which, notwithstanding certain faults of attitude and method, was responsible for memorable achievements and had its vindication in splendid Jewish types. It was the period when the Jews of Western Europe and America looked down somewhat patronizingly on their persecuted brethren elsewhere, but sacrificed themselves to the utmost to help them. They opened their purses generously for their relief if they were struck by disaster. They used every particle of influence they had to secure the intervention of enlightened governments on their behalf. They were convinced that, in the end, such efforts would be successful and Jews everywhere would reach the happly pinnacle of their Victorian coreligionists. This attitude was universal until, at the end of the century, Theodor Herzl * shattered their complacency with the bombshell of political Zionism.

Missionary for Jews

Henceforth, and down to the end of his prodigiously long life nearly half a century later (he was to celebrate his hundredth birthday before he passed away, active almost to the end), Montefiore was regarded more as an institution than as a personality in the Jewish world. Whenever and wherever the position of Jews was menaced in "backward" countries, the tall handsome English Jew, whom his Queen had delighted to honor, was, before long, on the spot, always enjoying British sympathy and diplomatic support. It was not so much *what* he achieved as *the spirit* in which he tried to achieve it. On occasion, he even used his unique experience for the benefit of oppressed Christian minorities in Muslim countries, as, for example, in North Africa.

By 1858, the political emancipation of English Jewry had been completed, the first Jew Lionel de Rothschild having taken his seat in Parliament in that year. Sir Moses was now an honored personage, enjoying the full rights of a citizen of what was then the world's most powerful and respected country. In spite of his own personal distinction on the British scene, Montefiore never hesitated to identify himself in the fullest possible sense both with the religious traditions of his fathers and with suffering Jews in other lands: the universal respect and veneration he enjoyed was not in spite of this but because of it. So highly was he regarded as a representative of British humanitarian rather than sectarian interests in these activities that, on his return from Damascus, he was authorized by the Queen to add to his coat-of-arms what are termed "bearers" (i.e., heraldic beasts holding a pennant), including the word "Jerusalem" in Hebrew, in specific recognition of his mission and its humane significance.

* See Chapter 8.

Numerically Anglo-Jewry was small—numbering perhaps only some ten thousand at the time of Montefiore's birth. Immigration and natural increase had brought it up to no more than forty-five thousand at the most by the time of his heyday, as against some two hundred and fifty thousand at this date in the United States. Nevertheless, Montefiore's self-sacrificing activity made him for many years outstanding among the Jewish communities of the world as the exemplar and champion of Jewish rights.

The perpetual problem of Jewish life in the course of the nineteenth century was the condition of Jews in Russia. Owing to her annexation of the greater part of Poland, that country now ruled over a majority of the world's Jews and—particularly under Czar Nicholas I, "the Russian Haman" (1825-1855)— was determined to put an end to their separate existence as a people. A network of oppressive regulations deprived Jews of basic human rights, restricted their opportunities of livelihood, excluded them from vast areas of the empire, and even suppressed many of their traditional institutions.

The success of the Damascus Mission made Jewish leaders hope that something of the same sort might be attempted here, with equally satisfactory results, and the well-tried Anglo-Jewish knight was obviously the man to undertake the task. Time after time Russian Jewish delegations implored Montefiore to intervene. The climax came in 1846 when an order expelling all Jews from the thickly populated frontier zone bordering on Germany and Austria was about to be put into effect. Something had to be done—and at once.

Efforts to Help Russian Jewry

At the close of the severe Eastern European winter, Montefiore, accompanied by his wife, journeyed to Russia. He was armed, as always, with useful diplomatic introductions and was fully backed by the English diplomatic representatives everywhere. He was acclaimed by the Jews with almost royal honor, amid the greatest possible popular enthusiasm wherever he passed on his way. Was this not the modern Mordecai, the Jew whom kings delighted to honor, and who, even in the royal court, remained meticulously faithful to his Jewish traditions? Among general circles, too, the courtly English gentleman created, as always, a most favorable impression. He was received in audience by the redoubtable Czar; he conferred with the minister responsible for Jewish affairs, and saw other persons in authority. As a result, he was ostentatiously given every facility to travel through the Pale of Settlement, in the sectors of the country to which Jews were for so long restricted by law, in order to observe the conditions of Jewish life there, and was invited to submit a report giving his personal recommendations for improving the conditions and status of Russian Jewry.

Montefiore did this with characteristic punctuality, attention to detail, and, it may be added, deference to authority. The ostensible results seemed at the time to be highly promising. The hated edict was withdrawn, and the Jews of the frontier districts were allowed to remain in their former homes. For a short while, it almost seemed as though a more friendly spirit had begun to pervade Russian governmental circles. Certainly they could no longer pretend, after their encounter with this proudly Jewish English gentleman, that the Jews were an unassimilable and parasitic element in national life.

On his way back through Germany, Montefiore was enthusiastically welcomed by the Jewish communities. Shortly after his return to England the Queen raised him to the hereditary rank of baronet "in the hope that it may aid your truly benevolent efforts to improve the social condition of the Jews in other countries by temperate appeals to the justice and humanity of their rulers."

But in the long run, the Russian mission proved to have aroused false hopes. Czar Nicholas had no desire to ameliorate the condition of his Jewish subjects so long as they remained Jews, and demonstrated the fact very clearly. His successors generally followed his lead, though not always with the same brutality. Thus, down to the close of Montefiore's life, the state of Russian Jewry continued to be a central problem in the Jewish world and one of his own constant preoccupations. There was an all too brief interlude after the death of Czar Nicholas I in 1855, when his son Alexander II attempted to initiate an ostensibly more liberal era in his empire, and relieved

Jewish subjects of some of their former crushing disabilities. Undoubtedly he had before his eyes the picture of Montefiore as a potential type of Jew who could emerge under conditions of emancipation.

In 1872, the now aged baronet went again to St. Petersburg—this time to bear a congratulatory message from the Board of Deputies of British Jews in London on the occasion of the bicentennial of the birth of Peter the Great. Again he was received with the utmost courtesy, was able to compare existing conditions with those on the occasion of his previous visit, and had the impression (as he reported on his return) that a new age in Russian-Jewish life, for which he had worked so devotedly, had dawned. But it proved to be a false dawn. After the Czar's assassination in March, 1881, the Russian government embarked on a policy of the blackest reaction, with the Jews again as the principal sufferers. The wave of massacres which broke out in the following year, adding the word "pogrom" to the English language, was a tragic landmark in Jewish history. The indomitable patriarch, now nearly one hundred years of age, offered his services to go to St. Petersburg once again to intercede. Whether he could have done anything is more than dubious, but the heroic spirit of the man commands admiration even now.

Meanwhile, in 1867, he had gone to Rumania on a similar mission—this time with the support of all the Great Powers, including even Russia—to make representations against the inhuman treatment to which Jews of that newly emerged petty state were being subjected. On that occasion, notwithstanding the protection of the Rumanian government, his life was actually threatened by an anti-Semitic mob in Bucharest. The heads of the state treated him with respect, not to say deference, struck hypocritically pious postures, and personally promised to carry out reforms: but actually this was the least successful of Montefiore's missions. Nothing was done, and notwithstanding treaty obligations and the most solemn undertakings, Rumania was to remain one of the dark spots on the map of the Jewish world, down to our own day.

The Mortara Case

At this period, although the Jews had been fully emancipated in the kingdom of Sardinia (the area which was to expand in the course of the nineteenth century into the kingdom of Italy), the Jews of Rome and the Papal States were still subject to the degrading restrictions and humiliations that had been imposed on them by the Popes at the time of the Counter-Reformation in the sixteenth century. One of the nightmares of their life was the threat of forced conversions. Although the Popes had always condemned baptism by naked force, any Jewish child over which the church could claim even a semblance of authority for some reason or other (frequently of the most shadowy description) might be dragged away from the bosom of his family to be brought up as a Christian.

One day in 1852, in Bologna, an ignorant nursemaid in a Jewish family named Mortara, imagining that Edgardo, the year-old baby in her charge, was about to die, performed her own makeshift baptismal ceremony over him with ordinary water so as to save his soul. Six years later, in 1858, she related this to her confessor, who instructed her to inform the authorities. In consequence, a squad of papal gendarmes was sent to the Mortara home to seize the child. He was whisked away to Rome in order to be brought up in the Catholic faith, sedulously removed from any family influence. A wave of horror spread through Europe, not confined by any means to Jews alone, and arousing impressive echoes in America as well. In Paris, where feelings ran high, the episode demonstrated how inadequate Jewish organizations were for dealing with such an emergency. In consequence the Alliance Israélite Universelle (which still does outstanding work) was formed, under the auspices of Montefiore's old colleague Adolphe Crémieux, later to be imitated by the now defunct Hilfverein der Deutschen Juden in Germany and the solidly-established Anglo-Jewish Association in England.

In the Mortara case, Montefiore followed what had become his normal pattern of action in such emergencies, traveling in person to Rome armed with letters of introduction to the most influential persons there, and receiving, as always, demonstrations of support from the English diplomatic representatives on the way. This time, however, he achieved nothing. It was a specific issue which could not be met, as on other occasions, with vague promises, expressions of sympathy, or promises of amelioration at some time in the future. And on the main issue the papal authorities were adamant: Edgardo Mortara continued to be brought up as a Catholic, subsequently becoming a priest and in the end a missionary.

In spite of this failure, however, Montefiore's position in the Jewish world was clearly that of its accredited representative at all times of stress and on all occasions when injustice against Jews anywhere in the world became manifest. He was more successful a few years later (1863) when the problem concerned a Muslim state, Morocco, where at that time power politics were inoperative and he could make the appeal on humanitarian grounds alone. This time his mission was not exclusively on behalf of the downtrodden Jew, who, besides suffering from all manner of galling medieval disabilities, had long been the target of maladministration and, now, of unfounded judicial charges which might well have resulted in a general persecution; the native Christian population was treated little better. The Sultan received Montefiore with barbaric splendor. The visit certainly created a deep impression throughout the world, and the American consul thought it significant enough to submit a detailed report on it to his government.

In 1872, when Montefiore was in his eighty-eighth year, he wanted to go to Persia, where the condition of the Jews, always wretched, had been rendered even more miserable by famine and popular turbulence. Again, in 1877, at the time of the Russo-Turkish War, when he was ninety-three years old, Sir Moses was restrained with difficulty from proceeding to the seat of hostilities in the Balkans, to see if his presence might help to expedite the relief work among the civilian sufferers—this time, predominantly non-Jews.

Montefiore and Palestine

Palestine was for Montefiore, as was natural and proper, an integral part of Jewish life and experience, and he visited the country seven times all told. At the time of his first journey there were perhaps some ten thousand Jews in all, mostly living in the four "Holy Cities"—Jerusalem, Safed, Tiberias, and Hebron: deeply pious, but without visible means of support, and nearly all dependent for their existence on the charity of their brethren abroad. Though his first visit was, as has been indicated, in the spirit of a medieval pilgrimage, Montefiore later became absorbed in the idea of revitalizing the land and its Jewish communities. It was not simply a question of charitable sentiment, as it was with some others. This stalwart Jew looked forward to the realization of the Messianic dream and the renewal of Jewish polity on the ancestral soil. "I do not expect that all Israelites will quit their abodes in those territories in which they feel happy, even as there are Englishmen in Hungary, Germany, America, and Japan," he wrote. "But Palestine must belong to the Jews, and Jerusalem is destined to be the seat of the Jewish Empire."

But Montefiore did not think in terms of the revival only in Messianic terms, for with all his piety he was severely practical. "Begin in the first instance with the building of houses in Jerusalem," he insisted. And his interest was by no means theoretical. Already in 1838, on the occasion of his second visit, he had submitted to Mehemet Ali of Egypt, then in control of the country, a detailed plan for establishing Jewish agricultural colonies, in advance of its day for its combined sound organization and religious idealism. A change of rule shortly afterwards made it impossible for the scheme to be carried into effect, although it had been seriously entertained. Nevertheless, to the very end of his life, Montefiore's enthusiasm for the idea never faltered, and he managed to put a good deal into effect. During each of his visits to Palestine, down to his extreme old age, he did something to forward fresh agricultural or industrial undertakings so as to improve the economic and moral status of the *Yishuv*, or to ameliorate the conditions of the country as a whole. Among his memorable achievements there was his helping pious Jews from the overcrowded cities to establish themselves on the soil, his sending young men for training in English textile mills in the hope that they would introduce new skills to the Holy Land, his trying to bring a better water supply to Jerusalem, his encouraging the removal of the densely packed

Jewish population of Jerusalem to newly built quarters outside the city walls (the nucleus of what is now, in fact, the capital of the State of Israel), and his improving conditions for those who went to pray—as he himself did so often—at the Western ("Wailing") Wall of the former Temple site.

In England and, indeed, in Europe as a whole, Montefiore was at the heart of various organizations for improving the lot of the Jews of Palestine, and more than once he pressed the need for systematic and practical action (though in vain) on the somewhat languid Board of Deputies in London. When the American philanthropist Judah Touro of New Orleans died in 1854, it was natural that, although he had never met Montefiore, by his will he appointed the latter to administer his considerable benefactions for the development of Jewish life in the Holy Land. Indeed, Montefiore's fourth visit to Palestine in 1855 was largely for the purpose of arranging for the use of Touro's bequest.

Sir Moses is thus in the tradition of Joseph Nasi, Duke of Naxos, who had made an early experiment in establishing a self-supporting Jewish settlement in and around Tiberias in the sixteenth century. On the other hand, Montefiore also helped to pave the way for Herzl, founder of political Zionism in its modern sense. He was, moreover, the father of the agricultural *Yishuv*, which was one of the most important factors in the recreation of a Jewish polity in Palestine in our own day. "Begin the hallowed task at once," the aged baronet wrote in his diary, on the occasion of his last visit to the country at the age of ninety, "and He who takes delight in Zion will establish the work of your hands."

The Philanthropist

In his private life, Montefiore achieved, with some degree of success, a synthesis of the life of the traditional Jew and the English country gentleman. He had purchased a great house and estate on the outskirts of the seaside town of Ramsgate, in Kent, not far from London. Here he entertained, squire-like, his neighbors and relatives, sometimes on a grand scale. The little Princess Victoria was given the run of the grounds before she became Queen in 1837 and long remembered this kindness. In 1846 Montefiore was appointed the High Sheriff of Kent—an honor reserved for the most esteemed of the country gentry.

To commemorate his first memorable visit to the Holy Land, he had built in 1833 a little synagogue adjoining his house, frequented by his household and the handful of Jews who lived in the neighborhood: here services were regularly conducted by an employee, who was in effect Montefiore's domestic chaplain, according to the Sephardi tradition in which he had been brought up; and when the aged baronet could no longer walk so far, he was carried in his sedan-chair—one of the last in regular use in England.

In Ramsgate, and in Kent generally, Montefiore was regarded with enormous affection by the whole population, and his hundredth birthday was celebrated as a public holiday—as it was in Jewish communities everywhere. His charities were unscientific indeed, but lavish; on a single evening, he dealt, he records, with applications for help from sixty widows. On the Sabbath he carried food-tickets with him so as not to have to handle money. In his later journeys, at least, he had with him his own *shohet* (kosher butcher), to ensure a supply of ritually acceptable food wherever he might be. And a scribe in Eastern Europe was kept perpetually occupied in copying Torah-scrolls—one a year—which Montefiore distributed among the Jewish communities far and near whom he honored with his patronage.

Sir Moses could and did read the Hebrew prayer book and the liturgical passages of the Bible, but, it seems, little or nothing more. It may be said, in this respect, he symbolized the gravest shortcoming of the Jewish communities in the English-speaking world, on both sides of the Atlantic, both then and in our own day.

On the other hand, Sir Moses had the positive attitude toward Jewish learning of the old-type Italian Jew. He took a remarkable Orientalist, Louis Loewe, into his service as his secretary, to accompany him on his journeys, to interpret for him when there was need, and to deal with the Hebrew correspondence which reached him in increasing volume from all parts of the world. Often, the patriarch would add to the letters sent out in his name his signature, in increasingly shaky square Hebrew characters, as he also did when he made his will. He lent the prestige of his name too to Jewish learned societies, such as the once-famous Mekitze Nirdamim, which was to edit and produce so many hitherto unpublished Hebrew works.

When his wife Judith died in 1866, Montefiore established in her memory next to his residence at Ramsgate a *yeshiva* of the traditional Sephardi or Italian type, well endowed, where resident scholars could perpetually study Jewish religious lore. The institution, still at Ramsgate, has since become modernized and has changed its complexion more than once. Recently, it was converted into an institution for training North African youths for the rabbinate, partly with a view to working in Israel—a cause which would certainly have been close to the heart of its pious founder.

The Legacy

In the course of his long life, Sir Moses Montefiore became an institution. Here was no timorous Jew, but a generous-hearted, warm-blooded one, for whom nothing that could adversely affect his brethren in any part of the world was a matter of indifference. After his first brilliant success in the Levant in 1840, his subsequent achievements, in political terms, were not perhaps great. But his spirit remained a permanent example and inspiration: a truism testified by the fact that his name was so frequently used for Jewish institutions in every country, in his lifetime and long afterwards.

Playing an honored part in English public life, Montefiore was at the same time completely loyal, as was well known, in his religious observance. Jews throughout the world of every type and in every land were his brethren; his life and background as well as his activities symbolized the unity transcending the differences between East and West, between Sephardim and Ashkenazim.

British Jewry had attained emancipation, but in his view this was not to be considered as their privilege alone. Sir Moses believed that it was the duty of the emancipated Jew to work for those yet unemancipated, wherever they might live, and to use the fact of his emancipation as an instrument for striving the more effectively in their behalf. Moreover, Palestine and the regeneration of Palestine were for him a practical ideal: not related to liturgical hopes or traditional charity, but translated into practice and reinterpreted in terms of nineteenth-century experience.

The old Jewish spirit of compassion, or *racamanut*, formerly restricted in operation to a single area, had its extension, under the circumstances of nineteenth-century life, to the whole world. The handsome, bewhiskered figure of Sir Moses Montefiore remains a symbol of its idealism and of the generous, self-sacrificing, ardent spirit that inspired it.

FOR FURTHER READING
Books about Moses Montefiore

GOODMAN, Paul, *Moses Montefiore* (Philadelphia: Jewish Publication Society, 1925). An excellent biography, it originally appeared in a series entitled quaintly "Jewish Worthies."

ROTH, Cecil, *A History of the Jews in England* (Oxford: University Press, 1964). The third edition of the best history of the Jews in England is immensely readable. The notes are very helpful.

LIPMAN, V.D. and Sonya, *Century of Moses Montefiore* (Oxford: Oxford University Press, 1985). An important new study that analyzes the key events in Montefiore's life and places them in the context of the times.

WOLF, Lucien, *Sir Moses Montefiore, A Centennial Biography, With Extracts from Letters and Journals* (London: John Murray, 1884). Though hard to obtain, this volume is a rich source for material about its subject.

RELIGIOUS
LEADERS

One of the greatest challenges confronting the Jew in the nineteenth and twentieth centuries has been that of reconciling his religion with the changing conditions of the modern world. Few intellectual challenges reached the Jew in the isolation of the ghetto. The limited sphere of economic activities allowed him—moneylending, petty trade and commerce—was harmonious with his religious and cultural life. As he emerged into the modern world at the end of the eighteenth century, however, the variegated economic pursuits which opened up to him made religious observance more difficult. The impact of modern rationalistic philosophies, science, and Biblical criticism awakened doubts and caused him to question the principles of traditional Judaism. The long struggle for emancipation, particularly in Germany, made the Jew anxious to eliminate the differences which separated him from his non-Jewish neighbor.

Wealthy privileged Jews began to mingle in Berlin salons, where they met bankers and diplomats on terms of equality. Yearning for complete social acceptance and regarding their Jewishness as a stigma, they began to identify themselves completely with German culture. Many prominent Jews even went so far as to embrace Christianity. Indeed, by the end of the first decade of the nineteenth century, more than ten per cent of Berlin's Jews had converted. In the following four decades more than four thousand Jews were baptized in Prussia alone. Four of Mendelssohn's children and all his grandsons save one underwent baptism. To help the Jew meet the impact of Western culture, and to counteract this flight from Judaism, Jewish leaders felt that some effort had to be made to render Judaism more acceptable.

The beginning of the Reform movement is usually associated with Israel Jacobson (1769-1828), a wealthy businessman of Westphalia. In 1810, at his own expense, he built a small synagogue, which he called a "temple," where he introduced a trained choir, hymns in German, and strict decorum. The sermon in the vernacular was a regular feature. The chanting of the prayers was accompanied by an organ, and a confirmation service for boys and girls was held. This experiment did not last long, for with the downfall of Napoleon, the Westphalian consistory was abolished. Jacobson, however, moved to Berlin and in 1815 arranged for a modified religious service in his own home.

When Jacobson's home synagogue proved too small for those who wanted to attend, a similar type of service was instituted in the home of Jacob Herz Beer, a Jewish banker, and was attended by hundreds from among the cultured classes of Berlin Jewry. But the Prussian government, fearing that religious reform might lead to civil disorder, ordered the synagogue closed. In December 1823 the king issued a cabinet order that henceforth "divine services of Jews must be conducted in accordance with the traditional ritual," thus terminating the efforts of Reform in Berlin for many years.[1]

A more successful effort got under way in Hamburg. Eduard Kley, one of the preachers at Herz Beer's private synagogue, became director of a school in Hamburg, and in 1818 established a temple in that city. An imposing building was erected and Gotthold Salomon, a gifted speaker, was engaged as preacher. Here also the organ, as well as vocal and instrumental music, was introduced, and the traditional cantillation of the Torah abolished. The first Reform prayer book was compiled in which some of the Hebrew prayers were replaced by German selections, while prayers for the return to Zion, for the coming of a personal Messiah, and for the restoration of the sacrificial cult were modified or eliminated. But in spite of many attacks by traditional leaders and several appeals to the Hamburg Senate, the temple remained open.

These first efforts at Reform were a spontaneous effort of laymen, small and experimental in character, seeking primarily to establish order and beauty in the synagogue. No organized attempt was made to develop a systematic philosophy of Judaism. Time had to elapse and a generation of rabbis and scholars trained in modern philosophy and alert to the trends of thought in Germany had to arise before any real effort at intellectual reconstruction could be undertaken.[2]

Foremost among these intellectual trends which influenced the new generation of Jewish leaders to become interested in reconciling Judaism with the new age were the rise of German nationalism and the glorification of the German state and culture. In the generation from 1815 to 1848 national consciousness became very strong in Germany. Reform leaders, anxious for full acceptance, toned down the national or ethnic elements of Judaism and other characteristics which separated the Jew from the non-Jew. They gave up the belief in a personal Messiah, repudiated the idea of a restoration to Palestine, and emphasized instead the universal aspects of Judaism.

Another factor which influenced the leaders of Reform was Protestantism—its concern with theology or creed, its opposition to ornate ritual and ceremonialism, and its emphasis on the Bible, with the right of each individual to interpret Scripture according to his own conscience. They envied and sought to imitate the decorum of the Protestant church, the hymns and prayers in the vernacular, the organ music and choir, and the sermons on universal moral themes.

Reform was also influenced by German idealistic philosophy, particularly that of Hegel. What Aristotle had been for the philosophers of the Middle Ages, Hegel became for Jewish thinkers of the nineteenth century. Indeed, Jewish thought in this period is often little more than a Jewish version of the philosophical idealism of Kant, Hegel, and Schelling.

Finally, the romantic outlook with its ardent interest in all forms of folk culture and its stress on history also had an impact on Reform Judaism. To understand a belief, custom, or institution, it was felt, one had to trace it from its beginnings.[3] This new emphasis on history led to the emergence of a group of German Jewish scholars who began to apply critical methods to the understanding of many neglected areas of the Jewish past. The founder of this new scholarly movement in Germany, known as the Science of Judaism (*Wissenschaft des Judentums*), was Leopold Zunz (1794-1874). His volume on the *History of the Sermon* (1832) demonstrated that the sermon was an ancient institution and that including it in the service was one of the best ways to revitalize public worship. His study of synagogue poetry of the Middle Ages (published in 1855) showed that since the prayer book was the work of several generations, the present generation could also make changes.[4]

The most prominent of the new theoreticians of Reform was Abraham Geiger (1810-1874), who enriched Jewish learning by a series of original and penetrating studies on the development of the Bible, medieval Jewish literature, and the history of the Jewish religion. Geiger was interested not only in reconstructing the Jewish past but in utilizing the knowledge thus acquired to chart the direction of the new Reform movement. To him Judaism had always been an evolving religion. By studying its growth and development, the scholar was able to distinguish between the essence of the faith—which lay in the universal ethical principles of Judaism taught by the prophets—and the accretions of history made up of the national aspects and the complicated system of laws and ceremonies. The latter had once served a useful purpose, but were now an obstacle to the fullest manifestation of the unique spirit of Judaism. It was the mission of Israel to preach these universal principles and make Judaism once again a world religion. If many contemporary Jews regarded their own religion as inferior and were attracted by Christianity, it was because of its narrow nationalism. Since the Jew has a unique gift for religious insight bordering on genius, once its national element was removed Judaism would become again a universal religion and prove its superiority to Christianity.

Geiger, therefore, objected to references in the traditional prayer book to the "chosen people," the coming of a personal Messiah, and the restoration of the Jews to Palestine. For the sake of continuity he wanted Hebrew to be retained in the prayer book but kept to a minimum in the actual worship service. Though he himself wrote essays in Hebrew, he felt that history had given its judgment against the language. He personally observed the dietary laws but primarily out of respect for his congregation. In private, he questioned their value because he felt they made for a separation between Jews and Christians. He also saw no objection to praying with uncovered head, though he made no attempt to carry out such a change in any of the congregations with which he was associated.[5]

Samuel Holdheim (1806-1860) was more radical than Geiger in his approach to Judaism. He officiated at mixed marriages between Jews and Christians, urged the transfer of the Sabbath to Sunday, and saw no need for the dietary laws or for circumcision. To Holdheim the healthy and permanent aspects of Judaism could be saved only by removing the diseased parts. He glorified the German state to so great an extent that in his view it was a special obligation to violate the Sabbath in order to work for the state.[6]

The differing views expressed by Geiger, Holdheim, and other Reform leaders might well have developed into a variety of sects had they not gotten together at a series of rabbinical conferences in Brunswick, Frankfurt, and Breslau (1844-1846), where major issues which confronted them were thoroughly thrashed out. The majority agreed that while there was no objective necessity in Jewish law to retain Hebrew throughout the service, it seemed "advisable" to do so at least for the basic prayers. It was also decided to continue to give the Messianic idea a prominent place in the liturgy, but references to a restoration of the Jewish state were to be eliminated. The Torah reading was to be based on the triennial cycle, and *Simhat Torah* celebrated only once every three years. Hold-heim and others recommended the abolition of the *Aliyot* or *aufruf-fen*, but the majority felt otherwise. It was unanimously agreed to allow the playing of the organ at services. At the third conference, held in Breslau, the Sabbath question was debated at length but no radical changes were recommended.[7]

The only radical Reform temple in Germany that continued through the nineteenth century was that of Holdheim. Almost the entire service was conducted in German, and the congregation worshipped without hats. Men and women were seated on the same level, though not together. Female voices were included in the choir, and services were held on Sunday instead of Saturday.

Aside from Holdheim's synagogue, however, Reform did not strike deep roots in Germany. There were many reasons for this: the opposition of Jews in the villages and small towns who constituted a large section of the population through most of the century, the attitude of the government which preferred to deal with officially constituted Orthodox congregations, the German climate which emphasized respect for tradition and authority, and the fact that the Reform Jew had to support the official congregation as well as his own synagogue.

Throughout this seminal period of the 1840's there were other rabbis and scholars who, while recognizing the need for change in religious life, were opposed to what they regarded as the radical tendencies of Reform. They did not organize themselves into a movement as Reform did. Nevertheless, based on the writings and expressions of opinion of its leaders they formed a "third party," the forerunners of what later came to be known as the Conservative tendency in Judaism. In many ways these scholars reflected the influence of the Science of Judaism as well as of the romantic outlook with its stress on history and tradition. While they recognized the necessity for modifications in Jewish life, they wanted to preserve the authority of Jewish law, the existence of Jews as a national entity, the survival values of Hebrew, and the hope of a Jewish restoration.

The outstanding spokesman of this group was Zechariah Frankel (1801-1875). Though steeped in Jewish classical sources, Frankel was a modern scholar, and made outstanding contributions to the history of Jewish law in his volumes on the Septuagint, the Mishnah, and Talmud. After serving as rabbi in Dresden for eighteen years, he was elected in 1854 as head of the Breslau Seminary, where he influenced a generation of rabbis in what came to be known as the "historical-positive" approach to Judaism.[8]

Frankel recognized that Judaism had always allowed changes through interpretation. He felt, however, that these changes could not be produced by theologians alone but must come from the people. Only those practices which the people had allowed to fall into disuse could be abandoned. He attended the first two rabbinical conferences in 1844 and 1845 in the hope of exerting a restraining influence and guiding the conference toward a moderate position. But when it was decided to retain Hebrew in the service only out of respect for the feelings of the older generation, he walked out of the conference in a dramatic protest against what he regarded as its radical trend.

To Frankel Judaism meant more than the universal principle of ethical monotheism emphasized by the Reformers. In his view, to neglect the national and historical elements which live in the consciousness of the Jewish people was to destroy Judaism. While his concept of nationalism did not include any actual steps for the restoration of Palestine, he felt that a belief in the ultimate return of Jews to their ancestral homeland had the power to arouse the enthusiasm of the Jew and was in line with Israel's Messianic hope.

Frankel stressed particularly the importance of Law, which had become in the course of time the Jewish expression of religiousness. Religion required outer symbols such as the *mezuzah, tephillin,* and observance of the Sabbath. The sanctity of these customs did not necessarily derive from their supernatural origin, but from the fact that for thousands of years they had found acceptance in Jewish life.[9]

These attempts of Frankel, Geiger, and Holdheim to reconcile Judaism with modern conditions did not go unopposed by the leaders of traditional Judaism. In Germany, Hungary, and Poland rabbis who espoused the age-old principles and practices of Judaism joined in condemning innovations in the Jewish religion. While it was not until the second half of the nineteenth century in Germany, when traditionalists often found themselves a minority in the communities where they lived, that they felt it necessary to organize a separate religious movement; even in the first part of the century those who refused to compromise with Jewish belief and practice came to be known as "Orthodox" * in contradistinction to the reformers and advocates of positive historical Judaism.

Among the outstanding Orthodox leaders in the first half of the

* The term "Orthodox" was applied to Jews for the first time by Abraham Furtado, president of the Paris Sanhedrin convened by Napoleon in 1807, and was afterwards used by Reform Jews to describe strict followers of tradition.

nineteenth century was Akiba Eger (1761-1837), rabbi in several important European communities and from 1816 to 1838 spiritual head of the province of Posen. This leading Talmudist and authority on Jewish law, to whom all the scholars of his generation turned for guidance, opposed with all his strength the attempts to introduce changes in the traditional prayer book. He forbade the use of any language but Hebrew in public prayers or any omissions or changes in the form of the religious services except for an occasional or incidental prayer. To him Hebrew was the national language of the Jewish people and the basis of Jewish unity. He, therefore, rebuked the champions of Reform for accepting with equanimity the people's lack of knowledge of Hebrew. "This prevalent ignorance," he wrote, "is a great evil." He blamed parents who taught their children French, Latin, and other languages but not the sacred tongue. "We are, then, worse than all the nations for each of them cultivates its own language while we neglect ours."

His son-in-law Moses Sopher (1762-1839), better known from his most important work as *Hatam Sopher*, head of the famous *yeshiva* in Pressburg (then part of Hungary) and one of the greatest Talmudic authorities of the nineteenth century, also combatted with great vigor and with the full weight of his authority the Reform movement. He condemned the three main innovations of the Hamburg movement—use of instrumental music in the synagogue, substitution of German for the Hebrew language in worship, and the omission of all prayers relating to the Messianic redemption of the Jewish people. To the *Hatam Sopher* Reform Judaism was a group defection like the Sadducees during the days of the Second Commonwealth and the Karaites in the eighth century, and had, therefore, to be fought.

While his Responsa are characterized by considerable rationalism, they are uncompromising in their attitude toward religious innovation and against any attempts at secular education in his own community. His spiritual testament *Tz'avot Moshe* forbade his children and descendants to have a secular education, an attitude which influenced Hungarian Orthodoxy throughout the nineteenth century. It was due chiefly to the influence of Moses Sopher that Reform made little headway in that land.

In Germany also there arose outstanding Orthodox leaders who put their emphasis on Torah study and tried to check the trend toward Reform. The progress of enlightenment in Germany was so far advanced, however, that even the Orthodox recognized that the needs of the times must be reckoned with. Thus, in Hamburg the community decided in 1821 to try and check the new movement

by calling to the pulpit Isaac Bernays (1792-1849), a strictly Orthodox rabbi, who had studied at the University of Wurzburg and was
equipped with a modern education. He was the first Orthodox rabbi
to preach in German, drawing on his philosophical background for
his discourses. He gradually enlarged the curriculum of the Talmud
Torah in Hamburg, which had previously taught only Hebrew and
mathematics, by adding courses in German, natural sciences, and
other secular subjects.

Bernays had a great influence on young Samson Raphael Hirsch,
who studied with him while completing his general studies at a local
gymnasium. As he grew to maturity, this young student recognized
that the world had entered a new period and that traditional Judaism, without compromising its basic beliefs, had to be interpreted
in the light of modern thought. His symbolical interpretation of
Jewish ritual, his emphasis on the values of observing Jewish law
and its influence on the perfection of the individual, his concept
of the Jewish mission, the role he gave to Jewish education, his
sermons delivered in German, especially the addresses at weddings,
his introduction of the synagogue choir and clerical attire for rabbis
and readers, all add up to a new and modern approach to Orthodox
or traditional Judaism. This approach has served as a source of
inspiration to many perplexed Jews during the past century. It is
to the life and teachings of the foremost representative of German
Orthodoxy that we now turn.

3. . Samson Raphael Hirsch

[1808–1888]

EDWARD W. JELENKO

S A M S O N Raphael Hirsch was one of the most outstanding—
and controversial—leaders of West European Jewry during the
nineteenth century. He succeeded in saving the heritage of the
Jewish people from the rapidly progressing disintegration and
in securing the continued existence of observant Jews in Germany. To this end, Hirsch reformulated the theology of Orthodoxy[1] and established an Orthodox Jewish community on new
foundations. He was the first among traditionalist rabbis to
develop successfully a synthesis of adherence to Talmudic
Orthodoxy with the study of the literature, philosophy, and the
social values of the non-Jewish world. Through his pioneering
spirit he created the movement of German neo-Orthodoxy.

Hirsch fought the Reform movement with all his power and
strengthened the influence of the Law, restoring it as a vital
element in the life of the Jew. He revised the system of religious
education and widened its scope by including the fundamentals
of secular culture.

Hirsch's forceful personality, his oratorical fire, his gifted
pen, and his unyielding perseverance, in addition to his scholarly
and literary achievements, won him a major role in the religious
revival of German Jewry. His influence as regenerator of traditional Judaism, manifest from the outset of his rabbinical career,
reached well beyond the borders of his own country. His system and his ideas found a particularly receptive atmosphere in
other countries where Jews were confronted with the same

problems which German Jewry had had to face during the nineteenth century.

Traditional Roots

Born on June 20, 1808, in Hamburg, Hirsch was a descendant of a family celebrated for both learning and piety. His father was a man of strict observance and high intellect who, though a merchant, devoted much of his time to Talmudic studies. His grandfather, Rabbi Mendel Frankfurter, a disciple of Jonathan Eybeschütz, the famous Chief Rabbi of Hamburg, had been, in his day, well known as a Jewish scholar and the founder of a large Talmud Torah. A grand uncle of Rabbi Hirsch, Rabbi Yehuda Loeb Frankfurter was the author of two Talmudic works.

The religious spirit pervading the Hirsch home and the adherence to traditional practices decisively shaped the boy's affinity to Orthodoxy. In addition to this early indoctrination, Hirsch's attachment and lasting fidelity to his heritage were intensified by the controversy brought about by the rise of the Reform movement in Hamburg.

The immediate cause of this controversy was the organization of a Reform society by Eduard Kley, a former preacher of the Reform temple in Berlin who, in 1817, became principal of the Jewish Free School in Hamburg. Kley immediately took active steps to create the Hamburg Reform Union Temple, which was dedicated a year later. The Hamburg rabbis violently denounced the "heresies" of the new movement and unsuccessfully attempted to have the temple closed by the government, whereupon a long and bitter struggle ensued among Hamburg Jewry. Since much of the discussion on the strategy to be followed by the Orthodox forces took place in the Hirsch home, the boy undoubtedly absorbed something of their ideas and arguments; these influenced his philosophy throughout his life.

Since the old-school *dayanim* (judges of the *Bet Din*, the rabbinical court) lacked training in modern knowledge and were therefore ill-prepared for the contest, the Hamburg community decided in 1821 to appoint Isaac Bernays as the spiritual leader or *hakham*, as he preferred to call himself, of its congregation. Although Bernays' scholarship and secular education were widely respected, his efforts to stem the tide of Reform proved unsuccessful. This was partly because of his inability to present the case for Orthodoxy in simple, understandable terms,[2] and partly because of his open contempt for the radical wing of the Reformers, whom he accused of contracting the majestic spirit of Judaism within narrow bounds.

Bernays had ability, however, to inspire his students with devotion to their faith. As Hirsch's first teacher, Bernays undoubtedly influenced him to choose the rabbinate rather than the commercial career for which his parents had designated him.

Student Days

In furtherance of his plan to become a rabbi, Hirsch went to Mannheim where, under the guidance of Rabbi Jacob Ettlinger, who later became the renowned rabbi of Altona, he devoted himself assiduously to Talmudic studies. While Bernays had opened Hirsch's eyes to the beauty of the Bible, it was Ettlinger who introduced him to the world of the Talmud.[3]

After a year at Mannheim, Hirsch matriculated at Bonn University in 1829. There he was brought in contact with a number of intellectuals among his fellow students, one of whom was Abraham Geiger.

With Hirsch and other Jewish theological students at Bonn University, Geiger founded a debating society which met in his room on Saturdays for homiletic exercise and candid criticism. Hirsch was the first to preach. In the discussion that followed his sermon, Geiger learned to respect Hirsch's "extraordinary eloquence, his ingenuity, his clear and rapid comprehension." This was all the more noteworthy since their viewpoints, even then, were conflicting enough to create misunderstanding. But in the course of studying Talmud together and exchanging friendly criticism for two semesters, their fellowship grew into mutual esteem.

It is strange indeed that two warm friends, descendants of families of similar background, both sincere and both inspired by a genuine desire to work for the welfare of the Jewish people, should have sought the realization of their ideals upon roads so utterly divergent, leading to goals so diametrically opposed. History assigned to these men the leadership of opposing camps in a partisan struggle which, at times, was bitter and marked by personal attack, though both made every possible effort to avoid overt conflict. Years later, during Geiger's Frankfurt incumbency, when they lived in the same community, they avoided direct contact or any open manifestation of their disdain for each other's ideas. In his posthumously published writings, Geiger acknowledged that his fellow student, who eventually emerged as his antagonist, had exerted great influence on him and had contributed largely to his enjoyment of the Bonn days.[4]

Rabbi in Oldenburg

Hirsch had hardly spent a year at the university when, in 1830, at the age of twenty-two, he became rabbi (*Landesrabbiner*) of the Grand Duchy of Oldenburg. He succeeded Rabbi Nathan Adler, later Chief Rabbi of Great Britain, who, upon his own departure from Oldenburg, proposed Hirsch for the vacancy, writing to the Oldenburg authorities: "Among all the candidates who have applied for this office, Samson Raphael Hirsch seems to me the most appropriate one." [5]

The position in Oldenburg was replete with many practical difficulties, but they failed to discourage Rabbi Hirsch. The impact of his Bonn experience, which had brought him face to face with religious problems vexing Jewish intellectuals, created in him the impetus for action. After hard study and reflection, he was resolved to secure the widest possible dissemination of the true meaning of Judaism as he understood it.

Nineteen Letters of Ben Uziel

Hirsch's first plea for Orthodoxy as a vital faith took the form of *The Nineteen Letters about Judaism of Ben Uziel*, one of his most significant and characteristic writings, published in 1836.[6] Conviction, strength of mind, and sincerity vibrated through every line. Their impassioned appeal and forceful style attracted wide attention, although the era was dominated by men such as Ludwig Börne and Gabriel Riesser, both vigorous advocates of emancipation, whose literary and philosophic writings negated many of the precepts of Judaism.

The *Letters*, patterned after the "dialogue" method used by Judah Halevi in his *Kuzari*, are a fictitious correspondence between a young rabbi called Naphtali and his youthful friend Benjamin, who, though originally religious, had lost his early religious beliefs through contact with the world and the reading of non-Jewish literature. In the first letter Benjamin complains about the set prayers, the rituals of Judaism, and the restrictions it places on all enjoyment. Judaism, he writes, distorts the intellect, begets a brooding disposition, and by its laws of separation, generates mistrust and suspicion. An understanding of one's age is needed, he maintains, and the striving for happiness and perfection must be man's goal.

The letters that follow are devoted to an exposition of the Jewish way of life, guiding the "perplexed" back to the wisdom of his ancestors. Beginning with the fundamental premise of the existence of a supreme power, the ruler of the universe, Hirsch concludes that the human race must reflect the infinite potentiality of the good in God. But with freedom of the will comes the inevitable conflict and confusion between good and evil—hence, the need for a community which will dedicate itself entirely to the mission of teaching humanity to seek the good or, what is synonymous, to obey the will of God. Such a people must have distinctive laws and customs to distinguish it from the mass of humanity so that it may be consecrated to the service of God—a duty historically assumed by Israel.

There follows an analysis of the Torah and the demonstration that its every part is essential and necessary, either to the furtherance of the ideal of good on the part of mankind or the establishment of Israel in its character of "servant of the All-One." No human authority, say the *Letters*, has power to abrogate any of the divine institutions.

Hirsch sees the divine spirit reflected in the harmony of every line of the Bible, the *Halakhah*, *Aggadah*, and the Midrash. To him, the Sabbath, for example, is not decreed merely as a day of rest from toil, but as a testimony of God's creation and might and as a sanctification for the days of the coming week, in keeping with *Halakhic* interpretation.[7] Since the Sabbath came to be regarded as a sign of loyalty to God, Hirsch treats with special detestation those who violate it.[8]

Yet, in this early work, he speaks of Reformers with mild

regret and pity for their erring ways, in sharp contrast to the fulminations of his later days during which he often misrepresented and distorted the position of his opponents. At this stage he did not "attempt to counter the attacks by the medium of apologetics, nor to conciliate opponents by means of feeble compromises between faith and science. His aim was rather to present the Judaism of old in such a light that sheer beauty of its form and the sublimity of its contents would win over those capable of religious feeling." [9]

The style of the *Letters* has been called "classical" by some of the author's admirers, although its extremely long sentences and other literary mannerisms often prove taxing to the modern reader.

Rabbi Hirsch published the *Letters* under a pseudonym—an action characteristic of the intensity of his feelings and his singleness of purpose. He did not seek fame; neither did he wish to use his name to procure a favorable reception for his book. His sole motivation was to give his fellow Jews food for thought. Nevertheless, his authorship did not long remain a secret, and it soon became known that the youthful rabbi of Oldenburg had written an eloquent and original defense of Orthodox Judaism.

The Nineteen Letters was praised by both friend and opponent. Isaac Marcus Jost, an historian, Reform leader and teacher in the Jewish schools in Frankfurt, wrote: "The decisive way in which he defends a cause which one had almost deemed lost, the enthusiasm and lively eloquence with which it was presented, could not fail to arouse a certain enthusiasm." [10] Geiger, in his evaluation of the work, gave expression to the "admiration and friendship" he felt for Rabbi Hirsch, and his sadness at the opposite roads the two men had taken:

> We recognized in its every feature, in its clarity and incisiveness, in its burning zeal, in the strength of its independence, in the fear of conceding anything to the prejudice of his cause, as well as in his victory over that fear—in these inestimable advantages of mind and heart, nay in the very weakness of the trend, to which we could not close our eyes—in all these we recognized a dear friend, who has won our admiration and friendship at first sight and who will keep these forever. Who will bear me a grudge if I confess to having felt a pang because we were going in different

directions, when such divergence makes for a break, not only of ordinary contact, but of intimate personal ties? Who will blame me if I here give expression to that pain. . . .[11]

The Horeb

In the last of *The Nineteen Letters*, "Ben Uziel" drafted his plans for the publication of a work about the commandments of Judaism, "extracts from the four-fold code, the *Shulkhan Arukh* . . . everything shall be treated popularly, directly for life . . ." [12] In 1838, Hirsch thus published in Altona his *Horeb—Essays on Israel's Duties in the Dispersion,* although he had actually written it earlier than the *Letters* because he considered "as our nearest and most fundamental evil the false opinions and notions which prevail concerning the extent as well as the meaning of our *mitzvot*." The purpose of the volume was to prevent people from looking upon what he said about Israel as "a mere dream picture, a creation of the enthusiastic fancy, nowhere existing in reality."

Realizing the necessity of bringing the contemporary Jew to an understanding of the reasons for the religious commandments, he adopted neither the pedagogical and utilitarian principles of explanation frequently resorted to by Maimonides, nor the mystical-allegorical method of interpretation of *Kabbalistic* and *Hasidic* literature. Like Mendelssohn, he stressed the psychological and symbolical meaning of the *mitzvot*, applying his method with great ingenuity, yet in a way which may often seem somewhat arbitrary and not quite plausible.

Horeb, the mountain in the Sinai desert on which God promulgated the Law through Moses, was indeed an appropriate title for a work in which Israel's duties were set forth and explained. Each law—ceremonial, ethical, and devotional—is thoroughly expounded and interpreted according to its part in the vast edifice of the ordinances. Although written "in the first place for Israel's thinking youths and maidens," the book is not easy reading. Nevertheless, it became a favorite source of edification in many families because of its powerful plea for purity and chastity.

The effect of both *The Nineteen Letters* and *Horeb* was pro-

found. In them Hirsch tried to find, and at least partially succeeded in finding, a new rationale for the "yoke" of the Law, the
severity of which was burdensome to the Western Jew. He
felt that some sort of reinterpretation was indispensable to
preserve Israel's devotion to the God idea. He strove to clarify
misunderstandings and, ultimately, to eliminate the diffusion of
Jewish spiritual verities.

Hirsch and Graetz

The idealistic tone of Hirsch's description of Israel's mission
was admirably adapted to reach the hearts and minds of impres-
sionable "educated young Jews." Among these young people
was Heinrich Graetz, a particularly gifted student who became
fascinated with Hirsch's writings and determined to devote himself to serious Talmudic and Biblical studies in order to be able
to champion the cause of Orthodox Judaism. To this end,
Graetz, then in his twentieth year, wrote to Hirsch, whom he
considered the only trustworthy guide, and was invited to live
with the already renowned Oldenburg rabbi. For more than
three years, Hirsch provided for almost all of Graetz' needs,
devoting a great deal of time and effort to his instruction as well
as to the supervision of his moral and religious conduct, while
Graetz, in turn, performed duties of companion and secretary.
This relationship between the fatherly teacher and the brilliant
pupil has been described by Graetz' biographer, Philip Bloch,
who gives a portrayal of the personality of Hirsch:

> In Samson Raphael Hirsch he (Graetz) met a man whose spiritual
> elevation and noble character compelled his profound reverence,
> and who fully realized all the expectations that he had harbored
> concerning him. Hirsch was a man of modern culture, and his
> manner was distinguished, even aristocratic, although he kept
> aloof from all social intercourse. He was short in stature, yet
> those who came in contact with him were strongly impressed
> by his external appearance, on account of his grave, dignified
> demeanor, forbidding familiarity. With great intellectual gifts
> and rare qualities of heart, he combined varied theological attain-
> ments and an excellent classical education. . . . He was the only
> teacher from whom Graetz's self-centered being received scien-
> tific stimulation; perhaps the only man to exercise, so far as the
> stubborn peculiarity of Graetz's nature permitted it, permanent
> influence upon his reserved, independent character.[13]

Five years after Graetz left Oldenburg, he dedicated his doctoral thesis, *Gnosticism and Judaism*, to "Samson Raphael Hirsch, the brilliant champion of historical Judaism, my unforgettable teacher and fatherly friend, in love and gratitude." [14]

Chief Rabbi of Moravia and Austrian Silesia

After eleven years in Oldenburg, Hirsch, now widely known as the champion of the "Old-Believers" (*Alt-Gläubige*), was called in 1841 to Emden as rabbi of East Frisia. Here he remained six years, active as he had been in Oldenburg with the organization of schools and charitable institutions, deeply concerned with the regulation of the service, serving as a dignified and tactful mediator between his people and the government.

In 1847, he received the highest tribute which could be paid an Orthodox rabbi in the West—a call to the rabbinate of Nikolsburg in Moravia, a position of distinction because of the outstanding Talmudic scholars who had previously occupied it, including Mordecai Benet and Nahum Trebitsch. A still greater tribute or recognition came to Hirsch in his elevation in the following year to the position of Chief Rabbi of Moravia and Austrian Silesia, inhabited by approximately 43,000 Jews, where his predecessors included Yom Tov Lipman Heller, Chief Rabbi of Prague and author of the *Tosafot Yom Tov*, an important commentary on the Mishnah, and Nahman Krochmal, founder of the Cracow Yeshiva. Hirsch was inducted into this office by Isaac Noah Mannheimer, an outstanding preacher in Vienna who had begun his career as the leader of the Reform movement in Denmark only to completely change his views, and who, in a letter to Geiger, denounced the "work of destruction" of the Reform movement at the rabbinical meeting in Breslau in 1846. [15]

In Nikolsburg (the seat of the chief rabbinate), Hirsch had to face adversaries on two fronts. Those who remained loyal to tradition looked to him as "a man in whom God's spirit is immanent," as Mannheimer characterized him, and who expected him to undo the Reform measures. The Reformers, on the other hand, hoped that a rabbi of modern education would appreciate their point of view and would conform, at least in part, to their ideas. What made his position still more difficult was that many of the Orthodox Jews felt that they could not subscribe to his modernism. Thus, all his attempts to establish an efficient congregational and educational organization failed, and he was *Oberlandesrabbiner* in name only. Hirsch nevertheless remained in Nikolsburg for four difficult years, and in 1851 accepted the rabbinate at Frankfurt-am-Main. He regarded the change as a great blessing.

Rabbi of Frankfurt

For decades, Frankfurt had been the acknowledged home of Torah study in Western Europe. But prior to the coming of Hirsch, the traditionalist minority in the Jewish community had found itself in a highly critical and dependent situation. German Jewry was organized in *Kehillot* or *Gemeinden*—rather than in congregations, as we know them in the United States—with virtually every Jew belonging to the all-embracing community organization. Synagogues, educational and charitable institutions were subordinate organs of the united community. In administrative as well as in purely religious questions the rabbi had to recognize the Jewish Community Council, a kind of directorate, as his superior authority.

Two-thirds of the Frankfurt Community Council members were strong protagonists of Reform; any proposal put forward by the Orthodox minority was, from the outset, doomed to defeat.

A comprehensive description of the situation is presented by Steven S. Schwartzchild:

> During the first generation of the rise and eventual preponderance of religious liberalism, i.e. up to about 1860, Jewish Reform was ideologically and politically quite radical and aggressive. Where, as in the ancient and great community of Frankfurt on the Main, the liberals achieved majority status on institutional boards, they did not hesitate to ignore the Orthodox minority. They often violated traditions unnecessarily, and, in the proud awareness of being enlightened and the majority, even abolished, at times, the facilities which the conservatives needed for the practice of Judaism as they believed in it.[16]

As early as 1818 when a member of the community donated 50,000 guilders toward the founding of a new school for the teaching of the Bible and Talmud, the plan was voted down. When, in spite of contrary regulations, the Talmud instructions had continued, the police were called, and teachers and pupils alike were hunted down and banned from the city. Citizens harboring such offenders were fined fifty florins. A *"Tsitsit* Society" for private Sabbath study of the weekly Bible sections had been forced to disband. The provision of kosher food for prisoners and hospital patients had been stopped. Such was the plight of Frankfurt's Orthodox Jewry during the years prior to Hirsch's arrival.[17]

Eleven pious members of the community had met in 1849 and drawn up a petition to the Frankfurt Senate, asking for permission to establish a new Jewish communal organization with all the necessary institutions. The petition was granted on condition that the new organization constitute itself not as a communal but as a religious association, and that its members settle their financial obligation with the official Jewish community.

By the middle of 1851, the newly established religious association (Israelitische Religions-Gesellschaft) had about one hundred members. It became necessary for them to seek a rabbi and the position was offered to Hirsch. Although he was not unaware that the numerical strength and financial resources of the Frankfurt community were in the hands of his opponents and that only a little-known private organization with no synagogue building of its own awaited him, Hirsch left his fairly lucrative position as Chief Rabbi of Moravia and Silesia, which had been invested with state authority, to accept the new post.

A few rooms had been rented and converted into a place of worship. Through years of hard work and struggle, Hirsch succeeded in arousing enthusiasm among his congregants and in attracting new followers among the leading Jewish families. He transformed the original group of eleven men into an impressive model congregation which numbered some five hundred families at the time of his death in 1888. Among them was the Frankfurt branch of the Rothschild family, which made a generous donation toward a new, imposing synagogue built in the Schuetzenstrasse, consecrated two years after Hirsch's arrival.

Unlike his teacher Bernays, who clung to the old disorder in the synagogue, Hirsch introduced strict discipline and decorum into the services. Some of the changes which he made, however, evoked opposition; in fact, in certain circles outside of Germany, Hirsch was regarded as a Reformer. Among the purely external changes introduced were the German sermon, the synagogue choir, and clerical attire for rabbis and readers. When in the *Bet Hamidrash* (House of Study) the Psalms were translated and explained, the *dayanim* would remark with a sigh that "in former times they 'learned' the Gemarah and 'said' *T'hillim*, while now they 'said' the Gemarah and 'learned' *T'hillim*."

Expansion of Jewish Education

But Hirsch did not confine his efforts to the synagogue. As educational philosopher, he sought and found solutions to the problems of integrating Jewish and European cultures and effecting a complementary relationship between sacred and secular studies in the school. The establishment of an elementary and secondary school for boys and a high school for girls was one of his most significant achievements.

There were a number of Jewish elementary schools in Central Europe, but the humanities were the primary subject matter of instruction, while their educational goal was the preparation for occupational life; there was little concern for the strengthening of Judaism. The majority of children did not attend Jewish school and came under Jewish influence only during religious exercises. Those children who did receive religious instruction could not pursue it in a systematic manner because they had little time for anything but their secular studies.

To remedy this situation, Hirsch addressed a letter to the Religions-Gesellschaft a few weeks after his appointment as rabbi in Frankfurt, proposing the establishment of a school "in which the elements of religious living and of general social education should be cultivated and furthered with an equal amount of care." The congregation supported the proposal and the Frankfurt Senate gave its consent. Thereupon Hirsch, like his grandfather, Rabbi Mendel Frankfurter, who had established the Hamburg Talmud Torah, had to go from house to house, virtually begging for contributions and pupils. Finally, a building was acquired and the school was opened on April 1, 1853, with an enrollment of eighty-four boys and girls. Recognized by the government, by Jews and by non-Jews, as a model school, it constantly grew until the number of pupils reached six hundred. In 1881, it moved into a new, well-equipped building, donated by Baron Karl von Rothschild, where it remained in existence until the Nazi ascendancy to power.

Of the school's educational methods and approach, Professor Zvi E. Kurzweil gives the following description:

It was characteristic that the secular studies were also imbued with a Jewish spirit in the sense that there was an attempt to teach general subjects from a Jewish point of view. For instance, in German lessons, literature showing a Biblical influence was chosen for study, such as the works of Schiller, the plays of Goethe like "Iphegenia" and "Faust," which were influenced by the Bible. Lessing's dramas reflecting his tolerant and broad outlook on matters of religion were also chosen for study. The integration of national consciousness and humanism in the works of Herder was especially valued. In non-German literature, too, preference was given to those works which portrayed Jewish characters, and the historical and social background that brought about this portrayal in various literatures was clearly demonstrated. The question of what was "the attitude of the Torah" toward various problems that arose in literature was frequently posed. This might seem to be of doubtful value esthetically, but educationally it was of great importance to emphasize that the approach to such literary creations was Jewish and it was as Jews that the students read and evaluated them. History and science were taught from a religious point of view and divergences between science and the Orthodox Jewish attitude to the world were considered and became subjects for debates. The aim was not to teach the Jewish and secular subjects separately, but to show their inter-relationship. Thus the teacher tried to foster in his pupils a fine Jewish outlook based on a profound grasp of Judaism. This explains the fact that so many pupils remained Orthodox after leaving the school.[18]

Hirsch recognized that education was a potent instrument for the preservation of Judaism in an alien environment, and an effective weapon in the war against the corrosion of assimilation. In fact, his lifelong interest in the religious development of the young was amply justified, for he was able to imbue his pupils with a lasting devotion to Judaism.[19] They translated into reality the motto inscribed on the school's banner by its founder: *"Yofe Talmud Torah in Derekh Eretz"* ("Study of the Torah in harmony with the prevailing civilization").

The Secession Movement (*Trennungs-Orthodoxie*)

During all these years Hirsch struggled for freedom of conscience by seeking to abrogate the law which compelled Jews either to remain contributing members of the Jewish Community Council or to renounce Judaism. In order to shake off this supremacy of the Council, Hirsch issued two pamphlets *Das Prinzip der Gewissensfreiheit* (The Principle of Freedom of Conscience) in 1874, and *Der Austritt aus der Gemeinde* (Secession from the Community) in 1876, in which he demanded the right to secede, aiming at the complete separation from the Frankfurt Community as well as the legal recognition of the Religions-Gesellschaft as an independent congregation. He also sent an appeal to the Prussian Diet wherein he declared "before the Lord, the God of truth, that between none of the various denominations existing within the Christian church is there a more thorough-going antagonism than between Reform Judaism and Orthodox law-observant Judaism." He therefore asked that serious consideration be given to this profound diversity of conviction, especially since the adherents of these two main movements in Judaism had long ceased to have a community of interest.

In spite of far-reaching concessions granted by the community which feared a disruption into sects, Hirsch remained adamant. His rejection of any compromise was strongly disapproved by Orthodox authorities who saw in the secession an open and incurable split in the Jewish ranks. Numbered among them were Rabbi Seligman Baer Bamberger of Würzburg, a Talmudic scholar of renown, and Moses Loeb Mainz and his brother, two wealthy merchants who had been instrumental in Hirsch's appointment as rabbi of the Religions-Gesellschaft.

But Hirsch stood firm, insisting that it was not he with his few adherents who separated from the great majority of German Jewry, but the majority who divorced themselves from genuine Judaism. He further vindicated his point of view by emphasizing that secession was an "obligation" decreed by religious law and should not be looked at from the viewpoint of political or practical considerations. His memorandum finally proved effective and, with the aid of Eduard Lasker, a liberal-minded member of the Diet who had an Orthodox Jewish background, the Secession Bill was passed by a large majority on July 28, 1876.

Last Years

Hirsch's last major work, completed when he was seventy-four, the *Translation and Explanation of the Psalms* (1882; second edition, 1898), was distinguished by elegance of rendition and strict adherence to the text. Like his translation and commentary on the Pentateuch, this work was also characterized by his unique method of exegesis, in which he uncovered certain kinds of symbolism which invested many of the passages with new significance.

In his last years he found consolation in his five sons and five daughters, all of whom were deeply devoted to their father's teachings. Hirsch had always held up to his sons his own Torah ideal. As professionals and businessmen, they demonstrated in their lives that it was possible even in the age of emancipation to combine Jewish learning and religious observance with participation in the cultural and economic life of their country.

Although his health was failing, Hirsch's mental capacity remained unimpaired and his zeal undiminished. This enabled him to work until the very end, which came quietly and without pain on December 13, 1888.

What Hirsch Believed

Hirsch did not accept the division between internal religious feeling and the external ritual, between the intention underlying a religious act and the act itself. He stressed that the Torah is concerned, first and foremost, with the reality of life; it was not revealed in order to inform man about the supernatural reality and to impart to him "dogmatic" truths, but to teach him the way he should go "in order to live." Hence, the principle of Jewish faith cannot be separated from the "ceremonial" law.

Stating that the belief in one God converts a heathen into a man, and that the fulfillment of the Law converts a man into a Jew, Hirsch hastened to draw the conclusion that the difference between a liberal and an Orthodox Jew is greater than that between a Protestant and a Catholic. "It was not the so-called Orthodox Jews," wrote Hirsch, "who introduced the name of Orthodoxy into the Jewish sphere. The term was first used in a derogatory sense by the 'advanced' Reformist Jews of their 'old backward' brethren. These thought the name insulting and, indeed, Judaism does not recognize any variants. It knows of no Mosaic, prophetic or rabbinic, and of no Orthodox or progressive Judaism. It either is Judaism or is not."

In his deeply spiritual justification of the commandments, he safeguarded his Orthodoxy by stipulating, as required by Jewish law and tradition, that while the practical execution of the laws is mandatory, their intellectual explanation is optional. Therefore, obedience is beyond any question, even when one lacks an explanation or disagrees with his interpretation. His reasons for the *mitzvot* are often far-fetched though lofty in their presentation. For example, without offering any reason or justification for God's command of the covered head, Hirsch indulged in a weak defense, based on a still weaker logic:

> . . . only those parts which principally serve as tools for human work, as face and hands, shall be visible; but everything which mainly subserves animal function, shall be covered; that to the corporeal eye, too, only the human in you may appear, the best remain under cover, that your very presence may remind: you are here for a divinely human vocation, not for a bodily-beastly. And as you withdraw the beastly part of your body from the eye, you may not, in any way, bear your body as if imposing esteem, so as to stride along with loftily rigid neck, adding, so to say, to your animal size, and, as if that were your greatness, forcing that upon the eye.

Although Hirsch strictly obeyed the Biblical injunction whereby nothing may be added to the commandments and nothing may be taken away therefrom (Deuteronomy 13:1), one gains the impression that, since the conclusion of the Talmud, the distinction between minor and major *mitzvot* has disappeared. Nonetheless, Hirsch succeeded in creating in the minds of many thousands of Jews in many parts of the world the feeling of joy in performing the religious duties. Hirsch is the founder of what later came to be known as "neo-Orthodoxy." [20] Rabbi I. Grunfeld, however, maintains that this term for the new movement is a "complete misnomer. In reality, Hirsch's conception of Judaism was not new; it was merely an application of the old, i.e., traditional Judaism to post-emancipation conditions." [21]

The Struggle Against Reform

As a supplement to his *Ben Uziel*, Hirsch published in 1838 his *First Communication from Naphtali's Correspondence*, followed in 1844 by his *Second Communication from Correspondence Regarding the Newest Jewish Literature*.[22] Through these polemic essays, Hirsch actively joined in the prevailing controversy aroused by the sweeping reforms of Samuel Holdheim, then rabbi in Frankfurt-on-Oder, the oldest and probably the most radical of the triumvirate of leading Reform apostles, consisting besides Holdheim of Abraham Geiger and Ludwig Philippson.

In this dialectic role, Hirsch proved himself a master. With persuasive reasoning and biting satire, he tried to expose what to him were "the shallowness and unworthiness of the Jewish Reform movement." He pointed out how the movement had started cautiously, beginning with merely external changes in the ritual, such as the introduction of shorter prayers in the vernacular and German songs in the divine service. (At that time, German was hardly spoken by Frankfurt Jews; some sort of Yiddish—one might call it "Judeo-German"—was the common language.) "Religious assimilation began with an attempt to level down the Jewish synagogue service to that of the Protestant church." [23]

Holdheim and his circle, including David Einhorn, Chief Rabbi of Mecklenburg, Moritz Abraham Stern, Professor of Mathematics at the University of Goettingen, and Theodor Greizenach, one of the principal founders of the Frankfurt Jewish Reformverein, "enriched neither credal nor ceremonial Judaism." [24] Instead they introduced new forms and methods, borrowed from the church, such as the substitution of Sunday for Sabbath services, with men attending bareheaded, as well as a liturgy, which apart from a few Biblical quotations and the *kaddish,* deviated fundamentally from tradition. Holdheim not only removed the "noisy" features, especially the sing-song praying, from the services, but also shifted the center of gravity in worship from the congregation to the minister. He also officiated at "mixed" marriages and promoted the ceremony of confessing the faith (confirmation) for boys and girls—an idea considered by Hirsch to have no roots or meaning in Judaism.[25] Furthermore, Holdheim advocated the abolition of circumcision.[26]

In diametric opposition to all of these Reform efforts was the stand taken by Hirsch. In his *First* and *Second Communications* he stressed his absolute belief and dependence on the Sinai revelation and its implications. For him, this revelation comprises the entire body of Jewish tradition, and he asks his readers to accept Judaism as an historic phenomenon. Its only monument being the Torah—the "Written" and the "Oral"— he asks that it be read for the sole purpose of finding out what Judaism is. "For we want to know Judaism . . . Only when Judaism is known from itself, known as it exhibits itself, and then is found to be in itself untenable and objectionable—then only let him who likes reject it."

The following passage of the *Communications* gives insight into the line of reasoning Hirsch follows:

> Let us read the Torah, unmindful of the trouble which the reading of these writings caused us in our youth, unmindful of all prejudices which may have been instilled in us against them from many sides. Let us read them as if we never had read them before. Let us put ourselves the question: What is the world to me— within me and without; what am I as man and Israelite combined as "*Ish Yisrael,*" as "Israel-Man."[27]

The "Israel-Man"

Hirsch saw the "Israel-Man" bound to the task of re-establishing communion with God by fulfilling the duties prescribed in the Torah, that is, in the entire body of Biblical and rabbinic laws. "The reform needed by Judaism is education of the present generation in the Torah, and not levelling the Torah to the need and spirit of present times," he stated.

But Hirsch believed that these two apparently antagonistic forces can be reconciled and synthesized in the life of the "Israel-Man," who is entirely devoted to his faith and, at the same time, shares in European civilization.

The life of the truly religious Jew, of the complete "Israel-Man," has two aspects: its center is eternal and unchanging, while its periphery is a product of history, continuously assuming new forms in accordance with the circumstances of the time.

Hirsch's personality demonstrated that one can be a strictly observing Jew and nevertheless shine forth in the glory of European culture. His vision of an ideal type of Jew is one who remains faithful to his religion and, at the same time, is a modern European and a loyal citizen of his country. What Hirsch feared and fought was the grave danger of disintegration of Judaism in the clash with enlightenment and assimilation, as exemplified by the Reform movement.

Jewish Acculturation—"Torah im Derekh Eretz"

Through this verse, culled from the Mishnah,[28] Hirsch expressed his conviction of the possibility of a harmonious blending of all the dominant cultural values of his time with Torah and Talmudic Judaism. He did not seek to adapt the world of the old Jewish faith to secular culture, which some leaders of Orthodoxy considered alien. His objective was merely to stem the tide of the de-Judaization of a lost generation which had succumbed to complete assimilation, and to lead it back, within the framework of the Torah, to the sources of the Jewish spirit.

The crumbling of the ghetto walls at the turn of the nineteenth century stirred the Jewish intelligentsia into a fervent longing for emancipation, culminating in their entry into the hitherto impregnable fortress of foreign cultures. The consequences were detrimental to the perpetuation of the Jewish communities; in the wake of emancipation came assimilation and with it a growing determination in many Jewish circles to seek complete acceptance of and acclimatization to the new mode of life. The continuation of Orthodox Judaism as it had existed in the ghettos, where it regulated every aspect of Jewish daily living, was considered virtually impossible. It was particularly the strict observance of the Sabbath and the dietary laws which leading Jews of "society life" felt to be in their way.

The glaring light of European society life outside the ghetto had dazzled and blinded the eyes of many of Israel's sons and daughters. "*Niheye kagoyim*" (Let us be like the other nations) had become the motto of the day. What happened to the generation which followed Mendelssohn's acculturation was not only emancipation of the Jews in the political sense, but their emancipation from historical Judaism.

The efforts of prosperous and cultural Jews were now directed outward; the Jewish community was no longer the center of their activity. Professions, politics, society were the focus of attention. It was no longer religion that controlled their lives. The road was open and they wished to press onward. As free citizens of the enlightened nineteenth century, they felt they had no need for external ties with an age that had departed. It was of small concern to them whether Judaism could survive with such an attitude. Moreover, to gain civic equality and to eradicate economic discrimination, some leaders openly advocated apostasy.[29]

In the face of this situation, Hirsch maintained that precisely because Jews must uphold "the sovereignty of the Torah within a given civilization," modern emancipated Jews had simultaneously the obligation to acquire all the cultural values of the non-Jewish world. For only with them could they defend and promote adherence to the Torah properly in the new environment in which they now lived. In the ghetto there had been no need to safeguard the Torah with the equipment and methods of modern civilization.

True, the rabbis of the old school, too, recognized the dangers arising from the new political development and resultant social stratification. They also saw that the old order of things was dying and that the Torah way of life threatened to go down with it. But, unlike Hirsch, they still held on to the old concept of life. They could not easily comprehend Hirsch's real objective nor his interpretation of *Torah im Derekh Eretz*. They had no understanding of the revolutionary courage with which he discarded the obsolete ancient *Derekh Eretz* and accepted the

vital new one which was emerging. He was revolutionary in
that his ideas prevailed over the power of centuries-old customs
which recognized the Torah only in connection with a definite
kind of *Derekh Eretz*.

Hirsch also felt that the term *Derekh Eretz* should be understood in the sense of economic activity, based on an important
Halakhic viewpoint. He explained its significance as follows:

> *Derekh Eretz* embraces everything which is conditioned by the
> fact that man has to cope with his existence upon earth, his
> destiny and his common life with others, and has to achieve this
> by the earthly means at his disposal. Hence it signifies especially
> the means of subsistence and of a respectable conduct of life, as
> well as everything connected with general human and civil edu-
> cation.[30]

In all his sermons and writings Hirsch deplored the narrow-
ness and the ghetto mentality which estranged Jews from the
world in which they lived and worked. The extremists to the
right refused to acknowledge that only Hirsch's refined form
of Orthodoxy (which he adapted to the socio-political realities
of life while, at the same time, retaining strictest observance of
the Law in all details) could attract recruits.

Dawn of Emancipation

There was one field of common endeavor in which all factions
of German Jewry could meet: the acquisition of political rights
and civil equality. It is characteristic of Hirsch's versatility that,
in spite of his manifold tasks, he found time to write and speak
for that cause. He saw no essential antagonism between Judaism
and humanism; Judaism is, in fact, the only way toward the
realization of ideal humanity. The divine law is the source of
righteousness, and the way of the Law is the only one which
leads to the consummation of the ideal of absolute justice and
equity.

Hirsch sincerely welcomed the dawn of emancipation in
Germany but the freedom he envisaged is well-defined in the
following quotation from one of his messages: "For truly, my
brethren, what would we have achieved if, now that we are
soon to become free Jews, we wished to stop being Jews?"
He rejoiced at the thought of emancipation as long as it is not

"degrading" and not motivated merely by "lust and narrow selfishness," as expressed in the sixteenth of *The Nineteen Letters*:

> I bless emancipation . . . the regard for the inborn rights of men to live as equals among equals, and the principle that whatsoever bears the seal of a child of God . . . shall be willingly acknowledged by all as brother . . . as a primary step to the universal recognition of God . . . But for Israel I only bless it if, at the same time, there awakens in Israel the true spirit, which, independent of emancipation or non-emancipation, strives to fulfill the Israel-mission; to elevate and ennoble ourselves to implant the spirit of Judaism in our souls, in order that it may produce a life in which that spirit shall be reflected and realized. I bless it, if Israel does not regard emancipation as the goal of its task, but only as a new condition of its mission, and as a new trial, much severer than the trial of oppression; but I should grieve if Israel understood itself so little, and had so little comprehension of its own spirit, that it would welcome emancipation as the end of the *Galut*, and the highest goal of its historic mission . . . We must become Jews, Jews in the true sense of the word, permitting the spirit of the Law to pervade our entire being, accepting it as the fountain of life, spiritual and ethical; then will Judaism gladly welcome emancipation as affording a greater opportunity for the fulfillment of its task, the realization of a noble and ideal life.

Hirsch's Anti-Zionism

In addition to emancipation, there was another aspect of Hirsch's thought which coincided essentially with the position of his adversaries in the Reform camp. But whereas he agreed with only the ultimate political and humanitarian objectives of emancipation, he fully subscribed to the Reformers' absolute negation of Zionism.

Hirsch regarded the Jewish community not as a people (i.e., a living, organic, collective entity), but as a religious congregation, united by a strictly defined creed and by certain principles of behavior rather than by the feeling of a common destiny and solidarity.

He also believed in the historic meaning of the Diaspora situation and the universal mission of Israel's religion which was to be fulfilled through the dispersal of the people of Israel. His was the passive hope of bringing the redeemer through righteous conduct rather than by active participation in the attainment of political independence of the nation.

This theory was based on the supposition that the modern state, being purely "humanistic," has no concern with any religious ideology and that, therefore, loyalty to and full participation in all activities of a Christian society do not encroach upon the content of Judaism. This was based on a concept which was common to Hirsch as well as to his assimilationist opponents: the notion that the Jewish religion has no connection with political reality and the national existence of the Jewish people.

But Hirsch and his followers predicated their vigorous opposition to Jewish nationalism also on other religious arguments. They held that only divine providence can bring about the realization of the Messianic hopes and that only God can redeem Israel. Therefore, to put one's trust in political arrangements would reflect upon divine power. But beyond this, the Torah is the sole criterion and the basic purpose of Jewish peoplehood.

> The Jewish people became a nation, possessed a land and formed a state only through the Torah and for the Torah. Land and state were but a means to attain Torah (which explains why the Jews had become a nation long before they lived in their own land and organized their own state). It explains why the Jews remained a nation even after their state broke apart. They will remain a nation so long as they do not lose their Torah . . .

Some of Hirsch's critics ascribe another motivation to his opposition to Zionism. They maintain that to him, just as to his Reform adversaries, Jewish nationalism seemed incompatible with German loyalty and patriotism, which were constantly stressed by both traditionalists and modernists alike. Unwittingly, he was driven thereby to surpass his Reform opponents (including Holdheim) in their denial of Jewish nationality. To be sure, both factions affirmed the cultural and political integration into the fatherland. But this consideration seems to have been of far lesser importance than the religious reasons, as far as the Orthodox community was concerned.

Dissemination of Hirsch's Ideas

Hirsch by no means limited his concern to the advancement of his own congregation and to the organization of two schools. He promoted Jewish life in general. In order to disseminate as widely as possible his theories of Torah and *Emunah* (Law and belief), he founded in 1854 a religious monthly, *Jeshurun*, which he published until 1870. Its publication was resumed in 1883 under the editorship of his son Isaac and, in 1887, it was merged with the *Mainzer Israelit* of Dr. Marcus Lehmann, rabbi of the Religions-Gesellschaft in Mayence.[31]

In addition to numerous contributions in *Jeshurun*, Hirsch produced between 1866 and 1878 a number of scholarly works. In those twelve years he published a course of lectures *Translation of the Pentateuch with Commentary*. The principal purpose of this work, which was printed in a number of editions, was to prove the historical unity of Judaism—that it cannot be divided into different forms and distinct periods of development, but that its latest manifestations were the logical and necessary postulates of Biblical revelation. With painstaking conscientiousness, he annotated every Biblical verse with the corresponding passages from the Talmud and the Midrash, down to the minutest detail. With this method Hirsch demonstrated how the *Halakhic* development is already nascent in the Biblical text itself.

Impact of Hirsch

In appraising Hirsch's position in modern Jewish history, one phenomenon becomes apparent: here was a leader whose personal integrity, piety, courage of conviction, and religious genius impressed friend and foe alike. He has been violently attacked and fervently adored at the same time, not infrequently by one and the same man. Speaking on the occasion of the centenary of Hirsch's birth, Kaufmann Kohler, leader of American Reform Judaism, declared:

> I, for my part, gladly offer on this occasion my tribute of regard and admiration for him whom I proudly call my teacher and to whom I am indebted for the very best part of my innermost life.

It may sound paradoxical, and yet it is true, that without knowing it, Samson Raphael Hirsch liberated me from the thralldom of blind authority worship, and led me imperceptibly away from the old mode of thinking, into the realm of free reason and research. His method of harmonizing modern culture with ancient thought, however fanciful, fascinated me. His lofty idealism impressed me. He made me, the *yeshiva bakhur* from Mayence and Altona, a modern man. The spirit of his teachings electrified me and became a lifelong influence to me.

Hirsch made a definite contribution to the study of Judaism, and his works hardly merited the disdain with which they were viewed by many of his adversaries. His symbolism of the Law, an apotheosis of the *Shulkhan Arukh*, for example, is a combination of sound and practical wisdom. As a matter of fact, Kohler, who was most vigorous in his denunciation of Hirsch's ideas and who characterized his view of the Bible and tradition as "naive, childish" and "nonsense," still held that "all his writings furnish valuable suggestions to the modern rabbi." Kohler further maintained that Hirsch's "universalism, his optimism, his conception of Judaism as a religion of joy, of hope, of faith in humanity and humanity's future, are still an inspiration to the Jewish reader."

For two generations his books have commanded the attention and stimulated the thoughts of scholars. This is evidenced also by the fact that, a quarter of a century after Hirsch's death, his collected literary legacy was published, and during recent years many of his books have appeared in English translations.[32]

As to the perpetuation of his teachings, a number of his articles in Hebrew translation are included in anthologies of Jewish thought and used in religious high schools and *yeshivas* in Israel. He is also given an honorable place in textbooks of Jewish history used in Israeli schools. A fine English edition of his translation of the *Ḥumash* by his grandson Isaac Levy appeared recently in London. In 1947, the Rabbi Samson Raphael Hirsch Society was founded in New York with the object of spreading Hirsch's religious philosophy and of publishing English editions of his writings.

The rapidly growing congregations and educational institutions in many Jewish communities throughout the world, established by Orthodox Jews from Germany reared in the Hirsch schools, are testimonials of the impact of his legacy. Thus, for example, the large and prosperous congregation K'hall Adath Jeshurun in New York, with Dr. Joseph Breuer, a grandson of Hirsch, as its spiritual leader, has a Jewish all-day school with an enrollment of more than six hundred pupils.

Because, through an historical accident, Hirsch wrote in German, his writings are not widely known. Nevertheless, over the years, the fruits of his labors have become increasingly evident, even beyond the boundaries of Germany. For example, Hirsch won the esteem of Russian Jewry by coming to its defense: in 1884, when the Commission for Resolving the Jewish Problem—generally known as the Pahlen Commission because of its presiding officer, Count von Pahlen—convened in St. Petersburg, the Russian newspapers launched a vicious attack on Jews and the Talmud. To counteract this campaign of vilification, the Gaon Yitzhak Elkhanan Spector of Kovno asked Hirsch to help refute the charges; whereupon Hirsch wrote an essay "On the Relations of the Talmud to Judaism and to the Social Attitude of Its Followers." This treatise on the Jewish conception of life, based on about one hundred and fifty passages of the Talmud and Maimonides, was submitted to the Commission and reportedly was instrumental in improving the position of Jews at that time. Rabbi Yitzhak Elkhanan—no doubt one of the great Talmudists of the latter part of the nineteenth century—was a great admirer of Hirsch, with whom he carried on an extensive correspondence on a number of scholarly and practical questions.

Because of Hirsch's affinity to secular culture it was easy for the ultra-Orthodox masters of the *yeshivas* to exclude him from the community of their peers. To be sure, he was proud of his German nationality; he was devoted to Schiller and declared himself a product of modern culture, imbued with German romanticism, all of which, no doubt, would have caused his excommunication in another age and environment.

The Hirsch protagonists, on the other hand, who considered him one of the great commentators (*Mefarshim*) and proclaimed his system and commentaries as the consummation of all scholarship, were guilty of the same exaggeration.

Like all men Hirsch had his faults. He was an extremist who strongly opposed Maimonides, challenging the Cordovan philosopher for trying to harmonize Judaism with non-Jewish science instead of developing Judaism pragmatically out of its own sources.

Hirsch's deep religious spirit moved him also to shut his eyes to the historical facts of the time and to reject Jewish nationalism, waiting, as someone put it, "for a Jewish Palestine" instead of a "Palestine for the Jews." His theory was that, even in the period of Israel's independence, state and territory had been merely a means of the people's "spiritual calling."

Though Hirsch was deeply embroiled in controversy, he did not seek it out. Polemics were a heavy burden which he was compelled to shoulder when he saw that the foundations of tradition were threatened. There is ample testimony in his writings that his heart yearned for peace. But energetic measures were necessary to develop in Frankfurt one of the most distinguished continental Jewish communities of that period. Its distinction did not rest on its size—according to the official census of the German Reich it numbered in 1933 only 26,158 *Glaubensjuden* (confessing Jews)—but rather on its intense religious life, its scholarship, the strong feeling of kinship among its members, and their eager desire to fill the gaps in their knowledge of Judaism. The credit for having achieved this, in the midst of the struggle for emancipation and the bitter controversy with a rising Reform movement, belongs to Samson Raphael Hirsch. With unyielding will and uncompromising obedience to the will of God and His law, he helped revive the spirit of Judaism.

FOR FURTHER READING

Books by Samson Raphael Hirsch

Fundamentals of Judaism—Selections from the Works of Samson Raphael Hirsch, edited by Jacob Breuer (New York: Feldheim, 1949). Writings in which Hirsch argues for the primacy of Torah in Jewish life followed by essays by his disciples.

Introduction to Rabbi Samson R. Hirsch's Commentary on the Torah, translated by Joseph Breuer (New York: Feldheim, 1948).

From the Wisdom of the Mishle, translated by Karin Paritzky-Joshua (New York: Feldheim, 1976). Twenty-two essays on the themes of the Book of Proverbs offering guidance on the human condition.

Horeb; A Philosophy of Jewish Law and Observances, translated with an introduction and annotations by I. Grunfeld, Second edition (London: Soncino, 1968).

Judaism Eternal: Selected Essays from the Writings of Samson Raphael Hirsch, Isidor Grunfeld, editor (London: Soncino, 1959) two volumes.

The Hirsch Siddur, Translation and commentary of the German into English by the staff of the Samson Raphael Hirsch Publications Society (New York: Feldheim, 1969). Hebrew and English on facing pages.

The Hirsch Psalms, Translation and commentary by Hirsch rendered into English. The work closest to Hirsch's heart that brings his basic ideas to their mature fruition. (New York: Feldheim, 1984)

The Collected Writings of Samson Raphael Hirsch Volume One (New York: Feldheim, 1984). A definitive edition of the works of Hirsch has begun to appear. The scholarship of the first volume augurs well for a distinguished presentation of his complete writings. Eight volumes are projected.

Books about Samson Raphael Hirsch

ROSENBLOOM, Noah H., *Tradition In An Age of Reform: The Religious Philosophy of Samson Raphael Hirsch* (Philadelphia: Jewish Publication Society, 1976).

Isaac Mayer Wise

EDITOR'S NOTE
Beginnings of American Reform Judaism

The origins of Jewish life in the United States go back to 1654, when twenty-three penniless Jewish refugees from Recife, Brazil arrived at the Dutch trading community of New Amsterdam. Governor Peter Stuyvesant was very much opposed to the admission of these "Godless rascals." However, because of the influence of certain wealthy Jews of Amsterdam, stockholders in the Dutch West India Company, the refugees were allowed to remain. The newcomers gradually gained the right to trade, own land, and stand guard, but not the right to worship in public.

A decade later, in 1664, the English annexed New Amsterdam, and the future of the Jews in North America was joined with the fortunes of the British settlers. By the end of the century a certain place on Beaver Street was known as "the Jewish synagogue" though it was probably not a distinctive structure. Congregation Shearith Israel (Remnant of Israel), as it was called, in 1730 dedicated its first synagogue building on Mill Street, and the congregation has had a continuous existence until the present.

Jewish communities were soon established in several other places along the Atlantic seaboard: in Newport, Rhode Island (1658), where Roger Williams insisted that neither "Papists or Protestants, Jews and Turks be turned away"; in Philadelphia (1745) where William Penn guaranteed religious liberty to "all who acknowledged one Almighty and Eternal God as creator"; in Charleston, South Carolina (1750), the first community in the modern world to give the Jew the right to vote; and in Savannah (1733), where James Oglethorpe rejected requests from both the trustees and settlers to exclude Jews. By the time of the American Revolution there were approximately 2500 Jews in America, concentrated primarily in those five seaboard centers.

For the most part Jews of colonial America engaged in trade or commerce. Some became wealthy and maintained connections through family and friends with merchants in Amsterdam, London,

Lisbon, and other European ports. Several achieved prominence: for example, Aaron Lopez of Newport, whom Ezra Stiles described as "a merchant of the first eminence," and Jacob Franks in New York, who became one of the wealthiest men in the country. Jews were also artisans, storekeepers, and landowners, but it was primarily as merchants that they played a role in the economic growth of colonial America.

Until the end of the eighteenth century the synagogue served as the center of Jewish life. Services were traditional in character. Although there were many Ashkenazim in America, in the eighteenth century Sephardi ritual prevailed. In those early days the congregation assumed many of the functions undertaken by the *Kehillah* or organized community in Western and Eastern Europe. Since congregational autonomy was the dominant pattern of religious organization in North America it was not possible to transplant the concept of *Kehillah* to the United States. The synagogue, therefore, not only organized services, but it employed ritual slaughterers, arranged for *matzot* for the entire community on Passover, dispensed relief, and provided education for Jewish children. By 1731 Shearith Israel had organized a school where Hebrew, Spanish, and English were taught, as well as arithmetic and spelling. The *parnas* or president of each congregation, with his associates, wielded a great deal of authority, supervising every aspect of congregational life.[1]

There were no ordained rabbis in the United States until the fourth decade of the nineteenth century, and few of the laymen had even a limited knowledge of the Law. Since religious leaders were essential, the *hazzan* or prayer-leader tended to assume the role of rabbi. The outstanding religious personality during the colonial period was Gershom Mendes Seixas (1745-1816), a third-generation American who in 1766, at the age of twenty-three, became *hazzan* at Shearith Israel. Except for a brief interval during the Revolution, Seixas served this congregation for almost half a century. When the Revolution broke out, although most of the Christian ministers of New York sided with the English, the "patriot Jewish minister" influenced his congregation to close its doors rather than continue under the British. After a few years in Connecticut, he went to Philadelphia and helped to build up Congregation Mikveh Israel. After the evacuation of the British, when many of the members who had fled from New York returned to their homes, Seixas returned to his former position at Shearith Israel.

Seixas was responsible for several innovations in Jewish life in his times. He was the first American preacher to deliver regular

Thanksgiving sermons. He was one among thirteen clergymen who participated in Washington's inauguration, and he served for many years on the Board of Trustees of Columbia University. Seixas thus became the forerunner of a new type of spiritual leader that was to emerge in America.[2]

During the period between the outbreak of the American Revolution and the downfall of Napoleon only a few immigrants came to America. After 1815, however, large numbers of Europeans began entering the United States, including tens of thousands of Germans who settled along the eastern seaboard or joined the general movement westward. Among these immigrants were many German Jews who in Germany had been artisans, small traders and merchants, bearing a load of taxes and restrictions in the small towns where they had lived. After Napoleon's defeat many of the political restrictions of the pre-Revolutionary period had been reimposed, and in 1819 riots took place against the Jews in Germany. These circumstances, combined with the economic slump of 1836, led to the migration of thousands of German Jews to the United States. The Jewish population of the United States in 1840 has been estimated at 15,000; in 1850 it had reached 50,000 and a decade later 150,000. By 1880 there were a quarter of a million Jews in the country.[3]

For the most part, these immigrants, unlike the settlers of the colonial period, were poor. Many of them turned to peddling, roaming the countryside, and trading with the non-Jewish Germans who had preceded them. As the American hinterland became settled, they followed the routes of expansion. Eventually some accumulated enough money to open a drygoods or general store and to settle down in the new territory. Thus Jewish communities came into being west of the Allegheny Mountains.

The first Jew to settle in Cincinnati came from England in 1817 rather than from Germany. Joseph Jonas, attracted by the potentialities of the Ohio Valley, disregarded all the warnings of his friends in Philadelphia against settling so far west and migrated to Cincinnati, a city destined to play an important role in the development of American Judaism. Other English Jews soon joined him and a congregation was formed in 1824. After 1830 German Jews also began to arrive, and soon Cincinnati boasted of two congregations. In the 1840's congregations were established by German settlers in Cleveland, St. Louis, Pittsburgh, Louisville, and Chicago, though in many places it took a long time before synagogue buildings were erected.[4]

Meanwhile new Ashkenazi synagogues were springing up in the

east, the first of which had been founded in Philadelphia in 1802. In New York a secession from Shearith Israel in 1825 brought into being the B'nai Jeshurun congregation, formed by English, Dutch, and German Jews, with the German element predominating. In 1828 a number of German, Dutch, and Polish Jews left B'nai Jeshurun and formed the Anshe Chesed synagogue. The next three decades saw other secessions; by 1860 the city had twenty-seven synagogues. In most instances Ashkenazi patterns of worship were followed.[5]

Though the number of synagogues increased during the first half of the nineteenth century, the synagogue gradually lost its centrality and power over its members. Before the Revolution, non-conformists in matters of Sabbath observance or dietary laws had been denied membership in the congregation or were subjected to fines. By the end of the eighteenth century greater tolerance was shown toward laxity in religious observance. Thus, Shearith Israel, B'nai Jeshurun, and Anshe Chesed in New York each started out by excluding non-observant Jews from membership but in every instance this attitude was later relaxed.

As the community grew in size, organizations, institutions, and activities unconnected with the synagogue arose. The slaughtering of animals and the baking of *matzot* were taken over by commercial butchers and bakers. The establishment of the American public school system in the middle of the century led to the decline of synagogue Day Schools. The Sunday School, founded by Rebecca Gratz (1781-1869), was organized on a communal basis. Philanthropy, which traditionally had been closely associated with the congregation, became a separate concern as the problem of relieving destitute immigrants assumed larger proportions. Even cemeteries once supervised by the congregation came under private control.[6] Fraternal groups which sprang up cut across congregational lines.

The first and most important of such groups was the B'nai B'rith. Founded by twelve German Jews in a New York restaurant in 1843, it combined mutual aid with purely fraternal features. B'nai B'rith lodges soon developed in Cincinnati, Baltimore, and Philadelphia, numbering about fifty units by 1860. The 1850's also saw the founding of the orders B'nai Israel (1853) and B'nai Abraham (1859). Thus a basis for social unity was achieved which transcended synagogue membership.

The most influential American Jewish leader in the first half of the nineteenth century was Isaac Leeser (1806-1868). A native of Germany, he came to the United States in 1824 and worked for a time for an uncle in Richmond. In 1829, though an Ashkenazi, he was called to serve as *hazzan* of the Spanish-Portuguese synagogue in Philadelphia. In the following three or four decades Leeser pioneered in almost every area of Jewish life. He was the first to introduce the sermon in English as a permanent part of the service, though this was not achieved without a long struggle with the trustees. He translated the Sephardi and Ashkenazi prayer books into English. His translation of the Bible became the accepted version in all English-speaking countries for three-quarters of a century, until the appearance of the Jewish Publication Society Bible in 1917. In 1843 Leeser launched *The Occident*, a monthly journal which he made into a powerful weapon to defend the traditional faith.[7]

Meanwhile, a Reform trend began in the early 1840's parallel with the Reform movement in Germany. The first efforts at Reform in the United States had taken place some years before in Charleston, South Carolina, in 1824. At that time forty-seven members of Congregation Beth Elohim, influenced by agitations over the Hamburg Temple, petitioned congregational leaders for certain changes in ritual. Lacking knowledge of Hebrew and traditional background, they asked for an abridgment of the prayers, English readings, and an English discourse once a week. They also expressed misgivings about some of the traditional doctrines in the Maimonidean creed, such as the coming of the Messiah, the restoration of Palestine, and belief in a physical resurrection after death. When their petition was rejected, some of the signers founded a new congregation which they called the "Reformed Society of Israelites." They worshipped with uncovered heads, and laymen read the services and preached the sermons. But lacking the guidance of a rabbi and subject to opposition from the rest of the community the group soon dissolved.

In 1836 the Reverend Gustav Poznanski, who had come under the influence of the Hamburg Temple, was elected preacher. The original synagogue building having been destroyed by fire in 1838, a new building was erected and an organ introduced. This led to a great deal of controversy and an appeal to the civil courts. But the Reform group prevailed. While this "Charleston movement" marked the inauguration of Reform in the United States, innovations were made very slowly. Not until 1879 were family pews introduced and the women's gallery abolished.[11]

Similar tendencies manifested themselves at this time in other communities. In Baltimore a Reform Society was organized in 1842 by a group of young men who conducted their own services patterned after the Hamburg Temple. This group later developed into the Har Sinai Congregation. In New York, with the arrival of increasing numbers of German Jews, a "cultus society" was organized in 1844. The sponsors advocated a change in Jewish worship "to occupy a position of greater respect among our fellow citizens" and to enable them to worship with greater devotion. Leo Merzbacher, rabbi of several German synagogues in New York, joined the group, and with his help Congregation Emanuel, soon to be known throughout the city as the "Temple," was organized in April, 1845. In the beginning, the aim of the congregation was primarily to create orderly and decorous services. A German hymnal was introduced and the sermon made a regular part of the service. But the old prayer book was retained as well as the traditional type of cantillation. Men sat in the front rows of the small rented rooms and women at the back. Hat and *tallit* (prayer shawl) were worn. Gradually, however, the organ was introduced and other innovations were made. Within a decade family pews were accepted.[12]

These early manifestations of Reform, however, were no more than scattered episodes and in no way constituted an organized religious movement. It was Isaac Mayer Wise, by the force of his personality and the institutions he established, who made Reform Judaism the dominant religious organization in American Jewish life until World War I.

4 . *Isaac Mayer Wise*

[1819–1900]

ISRAEL KNOX

A M O N G the shapers and builders of Reform Judaism in America Isaac Mayer Wise was preeminent. Although he received his formal education in Europe and came to this country at the age of twenty-seven, he nonetheless adapted himself quickly and gladly to the New World. From the very beginning he decided to undertake the necessary task, as he saw it, of invigorating and renewing Judaism in this free and friendly land, of rendering it viable in a community so unlike any he had known in Europe. Reform had had its inception in Germany, but it struck no deep roots there or elsewhere in Europe; it grew and prospered and achieved stature in America. And Isaac Mayer Wise helped more than any other single individual to bring this about. David Philipson, who was intimately acquainted with the entire epic of Reform—its sources, its origin, its development—deemed it proper to state: "The history of Jewish Reform in the United States is yet to be written; but whatever be the point of view from which it will be regarded, one fact is certain: the historian will have to reckon with the life and doings of Isaac M. Wise." [1]

Role in Reform

To say this is not to assert that Wise was responsible for the very existence and flowering of Reform in America. Wise's merit lies in the fact that he appraised the situation in America correctly, that he seized the opportunity and refused to let go of it in spite of obstacles and personal hardships. He was the beneficiary—not the creator—of the factors that were conducive to the emergence of Reform in America. But Wise was largely responsible for the specific character and content of Reform in this land, for its relative moderation as an evolutionary variant of Judaism and not as a revolutionary break with it, for its steadfast acceptance of the principle of continuity with the Judaism of all time and not only of one particular period or century. He remained loyal to this conviction throughout his life, and in his presidential address in 1896 before the Central Conference of American Rabbis laid down the following requirement for a revised prayer book: "We want not only a text, but a Jewish text; not only a text for Jews and by Jews, but also a Jewish standard of the spirit." [2]

Reform—for Wise—was a new phase in an ancient faith, an attempt to strip Judaism of all that runs counter to reason. But Wise never rejected the ancient faith; he claimed authenticity for the Sinaitic revelation, and insisted that his modification of Talmudic law was in accordance with the law itself, with the *din*. It is in this sense that Philipson's further evaluation is accurate: "From the moment almost of his landing on these shores he (Wise) became a power in American Judaism. It is not too much to say that, more than any other man, he stamped his individuality upon the history and development of Jewish life in the United States. His is the most prominent rabbinical name in American Jewry. His activity of over half a century as organizer, editor, preacher, educator is part of the history of the Reform movement whose untiring advocate he was from the very beginning . . ." [3]

Isaac Mayer Wise was at once a man of thought and of action. He formulated the basic conception of a liberal Judaism on American soil; he provided Reform in the New World with an interpretation of Judaism and a theoretical justification for its own modification of the ancestral faith; he mapped out the path for Reform to pursue, and indicated a purpose and mission for it. But he was not content with this alone; he wanted to assure Reform's future in America. Wise was chiefly instrumental in the establishment of Reform's three institutions—the Union of American Hebrew Congregations, the Hebrew Union College, the Central Conference of American Rabbis. For many years—

to the day of his death—he was president of the Conference and the College, and carried through in practice a good deal of what might have otherwise remained in the realm of speculation.

As one compares and evaluates Wise's comments upon Pharisaic Judaism, upon the nature and function of *Halakhah* (Talmudic law) in the past, the net impression is unmistakable: Wise was not prepared or willing to delete *Halakhah*—as a discipline in conduct, as a guide for sanctifying life here and now—from Reform Judaism. Neither Wise nor anyone else in Reform has succeeded in pointing the way toward a contemporary *Halakhah*, continuous with the past and yet free and flexible, in harmony with Jewish experience and yet conforming to our highest values. The problem may be inescapable, but neither Wise (nor moderate Reform as a variant of Judaism) chose the easy solution—the repudiation of *Halakhah* as such.

Wise supplied Reform with a rationale for its own way and its own style of Judaism, but he was no proponent of an "easy Judaism" devoid of discipline and duty or of the *mitzvot*. He considered the observance of the Sabbath mandatory in Judaism, and one of his earliest and most earnest conflicts in Albany involved this very issue. He was strongly opposed to all proposals for a Sunday service—not only as a substitute for the Sabbath service but also as complementary to it. He did not absolve the members of his congregations—first in Albany, later in Cincinnati—from the obligation of setting up a religious school for their children.

The logic of events may have been such that Reform turned out to be an "easy Judaism" as compared with Orthodoxy and (later) Conservatism, but that was not Wise's intention. It is true that Wise saw no special virtue in a "rigorous Judaism" based upon prescriptions and injunctions without relevance to contemporary ethical reality, but he was a diligent student of Jewish history. Nor was he a stranger to *Halakhah* or its role in Jewish life as a discipline in conduct and as an experiment in holiness. Wise realized that Judaism is not merely a matter of participating in a service once or twice a week, that it cannot be confined to the "four ells" of the synagogue; it is rather concerned with all facets of existence, and reaches out to the home and all aspects of behavior. Whether the "rigorous" Judaism of Orthodoxy and the "positive-historical" Judaism of

Conservatism have succeeded in preserving the unique character of classical Judaism in America to a greater degree than has Reform is an open question. But this much is certain: Wise's fervent hope was to plant a Judaism in America that would be sturdy, inspiring, and effective in the lives of its adherents.

Nor did Wise try to wash away the differences between Judaism and Christianity so as to make Judaism appear respectable and fashionable. He was a staunch unitarian in his view of God, regarding that approach alone as completely compatible with ethical monotheism; he eschewed the trinitarian notion of God as alien to the spirit of Judaism, and he was unsympathetic to the concept of an intermediary between man and God, and to the corollary doctrines of original sin and vicarious atonement. He was scornful of missionaries who were seeking to convert Jews to Christianity, and soon after his arrival in Albany voiced his opposition at a local church meeting. He also wrote a series of articles in *The Occident*[4] challenging the Presbyterian synod of New York, which had issued a call for the conversion of Jews; and in his own *Israelite* he was indefatigable in the defense of the separation of church and state. Indeed, Wise's proud and passionate conviction in the truth of Judaism as ethical monotheism prompted him to declare repeatedly that by the early twentieth century Judaism would become the universal religion of all mankind.

Early Years in Bohemia

When Wise came to America, he was already an ordained rabbi. He was twenty-seven years old, married, and the father of a child. Before leaving Europe, he had attended as a spectator the second conference of Reform leaders at Frankfurt in 1846. The philosophy of Reform was not yet fully formulated, though its general outlines were quite clear. Wise was sympathetic to Reform, convinced that it was particularly suitable for America, and resolved to strive for its progress in the new land.

In his *Reminiscences* Wise is strangely silent about his childhood and youth in Bohemia, as though the rhythm of his life had become audible and distinctive only in America. Earlier he had written for *The Occident*, a monthly journal published in Philadelphia, a gentle and informative piece entitled "Recollections of Bohemia." [5] Thereafter, all his labors, thoughts, and sentiments were for America.

Wise was born on March 29, 1819 in the village of Steingrub in Bohemia. His mother, Regina Weis, was his father's second wife, and bore him thirteen children, of whom seven died in infancy. Isaac Mayer was the oldest surviving son. At the age of four his education began in the Jewish school which his father, a teacher or *melamed*, conducted. At six he was introduced to the Talmud. When at nine there was nothing more for the boy to learn at his father's school, he was sent off to his grandfather in the village of Durmaul.

Isaac Mayer's grandfather Isaiah was a physician who had studied medicine in Italy, as had his father Leo before him, but he was not estranged from Jewish learning and was even interested in the mystical books of *Kabbalah*, which he perused in seclusion in the solitary hours of night. Isaac Mayer continued studying the Pentateuch, Rashi's commentary,* and the Talmud during the day in *heder*, and in the evening at home with his grandfather.

In 1832, after the death of his grandfather, Isaac Mayer, at the age of twelve, set out on foot for Prague, which was the seat of learning in Bohemia. There he enrolled in the *bet hamidrash*, the house of study, and was assigned, in the manner of the time, for board in a separate family each day of the week. From the *bet hamidrash* and *yeshiva* in Prague Isaac Mayer went on to Jenikau, the most famous and most modern rabbinical academy in Bohemia, conducted by Aaron Kornfeld. Wise rounded out his formal education by attending the University of Prague for two years and the University of Vienna for one year. Wise was now twenty-three and felt confident that he was ready for his vocation. In 1842 he received *semikhah* (rabbinic ordination) from a *bet din* (religious court) of three outstanding rabbis.

Wise spent several years as rabbi in the small town of Radnitz. There he married Theresa Bloch, a pupil, and in 1846 their first child was born. Wise was not happy in Radnitz, being at odds with his congregation and with rabbis in nearby

---

*Creators of the Jewish Experience in Ancient and Medieval Times, Chapter 9, Washington, D.C., B'nai B'rith Books, 1985

towns. He also defied the government's law which imposed a quota on the number of Jewish marriages, and was able to get it rescinded.

Journey to the New World

Wise thought of himself as an American while yet in Bohemia. He looked upon it as a sort of Promised Land for Reform, as almost divinely chosen for a happy consummation of Reform's program and tasks. On May 20, 1846, Isaac Mayer Wise set sail from Bremerhaven, without a passport, with his wife and small daughter. The voyage lasted sixty-three days, and on July 23 he arrived in New York, never to return to the Old World, not even for a visit.

When Wise came to the United States in 1846, there were probably no more than sixty thousand Jews in the entire country. Besides synagogues and a charitable institution here and there they had no corporate life of their own and no recognizable cultural activities. The first wave of Jewish immigration to the New World—in Colonial America—was mostly Sephardi, coming from Holland and other places where Jews of Spanish-Portuguese origin dwelled. After 1830 there was a steady stream of German-speaking Jewish immigrants, which gained momentum after the unsuccessful revolutions of 1848.

There were only three non-Orthodox synagogues in the entire country: Beth Elohim in Charleston (South Carolina), Har Sinai in Baltimore, and Temple Emanu-El in New York. After meeting Max Lilienthal, who was serving simultaneously as rabbi of three minor Orthodox synagogues but who had been associated with Reform in Europe, Wise was more convinced than ever that what was needed in the New World was a Judaism with a style of its own, in the manner of Reform and with an orientation toward America, a Judaism that could be fittingly described as a *Minhag America* (American practice). Through Lilienthal's recommendations, Wise traveled to New Haven and Syracuse to dedicate synagogues, and to Albany to preach. After a brief sojourn in New York City, he was elected rabbi of Beth El in Albany, where he settled for eight eventful years.

Albany: First Pulpit (*1846-1854*)

Albany was a laboratory for Wise. Whether so intended or not, his innovations there took on the aspect of an experiment, and it was in Albany that he paid in grief and suffering for his courage and integrity and his stubborn refusal to compromise. Convinced that only by the immediate inauguration of pressing reforms could the case for Reform be demonstrated beyond doubt and win the adherence of a majority of Jews in the United States, Wise set up a choir, put in an organ, abolished the women's curtained gallery, cut or excluded some traditional Hebrew prayers, eliminated the sale of *aliyot* (the auctioning off of various roles in the ritual reading of the Torah on the Sabbath), introduced the weekly sermon, and substituted the confirmation ceremony for both boys and girls instead of the *Bar Mitzvah* for boys alone.

It required much effort and persuasion to get the assent of the members of Beth El to these reforms. They were plain hardworking folks, mostly peddlers not completely sure of themselves and their moorings in the new land, with a minimum of education, and with no special sensitivity to theological nuances. They were not inclined to agree to religious innovations, or to move too far from the customs and beliefs of their parents. Because in their normal daily affairs they had adapted themselves rapidly and without much heartache to the economic conditions of their environment and thereby transgressed many of the precepts which they had formerly observed, their conformity to Orthodox ritual and liturgy in the synagogue became all the more rigid and literal.

Beth El became a house divided; a split in the congregation was inevitable. By background and habit, by virtue of what they remembered of Judaism in the "old country" and of what they needed here for a sense of continuity with their past, a majority of the members were predisposed toward the stable and ancestral type of Judaism—toward Orthodoxy.

The split came in 1850, after Wise's trip to Charleston, South Carolina, where he had preached and lectured with astonishing success in the Reform temple before sophisticated audiences, including some Christians. During his visit there he had been present at a debate between Gustav Poznanski, rabbi of the Reform temple in Charleston, and Morris Raphall, rabbi of B'nai Jeshurun in New York and the leading figure in Orthodoxy. In the course of his talk Raphall suddenly addressed himself to Wise with two questions: "Do you believe in the personal Messiah? Do you believe in the resurrection of the body?" Wise's reply was short and precise: "No!" Whereupon Raphall walked out of the hall.[6] Wise was subsequently bitterly attacked in the *Asmonean* and *The Occident*, two Anglo-Jewish journals, as unfit to hold the office of rabbi.

This larger controversy beyond the borders of Albany became interconnected with a quarrel in Albany between Wise and the president of Beth El. The tension was so sharp that a fight broke out in the synagogue on *Rosh Hashanah*, which was stopped only by the police. With Rabbi Wise, a sizable minority left the synagogue and organized a new congregation which held *Yom Kippur* services. Anshe Emeth (Men of Truth), as the latter was called, throve, thanks to Wise's enormous talents as organizer and to the enthusiasm of his followers. Some thirty-five years after its founding Anshe Emeth and Beth El healed the breach and united as one synagogue, Beth Emeth (the House of Truth). A new generation had arisen, bolstered by recent immigrants (following the abortive revolutions of 1848 in Europe); for them the quarrels of yesteryear were just a story told by their elders, and Wise's reforms were neither heretical nor incomprehensible. In May, 1889, the new temple of Beth Emeth was dedicated, and Wise participated in the celebrations.

Wise's last years in Albany were happy and fruitful. There was peace in his congregation, and he was now able to do a good deal of writing. In 1854 he published the first volume of his *History of the Israelitish Nation*, which provoked extensive polemical discussion and several fierce attacks.[7] Wise was not unduly disturbed because he accepted the fact that by the nature of things all his work was bound to incite both anger and enthusiasm. In this volume he omitted miracles as irrelevant to the enterprise of the historian, and he depicted the First Commonwealth from the perspective of an anti-monarchist, not sparing even David. Wise was writing Jewish history in the light of the American and French Revolutions.

The Years in Cincinnati

In April, 1854 Wise accepted an invitation from Congregation Bene Yeshurun of Cincinnati to serve as its rabbi, a post he was to hold for the remaining forty-six years of his life. Wise started out on this venture with some trepidation. He had finally surmounted all obstacles in Albany, Anshe Emeth was flourishing, his reforms were pleasing to his congregation, he was enjoying repose and was writing profusely. Cincinnati was a journey into the unknown, a plunge into the dark. Would he have to do over again much of what had already been settled in Albany? To what extent could he hope to succeed? As it developed, though, he discovered before long in Bene Yeshurun a friendly and cooperative congregation, not inimical to fundamental reforms and not averse to experimentation in ritual and liturgy.

The years in Cincinnati were joyous. Under Wise's guidance Bene Yeshurun rose to occupy the position of a sort of First Temple of Reform. The congregation, on his arrival, had consisted of men and women with a predilection for Reform but who still clung to the mode of Orthodoxy out of inertia and lack of leadership. Wise took them by the hand, showed them the ways of Reform, and illumined for them the meaning of their religion. He converted a round of duties and a set of ceremonies which they had accepted with the acquiescence of custom into a delightful and ennobling experience.

Wise was able to dispose quickly of the vestiges of Orthodox procedure in the synagogue which were not to his taste. Bene Yeshurun abolished without much prodding the sale of *aliyot*; it soon eliminated the *piyyutim* from the prayers (an old form of synagogue poetry that originated in the early Middle Ages, as well as the improvisations—in Ashkenazi liturgy—of many local cantors and composers); a choir of men and women was organized (later, with some non-Jewish professional singers) and an organ was purchased (and used even on the High Holy Days). Wise also abolished the "second holidays" of the three festivals—*Pesah, Shavuot,* and *Sukkot*. He waited fourteen years before proposing in 1873 the two most drastic reforms of all: the cessation of the observance of the second day of *Rosh*

Hashanah, and the discontinuance of the custom of worshipping with covered heads. It was not only an exercise in patience for Wise; it was an expression on his part of a more sympathetic and imaginative discernment of the process of spiritual change as gradual and organic than he had manifested in Albany.

During his long tenure at Bene Yeshurun, Wise inaugurated other reforms which gave it a content and style of its own. He fashioned new rituals for Friday night and Saturday morning and increased considerably the English portion of the service, shortening the Hebrew portion correspondingly. In 1867 he began to deliver lectures on Friday evenings. The lectures dealt with philosophical and historical themes, and some of the series were published as books: *The Cosmic God*; *Judaism and Christianity*; *The Ethics of Judaism*; *Jesus, the Apostles, and Paul.*

Shortly after his arrival in America Wise had embarked upon the publication of a weekly, the *Israelite*, the first issue of which had appeared in July 1854, and which he edited until his death; in 1874 its name was changed to *American Israelite*. This journal attempted to clarify the character of Judaism and to ward off and unmask all manifestations of social and religious anti-Semitism. It was vigilant in its defense of Jewish rights on grounds of human rights and democratic principles. There was, however, one serious lapse in the *Israelite*'s fealty to the cause of human rights and in its championship of justice. Neither Wise nor his journal took a firm stand against slavery, and Wise's position during the Civil War was anomalous. Wise also published and edited an eight-page weekly in the German language, *Die Deborah*, which he lovingly referred to as his "waste-basket" and in which he published his *Reminiscences* serially from July, 1874 to August, 1875.

Union of American Hebrew Congregations

The *Israelite* helped Wise to create a favorable atmosphere for the three major institutions of Reform and for focusing attention upon the urgent need for them. Wise was the architect and builder of these organizations, and had he done nothing else, this alone would have assured him a lasting niche in the history of American Judaism. While yet in Albany his observations of the American scene prompted him to send out a call for a conclave of rabbis and delegates from all synagogues in the United States to form a permanent synod and conference. The call was premature and without effect. In 1855, just after he had settled in Cincinnati, a conference was held in Cleveland with rabbis from both Orthodox and liberal synagogues. After much deliberation, a majority of the conference approved the following resolution, which both groups chose to regard as a victory: "The Bible, as delivered to us by our fathers and as now in our possession, is of immediate divine origin and the standard of our religion. The Talmud contains the traditional, legal, and logical exposition of the Biblical laws which must be expounded and practiced according to the comments of the Talmud." [8]

Wise presided at the conference and was one of the authors and sponsors of the resolution. He was elated at the outcome, and felt confident that it was a prelude to better things in the future. To his surprise he was vehemently assaulted for his role in the conference by the radical wing of Reform, spearheaded by David Einhorn.

Not until 1873, almost two decades later, was Wise's original summons heeded. On July 8 of that year delegates from thirty-four synagogues convened in Cincinnati, and the Union of American Hebrew Congregations was finally constituted. Wise wrote in the *Israelite* (July 18): "On the eighth, ninth and tenth days of July, 1873, in the convention held in Cincinnati, the youngest child of Israel was born, the Union of American Hebrew Congregations was organized, constituted and established." It was the youngest child but represented only a segment of Israel. Wise had planned and toiled resolutely and long for the Union. It was fitting that he should be elected as its president.

Hebrew Union College

With the Union a reality, Wise might have settled down to a quieter existence. But there was a dream, dearer to him above all others: Wise wanted to establish a college in America for the preparation of rabbis with a rounded knowledge of Judaism and imbued with the spirit of America, for whom the ways of Reform would be normal and natural, with no special memory of strife and discord. A college for rabbis—from a generation that was of this land and accustomed to its democratic temper and its freedom of inquiry—was to Wise a symbol of an indigenous Judaism, rooted in the soil of America, capable of growing and prospering under its benign sun. In 1855 he had made a start with Zion College, but it had been too early, and the College did not survive. But now, twenty years later, Wise launched—with the unstinted support of the Union—the Hebrew Union College. Wise assumed the office of president, and he taught a number of courses (which provided much of the material and the impetus to complete the second volume of his *History* and his *Pronaos to Holy Writ*).

Central Conference of American Rabbis

In 1899, again primarily owing to Wise's efforts and perseverance, the third major institution of Reform came into being —the Central Conference of American Rabbis. Wise had learned the wisdom of patience, and he therefore waited for a younger generation of rabbis to emerge, mostly graduates of the College, so that they might form the solid core of the Conference. The presidency of the Conference was conferred upon him, and he was repeatedly re-elected until his death. His addresses at the annual gatherings of the Conference were a weighty contribution toward shaping Reform policy and practice.

A Life of Achievement

Wise's forty-six years in Cincinnati were marked by personal happiness and tremendous achievement. His congregation cherished him and was proud of his vital role in Reform, and Wise, who was not inclined to underestimate his own worth and talents, was grateful for the courtesy, generosity, and consideration accorded him. He traveled much, speaking and lecturing on behalf of Reform, and he engaged in many enterprises. There were no objections from his congregation—on the contrary, his outside activities enhanced his reputation in Cincinnati. It flattered his congregation to learn that others esteemed his work too. On the fiftieth anniversary of his ordination as a rabbi—

October, 1893—he explained in the sincere and solemn language of a sermon: "There are few congregations in the land in which such pleasant relations between the congregation and the minister have been so uniformly sustained so long a time. It seems sometimes that we were made for one another. When I came here you, as a congregation, were twelve years old, I, as a rabbi, eleven years, and so we have lived our best years together." [9]

The equilibrium of Wise's personal life was disrupted in 1870 when his beloved wife became an invalid. She died four years later, at fifty-three, a friend and companion who had always been at his side to comfort him. In 1876 Wise was wedded to Selma Bondi, the daughter of Rabbi Jonah Bondi.

Wise's life came to an end on March 26, 1900. On Saturday morning, March 24, he preached in his temple and met with one of his classes in the early afternoon. As he arose from the chair a sudden stroke came and he fell. Wise was survived by his wife Selma, and eleven children—five daughters and six sons.

Philosophy of Judaism

What was Wise's professed philosophy of Judaism? How did he reconcile Reform with Judaism? Wise was an advocate of moderate Reform, and in some ways was more traditional than many of his followers and, indeed, of a goodly number of spokesmen of what was later to be Conservatism.

Wise differed from most defenders of Reform of his own day and of the succeeding generations in his belief that the Sinaitic revelation was an actual historical occurrence. He regarded it as an empirical fact, observed by six hundred thousand witnesses, and recorded by an unimpeachable author, Moses, who shared dramatically in the event. Like Judah Halevi* and Maimonides* seven centuries before him, he thought that this was irrefutable testimony. But he also maintained that the Sinaitic revelation was a self-evident truth, a central episode in human history, the "Great Divide" between darkness and light. He summed it up epigrammatically: "We must insist upon this one article of faith, 'I believe in the revelation of God and the God of revelation.' " [10] This was axiomatic, and apart from the

Creators of the Jewish Experience in Ancient and Medieval Times, Chapters 7 and 8, Washington, D.C., B'nai B'rith Books, 1985

witnesses, it was self-evident and self-certifying; it was the basis of morality and the heart of religion, and could have been neither invented nor imagined.

Wise, however, parted company from Orthodoxy in holding that only the Decalogue was of immediate and direct divine origin. He was averse to Biblical criticism, and insisted that Moses was the sole author of the Pentateuch. But Orthodoxy, despite its contention that Moses was the greatest of the prophets, extolled him only as the recipient of the Pentateuch, the Torah, and not as its author. The author of the Torah, according to Orthodoxy, is God, and the Torah is His word, perfect, definitive, and absolute.

By declaring only the Decalogue to be of divine origin and identifying it with the Sinaitic revelation, Wise was able to draw a sharp distinction between the permanent and the so-called temporary aspects of the Pentateuch and of the Scriptures as a whole. The Decalogue was universal, transcendent in time and place, valid for all groups and individuals, sublime in its theological and ethical import, at once the word of God and the crystallized and sustained wisdom of human experience. The rest of the Pentateuch was, for a specific period and people, the profound product of a superb mind and an unequalled lawgiver, possessing nuggets of truth for subsequent periods in history and for other peoples in other lands. It was all that but no more—not "from heaven," *min hashamayim*, in the immediate and direct sense in which the Decalogue was. The laws of the Pentateuch, therefore, as an aggregate and as single commandments, ordinances, or prohibitions, were not binding upon the present and did not constitute an inalienable element in basic Judaism. If they did, then Judaism would cease to be universal, a religion with a message for all mankind, and would properly fall into the category of particularistic religion, suitable for a specific tribe or nation.

This distinction between the permanent and the transient, between the essential and the incidental, marked off Reform from Orthodoxy from the very beginning. It did not matter that Wise's belief in the Sinaitic revelation was quite traditionalist and literalist. This did not clash with the general ideology of Reform. What did matter was the approach to the Scriptures as containing both permanent and transient elements, with the inference that only the permanent elements were of abiding value. It was in this mood that Wise wrote: "The difference between us and our opponents is simply this: we understand Judaism to be a religion, or rather, the only universal religion peculiar to the Jewish people." [11]

Wise was a staunch advocate of moderate Reform. It is therefore ironical that it should have been his traditionalist acceptance of the Sinaitic revelation that brought him now and then to the very boundary of radical Reform. There was a passion in Wise and a flaming zeal to show the world that Judaism was a universal religion, a faith for all mankind in an era of enlightenment. By contrast, other revelations appeared to be partial and particular, perhaps even to cancel each other out. But the Sinaitic revelation, though addressed to the children of Israel and verified by six hundred thousand witnesses, was also the inheritance of Christianity and Islam. Wise was convinced that by the twentieth century Judaism would emerge as *the* universal religion, and that its majestic and sovereign imperative— "Hear, O Israel: the Lord our God, the Lord is One"—would be avowed by the rest of mankind as the purest and noblest expression of ethical monotheism.

It was not easy for Wise to formulate those conclusions and announce them publicly. There was inner tension between his eagerness for accommodation and his wish for preservation. Accommodation was necessary if Judaism was to fulfill its destiny as the universal religion. The condition was stark and certain: Judaism must be "denationalized," all that is parochial in it must be shed, and only its sheer, shining essence—the Sinaitic revelation—must remain. But this was not easy. Wise was a proponent of Reform, not of revolution, and he was too keen and realistic not to suspect that essence torn out of its context and divorced from its concrete embodiment is abstract and ambiguous. He was aware of the vast riches of post-Biblical Judaism. He cited with warm approval Moritz Lazarus' famous comment that Israel's particularism has its source, motive, and aim in its universalism. Wise came close to the proponents of extreme Reform in his willingness to delete from Judaism all its Orthodox content, its ritual, ceremony, and Law, so as "to launch the universal religion based exclusively on the Ten Commandments." [12]

Judaism as a Rational Religion

Wise's traditionalist acceptance of the Sinaitic revelation was not at odds with his belief that Judaism was a consistently rational religion. A child of the Enlightenment, Wise spoke of reason very much in the same sense in which Thomas Paine argued in Revolutionary America that reason was the sole means through which man could discover God; he invoked the Sinaitic revelation in the same sense in which Jefferson's Act for Establishing Freedom in Virginia began with these memorable words: "Well aware that Almighty God hath created the mind free . . ."

The concept of rational or natural religion, that is, of religion without dogma, mystery, and miracle, and without the arrogant claim that any single expression of it is in possession of absolute truth, was one of his cherished ideas: "Judaism teaches no dogmas or mysteries, on the belief of which salvation depends." [13] It was therefore entitled to be designated as a rational religion, perhaps as *the* rational religion. Nor would there be serious disagreement on this among partisans of Orthodoxy, Conservatism, and Reform. But Wise was constrained to add: "Legalism is not Judaism nor is mysticism religion; the belief in fiction is superstition. Judaism is the fear of the Lord and the love of man in harmony with the dicta of reason . . ." [14] This interpretation of Judaism is valid for Reform but would call forth earnest objections from Orthodoxy and Conservatism. On the positive side Judaism is a rational religion because in its doctrines and duties it is "humane, universal, liberal and progressive." [15] "Therefore Judaism is the religion of the future generations, as it was the teacher of the past ones," Wise concludes.

Wise was thus commending Judaism as rational because of the absence of dogma, sacraments, and mysteries in its simple yet awe-inspiring theology. The Sinaitic revelation was not dogma: on the one hand, it was corroborated by a multitude of witnesses; on the other hand, it was no infringement of the criteria of reason. In science as in religion, one must begin somewhere: in science, the starting-point is the world, apart from such questions as how it came into being; in religion, the starting-point is God, warranted by a revelation which Judaism, Christianity, and Islam now share as a common inheritance and which is not repugnant to reason.

Judaism's disavowal of the efficacy of sacraments, through the mediation of a priesthood, is no mere negation. It is predicated upon the positive principle—"the priesthood of all the people." This principle was already communicated to Abraham (Genesis 17:1): "I am God almighty; walk before Me, and be thou perfect." This was applied by Moses to the congregation of Israel in its entirety: "And ye shall be unto Me a kingdom of priests and a holy nation" (Exodus 19:6).

Judaism is a rational religion not only for what it is not, but more so for what it is and for what it professes to be. And it professes to be "humane, universal, liberal and progressive." It is humane by virtue of the ethics and social precepts of the Pentateuch, the injunctions of the Decalogue, and the teachings of the prophets and sages of Israel. It is humane in its this-worldly orientation, in its hallowing of life here and now, and because it holds no threat of eternal damnation for its own adherents or for those of other faiths. It is humane because it counsels no asceticism and discountenances withdrawal from the affairs of men and the obligations of society (in Hillel's utterance in *Pirke Abot*: "Thou shalt not separate thyself from the community").

Then again Judaism is a rational religion because it is universal in quality, in the depth of its vision, and in the comprehensiveness of its solicitude for all mankind. Judaism proclaims in the Talmud (*Tosefta Sanhedrin* 13:2)—"The righteous among the Gentiles will have a share in the world-to-come"—and does not make explicit affiliation with Judaism the ground for salvation, as Christianity does. *Extra ecclesiam nulla salus* (outside the Church there is no salvation)—has no equivalent in Judaism, and is remote from its spirit. There is a reverence in Judaism for all who hunger for God, and Judaism grants their right to serve God and society through their respective faiths.

A rational religion, Wise states, must be "liberal and progressive," must help to free men from fear, superstition, selfishness, and pride; it must also help them to assume legitimate dominion of the world through knowledge and understanding. Judaism is liberal and progressive because it is not primarily otherworldly (the very term *olam haba*, literally translated, is "coming world"), and it is not anti-naturalistic. Judaism erects no wall between man and nature, and it does not condemn man to be a stranger in this world. It is a lamp to light his way across the earth, which is his home, and it is a teaching to sanctify and spiritualize his experiences in the realm of nature, in the world where men live, work, dream, and hope.

Judaism as "Non-Legalistic"

Wise had stated that "Judaism teaches no dogmas or mysteries, on the belief of which salvation depends." It is possible, without sophistry and evasion, to show that this is so. But Wise had also written that "legalism is not Judaism nor is mysticism religion . . ." And in the introduction to *Judaism—Its Doctrines and Duties*, he announced: "The author of this little volume ignores the three Talmuds (Jewish, New Testament, Koran), reads the Bible from its own standpoint, and proves that it contains the complete and rational system of religion for all generations and countries."

Wise was not against Jewish law. Indeed, he had criticized Paul for his negative attitude toward the Law, for his identification of religion with sheer faith, and for his notion of salvation as a divine gift—the fruit of faith and dissociated from good works.

For Wise, no rejection of the Law as such was tenable, and surely Paul's alternative must have seemed to him quite mystical and theological. Wise's differentiation was not between the Law and faith, but between the permanent core of the Law and the transitory elements, the specific application for a locality and a nation, a place and a period. He did not accept the view of Paul—and of most Christian theologians after him—that the Hebrew Scripture was the "Old Testament," to be searched for adumbrations of the future advent of Christ—a corridor to the New Testament which nullifies the validity of the Law. For Wise the Hebrew Bible contained a set of principles and a program for living.

That a portion of the Law had lost its validity Wise would not hesitate to concede, but not because of the new dispensation superseding the Law. This happened only because much of the Law had been fashioned for a specific period and place, and was not intended to last for all time as finished, static, and immune to change.

Yet at one point the positions of Paul and Wise coincided. Both were obsessed with a passion for a universal religion: Paul wanted it to be one for "Jew and Greek" (Galatians 3:28), and Wise wanted it as the "complete and rational system of religion for all generations and countries." Wise was probably thinking not so much of institutional or creedal victory for Judaism as he was of its social and spiritual influence upon other religions—an influence that would impell them to look more closely and more sympathetically toward their common source and origin in Judaism.

Wise spent most of his life and energy within the house of Judaism and was constantly preoccupied with the pressing problems confronting Judaism and Reform especially. Whenever his ardor for a universal religion subsided, he was the proponent of moderate Reform, trying to set his own house in order, building the external structure of Reform (the Union, the College, the Conference), and defining its internal content— the conception of the oneness of God, the election of Israel, the Messianic hope. Nor was this all. He rose in defense of the Talmud against its detractors in the camp of radical Reform, he immersed himself again and again in its tomes and drank of its wisdom, and he lauded it for its high morality, its preoccupation with justice in the community and among individuals, and its making concrete the prophetic pronouncement (Micah 6:8)— "It hath been told thee, O man, what is good, and what the Lord doth require of thee: only to do justly, and to love mercy, and to walk humbly with thy God." It was Wise's boast that whatever he did was warranted by *Halakhah*, that he stood on historic ground: "To be sure, I am a reformer, as much as our age requires; because I am convinced that none can stop the stream of time, none can check the swift wheels of the age; but I have always the *Halakhah* for my basis; I never sanction a reform against the *Din.*" [16]

Wise was cognizant of the role of *Halakhah* in the Jewish past, in preserving the Jewish people in a scattered environment. Without power and pomp, without an intricate theology and without a tightly unified ecclesiastical organization, without a

mystical, supernaturalist doctrine of the synagogue as the ex-
clusive medium of salvation and without a hierarchical priesthood, Judaism nonetheless remained intact (with one or two
minor "schisms"); in spite of intermittent persecution and
constant hostility, it did not fall away from its covenant and
commitment. The prophets supplied Judaism with a reason, the
"why" for its being; the Law, *Halakhah*, supplemented and
implemented the "why" with a "how"—the "how" of survival.
Halakhah as a discipline in conduct, as an experiment in holiness, was at once Judaism's *imitatio Dei* (imitation of God) and
its plan for the human enterprise upon this earth. It was
summed up by Rab (as related in Midrash *Breshit Rabba*, 44):
"The commandments were given to Israel only in order that
men should be purified through them. For what can it matter
to God whether a beast is slain at the throat or at the back of
the neck?"

Wise knew that *Halakhah* was responsible for the lofty
quality of Jewish life in the Diaspora, both individual and
corporate, for the rarity of drunkenness, the absence of adul-
tery, the decent treatment of wives, the negligible number of
crimes of violence, the love of learning, and the widespread
practice of charity. Nor was Wise alone in this. Kaufmann
Kohler, Reform's eminent theologian at the beginning of the
century and later president of the Hebrew Union College,
defined religion similarly: "The true object of religion is the
hallowing of life rather than the salvation of the soul." [17] In
applying this definition to Judaism, Kohler wrote: "Judaism
is a religion of *life*, which it wishes to sanctify by duty rather
than by laying stress on the hereafter . . . Nor is it a religion
of redemption, condemning this earthly life . . ." [18]

Why then did Wise inveigh against "legalism"? What meaning did he ascribe to it? Was he antinomian (anti-legalistic), as
the advocates of radical Reform were, or was he in favor of a
"legalism" that would be compatible with the spirit of the age,
with the mood and movement of the times, and with the logic
of contemporary experience? Wise was no despiser of *Halakhah*
as Law, as a hallowing of life. But he was antagonistic to *Halakhah* as a closed system, without room for addition or modification and with no precedure for repeal of any part of it. *Halakhah* was no longer coextensive with the entire range of Jewish

experience; much of it was obsolete and archaic, and some a hindrance and an obstruction in the progress of present-day Judaism. *Halakhah* was imperative for Jewish survival, and it was still distinctive to Judaism, but only if it were to be open and flexible, subject to revision and sensitive to ever-new situations, predicaments, and problems. That is why Wise had been anxious to establish a union of synagogues and temples so that such changes might be orderly and vested in democratic authority.

In the end, Wise concluded that what stood between him and Orthodoxy was nothing less than the Emancipation and all that it connoted. The Emancipation had broken down the walls of the ghetto, had permitted the Jew to face his neighbors on a footing of equality, had woven him into the fabric of modern society. Emancipation had wiped out the secular power of the church and state. But Orthodoxy, Wise felt, had shut its eyes and remained oblivious of this chapter in European history, had been putting up ghettos of its own, had been clinging to a medieval mode of religious observance, and had thus been jeopardizing the future of Judaism in America. Most of this, if not all of it, Wise subsumed under the term "legalism," which he consigned to the graveyard.

Impact on American Judaism

In appraising Wise's impact upon American Judaism and his role in Reform, it may be said that his contribution was first of all in the field of organization. The Union, the College, the Conference—these are enduring monuments to his memory and to his accomplishments. And in the process of doing, Wise gradually clarified his thinking, and became the theoretician as well as the master builder of Reform.

Within Reform itself, Wise's great merit was that he defended a moderate position and did not cut Reform off from historic Judaism, did not sever the branch from the tree. He was no scorner of *Halakhah* as such, conceding that it had helped to preserve the Jewish people as a group of high ethical character and as a congregation of holiness. At the 1953 convention of the Union of American Hebrew Congregations Wise's daughter rose to voice her distress that her father's ideas had been appropriated by some to serve the aims of extreme and radical Reform, and she reaffirmed with the strongest emphasis, out of her recollection as one who had lived with him under the same roof, his abiding love and concern for historic Judaism with its traditions and its Biblical language of Hebrew.

Whatever quarrels Orthodoxy may have had with Reform and its founder in America, it is indisputable that Reform here did not undermine Judaism (as some had predicted), did not impugn its validity, and did not serve as a bridge to Christianity. And this was mainly due to the influence of Isaac Mayer Wise during his lifetime and to the legacy that he left. In Western Europe, where Reform made little progress, there were numerous conversions and widespread assimilation. In Eastern Europe, with its compact Jewish communities, there was scant defection through conversion and only limited assimilation, but instead there arose vast secular movements which stressed some form of nationalism as the substance of Judaism (or Jewishness). In America, for many reasons—the Constitutional provision for the equality of all religions, the absence of legal and political disabilities for Jews, the enormous immigration from Eastern Europe in the several decades before World War I—assimilation did not find expression as an overt philosophy, and conversions were marginal.

But for a goodly portion of American Jews—of the second and third generation, and some of the first—it was Reform that sustained their linkage to Judaism and offered them an acceptable and meaningful religious faith. And when Conservatism appeared upon the American scene, its reception was rendered easier because Reform had already done much of the spadework and had created a favorable climate for liberalism in Judaism. For this also much of the credit, if not the major share, must be accorded Isaac Mayer Wise.

It is now clear that Judaism in America is bound to be pluralistic in ritual, ceremony, forms of worship, and attitudes toward *Halakhah*, while remaining single and unified in its essential and majestic affirmation: "Hear, O Israel, the Lord our God, the Lord is One." Whether he intended it or not, Isaac Mayer Wise, with his defense of moderate Reform, involving at once a reverence for historic Judaism and a sensitiveness for change and modification, charted a course that—in one way or another —all variants of American Judaism (except certain segments of Orthodoxy) have since been following.

FOR FURTHER READING

Books by Isaac Mayer Wise

A Defense of Judaism versus Proselytizing Christianity (Cincinnati: American Israelite Press, 1889)

The Essence of Judaism (Cincinnati: Bloch), 1868).

Judaism: Its Doctrines and Duties (The Israelite Press, Cincinnati: 1872).

Selected Writings of I.M. Wise with a biography by the editors L. Grossman and D. Philipson (Cincinnati: Robert Clarke Co., 1900)

Reminiscences Cincinnati: (L. Wise & Co. 1901; Central Synagogue of New York, 1945).

Books about Isaacs Mayer Wise

KNOX, Israel, *Rabbi in America, The Story of Isaac M. Wise* (Boston: Little, Brown, 1957). A sound biography that places emphasis on the Reform movement in America and Wise's role in shaping it.

HELLER, James G., *Isaac M. Wise: His Life, Work and Thought* (New York: Union of American Hebrew Congregrations, 1965). Maurice Eisendrath called this Wise biography the "definitive study." It certainly offers a rich story in the classic 'life and times' tradition, yet Wise's theology is also amply discussed. The bibliography is most complete and well presented.

KEY, Andrew F., *The Theology of Isaac Mayer Wise* (Cincinnati: American Jewish Archives, 1962). A modest and useful review of key concepts in Wise's understanding of Judaism.

Solomon Schechter

While Isaac Mayer Wise was laying the foundations of Reform Judaism in America, there was also emerging simultaneously a new religious trend known as the Historical School. Though this approach did not develop in America into a full-fledged religious movement until the present century, it had its protagonists throughout the nineteenth century. Differences existed among them, but in general members of the school were close in spirit to the religious approach of Zechariah Frankel, Graetz, and the Breslau school in Germany with its emphasis on the historical development of ideas and customs. For the most part they were from Western or Central Europe, and in a few instances native-born Americans. It is these men who established the Jewish Theological Seminary in 1886 and who constitute the forerunners of Conservative Judaism in America.

The outstanding figure of the Historical School was Isaac Leeser (1806-1868). Throughout his tenure at Mikveh Israel in Philadelphia until his resignation in 1853, and later as rabbi of Beth El Emes in the same city, Leeser worked for the preservation of traditional Judaism. Nevertheless, he recognized the necessity for "improvements" to meet the spirit of the times. Leeser cooperated with Wise and his Reform colleagues in several joint efforts. He participated in the synod convened by Wise in Cleveland in 1855 and looked forward to continuing cooperation. But in 1856, when Wise published his prayer book *Minhag America,* in which the prayers for the return to *Eretz Yisrael* and the rebuilding of the Temple were eliminated, Leeser and the Conservatives felt that cooperation was no longer possible.

Among those joining Leeser in his antagonism to Reform was Sabato Morais (1823-1897), who succeeded him at Mikveh Israel. Morais had been brought up in Italy in the spirit of the Italian Jewish scholar Samuel David Luzzatto, and after serving as a teacher in England for several years had come to America. Though strongly traditional in outlook, Morais was willing to accept the Ashkenazi rite in place of the Sephardi, eliminate passages in the prayer book about the sacrificial system, and introduce the triennial cycle of Torah readings—all this in the hope of achieving a uniform ritual for American synagogues. To Morais, however, changes in ritual had to be authorized by a "synod of learned and Godfearing ministers." [1] As a religious leader in Philadelphia, he inspired a group of men who studied with him and held him in high esteem. These included Mayer Sulzberger (1843-1923), jurist, communal leader, and Hebraist; Solomon Solis-Cohen (1857-1948), physician, communal leader and poet; and Cyrus Adler (1863-1940), a student of Semitics at Johns Hopkins University in the 1880's. These disciples later helped him to establish the Jewish Theological Seminary.

The Historical School also included rabbis who were close in spirit to the moderate wing of Reform. Benjamin Szold (1829-1902), father of Henrietta, had studied in Breslau, where he came under the influence of Frankel and Graetz. In 1859 he had come to America to head congregation Oheb Shalom in Baltimore, which was beginning to veer toward Reform. Szold prepared a prayer book *Abodath Israel* (1864) together with a German translation, which replaced the one by Wise which was then in use by the congregation. It abridged some of the traditional prayers and changed an occasional passage which was intellectually unacceptable to him; but it was primarily in Hebrew.

Similar in outlook to Szold was Marcus Jastrow (1829-1903), outstanding scholar of the nineteenth century. Jastrow had studied at the University of Berlin and with the help of Graetz was appointed rabbi of the German synagogue in Warsaw. A supporter of the Polish uprising against Czar Alexander II in 1863, he was imprisoned for several months and was saved by his German citizenship from banishment to Siberia. In 1865 Congregation Rodeph Shalom in Philadelphia, searching for a "star" to fill its pulpit, invited Jastrow to come to America. Like Szold, he too found himself constantly struggling against the Reform tendencies of his congregation. In 1871, together with Rabbi Henry Hochheimer (1818-1912) of Baltimore, Jastrow revised the Szold prayer book, providing it with an English translation. Gradually, the Jastrow prayer book came into use in a number of congregations.[2]

Whatever differences existed between the two wings of the Historical School, all agreed on the importance of lifting the cultural level of the American Jewish community. With the development of an American public school system, the Jewish Day Schools lost ground. It also soon became apparent that the one-day-a-week

Sunday School was not adequate to impart an historic tradition like Judaism. Leeser, Morais, Szold, and Jastrow therefore began to work for the establishment of congregational Hebrew schools. This required educational materials and trained teachers. There was also a great need, as Leeser pointed out, for a "ministry trained on the spot, who can speak the language of the country." The German immigration had brought in several preachers and theologians, but differences in background and barriers of language restricted their usefulness.

Thus began the movement for organizing a rabbinical school. Several plans were advanced, but it was Isaac Leeser who succeeded in launching the first Jewish school of higher learning in America. With the help of a group of laymen in Philadelphia, including Abraham Hart (1810-1885), outstanding publisher and civic leader, and Moses Aaron Dropsie (1821-1905), prominent attorney, pledges for endowment funds were obtained. With the backing of the Board of Delegates of American Israelites, the national association of representatives of local Jewish communities, and in partnership with the Hebrew Education Society of Philadelphia, the project got under way. Leeser had the support of several other members of the Historical School, including Mayer Sulzberger and Rabbi Samuel Isaacs (1804-1878) of Shaare Tefiloh Congregation in New York. Morais, though he felt that the movement was premature, readily joined the faculty, which included Jastrow and Aaron Bettelheim (1830-1890), a former classmate of Szold from Europe who shared the latter's point of view.

In spite of opposition from Wise and other Reform leaders who objected to the "Orthodoxy of the institution," Maimonides College, as it was called, opened its doors in 1868 with eight registered students. Several soon withdrew, however, and it gradually became evident that Morais' warning that "American boys were not sufficiently advanced in Hebrew learning to undertake rabbinic studies" was true. The death of Leeser in 1868 and the lack of both students and support forced the institution to close after graduating three men as rabbis. These initial organizing efforts of the Historical School, however, were not without value in that they paved the way for the Jewish Theological Seminary.[3]

Meanwhile, the period of the 1870's marked the seeming triumph of Reform Judaism in America. In 1869, at a conference of Reform leaders in Philadelphia, a program for Reform Judaism was drafted. This platform rejected traditional concepts such as the restoration of the Jewish state and the belief in bodily resurrection, abolished the distinction between kosher and non-kosher food, and insisted that Hebrew must be replaced in prayer by an intelligible language. In 1873 the Union of American Hebrew Congregations was founded by Wise, and in 1875 the Hebrew Union College came into being, designed to serve American Jews of all viewpoints. Sabato Morais served on its Board of Examiners, while Szold delivered the address at the first closing exercises. Agitations in favor of Reform began to develop in several traditional synagogues, such as Shearith Israel in New York and Mikveh Israel in Philadelphia, but little headway was made. Congregation B'nai Jeshurun in New York, however, was influenced somewhat by the new currents, and Shaare Tefiloh in New York and Rodeph Shalom in Philadelphia both accepted the Reform program. It began to appear that Reform was to become the dominant pattern of Jewish religious life in America.

Members of the Historical School, however, became increasingly dissatisfied with these trends. They were strengthened by the appearance of several new personalities in the 1870's who joined their ranks: Henry Pereira Mendes (1852-1939), a traditionalist like Morais, who had come from England in 1877 and was elected *hazzan* of Shearith Israel; Aaron Wise (1844-1896), father of Stephen Wise, who served as rabbi of Congregation Rodeph Shalom in New York (which later became a Reform synagogue), and Frederick de Sola Mendes (1850-1927), brother of Pereira, who came to America from Jamaica to serve as assistant to Samuel Isaacs, whom he later succeeded. (In the time of Schechter, De Sola Mendes was to change his views and join the Reform movement.) De Sola Mendes was the leading spirit in launching *The American Hebrew* (1879), a weekly publication which became a kind of unofficial organ of Conservative Judaism. The policy of the paper was made by an anonymous group of men which included Solomon Solis-Cohen, Pereira Mendes, Mayer Sulzberger, Philip Cowen (1853-1949), who became the publisher, and later on Cyrus Adler.[4]

The Conservatives had no clearly articulated ideology of their own but they were united in their opposition to several aspects of the Reform program. They were disturbed by the trend on the part of the radical Reform leaders in the 1870's to transfer the Sabbath to Sunday. They resented the attempt to remove Hebrew from the service. They felt strongly about the question of *kashrut. The American Hebrew*, for example, refused to accept advertisements for non-kosher products. When shrimp was served at the closing banquet of the convention of the Union of American Hebrew Congregations in honor of the first graduates of the Hebrew Union College in 1883, there was a bitter reaction among Conservatives

throughout the country.[5] De Sola Mendes influenced his congregation to resign from the Union of America Hebrew Congregations
as did other rabbis. Finally, after the pogroms and Russian May
Laws of 1881, most of the Conservatives, aside from Morais, followed the poetess, Emma Lazarus, in her call for the resettlement of
Jews in the Holy Land. They resented the denial of Jewish nationalism on the part of Reform Judaism.

This opposition to Reform was strengthened by the arrival in
1885 of Alexander Kohut (1842-1894), outstanding scholar and
representative of Jews in the Hungarian Parliament, to serve as
rabbi of Ahavath Chesed. The congregation was beginning to lean
toward Reform, but Kohut made it clear in his inaugural sermon
that he was opposed to "unauthorized radical Reform which has
gained such dominion among our coreligionists in this new world."
He described his own viewpoint as "Mosaico-rabbinical Judaism
freshened with the spirit of progress." [6] His public debates with
Kaufmann Kohler, who had succeeded his father-in-law at Temple
Beth El in New York, focused attention on the views of Historical
Judaism and made him its spokesman in American Judaism.

In November, 1885, nineteen Reform Rabbis gathered in Pittsburgh at the call of Kaufmann Kohler and drew up the Pittsburgh
Platform, which summed up the position arrived at by the Reform
movement. It was the most radical statement that had ever been
adopted either in Germany or America, rejecting Jewish nationalism and many of the principles and practices of traditional Judaism
which the Conservatives were trying to preserve. This platform
finally aroused the Conservatives to action. A movement got under
way to establish a new rabbinical seminary that would insure the
preservation of modern traditional Judaism in America.

The sparkplug of this effort was Sabato Morais, who became
the first president of the Jewish Theological Seminary, as the new
institution was known. Kohut worked closely with him, helping
him to plan, speak, and collect funds on its behalf. Pereira Mendes
offered to exchange positions with Morais so he could live in New
York and direct the activities of the Seminary. Cyrus Adler, as a
devoted disciple of Morais, felt a personal interest in the institution
from the day it started. In order to be of assistance he traveled to
New York during 1887 one day a week from Washington, where
he served as Assistant Secretary of the Smithsonian Institution.

Morais had wanted to call the new institution the "Orthodox
Seminary" to make clear its Orthodox leanings. Kohut, however,
preferred the more inclusive name of Jewish Theological Seminary,
and his suggestion prevailed. The official opening of the Seminary

took place on January 2, 1887. Classes were held at first in the vestry rooms of the Spanish-Portuguese Synagogue, located on West 19th Street in New York, and then for a brief time in the building of the Cooper Union. The institution finally moved to a large brownstone house on Lexington Avenue between 58th and 59th Streets, where adequate accommodations were available. This was the home of the Seminary until 1903, when it was transferred to a new building on 123rd Street, made possible by Jacob Schiff (1847-1920), communal leader and philanthropist.

The purpose of the Seminary as stated in its charter was "the preservation in America of the knowledge and practice of historical Judaism, as ordained in the Law of Moses and expounded by the Prophets and Sages of Israel." The faculty consisted of Morais, who taught Bible and Biblical literature, Kohut as professor of Talmud (his eight-volume, monumental Talmudic dictionary appeared in 1894), Pereira Mendes, who taught homiletics and Jewish history, and Bernard Drachman (1861-1944), an American-born rabbi who had graduated from Breslau Theological Seminary in 1885 and received his doctorate from the University of Heidelberg. Drachman taught various subjects from Hebrew language to the classics of medieval Jewish philosophy.[7]

Ten students, almost all of them born in Europe, where they had received their preparatory training, were enrolled. The first graduation took place in 1894. Among the seven students who were ordained was Joseph Herman Hertz, who was chosen Chief Rabbi of the British Commonwealth in 1913.

The early years were difficult for the Seminary. Its main support came from the English-speaking Orthodox element, that is, from the Spanish-Portuguese congregations, and from Hungarian and some second-generation German Jews. The hope that the East European immigrants who were pouring into America during this period would serve as a financial base did not materialize at this time. Between the East European immigrants and the Jews of Sephardi or West European ancestry there were basic differences in background, language, and attitude toward life and Jewish studies. In 1888 a federation of fifteen important East European congregations joined in bringing over Rabbi Jacob Joseph as the Chief Rabbi of New York Jewry. While the experiment of setting up the position of Chief Rabbi did not succeed, it was the beginning of an attempt on the part of the East Europeans to organize themselves.[8] In 1897 the Isaac Elhanan Theological Seminary was established as a higher institution for the study of Talmud along the lines of European *yeshivas*. At a convention of Orthodox congregations called in 1898 it became clear that it would not be possible for Eastern and Western Europeans to work together.[9]

Meanwhile, Alexander Kohut had died in 1894 at the age of fifty-two; three years later the founder of the Seminary, Sabato Morais, also passed away. In 1901 Joseph Blumenthal (1834-1901), head of the Seminary Association, also died. Lacking leadership and financial support, the institution began to decline. There was danger that it might suffer the same fate as Maimonides College a quarter of a century before. At this point Cyrus Adler succeeded in interesting Jacob Schiff, Mayer Sulzberger, and other Jewish leaders in the plight of the Seminary.[10] It was clear to these men that there was need for a modern institution of higher Jewish learning where the language of instruction would be English so that traditional rabbis could be Americanized and at the same time trained in the best spirit of Jewish tradition. With the help of Louis Marshall (1856-1929) the Seminary Board was reorganized and within a short time an endowment fund of a half million dollars was secured. Adler agreed to become president of the Board of Directors and to spend three days a week in New York.

At this juncture an outstanding religious leader was needed to revitalize the Seminary and to rally the forces of Historical Judaism. For several years negotiations had been under way to bring from England Solomon Schechter, well-known Jewish scholar of Cambridge University, as a member of the faculty. Schechter had visited America in 1895 and delivered a series of lectures at Graetz College in Philadelphia on the subject of "Aspects of Rabbinic Theology." After Morais' death, efforts were renewed to convince Schechter to come to America as the spiritual head of the Seminary. Finally, he agreed. His arrival in 1902 marked the beginning of a new era for American Jewry.

5 . *Solomon Schechter*

[1849–1915]

NORMAN BENTWICH

M O R E than a century has passed since Solomon Schechter was born in Rumania, and almost a half century since his death in New York. His was an era of relative security, but it was also marked by deep stirring of Jewish consciousness as a result of the murderous pogroms in Czarist Russia and Rumania, centers of more than half the world's Jewish population. It was the age, too, of the great emigration from Eastern Europe to the United States and other English-speaking countries, of the creation of institutions of Jewish culture in those countries, of the beginning of Zionism and the organized return of Jews to Palestine. In his own life Schechter embodied that movement of the Jewish people, passing himself from his native Rumania to the centers of Jewish learning in Vienna and Berlin, thence to England, where he lived for twenty years, and finally to the United States, where he became spiritual leader of the Jewish community for the last thirteen years of his life.

By his discovery and interpretation of the treasure of ancient manuscripts in Cairo, he added more than any man in modern times to our knowledge of post-Biblical and rabbinical Judaism, and Jewish history and lore in the early centuries of the Middle Ages. As president of the Jewish Theological Seminary he laid the foundation and set the tone for that outstanding institution which for decades after his death has been known as "Schechter's Seminary." Through his prophetic quality of tremendous personality, he exercised a strong influence on his generation and became pre-eminent in the development of Judaism in America.

Youth and Study

Solomon Schechter was born in the little Rumanian town of Foscani in 1849. His parents belonged to a special branch of the *Hasidim*, the philosophers among the mystics who stressed the joy of Torah and the virtue of study and learning. He was given the Hebrew name of Shneor Zalman after the founder of the sect to which they belonged. Imbibing a *Hasidic* enthusiasm, joyous mysticism, and simple piety, and devoted from childhood to rabbinic lore, he became a young prodigy of learning. His father was his first teacher, and at three he learned Hebrew and at five was already familiar with the Bible. At the age of ten he attended the *yeshiva* in a neighboring town. Here he became expert in the Talmud and while he mastered the jurisprudence of the rabbis, his preference was for the Midrash, the maxims, legends, and homiletical interpretations.

From his earliest years, however, Schechter was eager for knowledge of the larger world in which his people lived. Of that world he could only obtain passing glimpses. At the age twelve he read a Hebrew translation of one of the books of the first-century historian Josephus in the hope of learning the cause of anti-Jewish feeling in Rumania and the remedy for it. Since Josephus and the Hellenistic writers were regarded by the pious *Hasidim* of the neighborhood as heretical, Solomon had to read such books surreptitiously. He snatched glimpses too of the outer world through a weekly Hebrew paper *Ha-Maggid*, and began his philosophical studies with Maimonides' *Guide for the Perplexed*. Through the help of a *maskil* (modern scholar) of Foscani he was able to study the Hebrew work of Azariah de Rossi, an Italian Jewish scholar of the Renaissance. That book, entitled *Meor-Enayim* (Light of Eyes), was the first attempt by a Jew in modern times to deal with the Hellenistic development of Judaism and, as such, was the forerunner of a critical outlook toward Jewish authority.

At the age of sixteen Schechter entered the famous rabbinical school in Lemberg (Loov); but he was not happy in that Galician town and returned to Foscani. For some years he stud-

ied by himself until, at the age of twenty-four, he made his way
to Vienna where he became a student in its *bet hamidrash*. In
this cultural center he came under the influence of three outstanding teachers, who took a fatherly interest in him. These
were Meir Freedman, scholarly editor of Midrashic texts, Isaac
Hirsch Weiss, author of the first scientific survey of the legal
and theological doctrines of Judaism, and Adolph Jellinek, a
famous preacher. They initiated him into the mysteries of
historical science as applied to Jewish lore, and the principle
of going back to the original Jewish sources. From them Schechter learned what was to become the foundation of his own
contribution—devoted and exact study of the rabbinical tradition, the historical sense in relation to the Bible, and above all,
Jellinek's conception of the community of Israel—*Knesset
Yisrael*, or what Schechter was later to call "catholic Israel."
Simultaneously, he pursued, as an "extraordinary student,"
secular studies at the University of Vienna and subsequently in
Berlin. His concern was to find in Jewish tradition a living
doctrine for the modern age. Rejecting Yiddish as the vehicle
of Jewish scholarship, he developed an ardor for the revival of
Hebrew as a living literary language.

Either at Lemberg or at Vienna Schechter was affected by
the *Haskalah* and its striving to bring modern knowledge in
Hebrew to the young generation. He became critical of *Hasidism*, publishing two satirical essays in the Hebrew journal *Ha-
Shahar* in 1875 and 1877. The latter certainly, and the former
probably, were written by Schechter anonymously. Later he
repented that he had hurt his family, and his English essay on
Hasidism was a kind of atonement. In it he stated that there was
a time when he loved and a time when he hated the movement.
His subsequent recoil from the influence of the *Haskalah* was
more permanent because temperamentally he was opposed to
rationalism.

Schechter next accepted a post as assistant teacher in the
Berlin Hochschule, an academy of Jewish knowledge founded
in 1871 by Abraham Geiger, the intellectual leader of the Reform movement, for the purpose of teaching all schools of
Judaism. While yet in Vienna, Schechter had met Geiger's
successor, Pincus Frankl, and the two had become close friends.
Once in Berlin, the young scholar continued his studies with

Israel Levy, an authority on the Jerusalem Talmud and a radical critic, and with Moritz Steinschneider, the greatest Jewish bibliographer of the time; and he had as a pupil Richard Gottheil, who was later to become a professor of Semitics at Columbia University. At the Hochschule in Berlin, which was more Germanized than the *bet hamidrash* in Vienna, Schechter mastered German Christian theology, inspired by Max Weber and Adolf von Harnack, which was bitterly hostile to Judaism. According to them the Jewish God was remote, and Judaism took the soul out of religion. He realized that this was a form of academic anti-Semitism, and it was years before he expressed his own convictions.

The turning point of Schechter's life came in 1882, when he was invited to go to London by Claude Goldsmid Montefiore, a young English Jewish scholar of two famous families, who had come from Oxford to Berlin to extend his knowledge of Judaism. Montefiore, recognizing that Schechter, more than any rabbinical scholar he had met in England, understood and was able to harmonize Jewish law and doctrine with inward religion, persuaded Schechter to accompany him to England for a year as his personal tutor in Rabbinics. Schechter, never happy in Germany because of its spirit of militarism and the belief in "blood and iron" which was prevalent at that time, as well as because of what he later described as the "higher anti-Semitism" of German scholars, welcomed the opportunity. He knew of the great collections of Hebrew manuscripts and early printed books in the British Museum and the Bodleian Library of Oxford, greater, as he said, than any collection to which Maimonides had ever had access. In addition, he was attracted by what he had heard of the freedom of England and the almost complete absence in academic society of anti-Jewish prejudice.

London and Cambridge

Schechter's genius budded in England. With the encouragement of Montefiore and other English scholars, he prepared himself to become an interpreter of Judaism to Christian academic society and to the common man. During his first eight years in that country he held no academic post, except as an occasional teacher at Jews' College, London's rabbinical school;

but he was writing articles about Judaism in an extraordinarily expressive and scintillating style. He soon became the central figure of a band of Jewish laymen who sought to arouse Jewish consciousness and an interest in Jewish culture. They mingled Jewish knowledge with English humor. Included in this group were Dr. Moses Gaster, the *hakham* or chief rabbi of the Sephardi community, who, like himself, had come originally from Rumania; Israel Zangwill, then beginning his career as the novelist of the ghetto; Lucien Wolf and Joseph Jacobs—originally from Australia—the fathers of Anglo-Jewish history; Solomon J. Solomon, a distinguished painter; Asher Myers, editor of the *Jewish Chronicle*, then as now the principal weekly organ of the community; and Israel Abrahams, son of an English rabbi and tutor at Jews' College, who was later to succeed Schechter in the teaching of rabbinical studies at Cambridge University. The group, which called itself the "Wanderers" because they wandered to each other's rooms and from subject to subject, were in revolt against the official leaders of the Jewish community and what Schechter called their "red-tape or flunkey Judaism." Engrossed in the struggle for full civil and political rights, these religious and lay leaders were neglecting Jewish learning and culture. Schechter's passionate convictions about Judaism were roused by the clever skepticism of the rest. He would bear down on any rationalizing or cynical comment with a mixture of enthusiasm and indignation. Later, at Cambridge, in a circle of academic friends drawn from all sections of the University's life, "his Johnsonian flow of wisdom and tolerance," as one of the "dons" put it, exerted a similar kind of irresistible attraction. In the words of Joseph Jacobs, Schechter burst upon the Wanderers "like an explosive bomb or like a blazing comet in an intellectual sky . . . I can see him rising from his chair, pacing up and down the room like a wounded lion and roaring retorts."

Schechter's massive presence, his leonine head crowned with a shock of auburn hair, a shaggy beard, and flashing blue eyes, his burning faith and vehemence, and, above all, his overflowing humanity caused him to dominate the group, which became responsible for two notable Anglo-Jewish enterprises, the founding of the *Jewish Quarterly Review* and the establishment of the Jewish Historical Society of England.

In 1890 Schechter married Matilda Roth, a cultured Breslau woman then teaching in London. Herself cultivated in literature and art, she was an ideal helpmate for Schechter, serving as a critic of his writings and helping to create the kind of home that became a warm center of hospitality for his friends, students, and colleagues.

Three years later, Schechter was appointed Lecturer, and later Reader (i.e., Associate Professor) in Rabbinics at Cambridge University, and Keeper of the Hebrew manuscripts in the University Library. He had already published an English edition of a rabbinical text, the *Abot* (*Ethics*) *of Rabbi Nathan*, and his first volume of *Studies in Judaism*, a collection of popular essays which appeared originally in the *Jewish Chronicle* and other periodicals. His essay on the *Hasidim*, particularly, made a deep impression because it was the first sympathetic study of those joyous mystics of East European Jewry. At Cambridge Schechter, as the only professing Jewish "don" during the greater part of his twelve years there, had the opportunity of inspiring non-Jewish scholars of theology and Oriental studies like Charles Taylor, Master of St. John's College, Robertson Smith, the famous Biblical authority, as well as outstanding academic minds in other fields such as Sir James Frazer, author of *The Golden Bough*. Schechter had steeped himself in English literature, from which he could quote as easily as from the Bible and the Midrash. He expounded a full-blooded Judaism hitherto unknown to the scholars of the Christian university.

Adventure in the Geniza

Schechter's place in the world of learning was assured for all time when he identified, by a remarkable combination of learning and fortune, a fragment of the original Hebrew book of the Apocrypha, the Wisdom of Ben Sira or Ecclesiasticus, which had been lost for eight hundred years. Two Christian women in Cambridge, enthusiastic collectors of Hebrew and other Oriental manuscripts, had picked up a bundle of Hebrew fragments in Cairo. They consulted Schechter, who immediately recognized one of the fragments as belonging to the Book of Ben Sira. He published it with a commentary, which led scholars at Oxford and London to examine fragments of Hebrew manuscripts they had acquired from Egypt, and to find among them further passages from the Book of the Apocrypha. These findings confirmed Schechter in his suspicion that the common source for all the fragments must be the archives of an ancient synagogue in old Cairo which had been mentioned by medieval travelers as well as by some in the eighteenth century. This was known as the Geniza, meaning the buried archives of the Jewish community, a cemetery of books and documents which were no longer used. Since no writings in the sacred tongue were permitted to be destroyed, they were buried in order to preserve them from profanation. As Schechter described the Geniza, it was "a limbo to which were consigned remnants of good books to be preserved from harm, and of bad books to be preserved from doing harm." It was also a depository for legal contracts and official documents, a combination of sacred and secular record office—without a catalogue or attendant.

The Cairo depository, more than a thousand years old, had been attached to a synagogue in the old Byzantine-Christian city known to the Romans as Babylon. The synagogue, which had formerly been a Coptic church in one of the earliest hearths of Christianity, had been acquired for Jewish worship in the year 882. By a happy accident the documents placed in the Geniza (including many dating from the ninth century) had not been buried in the ground, as was the common practice; and when the synagogue itself was rebuilt in 1890 the Geniza fortunately remained untouched and unswept. The first attempt to ransack its treasures was made by Abraham B. Firkovich (1786-1874), a famous Jewish scholar from Russia who was building up an Oriental library in St. Petersburg. Though he had been unable to penetrate into the recesses of the Geniza, he had acquired from the guardians bundles of the manuscripts, which he had published and so set the learned world on their track.

Schechter convinced the authorities of the University Library that there was untold treasure to be found in the Cairo Geniza, and they sent him in 1896 to Egypt to prospect. Armed with only a glowing recommendation to the Chief Rabbi of Cairo from the Chief Rabbi of England, and with a sealed credential from the vice-chancellor of the University of Cambridge to the president of the Jewish community of Cairo, he was able not only to make a thorough exploration of the buried treasure, but also, by the persuasiveness of his personality, to take home to Cambridge nearly all of its contents. Though almost suffocated and blinded by the painstaking search through "the dust of the centuries," Schechter knew the immense importance of his findings, and of the hundred thousand fragments, manuscripts, and documents which he brought safely back and presented to the Cambridge University Library.

The Taylor-Schechter Collection, as it came to be known, was deposited in an upper room of the University Library. There for six years Schechter worked all the hours of daylight, clad in a dust-coat and wearing a nose and mouth protector. He himself sifted and classified the hundred thousand fragments which he had recovered. Surrounded by a row of common grocery boxes labeled Bible, Talmud, History, Literature, Philosophy, Rabbinics, Theology, and so on, he would pick out from the mass each piece of paper or parchment, look at it with his magnifying glass, and then place it in its proper box. It was a remarkable spectacle of the mastery of scholarship, and scholars came from Europe and America to see Schechter at work. The prizes he found, he stated, "I would not change for all Wall Street. I am finding daily valuable treasures. A whole unknown Jewish world reveals itself to us."

Importance of the Geniza Find

Nearly the whole of the Hebrew text of the Book of Ben Sira was recovered in different manuscripts; Schechter published an edition of it that marked a revolution in the knowledge of Hebrew of the earliest post-Biblical age because it was the only Hebrew writing which had come down from the Persian period of Jewish history. The discovery of the Geniza was as epoch-making for the study of the Bible and Jewish history from the time of the destruction of the Jewish state to the medieval period as the discovery of the Dead Sea Scrolls in our own day; and it covered a much longer period and a wider range of scholarship, including hundreds of copies of the Bible and Apocrypha books, a mass of fragments of the Talmud, some written in the eleventh and twelfth centuries, Arabic manuscripts, and innumerable other documents. It opened up a new world of Hebrew, Arabic, and Jewish lore. Its contribution to the knowledge of medieval

Jewish life and literature, Jewish history and law was immense.

In his first survey of the Geniza, Schechter described it as "a battlefield of books, and the literary brains of many centuries had their share of the battle. Their *disjecta membra* are now strewn over the battlefield. Some of the belligerents have perished outright and are literally ground to dust in the terrible struggle for space; while others, as if overtaken by the general crush, are squeezed into big, unshapely lumps." It was remarkable that the task of sifting, arranging, and interpreting the mass of manuscripts and print was done by one man alone, though he realized that he would not be able to complete the task. In fact, the work of publishing the texts—which has since engaged the minds of many scholars, Jewish and Gentile, in Britain, Israel, America, France, and Germany—is still far from complete.

Schechter's own contribution was outstanding. Besides the edition of Ben Sira, he published autographed letters of the heads of the rabbinical schools in Babylon, and of the medieval sage Moses ben Maimon,* and a portion of an unknown commentary or Midrash of Deuteronomy. He also edited fragments of Saadia Gaon,** the great tenth-century master of Jewish law and philosophy who lived in Cairo; included in this publication were documents about Saadia's life, and portions of his philosophical works formerly believed lost.

Still more important for the history of Jewish religion in the Middle Ages was Schechter's discovery of a large part of the Book of Commands of the most famous Jewish heretical sect, the Karaites, originally from Babylon, who rejected the rabbinical interpretation of the Torah. By piecing together the documents, Schechter was able to show that, far from rejecting the Law, the Karaites emphasized its strictness and the necessity for strict obedience. He revealed too the ancient origin of some of their fundamental tenets. Saadia and the rabbinical schools had charged the Karaites with the errors of a pre-Christian sect of Zadokites, associated mistakenly, as it appeared, with the Sadducees, who were opposed to the Pharisees. According to the Geniza documents the sect had its center at Damascus, and had fled from Jerusalem when the faithful were persecuted by a wicked priest. Schechter's discovery of the document of the sect became dramatically significant fifty years later, when copies

Creators of the Jewish Experience in Ancient and Medieval Times, Chapter 6, Washington, D.C., B'nai B'rith Books, 1985 **Ibid.,* Chapter 5

of the Manual of Discipline, or Rules of the Order, of a Jewish sect of the first century B.C.E., which tallied almost verbally with the Geniza fragment, were found among the Dead Sea Scrolls. The skepticism of some critics of Schechter about the authenticity of the sect proved unwarranted.

In the field of Jewish history he discovered another dramatic Hebrew document, a philosophic work of the twelfth-century sage Ibn Ezra describing the Kingdom of the Khazars (the subject of Judah Halevi's *Kuzari*),* of which little was known previously except by inference. The document tells how the rulers of the kingdom, which comprised the country of the Volga, the Crimea, and Caucasus, were converted to Judaism.

The findings of the Geniza and the scholarly editions published by Schechter enhanced his stature both at home and abroad. The Senate of Cambridge University recognized his services by conferring on him an honorary degree of D. Litt. (Years later he was the first Jew to receive a similar honor from Harvard University.) He was already well known in the United States, thanks to two prominent admirers, Mayer Sulzberger and Solomon Solis-Cohen, both scholarly Philadelphia leaders, who even before Schechter's epoch-making expedition to Cairo had induced him to go to the United States and deliver a series of lectures on rabbinical theology. While there, he had been urged to accept an important position at the Jewish Theological Seminary, which was then directed by its aged founder Rabbi Sabato Morais. Schechter's *Studies in Judaism* had been issued in an Amercan edition by the Jewish Publication Society. Schechter's fame was redoubled as a result of his Geniza finds, and a renewed effort was now made by certain American Jewish leaders to get him to settle permanently in the New World.

Call to the New World

Leaders in England, realizing Schechter's inspiration for the young generation, were reluctant to let him go. Though he held no official post in the community, Schechter's home in Cambridge was the meeting place for Jewish "dons" and graduates and the growing number of Jewish undergraduates, some of

*Ibid., Chapter 7

whom were to become leaders of English Jewry. On Saturdays the students conducted services in the small synagogue in Cambridge, while Schechter in *Hasidic* abandon, strode up and down singing the beloved tunes with lusty warmth and with little regard for the student who happened to be intoning the prayers. On Sabbath afternoons, all would gather at his home, as at a kind of *bet hamidrash*, for lively discussions of Judaism and related subjects. One member of that circle who felt "the touch of that great soul" has described the "joyous wit, the biting humor, the good fellowship, his (Schechter's) vibrant and even inconsequent storming of feeling—(his) trumpet-call to young and growing Jewry to love, live, and rejoice in the Jewish mode of life."

In spite of these warm relationships, however, Schechter yearned for a group, however small, of disciples who would dedicate their life to Jewish scholarship; he aspired, like a *Hasidic* rabbi, to have a following. The few Jewish scholars and rabbis who came to sit at his feet had either come from America or departed to America. His dream was to establish a school of Jewish learning for Jews, and he longed for an opportunity to dwell among his people with his family (he had three children). "I want to be a Jew and bring up my children as Jews . . . With Jews I can get understanding. I lose my life among Christians," he said on one occasion. Believing that "the future of Judaism is in America," he felt that the New World offered "a larger field of activity which may become a source of blessing for future generations." What induced him in the end to make the difficult decision to leave the academic circles of Cambridge, which he loved, was his sense of mission, as he felt it, "to act for God," to found in America, which was rapidly becoming the center of the largest Jewish community, a house of learning for the Law of Israel, its wisdom and doctrine. In 1901, when he was again invited to become president of the Jewish Theological Seminary, with a free hand and ample means to make it a school of genuine learning and a unifying cultural force among American Jews, his English friends could no longer prevail against that call. "I may become, if I am deemed worthy by God, the saving of Conservative Judaism."

Before Schechter left England, he wrote an *envoi*, which

was a declaration of faith provoked by correspondence appearing in the *Jewish Chronicle* about "Englishmen of the Jewish persuasion." It took the form of four letters entitled "Jews and Anglo-Saxons," "Jews as Missionaries," "Spiritual Religion versus Spiritual Men," and "Despising a Glorious Inheritance," which were published in 1900. In the first and second he attacked assimilation. Starting with a quotation, as was his practice, this time from the letters of Robert Louis Stevenson, about the noble ancestry of the Jews, he poured scorn upon the cry of "Englishmen of the Jewish persuasion," which was an imitation of an exploded German cry. "The doctrine professed by those who are not carried away by the new fanatical 'yellow' theology is, there is no Judaism without Jews, and there are no Jews without Judaism. We can thus only be Jews of the Jewish persuasion. 'Blessed those who remember!' " In the last two epistles Schechter turned on those who go about begging for a nationality, and clamoring everywhere "we are you"—and on those who prate about "a spiritual religion, which showed itself in an antipathy to the religion of Eastern Jewry and an insatiable appetite for new prayers." He also made a passionate appeal for the revival of Jewish learning.

In spite of the fact that these epistles aroused a flood of controversy in the Jewish press, Schechter took leave of England and its Jews on an affectionate note. He was well aware that this was to be a complete break and a change of emphasis in his life. Hitherto, he had been primarily the scholar and man of letters. Now he would be primarily head of a school, a leader of the Judaism of a vast Jewish community. He was to abandon the English academic cloister and to step into the crowded American arena of Jewish masses.

President of the Jewish Theological Seminary

If in England Schechter was a fiery force, the gadfly of the community, in America he became the sage speaking with authority, the unifying spiritual leader of the whole community. He arrived in New York in 1902, at a moment when the United States was becoming the center of gravity for the Jewish masses who had left Eastern Europe in search of freedom. The first decade of the twentieth century had brought

an immense growth of American Jewry: one hundred thousand
a year, comparable to the growth of the population of the State
of Israel in its first decade. In the period between 1900 and
1912, the Jewish population doubled. Schechter, conscious of
the opportunity, wrote from New York to Samuel Poznanski,
a Warsaw professor: "You must come to spread Torah and
Jewish knowledge in this land in which are hidden the future
events of our people."

The aims of the Seminary, which Schechter had come to
head, were defined in a charter granted under a law of the State
of New York: "The Jewish Theological Seminary of America
was incorporated . . . for the perpetuation of the tenets of the
Jewish religion, the cultivation of Hebrew literature, the pursuit of Biblical and archeological research, the advancement of
Jewish scholarship, the establishment of a library, and the education and training of Jewish rabbis and teachers." Louis Marshall, a leader of the bar, and later president of the American
Jewish Committee, an outstanding defender of Jewish causes
and one of the architects of The Jewish Agency for Palestine,
was the chairman of the Board of Trustees and worked devotedly with Schechter to realize those aims. Schechter chose as
the motto for the reorganized Seminary the words of the Bible
about the burning bush which Moses saw in the wilderness:
"and it was not consumed." That was the symbol of his faith
that the plant of Judaism and Jewish scholarship would flourish
in the Jew despite the fire through which the Jewish people
had passed.

In his inaugural address delivered in November 1902 before
an assembly of all sections of American Jewry, rabbis and laymen, Schechter insisted at the outset on the catholic purpose
of the institution. The community of America was drawn from
all parts of the globe. Each wave of arriving immigrants
brought its own rituals and dogmatisms all struggling for perpetuation. It was to be one of the aims of the Seminary to bring
unity into that diverse mass. It would be all things to all men,
reconciling all parties and appealing to all sections of the community.

The Seminary would stand for historical and traditional
Judaism. He quoted from Lincoln's address to Congress: "Fellow citizens, we cannot escape history . . . We must make an

end to these constant amputations if we do not wish to see the body of Israel bleed to death before our very eyes. We must leave off talking about occidentalizing our religion as if the Occident has ever shown the least genius for religion—for freeing the conscience by abolishing various laws . . . There is no other Jewish religion but that taught by the Torah and confirmed by history and tradition, and sunk into the conscience of catholic Israel." He was most concerned about the unity of Judaism in America. The Seminary was to give direction to the Reformers as well as to the Orthodox and Conservative. The unity of Israel, in his view, was a union of doctrines, precepts, and promises.

In April 1903, the new building of the Seminary on West 123rd Street, near Columbia University, was formally presented by Jacob Schiff. Like Schechter, the donor stressed the catholic aim of the institution "which should appeal to all desiring to prepare for the Jewish ministry."

Schechter set about gathering a band of scholars who could train and inspire a learned Jewish ministry able to interpret Judaism for American Jews. He found in the United States Louis Ginzberg, who, like Schechter himself, was a great master of Midrash, and J. M. Asher, who became Professor of Homiletics. From Europe Schechter recruited Israel Friedlaender of the Strasbourg University in Bible exegesis, and the historian Alexander Marx, who had just finished his studies at Königsberg. Later, Israel Davidson was engaged to teach medieval literature. In addition, Schechter's dream was to found a great library endowed with the most complete collection of Judaica in the world. In this task he was aided by Dr. Marx, and together they succeeded in establishing the largest Jewish library in America, with over a hundred thousand volumes and seven thousand manuscripts. Realizing also the great need in American Jewry for trained teachers, Schechter established in 1909 the Teachers' Institute as part of the Seminary, with Mordecai Kaplan as its director. Though Kaplan had not yet formulated his concept of Reconstructionism and of Judaism as a civilization, Schechter had already singled him out for his power of inspiring and stimulating.

There was no lack of candidates for admission to the Seminary, though only graduates of reputable American universities were accepted. Schechter sought to bring into the life of the institution something of that corporate spirit which he had learned to appreciate at Cambridge. His aim was to found, as it were, a Cambridge College of Jewish Studies.

While the first five years of his presidency were a period of achievement during which the Seminary grew in stature and increased in influence, the latter years were for Schechter a period of disillusionment. When Moses Dropsie left a fortune for an undenominational institution of Jewish and cognate learning and research, Schechter ardently hoped that the bequest would be used for the enlargement of the Seminary, or at least that the new institution would be bound up with the Seminary. He dreamt of a "Jewish academy with regular academicians which, by reason of its authority and scientific work, should give Jewish opinion the weight and importance in all matters related to Hebrew learning . . . Together with the Dropsie College as one institution we could do wonders in time; without it we shall only vegetate for some years and disappear in the end." The lawyers, however, advised that the bequest could not be used for the enlargement of the New York seminary and the idea of a merger with an institution in Philadelphia was found unacceptable.

As the years passed, Schechter apprehended a falling off of support on the part of the directors of the Seminary. The Orthodox section, which regarded the Conservatives as almost heretical, and the Yiddish press, which disliked English, made violent attacks on the Seminary and on himself. Having come to America with a mission to initiate a religious revival, he was sensitive to these attacks. He felt frustrated because of the financial problems which faced the institution and what he regarded as the neglect and indifference of some of the directors. Because of these difficulties, his scholarly interests could not be pursued as he desired. But despite moments of disappointment, Schechter, during the thirteen years of his presidency, laid the foundations of an institution which became the center of Conservative Judaism and one of American Jewry's important scholarly institutions.

Prophet of Counter-Reformation

Schechter was the center of a counter-reformation, standing for the Conservative tradition of Judaism against uncontrolled Reform. He found the Seminary established as the school for Conservative Judaism, but he did not define in any precise way what was meant by that term. He wanted "Judaism without adjectives and adverbs," what one may call "unhyphenated," and also without any geographical limitation. The fundamentals of Judaism must be the same in every country. "The observance of the Sabbath, the keeping of the dietary laws, devotion to Hebrew literature and hope for Zion are as absolutely necessary for maintaining Judaism in America as elsewhere. It cannot sufficiently be urged that the Atlantic forms no break in Jewish tradition, and that reverence for the Torah and devotion to religion are characteristic of the American gentleman." The talk of "deorientalizing Judaism" was "a piece of theological anti-Semitism."

Schechter realized that the Conservative synagogue was something different from the Orthodox, which was based on the divine revelation of every command, and he was deeply concerned that it should embrace all sections which were broadly loyal to the tradition. Though scornful while in England of organization, he nevertheless took the lead in America in organizing the Conservative communities into a union which could withstand the extremes of radical Reform and of unbending Orthodoxy. He brought the United Synagogue of America into being, and became its first president at a meeting in February 1913, attended by delegates of congregations, rabbis, members of the faculties of the Seminary, Dropsie College, and Graetz College in Philadelphia. He inserted in its constitution the following general clause: "It shall be the aim of the United Synagogue, while not endorsing the innovations introduced by any of its constituent bodies, to embrace all elements essentially loyal to tradition."

Because of that clause, the Sephardi congregation would not become a member of the United Synagogue. Schechter made no suggestion of changes in practice which might be introduced, and he strongly opposed the idea of a synod or San-

hedrin in America which might propose changes. He objected
to the creation of any reform of Judaism by resolution or conference. "I think synods, unless confined to purely administrative affairs, are useless and even harmful. Religion is one of the
things fitted to the heart which are vulgarized by public discussion. Besides, I think no man is capable of representing other
men in matters spiritual. Synods have also a tendency to create
among us a certain sacerdotalism, which is quite foreign to the
Jewish spirit." The evil which he particularly feared was a
permanent schism in the congregation of Israel.

Though his central interest was the Seminary, Schechter was
recognized as the spiritual leader of Jewry on the American
continent. His activities were manifold on behalf of the total
community. He was concerned about two things—the unity of
Israel and the diffusion of Jewish knowledge. To carry out the
latter, he served as chairman of the Jewish Publication Society's
Board of Translators of the Bible, which produced a new translation from the Hebrew based on American scholarship. He
also served as editor of the *Jewish Encyclopedia*, and co-editor
of the *Jewish Quarterly Review*, which he had helped found in
England.

In England Schechter had inspired a few, but in America,
despite his momentary disappointments, he was able to influence
many. His personality struck the Jewish public. He captured
them by storm. The man as well as the doctrine stirred them.
There was an enthusiasm for him in progressive as well as more
conservative sections. While he upheld with his old ardor the
teaching and practice of traditional Judaism, he was concilia-
tory to the leaders of Reform who had regard for the preservation of the Jewish faith. In his inaugural address at the Seminary he had said: "The ultimate goal at which we are aiming
is union and peace in American Israel. Although the Conservative spirit permeates it, an institution should not become a place
of polemics, but rather a spot where heaven and earth kiss each
other." The graduation ceremonies at the Seminary were outstanding features of Jewish public life, and Schechter's addresses were messages to the whole Jewish people. The Reform
and liberal rabbis before he came had started, in the infectious
atmosphere of uncontrolled individualism and secular Americanization, a movement to denationalize Judaism and shed its

distinctive practices. As the recognized master of Jewish learning, Schechter had the authority and conviction to check a process which imperilled Jewish survival and morals, to lay a foundation of knowledge in the training of rabbis, and to inspire, in at least a few of them, the love of research. He made learning an essential part of Judaism.

Attitude toward Zionism

A natural-born Zionist, Schechter issued in 1905 a statement of his faith, which, like his epistles to the Jews of England, was a call to a full Judaism. For him, the return of the Jewish people to the land of Israel was an integral part of his religious faith, in the fulfillment of Hebrew prophecy. Though he had visited Palestine after his exploration of the Geniza, and spent some time in a village with his twin brother, an agricultural pioneer from Rumania since 1882, he had hesitated to join the Zionist movement because he was apprehensive of the secular nationalism of many of its leaders. "You cannot sever Jewish nationalism from Jewish religion," he stated. In his view, the assimilation of Judaism to a modern nationalist revival was as dangerous as the assimilation of the Jew.

Schechter attended the Zionist Congress held in Vienna in the summer of 1913. On his journey he visited the graves of his parents and scenes of his childhood in his native Rumania. Though at the Congress great honor was paid him, he was not at home in its highly charged political atmosphere. His greeting to the assembly, delivered in Hebrew, briefly explained his views: "I do not divide the Jews according to their political condition and outlook. The main thing is that they are good Jews. As an American Zionist, I agree with the Westerners that Zionism is a religious movement." He was elected an honorary president of the congress for Hebrew language and culture which was also held in Vienna at the same time. He urged that the sittings should be devoted to literature which had the scientific spirit. What was called *belles lettres* was not beautiful. "I trembled to read the literature which, with our infinite vanity, we call the Hebrew Renaissance." It was about this time that Schechter made the personal acquaintance of Ahad Ha-am, whom he had long admired and with whom he had carried on a correspondence for several years.

Zionism at that time was strongly opposed by most of the lay-magnates of the community who feared that the national movement would endanger their standing as American citizens. For Schechter the return to Zion was essentially a spiritual and not a political rebirth, and it was as a bulwark against self-destructive assimilation and an assertion of a full Judaism that he championed it. "What I understand by assimilation is loss of identity, or that process of disintegration which, passing through various degrees of defiance of Jewish thought and of disloyalty to Israel's history and its mission, terminates variously in different lands . . . It is this kind of assimilation that I dread most, even more than pogroms . . ." His view made a deep impression, and influenced and inspired a group of young Zionist intelligentsia, including Judah Magnes, Henrietta Szold,* Horace Kallen, Max Radin, and Elisha Friedman.

The Hebrew University of Jerusalem did not become a practical project in Schechter's lifetime. He was, however, associated with the foundation of the Haifa technical school (Technion) in Palestine, an institution whose governing body was composed of representatives of Russian, German, and American Jewries. Schechter with Cyrus Adler, Judah Magnes, Louis Marshall, and Jacob Schiff were the American members. In 1913, when the controversial question of language for instruction arose and the German members pressed for German, Schechter recognized that Hebrew should ultimately be the language of instruction, but suggested that for a time it would be necessary to use German for technical subjects because of the temporary lack of Hebrew vocabulary and books. "If a workman used the wrong Hebrew formula, the boiler would still blow up." He was absolutely convinced of the importance of the Hebrew language as a link among all Jewish communities of the world; he himself used Hebrew regularly in his correspondence with Jewish scholars.

Schechter remained attached to England throughout his life. Though he did not live to know of the Balfour Declaration of the British Government favoring the establishment of a

* See Chapter 11.

Jewish national home in Palestine, he rejoiced when, in the early stages of World War I, after the Turks had thrown in their lot with Germany, the prospects of English rule in Palestine began to be discussed: "England is a Biblical country, reverential and practical, kind to our people, and able to understand our aspirations for and in the Holy Land. Any other power, even a civilized one, would secularize it soon enough. England in its sincerity and reverence would serve as a model to our radicals, and would save us from all sorts of assimilation. I mean assimilation of the Jew and Judaism."

Last Days

The outbreak of World War I caused Schechter deep agony and shortened his life. Yet he saw in it the instrument of God. The Prussian State was the embodiment of brute force and godless violence, and he foresaw its destruction. Every German victory was a blow. But he was confident that God would not forsake England and France.

Schechter had cause to invoke the Jewish concept of charity in the last years of his life. The destruction of the Jewish communities in Central and Eastern Europe during World War I weighed heavily on him. A child of Eastern Europe, he felt it as a personal blow. His last message to American Jewry, written in September 1915, two months before his death, was a moving appeal.

> It is not for me to pass judgment upon my people; but I cannot refrain from remarking that we have not realized the greatness of the disaster which overwhelmed our people, nor have we apprehended the full extent of our duty. Considerations of political economy, or rules of scientific charity, are out of place in this emergency. This is *the* Jewish question, and if Judaism should survive and the world should not become the graveyard of Israel, we must return to Israel's law. According to this law, no man has a right to more than bread and water and wood as long as the poor are not provided with the necessities of life.

On Friday, November 20, 1915, Schechter gave a lecture at the Seminary on the same subject of Jewish charity, which was so close to his thought. He was suddenly taken ill and brought to his home. He died the same day while reading a book by Sir Walter Scott. It was the eve of Sabbath, and rabbinical tradition regards it as happy to die at the ushering in of the day of rest. "I have not accomplished much," he once said, reminiscing about his own life, "but I think I have been loyal to a few principles and a few friends."

What Schechter Taught

Beyond Solomon Schechter's scholarship, public pronouncements, and fearless championing of the Zionist ideal in America, what mattered most was his conception of Judaism, which he inculcated in the spoken and written word. He was, above all, a religious genius, and learning was for him the ministering of a religious rather than a scientific purpose. He was not an innovator in religious thought; but he had a gift for making living and vivid what others had merely believed and known, and for communicating his enthusiasm to others.

His teaching of Judaism rested on the concept of continuity of the past and the present. In his view, the living Judaism of modern times must be linked with the Judaism of the ages, and it must represent the feeling of the mass of the Jews in its day. "Unless it is a present which forms a link between two eternities, representing an answer of Amen to the past and an opening prayer to the future, it will be a very petty present indeed."

A second basic concept for Schechter was that of "catholic Israel"—his own English rendering of *K'lal Yisrael,* which stands for the unity of the Jewish people and the Jewish faith in any era. He had a deep and passionate faith in an immortal, defiant Hebraism which had a destiny for mankind. He conceived Judaism as a universal religion, which meant ultimately that the world should become Jewish, and not that Judaism should fade out into the world. In modern terminology he was a fundamentalist, believing in the divine revelation of Moses and the prophets. But as a disciple of the Historical School of Vienna and Berlin, he believed also in a continuous revelation through the synagogue from generation to generation. The seat of authority was in the living body of Jewry and not in the actual words of the Bible; but he did not attempt to suggest what "catholic Israel" in his time would approve in the practice of Judaism. His account of the outlook of the Historical School is a little elusive: "skepticism combined with staunch conservatism, and with a touch of mysticism." But it is essential to the appreciation of Schechter to realize that he was more the prophet than the systematic thinker. He had immense knowledge of the tradition and of modern Christian theology, but was averse to formulating any change of practice or any new form of belief. Judaism for Schechter involved a positive doctrine of God and of man's duty in this world, as it was laid down in the Torah. It included specific doctrines, which he defined in one of his *Studies*, on "Dogmas": "You cannot be everything if you want to be anything."

At the same time, Judaism was a living organism, developing from age to age. That was the doctrine of the Historical School, and Schechter, while accepting that principle, still held that there were fundamental beliefs which could not change from age to age. Only that reform or development should be accepted which is adopted by the catholic conscience of Israel. That conscience was an almost mystical idea of a Jewish spirit which inspires the scattered communities, and determines which of the old ideas and practices might be rejected, and which of the new might be introduced.

While Schechter placed the center of authority of Judaism in the living body of "catholic Israel," there were times when he rebelled against that conception. The exaltation of tradition at the expense of the revealed Torah was "a sort of religious bimetalism, in which bold speculators in theology tried to keep up the market value of an inferior currency by denouncing the bright, shining gold of the Bible treasure—which is less fitted to circulate in the vulgar use of daily life than the silver of historical interpretation." Ultimately the Torah was the center of Judaism, and certain institutions, particularly the Sabbath and the dietary laws, were fundamental and should not be changed.

In his lectures at the Jewish Theological Seminary, Schechter's major concern was to give students a knowledge of Jewish ethics, particularly of the Jewish concept of charity, of which alone we have his notes. He made a great but unsuccessful effort to persuade Ahad Ha-am to come to America and give a series of lectures on those themes. In his own courses, he contrasted two attitudes of the rabbis to poverty. On the one hand, the poor are God's people, and on the other hand, Judaism considered poverty as the greatest of sufferings because it takes away man's independence and also may eliminate the possibility of his attaining the joy of the commandments. He pointed out that the rabbis as a whole were opposed to asceticism for similar reasons. The obligation to work was a definite commandment, no less than the Sabbath day rest.

Approach to Theology

In his written studies, as well as in his spoken addresses, Schechter avoided dialectic, and tried always to put his teachings simply and epigrammatically. That quality of scholarly simplicity is pre-eminently shown in *Aspects of Rabbinical Theology*, a collection of essays based on a series of lectures which he was constantly revising. His purpose was to state for both Jews and Gentiles the fundamental ethical teaching of the rabbis of the Talmudic and later periods. He emphasized the fundamental Jewish conceptions of God, Torah, the Messiah, and the establishment of God's kingdom on earth. Without making any attempt to compose a systematic body of doctrine, which he felt was not in conformity with the attitude of the rabbis themselves, he set forth their ethical aphorisms and stories, and their comments on the Bible. He stressed that the rabbinical teachings were "against the certain," and had the virtue of inconsistency: and he let the rabbis speak for themselves instead of through the mouths of their opponents. "Some interest may be felt in a theology which had a center of its own, namely God, and nothing else than God, and which contains elements of the eternal truth, and vital principles which enable it to withstand any hostile power's attempt to remove or destroy the center which made it what it is." Characteristically, he never mentions or refutes false conceptions about the teachings of rabbis. At the same time, he had deep conviction that Judaism would be the universal religion of the whole world after Israel had returned to Palestine. The idea of the Reformers, that the Jews in their dispersion had a mission, he dismissed as empty cant: "There can be no mission without missionaries, and the Jews in America do not produce them." There might, he said, be a passive mission of the Jew showing loyalty to his religion with material sacrifice; and ultimately there would be a Jewish mission and missionaries; but, for that, Western Jewry must be combined with the enthusiasm, warmth, and piety of Eastern Jewry.

Ahad Ha-am appraised the *Aspects of Rabbinical Theology* in a story after Schechter's heart. A Russian Jew consulted his friend about the registration of the birth of his child. If he antedated the birth, there would be difficulties; if he postdated it, there would be other difficulties. The friend suggested that he should register the true date. "Wonderful counsel!" exclaimed the parent. He had not thought of that course. Similarly, Schechter, reproducing the words of the rabbis, without any theories about them and without any glosses, presented a remarkable revelation of rabbinical theology as it actually was. He brought out the beauty of tolerance, the joy of the knowledge of God and the ceremonies, and the humanity of the Torah. The essential quality of joy, which Schechter had himself imbibed from his *Hasidic* family, constantly shines through, and this volume did much to dispel the legend of the "burden of the law." As a result, many Christian scholars were willing to re-examine the sources. Examples of such a new outlook among Christians are the treatise on *Judaism* by George Foot Moore of Harvard and that on *Pharisaism* by Charles Herford of Manchester (England), both of which were deeply influenced by Schechter's writings.

Schechter was concerned also to restore the ideal of the saint to its true place in the annals of Israel. In his studies on Jewish mysticism, he searched out the stories of individual saints from rabbinical literature, and once again, as in his *Aspects*, his essays were religious teaching by example. Regarding saintly characters as good and beautiful in themselves, he sought to make them so regarded by the Jewish people. "One of the ideas which the twentieth century would cherish about religion, in its reaction against the rationalism of the preceding age, is that soberness is good, but inspiration and enthusiasm are better; and that every religion which is wanting in the necessary sprinkling of saints and saintliness is doomed in the end to degenerate into commonplace virtues in action and Philistinism in thought."

On the relation of Judaism to Christianity Schechter, unlike many contemporary and later spiritual leaders of American Jewry, was reticent to express a view. Rabbinical literature, he realized, had much to teach about the times in which Jesus lived and about the origin of his sayings and teachings, and he contributed learned articles on that aspect to standard Christian works. At the same time, Schechter felt that the moment had not yet come for a Jew to write an objective life of Jesus from the Jewish point of view.

Legacy: The Writer and the Man

Schechter's written legacy to the Jewish people is contained partly in his scholarly studies of the rabbinical manuscripts and the Geniza treasure, and partly in his *Studies in Judaism* and *Aspects of Rabbinical Theology*, popular books illuminated by his wit and wisdom. It was his aim and achievement to bring the warmth and enthusiasm of living Judaism from Eastern Europe to the West, to restore the hold of Torah and tradition in the largest Jewish community of the world, and to build in it a center of Jewish learning. If it is regarded as essential that a religious leader should formulate precise views, then Schechter was weak as a thinker because he combined the greatest precision in scholarship with avoidance of precision about belief. His great contribution to Judaism in America was the authority he gave to the Conservative Seminary, which has grown during the last sixty years; and he laid a solid foundation of Jewish learning in the United States, which has borne fruit: there has been in America a steady revival of Jewish thought, and a recall to Jewish knowledge. More important even than these impersonal aspects of his legacy was his personal inspiration to his colleagues and students, and to many of the Jewish leaders who were not professionally Conservative. From his day on, traditional Judaism has been a growing religious force in this country.

As a man, Schechter's outstanding characteristic was his humanity. He was human in his strength and his weakness, his enthusiasms and his prejudices, his scholarship and his popular writing, his home and his public life. Whether he was searching old tattered manuscripts, or expounding the Talmud and rabbinic literature, describing medieval Jewish life in Egypt, Palestine, or Germany, portraying the founders of "Jewish Science" of the eighteenth and nineteenth centuries, writing obituaries of his teachers or friends, addressing students at the Jewish Theological Seminary, or discussing the politics and theology of the moment, his aim was to get at the man, to establish some direct human touch. He was not concerned with an "ism," but rather with the person who expressed the ideas. If Leopold Zunz was the great humanist of letters, Schechter was the humanist of life. He possessed what Zunz and other masters of "Jewish Science" lacked—the magic of revelation.

It was, above all, Schechter's religious passion and his deep knowledge of Judaism that marked him as a great Jew of his generation. If the nineteenth century was for Western Jews a period of *Haskalah*, of absorption of outside culture, the early part of the twentieth century was a period of *Hakhsharah*, a preparation for a revived Jewish life. And Schechter was a dynamic influence in that revival. Though this generation cannot be fired by his personality or stirred by his explosive talk, his written message—combining profound scholarship and abounding humanity, ardor for the Jewish nation and for a universal message of Judaism, the glowing vision and the practical teaching—is a lasting inspiration. He was in his own generation Hebraism incarnate, the inspiring master of Jewish tradition, and the inspired messenger of a living faith calling to an old-new loyalty.

FOR FURTHER READING

Books by Solomon Schechter

Selected Writings edited by Norman Bentwich (London: East-West Library, 1948).

Aspects of Rabbinic Theology with an introduction by Louis Finkelstein (New York: Schocken, 1969).

Studies in Judaism, Three series of collected essays (Philadelphia: Jewish Publication Society, 1896-1924). For a selection from these volumes see *Studies In Judaism: A Selection* (New York and Philadelphia: Meridian and the Jewish Publication Society, 1960).

Seminary Addresses and Other Papers, with an introduction by Louis Finkelstein (New York: Burning Bush Press, 1959).

Documents of Jewish Sectaries edited from Hebrew Manuscripts in the Cairo Genizah now in the Possession of the University Library, Cambridge, Solomon Schechter, compiler (New York: Ktav, 1970).

Books about Solomon Schechter

BENTWICH, Norman, *Solomon Schechter, a Biography* (Philadelphia: Jewish Publication Society, 1938). The most important single source for the life of Schechter.

MANDELBAUM, Bernard, *"A Special Ingredient—The Heritage of Solomon Schechter,"* Rabbinical Assembly, *Proceedings Volume 27 (1963)*.

SIEGEL, Seymour, "Solomon Schechter: His Contribution to Modern Jewish Thought," Rabbinical Assembly, *Proceedings* Volume 39 (1977). A valuable eassy that focuses on Schechter's theological writings.

PARZEN, Herbert, "An Estimate of the Leadership of Solomon Schechter," *Conservative Judaism*, Volume 5, No. 3 (April 1949), pp. 16-27. A distinguished historian assesses Schechter's leadership of the Jewish Theological Seminary and his role in American Jewish life.

MANDELBAUM, Bernard, *The Wisdom of Solomon Schechter* (New York: Burning Bush Press, 1963).

LITERARY
PERSONALITIES

The literature of a people has been described as the mirror of its soul, reflecting its aims and ideals, its achievements and failures. This has been particularly true of Hebrew literature during the modern era. From the beginning of "Jewish enlightenment" at the end of the eighteenth century until the reawakening of national feeling after the Russian pogroms in 1881, Hebrew literature reflected the efforts of the Jew to break loose from the confines of the ghetto and to seek a broader life. It recorded his struggle to adjust to the changing environment, to heed the beckoning call of the outside world. It was an educational force which attempted to teach the masses the rudiments of a general education and to guide them toward a greater appreciation of nature.

This *Haskalah* movement produced a literature that was secular and practical in character, stressing the importance of knowledge of the sciences and European languages, and the value of manual labor. It also emphasized the role of esthetics and beauty in life and produced poetry as well as novels, satires, and essays. Like the enlightenment literature in France and Germany it glorified reason, taught faith in human nature and a belief in social progress.[1] The writers of this literature lived for the most part in Eastern Europe—Galicia, Volhynia, and Lithuania, where life for Jews was hard and where they had to struggle against poverty, censorship, and persecution by fanatics. Though Jewish learning was highly valued and spiritual life intense, narrow-mindedness and superstition were often prevalent. Yet those writers laid the foundations for a great renaissance which began in the 1890's in Russia under the impact of Jewish nationalism. In this renaissance Hayyim Nahman Bialik was one of the towering figures. As background we summarize some of the earlier literary trends and the major writers who contributed to the development of Hebrew literature during the *Haskalah* period.

The first systematic attempt to revive Hebrew literature, which had declined in range and orginality after the expulsion of Jews from Spain, took place in Germany during the period of Moses Mendelssohn. Its most representative spokesman was Naphtali Herz

Wessely (1725-1805), who wrote poetry and essays. In a series of open letters addressed to the Jews of the Austrian Empire, *Divre Shalom Ve-Emet* (Words of Peace and Truth, 1782), Wessely applauded the Edict of Toleration of Emperor Joseph II which granted Jews greater rights and urged them to modernize their system of education to include secular studies. Although Jewish education up to this time had been limited primarily to the study of Talmud and Codes, he tried to demonstrate that secular studies were not incompatible with Jewish tradition. Wessely's major contribution to Hebrew literature was a long epic poem, *Shire Tipheret* (Songs of Glory), dealing with the Exodus from Egypt.[2]

There were few original writers in Germany during this first phase. Most of the works consisted of translations, digests of knowledge in various secular fields, and odes dedicated to contemporary kings and princes. These appeared in the Hebrew monthly *Ha-Measseph*, which was launched in 1784 in Königsberg by a group of educated young men and designed to promote the spread of modern secular knowledge through the Hebrew language. Its literary quality was poor and after a few years it ceased publication. By 1820 most Jews in Germany had emerged from the ghetto and had acquired a general education. Since the Hebrew language had been used primarily as a means to reach the masses, it fell into disuse as soon as knowledge of German became widespread. German *Haskalah* did succeed, however, in purifying the language of its medieval rabbinic style and laying a foundation for the spread of enlightenment to other countries, where it had a more lasting effect.

A more significant revival took place in Galicia, where the masses of Jews lived a complete, organic Jewish life and where knowledge of Hebrew was more widespread. In spite of the resistance of the *Hasidim*, who dominated Poland and Austria, enlightenment penetrated into cities like Lemberg, Brody, and Tarnapol, all of which had commercial contacts with Germany.

The most original thinker of the Galician *Haskalah* was Nahman Krochmal (1785-1840), the first to formulate a philosophy of Jewish history and to reconcile Jewish tradition with the philosophy of German idealism.[3] Krochmal was brought up in Brody, a large city in eastern Galicia, and after his youthful marriage settled in Zolkiev, a small town near Lemberg. Though he acquired a vast knowledge of modern culture in addition to his Talmudic learning, Krochmal published little during his lifetime, devoting himself to guiding his many disciples. His major work, *Guide to the Perplexed of the Time*, was published in 1851, eleven years after his death, by Leopold Zunz, to whom he had left his manuscript.

To Krochmal Judaism in modern times suffered from several evils: excessive enthusiasm bordering on mysticism, superstition, and a too mechanical or literal approach to Jewish law.[4] As a reaction to these distortions many people in his time had become materialists, denying tradition and the validity of the precepts. The remedy for this spiritual condition lay in gaining an understanding of the eternal rational values of pure religion. In this connection Krochmal analyzes the unique national spirit of Judaism which gives it its individuality and power. This he finds in a special gift of striving for the Absolute or God.

Jewish history, according to Krochmal, has been through three cycles of growth and decline: from Abraham to the destruction of the First Temple, from the restoration of the Second Commonwealth to the fall of Bar Kokhba in 132 C.E., and from Bar Kokhba to the middle of the eighteenth century. But because of the people's extraordinary power of religious self-awareness it has been able to survive periods of decay and renew the cycle of history. By concerning himself with the national spirit of Judaism Krochmal laid the foundations for modern Jewish nationalism. The book was written in Hebrew, and though poorly organized and never completed exerted a great influence on many subsequent thinkers.[5]

The Hapsburg Empire produced another Jewish scholar, less philosophical than Krochmal, but equally important in the development of Jewish learning—Samuel David Luzzatto (1800-1865), whose chosen field was Hebrew philology and Bible exegesis. Luzzatto, a native of Trieste, was appointed to the faculty of the newly established rabbinical college of Padua which had been set up in response to an Austrian government order that rabbinical students receive philosophical training. Here he taught Bible, Hebrew language, and related subjects for thirty-seven years. "Hebrew is my passion," he wrote, "and the revival of its literature the most beautiful dream of my life." Luzzatto's works included a Hebrew grammar, the first scientific study of the Aramaic translation of the Bible (*Targum*), a commentary on a large portion of the Bible, editions of medieval Hebrew poetry (with particular emphasis on the poetry of Judah Halevi with whom he felt a great affinity), and hundreds of articles, essays, and letters on many aspects of Jewish tradition. Unlike Krochmal, Luzzatto was opposed to metaphysics and abstract philosophy, which he called "Atticism" because of its Greek origin. The purpose of Judaism is not to teach philosophic truth but rather mercy, goodness and the qualities of the heart.[6]

From Galicia *Haskalah* spread to Russia, where Isaac Ber Levinsohn (1788-1860), often called the "Russian Mendelssohn," championed the broadening of Jewish intellectual horizons, and urged the importance of agricultural labor. While on a visit to Brody, Levinsohn had contact with Krochmal and other leading scholars of Galician Jewry. On his return to his native town in Volhynia he published in 1829 *Teudah be-Yisrael* (Testimony in Israel), in which he posed the basic questions which were to agitate Russian Hebrew writers for many years to come. Should a pious Jew study Hebrew language and grammar? Should he study foreign languages? Should he pursue secular sciences? Like Wessely in Germany, Levinsohn demonstrated from Jewish sources that Judaism is not opposed to such studies. In a later work he urged the establishment of modern schools where secular subjects would be taught in addition to Jewish subjects. These should include Hebrew, Bible, and grammar in addition to Talmud. Though not an original thinker, Levinsohn made a great impression on many Talmud students of his time who began to study Hebrew and Russian in spite of opposition from rabbinical leaders.

Within a decade after Levinsohn's pioneering efforts, *Haskalah* struck root in Lithuania, where the influence of the Vilna Gaon, who a century before had stressed the importance of secular knowledge, was still strong. In Vilna several poets arose who turned back to the Bible and glorified the past in the spirit of the romantic movement.[7]

The impact of romanticism on Jewish literature can be seen in some of the historical romances of Abraham Mapu (1808-1868), a teacher in the Jewish government school in Kovno. Though brought up in the poverty and squalor of Slobodka, a suburb of Kovno, Mapu let his imagination carry him back twenty-five centuries to ancient Judea for the scene of his novels. In *Ahavat Tziyyon* (Love of Zion, 1853) he unfolds a story of war and love and personal rivalries in the days of Kings Ahaz and Hezekiah and of Isaiah the prophet. Though the novel is not a great work of art, Mapu's account of life during the golden age of ancient Judea, written in the pure style of the Bible, his vivid descriptions of nature, the jubilant holiday celebrations in the streets of ancient Jerusalem, and the words of enlightened kings and eloquent prophets opened up a world of wonder and beauty new to the youth of his generation. It was read by thousands of young men in the *yeshivas* who wanted to escape the ghetto to a life of beauty and pastoral tranquillity. The book lifted the morale of a depressed people suffering from the autocratic policies of Czar Nicholas and aroused in them a desire for a better life. While there had been books before Mapu on Palestine, this pioneering Jewish novel aroused a longing for a return to Zion and intensified the dreams for political freedom which were later to result in the national awakening.[8]

The romantic glorification of the past gave way in the 1860's to a period of critical realism in Hebrew literature. The series of reforms promulgated by Alexander II (who reigned from 1855 to 1881) seemed to inaugurate a new era for Russian Jewry. Juvenile conscription was abolished. Jewish merchants were granted greater privileges, and graduates of higher institutions of learning became eligible for government service. Seeing a new hope of redemption from their disabilities, Jews turned away from a romanticized past and began to concern themselves with current realities. Also the works of Russian positivist writers like N. G. Tchernishevsky (1828-1889) and D. I. Pissarev (1841-1868) had a great influence on Jewish *Haskalah* writers.[9] Hebrew periodicals such as *Ha-Melitz,* established at Odessa in 1860 and *Ha-Shahar,* launched in Vienna in 1868, furnished outlets for essays and polemics on communal and religious problems and gave impetus to the development of a Hebrew literature concerned with the present rather than the past. Even the novels and poetry of the period reflected the new mood of realism which dominated Jewish as well as European literature in the 1860's and 1870's.

The outstanding poet of this period and one in whom the ideals and spirit of *Haskalah* found their fullest expression was Judah Loeb Gordon[10] (1831-1892). Gordon grew up in Vilna, and his early poems reflect an interest in the Biblical era. An historical poem "Between the Teeth of the Lion" (1868) dealing with the tragic fate of Simon the Zealot during the war with the Romans reveals the beginnings of the poet's protests against the over-spiritualization of Jewish life. "Woe is thee, O Israel. Thy teachers have not taught thee to conduct war with skill and strategem."

This new note is also apparent in Gordon's "Awake My People" (1863), which has been called the "Jewish Marseillaise," serving as a rousing battle call to the Jew to reform his outworn customs and embrace enlightenment. For the rest of his life, in satirical narratives, articles and poems, Gordon continued to attack what he regarded as the bigotry, decay and superstition of Jewish life. He was particularly disturbed by what to him was the hardheartedness of the rabbis in their literal interpretation of the Law. In "The Point of a Yod" (1876), one of his best-known poems, he laments the fate of the beautiful Bat Shua, a deserted wife, who is condemned to a life of loneliness because of a technicality in the spelling of a word in the divorce document. In 1878 Gordon was imprisoned on a false charge of revolutionary activity and while in prison wrote probably his greatest historical poem, "Zedekiah in Prison" (1879), in which he uses the king as his mouthpiece against the opponents of *Haskalah*. Contrary to the interpretation of the Bible, Zedekiah is pictured as a victim of circumstances and the representative of secular civilization who has been thwarted by the perverse spirituality of the prophet Jeremiah.

In his later years Gordon realized the emptiness of *Haskalah* reforms and their failure to bring about the changes needed in Jewish life. He, therefore, became pessimistic about the future of Hebrew literature. Nevertheless, Gordon exerted a great influence on his own time and on some of the writers who came after him. Not the least of these was Hayyim Nahman Bialik, to whom both Gordon's style and spirit of revolt served as a model.

The realistic trend in Hebrew literature can also be seen in the early writings of Moses Leib Lilienblum (1843-1910), champion of religious reform and probably the most extreme critic of Jewish life during the *Haskalah* period.[11] Influenced early in life by the writings of Wessely and Krochmal, Lilienblum began his literary career with a series of articles in *Ha-Melitz* entitled *The Paths of the Talmud* (1868), in which he contended that Talmudic Judaism was not a static religion and appealed to the religious authorities to ease some of the more burdensome legal restrictions. Branded a heretic and bitterly persecuted by the traditionalists in his Lithuanian community, Lilienblum was forced to flee to Odessa. But he soon became disillusioned by the petty careerism and lack of idealism he discovered among the "enlightened" in the city on the Black Sea. He also found it difficult to earn a living. In his autobiography *The Sins of Youth* (1876), one of his important contributions to Hebrew literature, Lilienblum laments his wasted existence, the years of misery, superstition, and struggle. "I have drawn up the balance sheet of my life of thirty years and one month and I am deeply grieved to see that the sum total is a cipher."

But he soon despaired of religious reform, lost faith in *Haskalah*, and began to concern himself with practical reforms in Jewish life and literature. He warned against the sins of idleness and urged the obligation of all to work, calling for the establishment of agricultural colonies as a remedy for some of the social ills of the ghetto community.

The same realistic approach which characterized the essays of Lilienblum and the later poetry of Gordon found expression also in the novels of Peretz Smolenskin (1842-1885), who represents the transition from *Haskalah* to the new era of Jewish nationalism. Smolenskin was born in a small town in White Russia; his life was marked by many of the hardships that were typical of the time: poverty, persecution, wanderings from town to town in search of a livelihood. In 1886 he finally reached Vienna, where by dint of superhuman sacrifice, he was able to launch the Hebrew monthly *Ha-Shahar* (The Dawn) dedicated to fighting the assimilationist tendencies of the enlightened as well as the fanaticism of the Orthodox. During the twelve years it appeared, this magazine was the outstanding Jewish periodical of its time. Smolenskin's six novels were published in installments in this publication as were his essays.

His best known novel *Astray in the Paths of Life* is a semi-autobiographical work portraying the hardships of an orphan youth, his experience in the *yeshiva*, at the court of the *Hasidim*, and his wanderings through Europe. Dealing with actual issues which agitated the youth of his time, it became a most widely read book in the 1870's.

Smolenskin's place in the history of Hebrew literature is also based on his essays, in which he advocated a cultural or spiritual form of nationalism. He was critical of the German Reform movement and German *Haskalah* for their servile imitation of Western ways, for giving up hope in national redemption, and transforming Judaism into a religious persuasion. "Even though it be pointed out that this hope of redemption will never be realized," he wrote, "we ought not to abandon it. For there are many fine ideals which are not realizable, and yet we do not refrain from teaching them." Smolenskin blamed Moses Mendelssohn for this trend, regarding the Berlin sage not as the liberator of Judaism but as its destroyer. To Smolenskin, Jews were a spiritual people, bound together by four thousand years of history, with the Torah and the Hebrew language as its foundations. Through the study of Hebrew and Jewish culture, rather than the humanistic emphasis of *Haskalah*, he felt, the Jew can recapture this national spirit.[12]

Smolenskin's concept of spiritual nationhood prepared the way for a spiritual revival of Jewish life and included the hope that ultimately Jews would become a people with a land of their own. But he advocated neither territorial repatriation for present-day Jews, nor any movement for the settlement of Jews in Palestine. When in the spring of 1881 a series of pogroms broke out against the Jews of Russia, and in their wake the *Hibbat Zion* (Love of Zion) movement was organized for the establishment of colonies in the Holy Land, Smolenskin became a political nationalist. In his later essays he urged that a million Jews migrate to Palestine.

The 1881 pogroms were more extensive than any previous riots against Russian Jews. Men of education and position joined the masses in attacking the Jews. After the riots were finally checked, the so-called May Laws were issued by the government, forbidding Jews to settle anew outside of towns and boroughs, forbidding them to manage estates, and imposing on them economic restrictions which led to the emigration of hundreds of thousands of Russian Jews.

These events shattered the cosmopolitan dreams of the leaders of *Haskalah* and the faith that emancipation for Russian Jews could be brought about through acquisition of secular knowledge. Bitterly disillusioned, they sought "new remedies, new ways," and many now saw the answer in resettlement in the historic land of their fathers.

The rise of Jewish nationalism ushered in a new age for Hebrew literature which, by the end of the century, saw a remarkable flowering of short stories, essays, and poetry. *Haskalah* ideals lingered on with some writers, but for the most part the literature of the nationalist period marked a reaction against *Haskalah* with its emphasis on secular knowledge and the Europeanization of the Jew. It concerned itself rather with the tragedy of the Jewish people, and the dilemmas of a generation torn between two worlds. It left social issues to the publicists and newspapers—even Zionism as a political and economic movement was not yet a frequent theme —and put its emphasis on lifting artistic standards. Post-*Haskalah* literature no longer satirized the obscurantism and superstition of the masses but approached the tradition with greater reverence and sympathy.

Among the important literary figures during the last two decades of the nineteenth century were David Frischman (1860-1922), a many-sided writer who made his mark as poet, short story writer, translator, and above all as a literary critic who tried to correct the provincialism in Hebrew literature and create a "taste for the good," [13] and Mordecai Ze'ev Feierberg (1874-1899), who in spite of his brief and tragic life, gave voice in his sketches, particularly in *Whither* (1898), to the dilemma of his age: how can the Jew hold on to his spiritual integrity and yet not isolate himself from the world.* But the writer who marked the climax to the remarkable development of Hebrew literature in modern times was Hayyim Nahman Bialik, the most representative figure of the modern Hebrew renaissance and the poet laureate of the Jewish people.

* Mendele Mocher Sephorim and Ahad Ha-am, both outstanding writers in this period, will be dealt with in subsequent introductions.

6 . Hayyim Nahman Bialik

[1872-1934]

M. Z. FRANK

H A Y Y I M Nahman Bialik is considered to be the greatest Hebrew poet in a thousand years and in some respects the most important Jewish literary figure since the writers of the Bible. In his lifetime he was called the "national poet of the Jewish people," the "Jewish poet laureate," and even "the modern prophet," designations which are still meaningful today. Wherever modern Hebrew literature is studied—in the schools of Israel and elsewhere—Bialik's works occupy almost the same importance as do Shakespeare's plays in the English-speaking world. Since Bialik's death in 1934, innumerable articles and books have been published which record the poet's conversations, explain his vocabulary and Hebrew style, comment on his poems, or interpret hitherto unknown letters and biographical details. His works have been translated into twenty-five languages, including Japanese, and are included in most anthologies of modern poetry.

Childhood in the Ukraine

Hayyim Nahman Bialik was the youngest child of Reb Yitzhok Yoissef and Dinah-Priveh, both of whom had had children by previous marriages. Reb Yitzhok Yoissef was a pious scholar and an unsuccessful member of a fairly prosperous merchant family whose main business was timber.

Hayyim Nahman was born in December, 1872 in the little Ukrainian village of Radi, where his father managed one of the family's enterprises, a flour mill, while also looking after some lumber business nearby.

Hayyim was left almost entirely to himself. In that village there was one other Jewish family, with a young daughter who was Bialik's only playmate. His mother was busy all day and had little time for the boy, while the father was at home only for the Sabbath, which he spent in prayer and study. Reb Yitzhok Yoissef had little patience with his son; he was an unhappy sullen man, full of resentment against his treatment at the hands of his brothers and brothers-in-law, on whom he was dependent economically for his livelihood. Being an imaginative child, full of spirits, Hayyim grew up without much guidance. He roamed the beautiful sunny countryside and found his playmates in nature: "any bird that flies, any tree with a shadow, any shrub in the woods, the face of the moon timidly glowing into the window . . . any bramble growing behind a broken fence, any taut golden ray reaching my eyes from the sun . . ." ("Radiance"). Whenever he darted into the woods or into a pool, Hayyim Nahman felt himself accompanied by "myriads of invisible sprites."

As Bialik relates in his autobiographical prose story *Wild Growth*, that first world was a happy and carefree one.

> That pristine world of my existence which I brought with me from the village and which still lives on in a secret compartment of my being—that strange, marvelous singular world—that, it seems to be, knew no autumn or winter. I can see the village of my childhood as made out of solid summer stuff. The sky, the earth, the vegetation, the animals—all are summer. Even little Feigele, my only playmate in the village, appears as a summer creature, . . .*

The golden summer of Hayyim Nahman's early childhood suddenly gave way to dreary winter when his father decided to defy his relatives and go into business for himself. He moved the family to Zhitomir, the provincial capital, where he opened a tavern in an outlying section called the Tarmakers' Suburb. To be a barkeeper was an occupation far less suitable to a pious scholar than the respected timber trade in which Reb Yitzhok Yoissef's family engaged. In a poem entitled "My Father"

* Unless otherwise indicated, translations from Bialik are by the author.

Bialik later recalled his father's face "floating above the smoke of the tavern as he stood behind the counter, immersed in some religious volume, as if seeking to insulate himself from the unclean surroundings of drinking and brawling, and leaving his book only now and then to serve a drink or to prevent a fight from getting out of hand. The sensitive child would nestle up to his father and, raising his eyes, would often see a tear running down the older man's face.

Unfortunately the business did not prosper. The poverty of the household was described by Bialik in a poem called "My Song."

On Friday nights our Sabbath festival profaned by want:
The table lacking the sacramental wine and even the Sabbath
    loaves;
The candlesticks pawned, and in their stead mud
Holding the few lean and wretched candles,
Their smoking flames sending the walls a-dancing weirdly;
While seven hungry sleepy children sat at the table,
As mother sadly listened to their chanting welcome
For the ministering angels of the Sabbath.
Father, with a guilty mien, in a dejected mood,
Cutting a dry small morsel of black bread with a blunt knife
And then a tail of a herring for the Sabbath fish—
And as, in misery and humiliation, we chewed upon
Our tear-soaked stale and tasteless crumb
We joined our father in the singing of the Sabbath hymns,
Singing on a hungry crying stomach, on a desolate heart,
The cricket then would join our mournful choir
Hailing, he, too, the Sabbath from his dismal crevice in the dark.

The transition from village to town proved difficult for the boy. As soon as the family moved to town, Hayyim Nahman was sent to the *heder* where the teacher, like so many ghetto teachers recorded in Jewish literature, had little sensitivity, imagination, or pedagogical skill. An assistant called for the children and brought them home, often carrying them through the town's mud, and drilled them in the Hebrew alphabet. Both master and apprentice, as Bialik recorded in *Wild Growth,*

knew only how to hurt, each one in his own way: The *rebbe* used to hit with a whip, with his fist, with his elbow, with his

wife's rolling pin or with anything else that could cause pain,
but his assistant, whenever my answer to his question was wrong,
would advance toward me, with the fingers of his palm distended
and bent before my face and seize me by my throat. He would
look to me then like a leopard or a tiger or some other such wild
beast and I would be in mortal dread. I was afraid he would
gouge out my eyes with his dirty fingernails and the fear would
paralyze my mind so that I forgot everything I had learned the
previous day.

Life with Grandfather

When Hayyim Nahman was seven, his father succumbed to
illness and died. The four oldest of the seven children were sent
off to live with relatives or were apprenticed to artisans.
Bialik's mother was left with her "three little striplings," for
whom she had to provide as best she could, working all day and
half the night, peddling, sewing, washing, and mending. The
task being beyond her, she decided to give Hayyim Nahman,
the youngest and brightest of the three, into the care of his
well-to-do grandfather. She bundled up the boy's few belong-
ings, prepared his favorite muffins, and then led him to the
other end of Zhitomir, to the suburb of the Timber Merchants,
where his grandfather lived.

Reb Yaakov Moishe Bialik was a widower of about seventy,
retired from active business and devoting his time to prayer and
study. The old man was annoyed at first at this disturbance in
his peaceful existence, but soon grew fond of the boy, even
though, like most pious Jews, he seldom showed any outward
signs of affection.

The *heder* which Hayyim Nahman now attended offered
better instruction than those most boys of his age were able to
attend. Reb Meir, who headed it, was a good teacher and endowed with a dramatic flair. He was able to make the stories
of the Bible come alive, drawing or building models of Noah's
ark or of Moses' tabernacle; he called the pupils' attention to
the beauty of the Hebrew language, and, in the summertime,
he held classes outdoors under the trees.

In this new atmosphere, the sensitive boy began to perceive
the inner light and warmth that shone through what had hitherto been to him only the exacting discipline of the Jewish

tradition. In a later poem, Bialik was to describe a winter evening at his grandfather's home when the *dayan* (assistant rabbi) of the neighborhood came to study; the two scholars would engage in a discussion of a point of Law, with the folio of the Talmud and other volumes before them on the table. The oven was hot; the kerosene lamp shone brightly. The grandfather's second wife sat in a corner, knitting a stocking and nodding her head. Though there was a strong wind outside tearing at the shutters, the little boy had a feeling they were all in a strong fortress, protected by the power of the Torah from the storms raging outside.

Living in his grandfather's house opened to young Bialik the world of Jewish learning and the spirit of Judaism, which were to provide so much inspiration for his future writings. One of the greatest influences was the old man's library, where the boy was able to delve into a large selection of Hebrew books.

Early Doubts

These books in his grandfather's library were nearly all of a religious nature. Only here and there he found a book dealing with the rules of Hebrew grammar, a story written for its own sake, or a book of philosophy. The latter type of book was not supposed to be taken seriously since it was not considered proper for a young boy.

Yet it was precisely such "frivolous" books that Hayyim Nahman bought secretly with his own few pennies, which he managed to save. Some of the titles would have shocked his grandfather: books written in the "holy tongue" which questioned and even ridiculed the very notions which pious Jews for centuries had held sacred and immutable; books of poetry extolling love and nature; novels, including translations from the French by Eugene Sue (*Mysteries of Paris*) which dealt with the Gentiles and their underworld. In Bialik's days those were books Jewish scholars read secretly or kept under their large folios of the Talmud, hidden from the eyes of the pure.

At the age of thirteen he began to have doubts about the value of the traditional Jewish way of life, with its total emphasis on piety and religious scholarship to the exclusion of secular knowledge, with its disdain for the arts and sciences, its com-

plete regulation of conduct, even of thinking and feeling, and
its toleration of so many superstitions.

The doubts which arose in the boy's mind resulted not only
from the influences exerted by secular books and by friends
who recommended such books to him, but also from the life
around him, which had changed since grandfather was a boy.
The district in Zhitomir where the Bialiks had lived did not
happen to be inhabited by Jews afflicted with a strong spiritual
thirst either for the old Jewish heritage or for the new Western
civilization which had at last penetrated the Russian provinces,
or even for the budding Russian literature which was just then
coming into its own. On the contrary, the Jews of the Tarmakers' Suburb, as described in some of Bialik's short stories
("Big Man Arieh," "Behind the Fence"), were "pennyworth
people with pennyworth souls." Yet, somehow, cultural influences stirred the air. Somewhere, it was said, there were Jewish
young men who went to Russian high schools and universities
or went to study abroad, in Germany, France, or Switzerland.
Somewhere there were Jews who shaved their beards, cut their
earlocks, wore European clothes—Jews who lived a richer,
fuller life, so different from the constricted life in the ghetto
which was hemmed in by innumerable regulations, fears, and
prohibitions, and was so narrow in its horizons.

And yet the old Jewish way of life had its fascination too.
The traditional sing-song of Talmud study was so sweet, the
old beliefs so heartwarming. So much blood had been shed to
keep Judaism alive—was it all in vain? The old tradition commanded Bialik's loyalties all the more because so few of the
Jews in the Tarmakers' Suburb in Zhitomir—or in the whole
town, for that matter—kept the old fire of studying Torah
alive. Hayyim Nahman was the only boy of his age who continued his study in the house of worship in his neighborhood,
where once there had been many. He was a solace to the older
men who frequented the *bet-midrash*. In later years one of
them was to recall nostalgically "the nightingale" Hayyim
Nahman, whose sweet cantillations as he studied the Talmud
had given them hope.

Volozhin: Pull of the Larger World

When he was fifteen years old, Bialik had a dream of going to Berlin to study at a modern rabbinical seminary, where loyalty to Judaism and Jewish scholarship could be wedded to knowledge of the larger world. But he did not dare breathe this thought to his grandfather. Instead, he ventured a far less daring suggestion: that he go to study at the famous *yeshiva* of Volozhin, established in 1803, in the province of Vilna in White Russia. In those days, the best Talmudic academies were to be found in Lithuania and White Russia. Each *yeshiva* had its own tradition and methods, and attracted students from all over Europe and even from other parts of the world.

At first, the old man would not agree to young Bialik's going to Volozhin because he knew that *yeshiva* to be a stronghold of opposition to *Hasidism,* of which he, like most Jews in the Ukraine, was a strong adherent. However, when the grandfather accidentally discovered that the boy had little faith in the *Hasidic* rabbis, he agreed to let him go to Volozhin; he hoped that would at least help to keep the skeptic young Hayyim Nahman within the fold of observant Jews.

The red-headed boy from Volhynia (he was called, in the fashion of the time, "*Der Zhitomirer*," the student from Zhitomir) presented a curious spectacle in Volozhin: he wore the long coat and earlocks, blue stockings, and sandals of the Ukrainian *Hasidim.* The "Litvak" *Mitnagdim* of Volozhin wore shorter earlocks, shorter coats, and more somber dress. In temperament, too, they were more sedate. Their method of studying Talmud also differed; the "Litvaks," especially at Volozhin, stressed thoroughness rather than quantity, and rational discussion rather than flights into mysticism. However, since many students came to Volozhin from other parts of the world, a certain tolerant attitude existed toward "outlandish" figures.

Bialik arrived at Volozhin at a tumultuous time in its history. The students were demanding that they be taught secular subjects, while the Russian governmental authorities were stipulating that the Russian language be taught. There were student strikes, mild riots, sabotage. Much time was consumed in the struggle, and a number of students studied Russian in secret or read forbidden Hebrew books. Bialik, one of the culprits, began also to learn Russian and joined a secret society of religious Zionists, which entrusted him with the task of drawing up its program.

During his first few months at Volozhin, Bialik managed to attain a high degree of scholarship according to its exacting standards. But, after a while, he grew tired of the confined life at the *yeshiva*, where the students' every hour was controlled and supervised, their letters censored, outside reading prohibited, and all study limited to the Talmud.

Yet there were certain features of the regime at Volozhin which made a lasting impression and engendered fond memories for Bialik. The methods of teaching were in some respects those of the most advanced colleges and modern universities— through seminars rather than ordinary lectures. Each student selected his own assignments, with the approval of the dean. The most memorable aspect of *yeshiva* life was the constant din in the study halls—a din which to the Talmudic scholars was more in the nature of heavenly music than the most solemn chanting in the synagogue.

Bialik spent his final months at Volozhin roaming the woods and the fields, watching the Byelorussian peasants at work, dreaming of Zion, and writing Hebrew verses. Finally, after a year and a half at the *yeshiva*, he decided to run away to Odessa. A hundred of his fellow students accompanied him to the stagecoach, singing Hebrew songs, and predicting future greatness for their friend Hayyim Nahman of Zhitomir.

Odessa: Launching of the Poet

Bialik hoped to find in Odessa what he had once dreamed of finding in Berlin—a synthesis of Judaism and modern European culture. Odessa, Russia's main port on the Black Sea, built by Catherine the Great, was perhaps the most cosmopolitan city in Russia, inhabited by Russians, Ukrainians, Greeks, Armenians, Tartars, Germans, and Jews from Germany, Galicia, and other parts of Russia. To Orthodox Jews of the smaller towns, Odessa was a den of iniquity, a godless city, where Jews did not obey the Law, dressed like Gentiles, and spoke Russian. During the latter part of the nineteenth century, the city had become the main center of modern Hebrew literature. It was the home of Ahad Ha-am (Asher Ginzberg), the great Hebrew essayist and philosopher whose ideas had been much discussed at Volozhin. Bialik had been very much influenced by him—perhaps no less for the unusual felicity of Ahad Ha-am's Hebrew prose as for his ideas. In fact, Bialik's flight to Odessa was in a sense a pilgrimage to see the writer, who was one of his heroes.

A rabbi in Odessa, the father of a classmate at Volozhin, had given Bialik a letter to Ahad Ha-am. When Bialik showed the great man one of his Hebrew poems, Ahad Ha-am arranged for its publication in a magazine. Entitled "Welcome to the Bird," the poem had a freshness of Hebrew style which commanded attention.

> Do you bring me friendly greetings
> From my brothers there in Zion
> Brothers far yet near?
> O the happy! O the blessed!
> Do they guess what heavy sorrows
> I must suffer here?

The success of this first poem did not assure Bialik of any immediate triumphs as a writer, nor did it provide him with food and shelter. Bialik suffered hunger and cold, and whenever he went to the homes where he had been engaged as a private tutor in Hebrew, he kept his torn trousers covered by his overcoat. But he managed to improve his Russian and to learn the rudiments of German. He stayed in Odessa only a few months.

From the World of Business to Education

When Bialik's grandfather was on his deathbed, the poet returned to Zhitomir. Shortly after his grandfather's death, Bialik married into a family of lumber merchants in the province of Kiev and became a businessman. Except for the circumstance that there were no children, Bialik's marriage with Mania Averbach was an eminently happy one, and so were the poet's relations with his father-in-law Reb Shevach Averbach. But his venture into business proved catastrophic financially, wiping out his wife's dowry. The years spent by Bialik in the woods where timber was being cut, however, produced some of the best-known poems in the Hebrew language, many of which were first scribbled on the backs of receipts, bills of lading, and other such documents, or written in the middle of the night, while singing, much to the bewilderment of the night watchman.

But Bialik was no businessman. After his failure in that endeavor he was forced to accept a teaching engagement in a town in Russian Poland on the German border. There, too, he tried his hand at business, as a coal merchant, and there again his principal achievement was producing poetry.

Eventually Bialik was offered a position in Odessa, teaching in a modern Hebrew school conducted by Zionists. The poet now had the opportunity to introduce improvements in an area of Jewish life in which he had suffered so much as a child. In the Odessa school he taught children to speak Hebrew, using a simple vocabulary before they began the study of Bible. In collaboration with his colleagues, Bialik compiled children's readers in Hebrew, an activity which led him into a career as publisher—starting with school textbooks—which he was to continue to the end of his days.

Conflict . of . Cultures

When Bialik returned to Odessa in 1900, he was twenty-eight years old and already recognized as the leading Hebrew poet of the age. Most of the poems he had written in the decade since his first visit to Odessa expressed nostalgia for the traditional house of study (*bet hamidrash*), Talmudic literature, and the inner conflict of the Talmudic student.

The generation of Jewish intellectuals in Russia and nearby East European countries (Galicia and Bukovina in the Austrian-Hungarian Empire, and Rumania) consisted, in large measure, of former students at the *bet hamidrash* or the *yeshiva*. This was a generation which had to move from one culture into another, a transition which, in most cases, was accompanied by loss of faith and abandonment of religious observance. In nearly all cases it was a painful process. Such young men were torn by two strong opposing sentiments: on the one hand, the pull of the old Talmudic Orthodox civilization, with its haunting

melodies, its habits of thinking and feeling, and the consciousness that there was an ancient civilization which preserved
Judaism through the ages; and, on the other hand, the lure of
the modern Western world, with its arts and sciences, the rule
of reason, and the promise of a better life.

Bialik struck a responsive chord in the hearts of his contemporaries with his description of the *bet hamidrash*:

> The spring whence strength of soul was drawn in evil days
> By those who gladly walked to meet their death . . .
> climbing to the stake,
>
> The stronghold where your fathers
> Salvaged their soul's desire and held the Law
> Holy above all holies to be saved,
>
> The biding spirit that kept
> Their mighty spirit and its essence pure.
> "On the Threshold of the House of Prayer"
> translated by Harry A. Fein.

But *bet hamidrash* was now abandoned, with few left to guard
it:

> A miserable remnant . . . a few stray sheaves of much lost,
> some shrivelled Jews . . . who lose their pain in faded Talmud
> page . . .
>
> Abandoned in the nest, the fledglings gone
> Like shadows vanished in the lofty trees.

The most important of Bialik's poems of that period is "*Ha-
Matmid*." ("The Talmud Student"), a long poem of some
twenty pages, written over a period of seven years. The most
emotional of Bialik's poems, it deals not only with the specific
problem of the conflict of cultures in the Jewish world but
also touches on the universal conflict between the hunger for
life and the hunger for self-dedication. Many tears were shed
by former Talmud students as they read the poem, which appeared in installments in *Ha-Shiloah*, a Hebrew magazine.

The poem dealt with the recluse scholar, the *matmid*, who
was not necessarily the brightest but by far the most dedicated
scholar, and who refused to take advantage even of the limited

time permitted at the *yeshiva* for rest and recreation in order to devote every possible moment to study the Talmud.

> A prisoner, self-guarded, self-condemned
> Self-sacrificed to study of the Law.

Bialik echoed what was in the hearts of thousands of his contemporaries:

> I, in my boyhood, was a listener
> Among the voices, and my youth was passed
> Among these wan sufferers, whose wrinkled brows
> And staring eyes implore the world's compassion.
>
> The heart in me cries out: Lord of the world!
> To what end is this mighty sacrifice?

This last question apparently is unanswerable. But there is an affirmative note in the final lines of the long poem:

> . . . How strong, how sturdy
> The seed must be that withers in those fields,
> How rich would be the blessing if one beam
> Of living sunlight could break through to you;
> How great the harvest to be reaped in joy,
> If once the wind of life should pass through you.
>   (translated by Maurice Samuel)

An even more vigorously affirmative note on the value of such devoted study is found in the last lines of "On the Threshold of the House of Prayer."

> Thou shalt not fall, Shem's tent, I'll build thee fast;
> From heaps of dust thy walls I'll resurrect.
> All palaces shalt thou alone outlast!
>
> With clouds dispersed, God's glory there will bide
> All flesh shall then behold that God holds sway;
> Buds fade, grass withers . . . God endures for aye.
>   (translated by Harry A. Fein)

Bialik espoused the Jewish attitude whereby man refuses to accept fate as inevitable but makes an intelligent effort to control his destiny. He based one of his most majestic poems, "The Dead of the Wilderness," on an ancient Talmudic legend about giant warriors who, in spite of divine injunction to wait, attacked the enemy as they were proceeding to the Promised Land, and their bodies are said to lie intact, still buried in the desert sands. Once every few centuries, they rise to renew their challenge to divine procrastination.

We are the mighty!
The last generation of slaves and the first generation of free men!
Alone in our hands is our strength.

Yea, on the tops of the crags in the thickness of clouds,
With the eagles of heaven we drank from the fountains of freedom.
Even now, though the God of vengeance has shut the desert upon us,
A song of strength and revolt has reached upon us, and we rise.

Forward despite the heavens and the wrath thereof.
                (translated by Maurice Samuel)

A year or so later, Bialik was very much moved by the pogrom in Kishinev, in which about two score Jews were killed. He wrote "The City of Slaughter," a poem in which he preached not an abstract doctrine against a philosophical kind of passivity, but a concrete form of revolt against the habit which Jews had developed, in centuries of oppression, of running away, hiding without offering a fight, and praying and weeping:

Come now, and I will bring thee to their lairs
The privies, jakes and pigpens where the heirs
Of Hasmoneans lay, with trembling knees,
Concealed and cowering—the sons of Maccabees!
The seed of saints, the scions of the lions!

It was the flight of mice they fled,
The scurrying of roaches was their flight;
They died like dogs and they were dead!

For great is the anguish, great the shame on the brow:
But which of these is greater, son of man, say thou. . . .

The traditional Jewish response to calamity was to view it as a punishment for sins, to repent, to pray for forgiveness, and, sometimes, to tighten control on the community or to look for culprits as scapegoats. The prevalent attitude was acceptance, which, Bialik felt, by the time of the Kishinev pogrom had lost whatever tragic grandeur it had once had. The poet seemed to hear the divine voice bidding him carry this message:

> Wherefore their cries imploring, their supplicating din?
> Speak to them, bid them rage!
> Let them against Me raise their outraged hand,—
> Let them demand!
> Demand the retribution for the shamed
> Of all the centuries and every age!
> Let fists be flung like stone
> Against the heavens and the heavenly throne!
>
> (translated by A. M. Klein)

As soon as "The City of Slaughter" appeared, Vladimir Jabotinsky translated it into Russian and Bialik himself translated it into Yiddish. In the three languages the poem became the rallying call of Jewish self-defense and its author was hailed as "prophet." It had a more far-reaching effect than any other poem in Jewish literature.

> Arise and go now to the city of slaughter;
> Into its courtyard wind thy way;
> There with thine own hand touch, and with the eyes of thine head,
> Behold on tree, on stone, on fence, on mural clay,
> The spattered blood and dried brains of the dead. . . .

The day that poem was written, states Jacob Fichman, a leading Hebrew poet and literary essayist, "was perhaps the most important date in the history of modern Hebrew poetry . . . In that poem of pain and shame Bialik attained the stature of a mentor and a chastiser of his people, the like of which was unknown in Hebrew poetry since the days of the Bible."

To "The City of Slaughter" is credited the fact that a year later, when a similar pogrom took place in Homel, White Russia, a formation of 450 young Jews fought off their attackers and put them to flight in spite of the encouragement the rioters had from the Russian police. In 1907, in Jaffa, Palestine, a number of veterans of such Jewish self-defense groups in Russia, including the leader of the group in Homel, met in the room of Itzhak Ben Zvi (now President of Israel) and formed the first military unit to defend Jewish life and property in the country. Out of that unit (called *Hashomer*, "The Guard") in time grew the Hagannah, the Jewish militia in Palestine, which, in turn, eventually became the present Israel Army.

Many of Bialik's "prophetic" poems are written in the mood recurrent in Jeremiah—the complaint by the messenger of God's word that the people fail to heed the divine message. Bialik saw the problem as the Jews' lack of courage, dignity, regard for their own historic heritage, or an earnest desire to reconstruct their national life on sound foundations. One of the most powerful of such poems was written by Bialik in Yiddish, presumably in order to reach wider masses. "The Last Word," still today the favorite of Yiddish school recitations, begins with the lines: "I have been sent to you by God . . ."

"The Scroll of Fire"

In "The Scroll of Fire," a long prose poem written in 1905, Bialik developed a philosophy of Jewish history. The central idea is that with the loss of their political independence and exile from their homeland, Jews can preserve their heritage only at the cost of foregoing the wholesome and normal enjoyment of life; and periodically they revolt against the heavy burden. Based on a Talmudic legend pertaining to the destruction of the Temple and the ensuing captivity by the Romans of hundreds of Jewish youths and maidens, this poem merges the story of Bialik's own life with the story of the Jewish people. The Biblical period is the happy years of the people's childhood —like Bialik's own in the Volhynia countryside. The austere Talmudic law imposed on the Jewish people is personified by an old man reminiscent of Bialik's grandfather or the dean at the Volozhin *yeshiva*. In the following passage, a solitary youth who managed to escape the Romans says to the maiden:

Tall standing corn and choicest fields blessed by childhood
And flourishing groves and the branches of the cypress trees
    took me into their secret.
And I loved the God of the earth, the God of the mountains and
    the valleys,
And revered the God of the heavens.
And one day a hoary-headed man of Judea

Found me flung down among the mountains with dawn
And the man was garbed in a cloak and his hair was wild
As he walked darkly and angrily.

And the aged man had compassion on me,
And he planted me in the innermost shelter of his tent,
And with the shade of his trembling white beard he covered me.
And he taught me his ways and caused me to worship his God,
And he restrained my soul from all delight and taught me to look
   to the heavens,
And all the blossoms of my youth he plucked forth one by one.

And my days became fasts as were his days,
And my nights became prayers as were his nights.
And I feared the old man exceedingly
As the flower fears the autumn.
My face grew thin and my forehead blanched from day to day.

See now, the heavens have mocked me
And with a cruel lie encircled me.
My youth, my everything, have they taken from me.
And nothing have they given me in return.

                                    (translated by Ben Aronin)

"The Scroll of Fire" is not the best-known of Bialik's poems,
though it seems to be one of his most ambitious. The poet's
purpose seems to have been to produce the equivalent of Dante's
Divine Comedy, Milton's *Paradise Lost*, Goethe's *Faust*, Push-
kin's *Eugene Onegin*, Mickiewicz's *Pan Tadeusz*—or, to use an
example from medieval Hebrew literature, Gabirol's *Crown of
Glory*. In other words, the poem was to give expression to the
spirit of a whole age, a people, or a total philosophy. But whereas
all the foregoing poems took years to produce, Bialik wrote his
"Scroll of Fire" in one month. Had he worked at it for seven
years as he did in the case of *"The Matmid,"* "The Scroll of
Fire" might perhaps have become Bialik's magnum opus.

Career as Editor and Publisher

Except for an interruption of two years, Bialik lived in Odessa,
from 1900 until he left Russia shortly after the Russian Revolution. During this period and until his death in 1934, editing and
publishing remained his chief occupation, first in Odessa, then
later for a brief period in Berlin, and finally in Tel Aviv. But

his publishing career was more than a business venture: it was closely linked to a vast project of historic cultural significance which Bialik in time came to consider as far more important than his own poetry.

The project which Bialik evolved and which today, a quarter of a century after his death, is still far from being carried out is comparable to the work of those who in centuries gone by edited the Bible and the Talmud. In each case, scattered expressions of the Jewish spirit covering many generations were examined, sifted, winnowed, and edited, and finally brought together in one great collection as an authentic body of literature representing the basis of Jewish culture. What Bialik had in mind was a new collection, edited in the spirit of modern secular Jewish nationalism, but with more modest pretensions to authority than the Bible, Mishnah, or Talmud.

With two colleagues, Bialik at first undertook to issue an abridged Bible for school children. This immediately aroused a controversy; not only the Orthodox but many irreligious Jews as well objected to any tampering with the Bible in its traditional form.

After the completion of the Bible series came a Talmud series, with special emphasis on the *Aggadah,* that part of the Talmud and Talmudic literature which deals with legend, folklore, and proverbs. Out of the *Aggadah* compilation for school use grew also a similar collection for adults. The Bialik *Book of the Aggadah* remains the standard modernized text, with the original Hebrew left intact as found in the old sources, and the Aramaic portions translated into the same style of Hebrew.

Bialik never tired of advocating what he called *Kinnus,* literally "ingathering" or "collection." His aim was the publication of a sort of Hebrew equivalent in Jewish literature of the Harvard Classics, including works written in Hebrew as well as translations from other languages. Among Hebrew works the first to claim his attention were the poems produced by the literary giants of the Golden Age in Spain—Solomin ibn Gabirol, Judah Halevi,* and the two Ibn Ezras—though he actually succeeded in publishing only the annotated works of Gabirol and Abraham ibn Ezra.

Creators of the Jewish Experience in Ancient and Medieval Times, Chapter 7, Washington, D.C., B'nai B'rith Books, 1985

After about 1905 or 1906 Bialik stopped writing poetry, except for an occasional rare piece, at a time when he was seemingly at the height of his poetic productivity. The surprised and disappointed public hoped it was a mere pause and vainly sought for explanations. One theory advanced by some critics (e.g., Jacob Fichman) grew out of Bialik's feeling that modern literature in Hebrew had little future unless the public had an adequate appreciation of the literature of the past. He seemed to consider the task of husbanding the literary heritage of the Jewish people and presenting it in readable Hebrew more important than that of writing his own poetry.

Bialik rendered into Hebrew Cervantes' *Don Quixote*, which he abridged, and Schiller's *Wilhelm Tell*. He translated into Hebrew from the Russian manuscript a play which became most famous in its Yiddish version—S. Ansky's *Dybbuk*. Bialik also gave the first renderings of some of Sholom Aleichem's stories from Yiddish into Hebrew, and collaborated with Mendele Mocher Sephorim in translating his Yiddish books into Hebrew.

Russian Revolution: Departure for Palestine

Bialik's publishing career was interrupted by the victory of the Bolsheviks in Russia in 1917. They declared the Hebrew language to be "counter-revolutionary," and forbade its teaching. All Hebrew schools were closed. The plates in Bialik's printing shop, including those prepared for the publication of Ibn Gabirol's works, were scrapped for metal.

Bialik's life was in danger on several occasions, but his fame as a poet and the prestige in which he was held in Russian literary circles saved him. He often quarrelled with Bolshevik leaders in Odessa, who included some of his most avid readers and admirers. Once he told the leader of the secret police, a Jew named Deutsch: "You are the second great lie in history . . . The first one was two thousand years ago, when, in the name of brotherly love, rivers of blood began to be shed." To his brother-in-law, Jan Gamarnik, a Bolshevik general, he said, "Some day you will die a shameful death at the hands of your own comrades." (Gamarnik really did perish in the first purge in the 1930's at the hands of Stalin's henchmen.)

Finally, as the result of efforts by Maxim Gorki and other great literary figures who were in his good graces, Lenin issued a permit to Bialik and a few other Hebrew writers to leave Russia, on the understanding that they would proceed to Palestine. Some petty Jewish officials in the Communist Party sought to sabotage the implementation of that permit, but the group managed to outwit them and left Russia, making their first stop Berlin. It happened that the German capital was at that time a gathering place for Hebrew writers—some who had lived there before World War I, others who were recent refugees from Soviet Russia or emigrants from Poland. With its facilities for producing books Berlin was for a while a center for Hebrew publishing. Bialik, too, started his Dvir Publishing House there, but even then the books bore the mark "Berlin-Tel Aviv." Within a couple of years Bialik moved to Tel Aviv, his original destination on leaving Russia. The Jewish city on the Mediterranean shared with Berlin and Warsaw the role of successor to Odessa as the center of Hebrew publishing in the world, and has in our time become the main center. Tel Aviv was the natural place for Bialik in which to take up residence. (It already boasted a colony of the leading Hebrew writers in Palestine, including Bialik's revered master, Ahad Ha-am, who had moved to Tel Aviv from London a short time before.) Many of these men taught at the Herzliah, the oldest and largest Hebrew secondary school.

On April 1, 1925, a year after Bialik's arrival in Palestine, when the Hebrew University was opened on Mt. Scopus by Lord Balfour, Bialik delivered the main address.*

* An English text of the address is to be found in *The Zionist Idea,* edited by Arthur Hertzberg (Doubleday, New York, 1959).

Bialik in America

In 1926 Bialik visited America in the company of his friend and associate in the publishing business, Shemaryahu Levin, on a mission to raise money for the Keren Hayesod as well as to interest individuals in the Dvir Publishing House of Tel Aviv. Bialik was given a royal welcome, and his visit left a lasting impression. But he was forced to travel for five months at a dizzying pace all over the country, making two or three speeches a day, listening to many more in his honor, and hearing himself introduced by chairmen who did not know how to pronounce his name and who did not know whether the man they were honoring was an alto, a soprano, or a cantor's apprentice (the Hebrew word *meshorer*, used also in Yiddish, means both a poet and a singer). Bialik described all his experiences at the end of his trip in a famous letter to Ahad Ha-am, in which he waxed sarcastic about American publicity and campaign methods, deprecated the lack of cultural and spiritual content in American Zionism, but expressed enthusiasm for the vitality and spirit of freedom of American Jewry and faith in its future potentialities. The growth and development of American Jewry within a single generation he termed one of the great marvels of Jewish history.

More than a decade earlier, when the great Yiddish writer Sholom Aleichem and his son-in-law, the Hebrew writer I. D. Berkowitz, first contemplated settling in the United States, Bialik, who was a close friend to both men, had strongly urged them to desist from such a step. There was no room, he argued, for men of talent and sensitivity in that brash, noisy country, with its vulgar plebeian spirit, its low-class Jews (for, after all, no respectable Jew in Russia would think of emigrating to "The Land of the Dollars"), its sensation-seeking Yiddish press, its rapacious and uncouth Jewish publishers.

In his letter to Ahad Ha-am, however, Bialik now showed a more benevolent attitude toward the boisterous nature of American Jewry, the first signs of appreciation of what he called "the miracle of Jewish history" in the rise of American Jewry, and some belief in its future. He frankly confessed that his previous prejudices were irrational and prompted by a fear of the unfamiliar and by the dread of the rustic for modern urban civilization, which, in his mind, was embodied in New York. He realized, he said, that America was a country in the process of becoming, and that what he had previously considered as "American bluff"—the brashness and lack of proportion—in reality represented vigor, "a superabundance of youthful forces"; here, he now felt, was "virgin soil" which some day would be capable of producing "spiritual power of incalculable dimensions."

He found encouragement in many of the meetings he had

with Jews in America, whether those meetings were formal or informal. He met American Jews who had a warm feeling for Judaism and Jewish learning, who "did not throw away the traditional Jewish concern" for Jewish survival. "They remained with that great concern in their new homeland." He came to the conclusion that even though the Jews of America might be overly optimistic about their own position, it was still the best of all Diasporas, and that next to the historic Jewish homeland in Israel America was the country in which the survival of Judaism had the best prospects.

Last Years

Bialik's years in Tel Aviv were the happiest of his life. He became the most beloved figure of the Jewish community of Palestine, attracting large crowds whenever he lectured; he was often seen dancing on the streets and on the beach with *halut-zim* (pioneers) and children. In an effort to give fresh meaning to traditional practices, Bialik introduced in Tel Aviv the custom of gathering on Saturday afternoons for discussions on questions relating to Judaism, which he called *Oneg Shabbat*—Sabbath Delight. The name is ancient, but its current widespread application to the Saturday afternoon cultural get-together owes its origin to Bialik.

The *Oneg Shabbat* took place in the Ohel-Shem (Tent of Shem) auditorium and was always filled to capacity: though Bialik was rarely the main speaker, he was nearly always the chairman, and the public, as a rule, was more interested in his comments and remarks than in the main lecture. The meetings usually started and ended with community singing, mostly of traditional and religious songs, with the poet himself, who had a good voice and a good ear for music, as a lusty participant. This institution of *Oneg Shabbat* has since spread far and wide in the Diaspora.

In his last years Bialik underwent several operations to cure an ailment from which he had suffered for a number of years. In Vienna, where he had gone in 1934 for another operation, a blood clot unexpectedly developed which choked him. "My heart," were the last words Bialik uttered. Only a few minutes earlier he had been rereading the Bible from the beginning, and had reached the end of the story of creation before he expired.

The poet was brought back to Tel Aviv to be buried beside Ahad Ha-am. His house numbered 22 has become the Bialik Museum, and the street has been renamed Bialik Street. The library of the Museum contains some thirty thousand volumes in Hebrew on subjects related to Hebrew literature and Judaism —the two subjects nearest the poet's heart.

The Legacy

Bialik was the favorite poet of Chaim Weizmann, Itzhak Ben Zvi, David Ben-Gurion, Moshe Sharett, Vladimir Jabotinsky and the whole generation which fought for the Jewish homeland and created the State of Israel. When men and women of that epoch spoke of themselves or of their children born in the homeland as "the last generation of enslavement, the first generation of freedom," they were using a phrase taken from Bialik's "Dead of the Wilderness." They did not merely derive esthetic enjoyment from his Hebrew verses: they drew inspiration for the great historic task to which they had set their hands. Though Bialik wrote few verses which contained a direct Zionist appeal, he evoked a mood for action as no other poet did.

The tribute Bialik paid Mendele—that he succeeded in blending the various Hebrew styles stemming from different historic periods into one homogenous idiom—applies more to Bialik than to Mendele. His highly developed sense of idiom combined with his profound scholarship and love of the language produced a Hebrew style the like of which had not been known in the past. No one else was as capable of using a Hebrew word or phrase with such a keen sense for its shadings, nuances, and connotations accumulated over the centuries. He was, however, primarily a poet, and his prose lacked the succinctness or unique character of his verse.

Outside of Hebrew, Bialik wrote only in one other language—Yiddish. Though Yiddish was his mother tongue, it was not a language he studied or cultivated. And yet the few poems he did write in that tongue gave Bialik an honored place in Yiddish literature. One such poem describes little boys at the *heder*. In both Hebrew and Yiddish, his poems revealed a genius for language and an uncanny sense of idiom. In each language, he knew how to select the sounds and the idiomatic expressions suitable for the effect he sought to produce.

Somewhat off the main track of Bialik's poetic contributions are his so-called *Songs of the People* and his many children's poems. In both Bialik displayed his genius for articulating motifs which had evolved in the Yiddish idiom in superb Hebrew. Most of his *Songs of the People* are based on motifs found in Yiddish folk songs, as, for example, "Between the Tigris and the Euphrates" and "By My Well," both of which have been translated into English. Bialik's *Children's Poems* still delight youngsters in Israel—as they always delighted children familiar with Hebrew in Europe, in Palestine, and elsewhere.

In general, Bialik defies classification. As an editor and publisher, he was a great affirmer of historic Jewish values. Though his poetry reflects many moods, it is deeply rooted in the past and at the same time is full of meaning for our own times. Bialik remains "the poet laureate" of the Jewish people, and, since the days of the Bible, its most impressive Hebrew writer.

FOR FURTHER READING

Books by Hayyim Nahman Bialik

Complete Poetic Works, translated from the Hebrew, edited with introduction by Israel Efros (New York: Histadrut Ivrit of America, 1948).

Selected Poems with English translation by Maurice Samuel, illustrated by Maida Silverman with the Hebrew text vocalized (New York: Union of American Hebrew Congregations, 1972). A splendid one-volume introduction to Bialik. The vocalized text allows the Hebrew speaker to enjoy the sounds of Bialik's lyric voice.

Selected Poems translated by Ruth Nevo (Jerusalem: DVIR and The Jerusalem Post, 1981) with English and Hebrew on opposite pages.

Poems from the Hebrew, edited by L.V. Snowman with an introduction by Vladimir Jabotinsky. (London: Hasefer, 1924). This admirable collection achieves a special stature because of Jabotinsky's excellent critical essay.

Bialik Speaks: Words From The Poet's Lips edited by Mordecai Ovadyahu (New York: Herzl Press, 1969) A collection of Bialik's thoughts that reveal the man and his view of the world.

Books about Hayyim Nahman Bialik

JESHURIN, Ephim H., *Chayim Nahman Bialik Bibliography* (New York, 1964). A useful guide for those who want access to the whole Bialik corpus.

There is a vast Bialik literature but it is mostly in Hebrew.

Sholom Aleichem

Throughout their history the Jewish people have spoken many tongues and developed literatures in several languages other than Hebrew. These have included Aramaic, Greek, Arabic, Ladino, and, during the last thousand years, Yiddish, a language which perhaps more than any other has reflected the soul of European Jewry.

Yiddish as a spoken tongue had its origins among the French and Italian Jews who moved to the highland regions of Southern Germany sometime between the tenth and thirteenth centuries. Those Jews who previously had spoken an old Romance vernacular began to shift to the Middle High German of their neighbors. But because of differences in interest between them and the Christians in feudal society, and the influence both of their religious practices and of the Hebrew books they studied as well as their general way of life, their German gradually changed its inflection and became interwoven with Hebrew. Increased contact between Jews in various lands when large numbers of Jews migrated from Germany to Poland after the Crusades resulted in many Slavic expressions creeping into their conversation. Thus the vernacular of Jews gradually developed into a distinctive language.[1]

In the course of time a literature was born, distinct from the scholarly works written in Hebrew, more folksy in character, and consisting primarily of translations and adaptations from Hebrew and German works. It was designed particularly for women and uneducated men, and until the middle of the eighteenth century was of two types: a secular literature designed for entertainment or amusement, whose major source was the bards or wandering minstrels of the surrounding non-Jewish world, and a traditional religious literature, didactic in purpose and dealing with moralistic themes drawn from Jewish tradition. Until the middle of the sixteenth century the minstrel type of literature predominated.[2]

In this early period we find Jewish counterparts of the wandering actor and troubadour of Germany, known as *Spielmann*, who sang of the exploits of knights and epic heroes. These Jewish *Spiel-männer* went about chanting chivalric sagas and romances in the courtyards, at weddings or other festivities, eliminating, however, passages referring to Christianity, skipping the parts about battles, and trying to humanize the more brutal scenes. Gradually trouba-dour romances based on Jewish sources began to appear. Jewish religious songs came into being, and stories of the Bible were trans-lated and retold in Yiddish. The most original of such productions was the *Shmuel Buch* (Book of Samuel) published in 1544, an epic poem of some grandeur about the life and deeds of King David based on the text of the Bible, and embellished by stories from the Midrash and *Aggadah*.[3]

After the invention of printing the minstrels became less impor-tant. The early anonymous figures gradually disappeared as individ-ual writers and storytellers with distinctive personalities began to emerge. One of the most interesting of these personalities was the colorful Hebrew grammarian and poet Elijah Levita, known as Eliyahu Bahur (the stroller), whose *Bova Buch* represents a high-light in the history of early Yiddish literature. A passionate romance of adventure and intrigue based on the adventures of Prince Bovo d'Antona, it fired the imagination of Jewish householders for centuries. Through a misinterpretation the words *Bovo Ma'aseh* (tale of Bovo) became *Bube Ma'aseh* (grandmother's tale) and remain to this day a synonym for any fantastic tale.[4]

From the second half of the sixteenth century until the middle of the eighteenth, the moralistic element which earlier had con-stituted a minor trend became dominant in Yiddish literature. Notes and comments on difficult words set down by teachers on the margins of Hebrew Bible texts led to the translation of various Biblical books. Soon prose paraphrases of the Pentateuch and other Biblical books appeared, the outstanding of which was the classic work known as *Tzenah u-Re'enah* (Go Forth and See). This Yiddish paraphrase of the Five Books of Moses, the *Haftorot* (prophetic por-tions), and the *Megillot*, with homiletic commentary drawn from Midrash, Talmud, and classic Jewish commentaries, was composed at the end of the sixteenth century by Rabbi Jacob Ashkenazi of Janow, Poland. Written in simple style for the benefit of the average person, it served as a kind of encyclopedia of Jewish knowledge for the Jewish woman. She used it every Sabbath in the synagogue and turned to it in her free moments at home. This book exerted a great influence, appearing in more than thirty editions in a little over a century.[5]

Translations of the prayer book were issued to help Jewish

women fulfill their religious duties in the synagogue. A number of women soon emerged as translators and editors of such special collections. A new type of prayer book known as the *Tehinot*, written especially for women and keyed to their personal needs, was developed. Rich in pathos and sentimentality, it contained prayers to be uttered at home as the Sabbath candles were lit as well as requests for family health and prosperity.

Even in works of fiction the moralistic element played an important part. The most important of these was the *Ma'aseh Buch* (Book of Stories), a collection of more than two hundred and fifty Talmudic legends and medieval folk tales embellished with additional material. Appearing at the beginning of the seventeenth century, this book overshadowed all previous works in its popularity and served as a model for various collections of stories and legends which were published in its wake.

Old Yiddish literature was largely a product of Western Europe and of Ashkenazi Jewry in Germany, Italy, and Amsterdam. With the coming of the Enlightenment, however, Yiddish declined both as a spoken tongue and as a literature in western countries. Mendelssohn, Wessely, and enlightened Jews of Germany were opposed to the "jargon" and urged their coreligionists to learn German. For a time Yiddish was still used in daily intercourse (Mendelssohn himself corresponded with his fiancee in Yiddish), but as the Jews of Western Europe abandoned Yiddish for the vernaculars of the countries in which they lived, cultural assimilation took place and the writing and publishing of Yiddish books, especially new works, ceased almost entirely. By the beginning of the nineteenth century the center of Yiddish literature had shifted to Eastern Europe, and the Germanized Yiddish of the West gradually yielded to a language more closely resembling the speech of the masses in Poland and Russia.

The rise of *Hasidism* in the middle of the eighteenth century opened up a new source for Yiddish both as a spoken language and as a literature.[6] This religious movement, which by the end of the century had captured the loyalty of half the Jews of Eastern Europe, particularly in the Ukraine and Poland, awakened the Jew to a life of fervor and joyful living and gave him greater dignity. To the *Hasidim* Yiddish was no longer the "speech of the ignorant and of women" but worthy of esteem alongside of Hebrew. *Hasidic* rabbis preached and frequently prayed in Yiddish and, of particular importance for the development of Yiddish literature, told their legends and folk tales in that language.

The most famous of these collections of *Hasidic* legends is the volume of miraculous tales about the Baal Shem Tov,* founder of the movement which sprang up in the half century following his death. These allegories and stories of the Besht, as he was called, were recounted orally by one *Hasid* to the next and finally assembled in book form and published in 1815 under the title *Shivche Ha-Besht* (Praises of the Baal Shem).

The leading storyteller among the *Hasidim* was the mystic dreamer Rabbi Nahum of Bratzlav (1772-1811), the great grandson of the Besht. Thirteen of his tales have been preserved, virtually every one of them a work of art, delightful to read and full of symbolic meaning. Though full of fanciful details about kings, princes, and demons, these stories are a vehicle for their author's religious or ethical message. Rabbi Nahman drew his material from Jewish and non-Jewish sources as well as from the inspiration of a journey to the Holy Land made in 1898. Among the most famous of his stories which are still read and remembered is "The Lost Princess," the story of a precocious child lost to her father and found after many trials; "The King's Son and the Servant's Son," an allegory of the exchange of two newly born children, the queen's baby and that of her gardener's wife, told at the time when one of his disciples spoke to Rabbi Nahman of the upheaval brought into the world by Napoleon, "a man of low birth who has become an emperor." [7] "The Seven Beggars," which took several days to recount, is rich in psychological overtones. All these stories were taken down literally as Rabbi Nahman told them by his most faithful disciple Rabbi Nathan of Nemirov. These fascinating tales, mystical and lofty in nature, constitute a link in the great narrative tradition between the seventeenth-century *Ma'aseh Buch* (reprinted in this period) and the later stories of Isaac Leib Peretz.

While *Hasidism* lent an impetus to the development of Yiddish literature, *Haskalah*, the Enlightenment movement of the nineteenth century, put its emphasis on the revival of Hebrew and the importance of European languages. Few works of talent and originality were produced during the early *Haskalah* period. The *maskilim* looked down on Yiddish, though many of them used it to write their satires against the *Hasidim* and as the medium best suited for disseminating general knowledge among Russian Jews. Many works from other languages were translated into Yiddish in order to reach the common people. It was also proposed to translate the Bible into Yiddish, as Moses Mendelssohn had done into German, but because of opposition to the use of the "slave language" for sacred purposes, only the Book of Proverbs was completed.

* See *Great Jewish Personalities*, I, Chapter 11.

While most of the *Haskalah* writers regarded their Hebrew works as more important, there were three men who wrote primarily in Yiddish and thus helped prepare the way for the later flowering of Yiddish literature at the end of the nineteenth century. Israel Axenfeld (1787-1866), a notary public in Odessa, wrote some twenty-five stories and novels in "ordinary folk Yiddish," describing life in the early nineteenth century. His purposes were both to amuse and to be of use to his brothers who suffered under the yoke of superstition. Though in his youth a disciple of Rabbi Nahman of Bratzlav, no one later fought *Hasidism* as bitterly as this erstwhile *Hasid*. Most of his works remained unpublished and were read in manuscript form. His play *Der Erster Yiddische Rekrut* (First Jewish Recruit), describing the upheaval in Russian Jewry caused by the edict of 1827 forcing Jews to serve in the military, was later performed on the Yiddish stage in the 1920's and 1930's with evident success. Axenfeld's sketches constitute interesting source materials and had an influence on the work of Mendele Mocher Sephorim.

The most talented and original among the *Haskalah* writers in Yiddish was Solomon Ettinger (1800-1855), a physician who studied in Lemberg and practiced for a time in his native Zamosc. Ettinger wrote fables, epigrams, poems, and dramas, most of which were not published until after his death. Of his plays the best known is *Serkele* (Little Sarah), the story of an unscrupulous woman who illegally acquired control of the property of her wealthy brother who was believed dead, and dominated his household until her plans were frustrated by his unexpected return. Ettinger was deeply concerned with improving the prevailing Yiddish style, his comedy and poems being the first works in Yiddish to possess a correct European form. As a forerunner of Mendele and other major writers he has been called the "great grandfather of modern Yiddish literature."

In the fifties, on the threshold of the new period, Isaac Meir Dick (1814-1893) a Vilna *maskil*, wrote several hundred tales and short stories which were read by educated as well as by untutored women readers. Unlike those of his predecessors, however, Dick's works were issued regularly by a Vilna publishing house. Like the stories written during the *Mussar* period, they are moralistic. However, his use of humor and folklore, which he was the first to draw upon, and the knowledge he revealed of the daily life of the people made his stories very popular. Though written in a curious Germanized style, they were to be found during the 1850's and 1860's in almost every Jewish home and played a role in the cultural development of Lithuanian Jewry.[8]

The seeds that had been planted by *Hasidic* storytellers and an occasional *Haskalah* writer developed in the last decades of the nineteenth century into a new age for Yiddish literature. Several factors explain this flowering. In October 1862 a weekly journal in Yiddish was issued for the first time, *Kol Mebaser* (The Herald), initiated by Alexander Zederbaum in Odessa as a supplement to the Hebrew magazine *Ha-Melitz*. This journal attracted a number of new readers aside from those who read Dick's weekly stories and served as a rallying point for new contributors. The new political rights granted Jews at this time by Czar Alexander II (1855-1881) increased the hopes of Russian Jews for emancipation. The beginnings of industrialization in Russia opened up new economic opportunities and made available positions for Jews in commerce and trade. The attitude toward secular education consequently changed and thousands of young Jews now flocked to the *gymnasia* and universities. Since Yiddish was the language of the masses, many now turned to it as a means toward ultimate enlightenment. The rise of Russian socialism in the 1870's (*Narodniki*), with its philosophy of going down to the people and working with them, found adherents among some *Haskalah* writers who began to develop a greater interest in the masses of Jews and a greater respect for their language. Thus in the 1860's and 1870's an increasing number of works began to be published in Yiddish and progress was made in poetry, drama, and other fields.

During the last decades of the century three literary giants came to the fore: Mendele Mocher Sephorim (Shalom Jacob Abramowitz), Isaac Leib Peretz, and Sholom Aleichem (Solomon Rabinowitz). They comprised the classical trio that transformed the despised jargon into a creative literary medium and brought into being the golden age of Yiddish literature.

The first of these great figures, Mendele Mocher Sephorim[9] (Mendele the Bookseller) (1835-1917), was actually the founder of modern Yiddish literature and affectionately called by Sholom Aleichem its "grandfather." Mendele was born in a small Lithuanian town in the province of Minsk and, like so many of his contemporaries, spent most of his youth studying at various *yeshivas*. Returning to his native town after the death of his father, he found his imagination fired by the tales of a well-known tramp, Abraham the Lame, and joined him in wandering and begging through Lithuania and Southwest Russia—Volhynia, Podolia, and the Ukraine. On the journey he became acquainted with the lowly aspects of Jewish life—the vagabond beggars, the poor and the disinherited—all of which he later described in his novel, *Fishke der Krumer*. In

Kamanetz Podolsk he met Abraham Gotlober, a Hebrew and Yiddish writer who influenced him to give up his aimless way of life and take up cultural pursuits. After serving as a teacher in Berdichev and living in other places for a number of years, he finally settled in 1881 in Odessa, where he became principal of the community Hebrew school, a post which he filled for the last thirty-six years of his life.

Mendele began his writing career as a typical *maskil,* with several works in Hebrew. Observing, however, that many of the people did not know that language and wanting to be useful, he decided to write in Yiddish, though he knew that most of the Jewish intellectuals still avoided the vernacular and regarded it with disdain. Mendele's novels and sketches in Yiddish are masterpieces of realistic fiction depicting in great detail the stark reality of Jewish life in the Pale during the 1860's and 1870's. With biting satire he points up the ignorance, pauperism, and dislike of manual labor which characterized Jews in the ghetto as well as the social injustices practiced by the *"Shayne Yiden,"* the aristocratic Jews, upon their ignorant and helpless brethren.

In *Fishke der Krumer,* published in 1869, the tender idyllic tale of two beggars, one lame and the other hunchbacked, is seen against the background of the paupers and beggars Mendele himself had associated with in his youth. Mendele's famous allegorical novel *Die Klatche* (The Nag), published in 1873, dealing with the oppression suffered by the Jewish people, is a strong indictment of the *Haskalah* attitude that Europeanizing himself will gain the Jew acceptance in society. In *Masa'ot Binyamin Hashlishi* (Travels of Benjamin the Third), published in 1875, a delightful story of two small-town Jews with a yearning to see the world, written in the spirit of Cervantes' *Don Quixote,* Mendele ridicules the visionary tendency and inflamed imagination of many people in the ghetto who were unfamiliar with the outside world.

But with all his irony and biting criticism about life in the Pale, Mendele describes the people themselves with tenderness, sympathy, and great concern for their suffering. He saw not only the ugliness and the external blemishes of ghetto life but also its inner spiritual beauty and nobility of soul. His work portrays Jewish life with such accuracy and artistic skill that it is possible to reconstitute the small-town life of East European Jewry from his realistic writings.

While Mendele was the supreme critic of Jewish life in the *shtetl,* Isaac Leib Peretz (1851-1915), the second of the trio of classical writers, was the psychologist of Yiddish literature.[10] In his famous folk tales and *Hasidic* stories he concerned himself with typical individuals, their struggles and their deep sense of values. Unlike Mendele, Peretz was a many-sided European writer, the hero of the intellectuals, who made Yiddish a cultural force in Jewish life and won for himself the name of "father of Yiddish literature."

Peretz was born in Zamosc, one of the early centers of *Haskalah* in Poland,[11] and spent the first thirty-five years of his life in that town. While studying Talmud at the local *yeshiva*, he was permitted by his parents to familiarize himself with Polish, Russian, and German, and to read secular books. After trying his hand at several occupations, he studied law and for almost a decade was a prosperous lawyer in his native Zamosc. In 1887 he was forced to give up the practice of law because of involvement in anti-Czarist activity. Settling in Warsaw he became an official of the Jewish community, retaining this position for the last twenty-five years of his life.

Peretz, like the other members of the trio, began his literary career in Hebrew and throughout his life retained his devotion to that language. But he felt the need to speak to the masses in the language they understood. His first work in Yiddish, a long narrative poem entitled "Monish" appeared in 1887. For a time in the early 1890's he wrote realistic short stories and devoted himself to the popularization of scientific material. It was not until the turn of the century, when Peretz was almost fifty, that he brought forth the romantic folk tales and *Hasidic* stories which represent his greatest contribution to Yiddish literature. These tales such as *Bontsie Shvaig* (Silent Bontsie), the *Meshulah* (The Messenger), and *The Three Gifts* deal with incidents in the lives of humble and lovable figures who practice humility, patience, and self-sacrifice in spite of their sufferings.

Many of his best-known stories—*If Not Higher, The Golden Chain, A Midnight at the Old Market Place*—stem from the world of *Hasidism*. Though he himself was far removed from the *Hasidim* in belief and practice, Peretz drew many of his themes and much of his inspiration from *Hasidic* sources. What atracted him to this movement was its attempt to rise above external piety to true spirituality.

Aside from the above, Peretz made a contribution to Yiddish literature by his interest in the Yiddishist movement which during the 1880's and 1890's attempted to raise the status of the language in the public esteem. Under the impact of Jewish nationalism a literary upsurge began to take place at the end of the 1880's, as many Jewish intellectuals who had drifted away from Jewish life returned to their people. New periodicals appeared, including one edited by Peretz himself. The collective creations of the people which had been ignored by *Haskalah* writers now became an object of study. A new group of writers came forward whom Peretz had introduced to Yiddish literature or encouraged in their work such as Sholem Asch (1880-1957), H. D. Nomberg (1876-1927), and Abraham Reisen (1876-1953). His modest home in Warsaw was a gathering place for poets, writers, and confused intellectuals who came out of Poland to make Yiddish literature their life's work. Gradually under Peretz's leadership Yiddish literature attracted an intelligent reading public and forged the language into a modern instrument. At the Yiddish language conference, held in Czernowitz in 1908, attended by many distinguished writers, Peretz was the dominant figure.[12]

It is against this background of resurgence of literary creativity during the last decades of the nineteenth century and of tremendous growth during the first decade and a half before the first World War that we must view the third of the great classical writers in Yiddish. Sholom Aleichem (1859-1920), one of the world's greatest humorists, is the most popular of Yiddish writers and the symbol of the ability of the Jew to triumph through laughter over adversity. It is to the life and contributions of Sholom Aleichem that we now turn.

7 . *Sholom Aleichem*

[1859–1916]

LOUIS FALSTEIN

S H O L O M Aleichem died on May 13, 1916. A correspondent from the *New York Sun*, sent to the modest apartment on Kelly Street in the Bronx where the writer's body lay in state, surrounded by an honor guard of distinguished Yiddish writers, described the scene as follows:

> To one who stood in the tiny room with six candles and the body of Sholom Aleichem, there was shown that the death of a jester who had touched the hearts of the people is a matter of greater grief than the death of a king. For the men and women, old and young, rich and poor, who turned from the face of the dead to the light of the outside day, there were few whose eyes were not moist . . . Some women, under the stress of extreme grief, broke into hysterics. . . .

What the reporter found incredible was "a grief so universal that it could bring tears to the eyes of full-grown men . . . men who had never before looked upon Sholom Aleichem, but knew him only through his books." All day long, the walk opposite the apartment building was crowded with mourners who overflowed into the street, causing all traffic to be rerouted. Though some wept, the great mass of people stared in silence at the shaded windows of the second-floor apartment. Later in the day and toward evening, delegations began arriving from Philadelphia, Pittsburgh, the Middle West, and Canada. Messages of condolence poured in from the Pacific Coast, England, and the Continent.

"When has a man died in poverty," asked the *Literary Digest* in a glowing summation of the writer's life, "and on the next day brought out more than thirty thousand mourners to his bier?"

The thirty thousand who escorted Sholom Aleichem to his final rest and the countless thousands throughout the world who lamented his passing had not the vaguest notion of the grinding poverty that was the writer's lot before his death. Those who mourned were bereaved because in his passing something of themselves had died. Sholom Aleichem had been the singer of their inarticulate desires, shattered dreams, small triumphs, and fragile hopes. No Yiddish writer had identified himself so completely with the masses of the Pale of Settlement who lived in the *shtetls* (small towns) crowded together as "tightly as herring in a barrel." He had touched the heart of the Jewish idiom, coming closer to it than any other writer. He did not attempt to poetize or alter the language which was rich in tenderness, intimacy, and affection. In his hands, vernacular Yiddish had seemed a perfect tool, as though it had been fashioned for his purpose. He was the first writer of stature—with the exception of Mendele Mocher Sephorim, whom he venerated—to work in the Yiddish language, and the most popular. He wrote no towering novels. Most of his works were short stories, monologues, and now and then a play—but they attained full epic stature because they embraced the fullness of life.

The World of Sholom Aleichem

The world of Sholom Aleichem was the impoverished *shtetl* of Eastern Europe. The towns were vast slums, congested, dirty, the roads impassable after a rain. The people lived in cramped, rickety wooden shacks—all but the wealthy—with thatched or tin roofs over their heads and mud floors under their feet. Sewerage was unknown. The market place was the town's hub, the source of bread. The synagogue was the spiritual as well as social center. The most crowded place was the cemetery, where many had lain since before Columbus sailed for America—Jews who had died natural deaths as well as those killed in pogroms.

With few exceptions, the people spoke Yiddish, the "mother

tongue." "Anyone with a sound reading and writing knowledge of Russian was a suspicious character; he was on the road to assimilation, to shortening of the beard and gaberdine, removal of earlocks, consumption of forbidden meats, and the final horror of apostasy." [1]

A large number of *maskilim* in the towns held Yiddish in low esteem, and instead conversed in Hebrew, read Hebrew books, and frowned on the pious. There were also in the *shtetls*, later made famous by Sholom Aleichem by such laughter-provoking names as Kasrilevka, Mazepovka, and Kozodoevka, some who clipped their beards and wore the short coats of Gentiles. But, by and large, those communities were strongholds of old Jewish ways. The Sabbath was a day of rest and renewal. Religion was the sun around which their lives revolved. The children crowded the *heders;* the bright boys went on to study in *yeshivas*, the fortunate among them being snatched up by in-laws of means who enabled them to pursue their studies without having to worry about filling their stomachs.

Learning was held in high esteem. One of Sholom Aleichem's most humorous stories describes a large household, the head of which took inordinate pride in his learned sons-in-law. The only son-in-law whose praises the man failed to sing was the one who worked to support the others and made it possible for them to study.

On occasion, there was a pogrom, with the acquiescence of the authorities. But the people managed to get along. They believed in miracles; indeed their survival from one Sabbath to the next was a miracle. Hordes of beggars marched from house to house. The difference between the beggars and the givers was often nonexistent.

The towns, for the most part, were *Hasidic* strongholds, where rabbis ruled like feudal princes, the movement of *Hasidism* having lost its spiritual purity by Sholom Aleichem's time. Hereditary priesthood was enthroned. Rivalries flourished among wonder-working rabbis whose courts were little islands of prosperity and opulence surrounded by a sea of wretchedness.

Jews without residence permits were excluded from the large cities, a great many obtaining such permits by bribing officials. Those who were desperate and could not scrape together a livelihood in the small towns clung to the cities without permits, changing their residences often, and keeping one step ahead of the Czar's police. Notwithstanding the many obstacles placed in their path, Jews became doctors, lawyers, engineers, well-to-do merchants, and revolutionaries. There were even a few who attained great wealth and whose names inspired almost as much awe among Jews in the *shtetls* as the mention of Roths-child.

The May Laws of 1881, following the assassination of Czar Alexander II, let loose a reign of terror. Jews were further restricted, driven from the countryside, and forced to flee the large cities as well. Anti-Semitism became an unsheathed sword. The population of the over-crowded Jewish towns increased, as did the ranks of *luftmenschen*.* This was the world Sholom Aleichem mirrored in his stories.

Growing up in "Kasrilevka"

Sholom Aleichem—his real name was Rabinowitz—was born on February 18, 1859, in the small Ukrainian town of Pereya-slav, in the Poltava region. "Of children there were a goodly number," he wrote many years later in his autobiography, *Fun'm Yarid*, "over a dozen; of all sizes and colors, black-haired, blond and yellow." The family moved to Voronko, a town smaller still than his birthplace, and which, not a quarter of a century later, Sholom transmuted into the famed Kasrilevka of his many stories.

In *heder*, where Sholom spent all his waking hours, he was the brightest if not the most diligent student. His rich fantasy life—he dreamt often of hidden treasures—frequently brought him into conflict with the *rebbe*. However, he suffered no humility from the canings, assured that the offended parts would "heal before one walked under the marriage canopy."

Sholom's father, Nahum Vevik's, a well-to-do merchant by Voronko standards, was a curious combination: a *maskil* and philosopher who at the same time was a follower of a *Hasidic* rabbi; a pious Jew who defied family tradition and sent Sholom to a school where he received a modern education. The chores

* Yiddish for "rootless persons," used to describe East European Jews who lived on peddling and petty speculation.

of rearing the large family and taking care of the store fell to the mother.

As a boy, Sholom believed firmly that Voronko was the center of the universe and its Jews the select of God; at the very summit stood his father, whose seat was near the east wall, second only to the rabbi's. In Sholom's opinion there was not a home in Voronko or elsewhere more resplendent, a father more distinguished.

Unfortunately, Nahum Vevik's lost his business, and the family was forced to move back to Pereyaslav. Reb Rabinowitz opened a small unattractive inn. The family fell upon evil times and eventually all their jewelry and silverware had to be pawned. But Sholom's gloom was dispelled by Pereyaslav's broad streets and wooden sidewalks. Soon after their arrival, his display of scholarship earned him the nickname of "Bible boy."

After a great deal of soul-searching on the part of his father, Sholom was entered in the county school, where he came in contact for the first time with the world of Gentiles. Although his Russian was far from adequate, he accomplished the unprecedented feat—for a Jewish boy—of winning a prize of 120 rubles for being a brilliant student. This event created a furor among the town's Jews, who streamed to the Rabinowitz house in great numbers to verify the truth of the rumor. Uncle Pinney, the most pious of the three Rabinowitz brothers, was bitterly opposed to the fuss made over the boy. He argued that "many of the Jewish boys attending the county school, instead of the *yeshiva*, where they belonged, departed so far from the ways of piety, they carried handkerchiefs on the Sabbath and conversed in Russian."

During those days epidemics sweeping through the countryside took their heaviest toll among the Jews crowded into small towns. The cholera epidemic that struck Pereyaslav claimed Sholom's mother among its many victims. "We did ourselves proud," Sholom Aleichem recalls in his autobiography, "when the six of us said *kaddish*. One of the visiting relatives said with envy: 'How could you not go straight to paradise with such *kaddish* readers?'"

After a decent interval, Sholom's father remarried. The new mother possessed a "hot temperament and a rich Berdichev stepmother vernacular." In dealing out punishment, "she did not favor her own children," treating all alike with scrupulous impartiality.

Although Sholom was pressed into service by his stepmother —his job was to stand outside the inn and coax passers-by to stop with them—he found time to read books, journals, and newspapers in both Russian and Hebrew. The first novel he read was in Hebrew, the language favored by the Pereyaslav intelligentsia. It was a famous work *The Love of Zion* written by Abraham Mapu, a modern Hebrew novelist from Lithuania, who was in great vogue among the "emancipated" youth. The boy read in the garret, away from the suspicious and prying eyes of his stepmother. He enjoyed the book thoroughly, weeping for the hero, and embracing the heroine.

With the few kopecks he had put by, Sholom bought a ream of paper, ruled the pages on both sides, and began himself to write a novel entitled *The Daughter of Zion*. He wrote at night, by lamplight. One evening his stepmother apprehended him in the attic. "She immediately created such a furor, the whole household woke in fright." He was forbidden, henceforth, to waste precious kerosene and to indulge in such idle and unbecoming pastimes. His father "confiscated" the unfinished novel, but instead of destroying it, as Sholom had feared, showed it to a friend. "Reb Nahum, you don't know what you have here!" the friend said prophetically. "This boy is going to be a somebody." Reb Nahum's friend insisted that Sholom must become a writer. In this he was echoed by others of the inner circle, the men who drank tea and played chess with the innkeeper.

Sholom liked the notion of becoming a writer. The question was whether to write in Hebrew or Russian. Yiddish was not even considered a possibility; it was for speaking, but writing in what was called "jargon" and *"irretaitch"* was "fit for women" and out of the question. A person who even carried Yiddish books might be ridiculed.

Sholom's first literary endeavor was a lexicon of his stepmother's invective, compiled and arranged in alphabetical order. Soon he was forced to interrupt his writing to give private lessons. After tutoring for a short time in Pereyaslav, Sholom, who had then turned seventeen, was engaged by a leather merchant from a nearby town to educate his children. But in view of the fact that his duties also included minding a newborn infant at night and performing other chores, he soon sought a livelihood elsewhere.

After several unfortunate experiences, the wandering half-starved young tutor was introduced to a wealthy Jewish land-owner, Elimelech Loieff, who was looking for a teacher for his thirteen-year-old daughter. Reb Loieff, who possessed "the voice of a lion and the bearing of a field-marshall," put Sholom through a gruelling examination before consenting to hire him. He tested Sholom's Russian and Hebrew as well as his knowl-edge of Rashi's *Commentaries*.*

The next three years, passed in the village of Sofievka, on the large estate of his employer, were the happiest of Sholom's life. "I lived like a prince," he later wrote. Reb Loieff, who treated him as one of the family, was generous and wealthy. Sholom's life was transformed, as if by magic, from one of privation to abundance. It was as though one of his own boy-hood reveries had borne fruit.

Romance in the Shtetl

In his three decades as a writer, Sholom Aleichem's plots were as varied as the types he portrayed. But the most wildly improbable, tenderly romantic plot was one he did not write; he lived it. Olga, Reb Loieff's only daughter—and after the death of her brother his only child—was Sholom's constant companion. Together they read Shakespeare, Dickens, Goethe, Schiller, Gogol, and sentimental French novels. During this period he wrote a great deal: novels that were "heart-rending," "noisy dramas," and "inextricable tragedies." As soon as he had finished a work, he read it to Olga. Both hailed each composi-tion as a masterpiece. But as soon as a new manuscript appeared, they enthusiastically crowned it as Sholom's glory, burning the previous one in the oven.

In one of his novels, *Yoselle Nightingale*, Sholom Aleichem dramatized the plight of two young lovers unable to consum-mate their romance in marriage. In the case of Sholom and Olga, it was Reb Elimelech who presented the final obstacle. Upon discovering that the two were in love, he dismissed Sholom

---

*Creators of the Jewish Experience in Ancient and Medieval Times, Chapter 9, Wash-ington, D.C., B'nai B'rith Books, 1985

and took Olga on a long journey. Although he was fond of the young tutor, Reb Loieff did not approve of his daughter's carrying on a romance without his knowledge and approval.

From Sofievka, the lovelorn, impecunious Sholom went to Kiev, where "eminent novelists and poets blessed by God" dwelled in great numbers. He arrived in Kiev without the residence permit required of Jews. During his first night in the great city, which later appeared in his stories as Yehupetz, the police raided the inn where Sholom stopped; he hid in the attic with other non-resident Jews.

Unable to obtain a residence permit, penniless, and disillusioned, he left Kiev and subsequently settled in the small town of Luben, where he served briefly as a government rabbi. Meanwhile, in Sofievka, Reb Loieff withdrew his opposition to Sholom as a son-in-law, and his marriage with Olga took place in 1883. The couple lived on the father's estate, with Sholom serving as its general manager. Reb Elimelech, of whom Sholom Aleichem wrote a masterful sketch in his autobiography, died in 1885 leaving his daughter a quarter of a million rubles. The young couple gave up Sofievka and moved to Kiev. Their money enabled them to obtain a resident permit without difficulty.

Writer in the Making

In Kiev, Sholom assumed a role in which he was sorely miscast, that of speculator on the stock exchange. Eventually he lost Olga's inheritance—but Yiddish literature gained by it. How else could he have written about the immortal character Menachem Mendl? It was during this period, while he was still in business, first as a speculator, broker, and later as a merchant, that the author assumed the pen name Sholom Aleichem (in Hebrew, "peace be unto you," and used as a greeting). The use of the pseudonym was in part due to his desire to keep his business colleagues from finding out about his literary avocation; moreover, he probably did not take his initial thrusts at Yiddish literature very seriously at the start.

Sholom Aleichem first broke into print in 1879, writing local correspondence for the Hebrew weekly *Ha-Tzephirah*. This was followed, in 1882, by articles on Jewish education in another Hebrew weekly *Ha-Melitz*. During this period of literary apprenticeship, he also wrote in Russian for *Yevreyskoie Obozrenie* (1884) and *Kievlianin* (1885).

Inspired by the phenomenal success of Mendele Mocher Sephorim, Sholom Aleichem also wrote a Yiddish tale, his first, called "Two Stones," which appeared in *Yiddishes Folksblatt* in 1883, and brought the author instantaneous recognition. "Penknife," a children's story, one of his best, came next. Other stories followed, rich in humor, compassion, and gentle irony. He won praise from eminent writers such as Mendele and later from Gorki and Tolstoy. His name was linked with Gogol, Dickens, and Mark Twain.

Temporary wealth enabled Sholom Aleichem to found a Jewish annual, *Die Yiddishe Folksbibliotek* (1888), a publication of high literary merit. To attract authors of distinction and talent, he paid large fees for contributions. Isaac Leib Peretz, who wrote in Hebrew but like Sholom Aleichem was inspired by Mendele's success to try his hand in Yiddish, appeared in the *Folksbibliotek* with his celebrated poem "Monish." Peretz and Sholom Aleichem remained friends long after the annual was discontinued for lack of funds.

After losing his wealth, Sholom Aleichem decided to move from Kiev to the more congenial climate of Odessa, where he planned to devote all his time to writing. In Odessa he was near Mendele Mocher Sephorim, whom he considered his master, and who exerted a powerful influence on him. On one occasion when "Grandfather," as the younger man had nicknamed Mendele, visited his home in Odessa, Sholom Aleichem gave the master a newly completed manuscript to read. After a brief lapse of time, Mendele lifted his eyes from a page he was reading and inquired of the host whether there was a fire in the oven. Sholom Aleichem, trembling lest his distinguished guest was hungry, replied in the affirmative, assuring him that a meal would soon be forthcoming. "If the oven is going," Mendele said calmly, handing Sholom his manuscript, "throw this in. This is not your genre." Years later, at a banquet celebrating the seventy-fifth birthday of Mendele, Sholom Aleichem publicly thanked "Grandfather" for his sound advice.

In Odessa, Sholom Aleichem became the center of a group of prominent Jewish writers. Among them were E. L. Levinski, who wrote a Utopian volume about a visit to Palestine a hundred years hence; Ben Ami, who wrote in Russian; J. H. Ravnitzki, a collaborator with Bialik on several anthologies; and M. L. Lilienblum, writer and philosopher. Unable to earn a livelihood in Odessa, Sholom Aleichem returned to Kiev, his mind alive with business schemes, determined once again to storm the battlements that had repulsed him in the past. But he forsook commerce finally and irrevocably in 1900, admitting failure. Henceforth he determined to stick to his last as a professional writer in Yiddish. During this period in Kiev, Sholom Aleichem did some of his best writing. Tevyeh, Sholom Aleichem's famous character, appeared in 1895. Kasrilevka, Yehupetz, and Boiberik were soon household words. But even though the name of Sholom Aleichem was becoming increasingly famous, he struggled desperately "not to let the world know how difficult things were," and how he was often forced to seek means other than writing to care for his wife and six children.

First Visit to America

The Kiev pogroms of 1905 profoundly shocked Sholom Aleichem. As a protest against a regime that permitted such atrocities, he left Russia. After settling his family in Switzerland, the writer toured Western Europe, lecturing before Jewish audiences. Later on, the dapper little man with the long hair, the merry twinkle in his eye, the velvet waistcoat, and flowing tie became a familiar figure on the American lecture platform as well. America enchanted and bewildered him. Unlike other countries he had visited, America was not completely strange. There were in its large cities many thousands of Jews originally from the *shtetls*. Sholom Aleichem listened to their tales, rejoiced in their triumphs, and grieved over their defeats. He lamented the loss of traditional values on the part of many of his former "little people." Some of them who achieved the status of *all-rightnik* (*nouveau riche*) placed material success above the spiritual. According to Sholom Aleichem, the *all-rightniks* looked upon the coming of the Messiah as a great catastrophe because they would have to abandon all their American material acquisitions and migrate to Palestine. Subsequently, a new element appeared in his stories: America as the one place on earth where Jews suffered no pogroms and spent all their energies "making a living."

Sholom Aleichem and Bialik

Sholom Aleichem returned to Europe in 1907 and went to The Hague as an American delegate to the Zionist Congress. There he met Hayyim Nahman Bialik.* The two embraced as though they were old friends. In Sholom Aleichem's account of his brief but pleasant stay in Holland's capital, a good deal was said about the joyous occasion of his meeting with the great Hebrew poet, their conversations, long walks, and reveries, but nothing about the Congress. Beyond the esteem each had for the other as a creative person, both dealt in their writings with the changing pattern of Jewish life in Russia, and revealed a strong attachment to the traditional ways of their people. Bailik wrote in Hebrew as a poet, on an intellectual plane, while Sholom Aleichem wrote in Yiddish on the level of the common man.

Before returning to Russia, Bialik visited his new friend in Switzerland. They talked, reminisced, and planned for the future, and sometimes they were joined by Mendele Mocher Sephorim, who, like Sholom Aleichem, was also a voluntary exile from the Czar's domain.

In 1907, Sholom Aleichem began writing one of his most humorous works, the saga of Mottel Peissi, the cantor's son. Sholom Aleichem continued writing about Mottel even after he became ill with tuberculosis and did not have enough money for rent. "When I look at the calendar," he wrote a friend,[2] "and see the date when I have to pay rent, and my wallet is as dry as a desert, it is bad. It is my jubilee of twenty-five years as a writer. So Jews in Russia have scraped together their pennies and there is already a special fund for me of a hundred rubles . . ."

His illness alarmed many of his friends, among them Peretz, who wrote often to urge Sholom Aleichem to take care of himself and achieve a quick recovery. He was at a German resort, surrounded by his large and growing family (two sons-in-law having been added), when World War I broke out.

* See Chapter 6.

Threatened with internment as an enemy alien, Sholom Aleichem fled to Denmark. In Copenhagen, he was struck down by
diabetes, a malady that two years later claimed his life. Writing
to a friend in Warsaw, Sholom Aleichem quipped: "Having
been told I have diabetes, I no longer fear of dying from hunger.
I'll most likely die from thirst."

Last Years in America

Sholom Aleichem arrived in the United States on December
3, 1914. Pardoxically, his arrival was reported more fully in the
New York Times than in any of New York's five Yiddish
dailies. In his first public appearance at Cooper Union, arranged
by the Committee of One Hundred that had brought him and
his family to the United States, Sholom Aleichem said:

> I came to America the first time in 1905. This is my second time.
> Both times I came in the wake of a catastrophe. My first visit
> here followed the bloody excesses of 1905 in Russia. This time I'm
> here because of the insanity, the war in Europe. If ever it becomes
> necessary for me to come a third time, I'm hard put to it to
> imagine after what kind of catastrophe that will be. The worst,
> it seems to me, has already happened.[3]

Although Yiddish-speaking residents of New York, where
he settled, came in large numbers to hear Sholom Aleichem
whenever he spoke, and read his works, the Yiddish newspapers
devoted little space to him. After he became a contributor for
one of the dailies, *Der Tog* (*The Day*), the four competing
Yiddish papers ceased printing his name altogether.

Ignored, neglected, suffering from poverty and ill-health, and
grieving over the loss of Jewish lives in the war, Sholom Aleichem nonetheless continued writing. There were still many
Mottel tales to be told—Mottel in America, growing up and
"making a living." There was also his own autobiography. "My
friends have often insisted," Sholom Aleichem wrote not long
before his death,

> that I should recount the story of my life. The time has come,
> they said, and it may even be interesting. I tried to listen to their
> advice. Several times I put the pen aside until . . . until finally

the right time came. Before I had reached the age of fifty, I had the honor of meeting his majesty, the Angel of Death, face to face. I was almost dispatched to that place whence one cannot write letters nor even send a greeting by messenger. In short, having been practically gathered unto my forefathers, I said to myself, "Now the time has come. Snatch the opportunity and write, for no one knows what tomorrow will bring! You may die suddenly. People who think they knew you and understood you will turn up with cock-and-bull stories about you. What will you gain by it? Better do the job yourself, for nobody knows you as well as you know yourself . . ."

Thus began the introduction to his final and, in many respects, his most significant work—the summing up, the autobiography, or, as he called it, "the return from the fair" (*Fun'm Yarid*). Unfortunately, he did not live long enough to complete this work. But the episodes he committed to paper, sections of which are available in English as *The Great Fair* (translated by the author's granddaughter, Tamara Kahana), are eloquent proof of the great loss suffered by Yiddish as well as world literature when Sholom Aleichem put down his pen for the last time.

Tevyeh the Milkman

Among Sholom Aleichem's major character creations is Tevyeh, about whom the author was writing as late as 1914, and who had a little of every Jew in him. A pauper with a philosophical bent, whose emaciated nag crawled along the dusty road between Anatevka and Boiberik, delivering milk, cheese, and butter to the summer homes of the wealthy Jews from Yehupetz, Tevyeh was the immediately recognizable symbol of the wretched Jew who refused to accept defeat. As though being a Jew was not in itself a sufficient liability in the Czar's domain, Tevyeh's business was bad, his horse old and stubborn, his wife ailing. Moreover, he was the father of seven marriageable daughters.

"Tevyeh the Dairyman" is not properly speaking a story. It is a catalogue of disasters, told in monologue form. Notwithstanding the fact that Tevyeh's tribulations were endless, he was astonishingly resilient. He believed implicitly in God, addressing Him intimately, sometimes imprudently, but always hopefully.

> Blessed are they that dwell in Thy house (Right! I take it O Lord, that Thy house is somewhat more spacious than my hovel!) . . . I will extol Thee my God, O King (what good would it do me if I didn't?) . . . The Lord is good to all (and suppose He forgets somebody now and again, good Lord, hasn't He enough on His mind?) . . . The Lord upholdeth all that fall, and raiseth up all that are bowed down (Father in heaven, loving Father, surely it's my turn now, I can't fall any lower) . . . Thou openest Thy hand and satisfiest every living thing (so You do, Father in heaven, You give with an open hand; one gets a box on the ear, another a roast chicken, and neither my wife nor I nor my daughters have even smelt a roast chicken since the days of creation) . . .[4]

Although he provokes laughter, Tevyeh is not a comedian. The millions of Jews who read the Tevyeh episodes as they appeared in Yiddish newspapers and between the covers of books laughed because they identified themselves with the milkman's dilemmas and his unique way of articulating them. Tevyeh, who misquoted the Holy Books liberally, was a traditional Jew, like any pious Kasrilevkite, but his contacts with the outside world were broader and he was more tolerant of those who did not believe as he did. Deriving from the old stable Jewish life, he was witness to the cataclysmic changes taking place in Russia and among the Jews. He was more than a witness. He was an unwilling participant. One of his daughters married a revolutionist whom she followed to Siberia and exile, with Tevyeh's acquiescence; another took a Gentile for a husband and became an apostate and was disowned by her parents. His wife died and the peasants of Anatevka, his former friends, descended on his hut during the incitements against the Jews in 1881 for the purpose of staging a pogrom. But Tevyeh survived.

Tevyeh was Sholom Aleichem's resounding answer to those who questioned the capacity and ability of the Jew to survive. Although not an observant Jew, the author knew better than anyone that Tevyeh could not have endured without his faith.

Menachem Mendl, the Luftmensch

As a character, Tevyeh was completely passive (what could a Jew do?), reacting to each catastrophe as it befell him. Menachem Mendl, on the other hand, was a person to whom action was imperative. Not that his action ever resulted in anything. Cane in hand, Menachem Mendl and his fellow-*luftmenschen* in the Jewish towns of the Pale literally became adepts at necromancy, trying to coax a living out of thin air. Denied access to the soil, excluded from the guilds, barred from the large cities, they were reduced to "deal in things you can't put your hands on." Sholom Aleichem introduces Menachem Mendl to the reader through a series of letters exchanged between the character and his wife, Sheineh Sheindl. Menachem Mendl writes from Yehupetz or Odessa, where he is playing the stock market with his wife's inheritance. His letters home are full of characteristic optimism and enthusiasm for the propects at hand. His wife's replies, just as characteristic, are heavy with skepticism; she has been married to Menachem Mendl for many years—there are hungry children in the house—and she finds little reason for optimism, since Menachem Mendl has never been successful in earning a living. He had tried a great many things, but the ruble always eluded him. As a marriage broker he once virtually consummated a match, but it turned out that both parties were of the same sex. So eager had he been to close the deal, he had failed to make a proper check. The luck of a *luftmensch!*

Menachem Mendl was not a fool. But his judgment was impaired after living too long on a merry-go-round that failed to stop. He was Sholom Aleichem's most tragic character. Unlike Tevyeh, who had his faith to sustain him, Menachem Mendl existed largely by self-delusion.

To many readers of Sholom Aleichem's tales, Menachem Mendl was not a fictitious character. Copied straight from life, he was someone they knew, were related to, met daily in the market place.

Tales about Children

Some of his saddest and, at the same time, most exuberant tales were about children. Sholom Aleichem retained until the day of his death the freshness of a child's viewpoint. He was the first Yiddish author to write about children. "Penknife," one of his earliest and most celebrated tales, dealt with a boy who stole a knife he desired more than anything else in life, only to find his days poisoned by feelings of guilt. In his final work, *Fun'm Yarid*, Sholom Aleichem returned to his childhood, to a world he loved and never really abandoned for any length of time during his three decades of creative writing.

There is a universality in Sholom Aleichem's youthful characters, though their reveries are different from those of Gentile neighbors. The Jewish boys about whom he wrote felt more kinship with the *Kabbalah* than with God's green fields and swift rivers. The fantasy life of these boys and girls never strayed far from the spirit of the Jewish people. The Kasrilevka boys, Sholom and Shmulik, searched for a hidden treasure. In this they were no different from Gentile boys, but it was the manner in which they proposed to find the treasure that differed: they meant to use the *Kabbalah* as a magic key that would unlock all secrets and lead them directly to their object. "Why do you think God created the *Kabbalah*?" Shmulik, the expert, inquired. The *Kabbalists* could do anything they pleased. Even Sholom, the skeptic, could see at a glance the incomparable advantage of being a Jew. The only complicating factor, the single obstacle preventing them from going to the spot where the treasure was buried and loading their pockets full of precious stones, was the ritual which must be observed. According to Shmulik, it was necessary to fast forty days and forty nights and recite forty chapters from the Psalms on each of these days before the mystery revealed itself. Sholom was prepared for this arduous ritual—but then Shmulik left town and never returned.

Sholom Aleichem's children were steeped in Bible lore. In a story titled "Song of Songs," ten-year-old Shimek said to the little girl, Buzie, whom he fancied: "Come, my beloved, let us go forth into the fields. Let us lodge in the villages. Let us get up early to the vineyards. Let us see if the vine flourish, whether the tender grape appear, and the pomegranates bud forth . . ."

The Jewish boys dreamt of romance fully and passionately, but they had their own unique ways of expressing their love. "And it came to pass," a boy wrote to a girl who captivated his heart, "that a Jew named Mordecai, who is Motelle in real life, and dwelt in the city of the Kingdom of Ahasuerus, called Shushan, which is none other than our own city . . . and the maiden was fair and beautiful, and she found favor in the eyes of Mordecai. But Mordecai instructed Esther to reveal no word thereof to any man . . ."

One of Sholom Aleichem's best-loved characters is little Mottel Peissi, the cantor's son. "Hurrah, I'm an orphan!" Mottel exclaimed after his father, who had been ailing for a long time, finally passed away. As an orphan, Mottel fancied himself the center of attention and the object of sympathy. Like Sholom Aleichem's grown-up Jews, Mottel did not realize how badly off he was. Being a child, he took his pleasures where he found them.

Mottel, Jewish to the core, possessed the universal child's sense of wonder and novelty in all the things he touched and experienced both in the *shtetl,* where he was born, and in America, where he finally went to live. Mottel, the child whose spirit was as free as a bird in flight, was Sholom Aleichem's perfect vehicle for his irrepressible humor. Mottel also served as a bridge between Russia and America. Sholom Aleichem was composing new Mottel episodes a few days before he died.

Genius of Sholom Aleichem

In all his creative life, Sholom Aleichem strove and succeeded to remain at one with the people about whom he wrote. On two occasions when he departed from the pattern—in his novels *Sender Blank* and *The Storm*—the results were not successful. *Sender Blank* (1888) explored the life of a parvenu and snob, a Jew who, having lost the traditional ways of his fathers, ends up as a miserable usurer. *The Storm,* written in 1907, after the defeat of the revolution in Russia and the disillusionment following in its wake, dealt with a group of young Jewish revolutionaries, among whom was Yashka Vorona, an apostate and stool pigeon. Sholom Aleichem, the man of compassion and gentle irony, made no attempt to conceal his hatred both for Sender Blank, who betrayed his heritage as a Jew, and for Yashka Vorona, who betrayed his fellow-Jews to the Czarist police. Although both these novels were important social studies, they were not his genre, as Mendele had said of another of Sholom Aleichem's works. Hatred was not his forte.

Sholom Aleichem was at his best as an indefatigable chronicler. He strikes the reader as a listener rather than a writer, an omnipresent eavesdropper, notebook and pencil in hand, wandering among the Jews of the small towns of the Pale, riding along on the temperamental narrow-gauge train known as the *ledig geyer* (loafer) that crawls interminably through endless Ukrainian steppes and towns, through Berdichev, Vinnitsa, Nemirov, Gaisin—and all the way to Kamenka on the Dnestr River. During the course of the journey, lasting a week—one or two days should have been sufficient—Sholom Aleichem talked with and listened to hundreds of Jews, each one of them with a tale as long as the Exile. Talk was not prescribed. The right to act having been taken away from them long ago, Sholom Aleichem's Jews were the world's most prodigious talkers.

Sholom Aleichem was a patient listener. He listened to all, and in particular to the poor, toward whom he was partial. The rich fared less well; he satirized and pitilessly "exposed" them in the manner of Balzac.

Before Sholom Aleichem's death and for many years afterward, critics debated his place among the famous triumvirate of acknowledged masters of Yiddish literature. Like Peretz, Sholom Aleichem became a folk hero while still alive. In addition to mirroring the lives of poor Jews in Russia—and this meant the vast majority—he was an active partisan in their ceaseless struggle to survive as a people. Like Mendele, he wrote about the *shtetl*. Sholom Aleichem's genre was humor, while Mendele excelled in satire. Peretz eschewed realism and achieved fame through his mystical tales of *Hasidism*. Each was supreme in his genre.

Some critics maintain that Sholom Aleichem's characters are not as complex as those of Mendele, that he was not as profound as Peretz, that he did not probe deeply, and that Tevyeh, Menachem Mendl, and Mottel were types who lack the dimensions of full-blooded fictional persons. What must be kept in mind is that this may have been Sholom Aleichem's intent; in recreating a prosaic and commonplace world, as contrasted with Peretz's mystic and exotic one, he sought the representational and familiar. His readers were the same people about whom he wrote. Were all history books of that era to vanish, Sholom Aleichem's tales could offer a complete and faithful picture of life among Russian Jews in the latter part of the nineteenth and beginning of the twentieth centuries.

Sholom Aleichem became the most popular of writers among the mass of Yiddish readers because his tales were simple, direct, and free of abstruse symbolism. He spoke to the heart and without circumlocution. Readers found his voice gentle and compassionate. More important still, he taught people to laugh at their own predicaments. He made them take pride in their virtues and laugh at their foibles. He taught them to be optimistic—in the face of a repressive, pogrom-ridden government that plotted their spiritual if not their physical extinction. He often romanticized the characters he created—though he did not neglect their weaknesses—portraying his "little people" not only as they were but as he might like them to be.

The jester, the mimic, the folk humorist who "discovered the liberating power of laughter" [5] has taken his rightful place among the immortals in world literature. Sholom Aleichem's greatness as a man lay in his broad humanity; his greatness as a Jew lay in complete self-identification with his people; his greatness as a writer lay in his ability to encompass in his works the manifold aspects of Jewish life in the Pale of Settlement. A pioneer in a new literature, he led a successful crusade on behalf of Yiddish, thus opening fresh vistas to writers of talent as well as to thousands of readers.

Sholom Aleichem's legacy to the world was his simple philosophy, an optimism that permeated his stories, faith in the inconquerable spirit of man, and hatred of tyranny. For Jews, his stories open a window on the world of their fathers, on values and traditions that were centuries in the making. He is thus a link with a tragic but proud, heroic past.

FOR FURTHER READING
Books by Sholom Aleichem

Adventures of Mottel, translated by Tamara Kahana (New York: Henry Schuman, 1953).

Inside Kasrilevke, translated by Isidore Goldstick (New York: Schocken Books, 1948).

Jewish Children, from the Yiddish of Sholom Aleichem (New York: Bloch, 1937).

The Old Country, translated by Julius and Frances Butwin (New York: Crown, 1946; illustrated edition, 1953).

Selected Stories of Sholom Aleichem, introduction by Alfred Kazin (New York: Modern Library, 1956).

Marienbad, translated by Aliza Shevrin (New York: Putnam, 1982). A marvelous comic novel of personal entanglements in cosmopolitan Warsaw at the turn of the century. Written in 1911.

In The Storm, translated by Aliza Shevrin (New York: Putnam, 1984). A powerful novel about Russian Jews at the time of the 1905 pogroms.

From the Fair, The Autobiography of Sholom Aleichem, translated, edited, and with an introduction by Curt Leviant (New York: Viking, 1985). Writing in *The New York Times,* Chaim Potok said, "Curt Leviant's introduction serves as a smooth entry into the world of Sholom Aleichem; his translation captures the bounce and effervescence of Aleichem's Yiddish."

Why Do The Jews Need A Land of Their Own? translated from the Yiddish and Hebrew by Joseph Leftwich and Mordecai S. Chertoff (New York: Herzl Press, 1984) originally published by Beth Sholom Aleichem, Tel Aviv, 1978, 1981. This collection of stories one act plays, a novella, essays and letters reveal the depth of Aleichem's understanding of and passion for a Jewish return to Zion.

Favorite Tales of Sholom Aleichem, translated by Julius and Frances Butwin (New York: Avenel Books, 1983). There are 55 stories here that originally appeared in volumes entitled *The Old Country* and *Tevye's Daughter.*

Books about Sholom Aleichem

SAMUEL, Maurice, *The World of Sholom Aleichem (New York; Alfred Knopf, 1956.*

ARCHITECTS
OF THE JEWISH
STATE

Alongside the achievement of emancipation by West European Jewry, the most important development in Jewish life during the modern period was the rise of Jewish nationalism at the end of the nineteenth century. The inauguration of the movement for the return of the Jew to his ancestral homeland introduced a new force which gradually transformed the character of Jewish existence.

Theodor Herzl is usually regarded as the personality who symbolizes the rise of modern Zionism, but the movement did not begin with him. Organized efforts for a return to Palestine had begun more than fifteen years before the launching of the World Zionist Congress in 1897, and the idea of the return as a practical solution to the Jewish problem goes back to the middle of the century. Herzl was not aware of these earlier proposals when he wrote his pamphlet *The Jewish State* in 1896, but he soon discovered that a great deal of Zionist sentiment already existed, particularly in Eastern Europe.

Although belief in the ultimate Messianic restoration of the Jews to Palestine was a cardinal principle of the Jewish religion throughout the centuries, proposals that Jews actually take the initiative themselves in colonizing the land were not seriously broached until the nineteenth century. Several factors account for this new interest in Palestine after the interregnum of almost seventeen hundred years. Foremost among them was the rise of nationalism in Europe with its emphasis on the linguistic and cultural heritage of national groups and their right of self-determination. Between the Congress of Vienna in 1815 and the Congress of Berlin in 1878 a nationalistic awakening took place throughout Europe, resulting in independence for a number of formerly subject peoples, such as the Greeks, Serbians, Rumanians, and Bulgars. Countries like Italy and Germany, which had been divided for centuries, now achieved national unity, and additional minorities like the Poles and Czechs either revolted against their overlords or began agitations for freedom.

Thus the idea of nationalism was in the air. The example of other peoples successfully struggling for freedom inevitably inspired the idea of a Jewish national revival among some of the bolder Jewish spirits of the age.

One of the earliest of such advocates was Tzevi Hirsch Kalischer (1795-1874), a traditional rabbi with philosophical interests who served for forty years in Thorn, Prussia, across the border from Poland. As early as 1836 Kalischer, in a letter to Nathan Mayer Rothschild, son of the founder of the banking firm, pleaded for the re-establishment of agricultural settlements for the poor Jews in Palestine.

In his most important work *Derishat Zion* (*Longing for Zion*), published in 1862, Kalischer urged the Jews to hasten the coming of the Messiah by taking the initiative and resettling the land through their own efforts and sacrifice. "Let no one think," he wrote, "that all of a sudden the Lord will descend from heaven and say go forth . . . Note how Italians, Poles, Hungarians risk their lives and their possessions for the reputation of their countries. Only we Jews who are heirs to a land which is the glory and joy of the world . . . . have nothing to say and act like a man who has no courage." [1]

Kalischer influenced a group to buy land for colonization on the outskirts of Jaffa. In response to his insistent request the Alliance Israélite Universelle, an international Jewish organization founded in 1860, made the first attempt at scientific farming in Palestine by establishing a Jewish agricultural school at Mikveh Israel, near Jaffa. But his ideas received little additional encouragement for the pious Jews who lived in the "Holy Cities" of Jerusalem, Hebron, Tiberias, and Safed, and who depended on the traditional collection of alms (*Halukkah*), opposed the idea of agricultural settlements fearing it would lead people away from study and open the door to heresies.

In the same year that Kalischer published his views, Moses Hess, the most original and profound of the precursors of modern Zionism, voiced many of the leading ideas of Zionist ideology.[2] Hess grew up in Germany, where he was given a traditional Jewish education. As a young man, however, he drifted away from Judaism, married a Christian woman of questionable reputation, and became one of the earliest German socialists. Like most of the young radicals of the time, Hess believed that Jews should disperse and become assimilated into the nations with whom they lived.

Through his studies of anthropology and the natural sciences, Hess became convinced that the Marxist doctrine was wrong when it held that nationalism was not a basic factor in history. He saw the unique role which national cultures would play in the future world order, and gradually began to devote himself to a critical examination of the Jewish question. The result was *Rome and Jerusalem*, which is widely regarded as one of the classics of nineteenth-century Jewish thought.

Influenced by the national awakening in Italy and seeing the failure of emancipation, Hess urged the Jews to recognize that homelessness was the heart of the Jewish problem. Germans were anti-Jewish racially, and neither religious reform, baptism, nor political emancipation would make the Germans regard them as part of the German nation. There was only one solution for the Jew—establishing a Jewish state on the banks of the Jordan in Palestine. He dreamed of a Jewish Congress with the support of the European powers and advocated the establishment of a Jewish colonization association. Palestine, according to Hess' plan, was to be a socialist state, with industry and agriculture organized on Mosaic or socialist principles and labor given full legal protection. The new state, as was true in antiquity, would become a "spiritual nerve center" which would stimulate Jewish life throughout the Diaspora.

The book met with a hostile reception because its suggestion that German Jews recognize themselves as a nation ran counter to the universal outlook of the time. Hess' proposal—like those of Kalischer and other early precursors of Herzl—had little influence on contemporary attitudes. In Western Europe belief in emancipation was at its heyday in the 1860's, and in Russia traditional Jews were still afraid that such a movement would lead to a breakdown of religious belief.

During the next two decades, however, insistent demands for national rights by the ethnic groups that made up the Austro-Hungarian Empire gave rise to a new non-political conception of nationalism emphasizing common historic memories and cultural aspirations rather than territory and statehood.[3] Since the Jews of Russia lived as a compact mass in the Pale of Settlement, speaking for the most part their own language (Yiddish) and conducting their own intensive religious and cultural life, they had many of the attributes of nationhood. If the Czechs and Ruthenians could claim national rights, why not also the Jews? Another factor was the emergence of Palestine and the Middle East on the political horizon, for the Congress of Berlin had assigned to Great Britain the island of Cyprus and turned public attention in the direction of the Middle East.

The outbreaks against the Jews in Russia, which began in April 1881, and the subsequent restrictive legislation shattered the dream of the *maskilim* that Russification would bring the Jew civil and eventually social equality. Bitter disillusionment followed from the fact that members of the revolutionary *Narodniki* movement as well as enlightened portions of Russian society had shown themselves indifferent to Jewish suffering. Jewish intellectuals who had drifted away from Jewish life now returned. Lilienblum, for example, who earlier had emphasized the importance of religious reform, now described religious differences among Jews as a "relatively minor side issue," and joined the *Hibbat Zion* (Love of Zion) movement which had sprung up after the pogroms.

The outstanding convert to Zionism at this time was the physician Leon Pinsker (1821-1891), often called the father of the Jewish national movement. In his pamphlet *Auto-Emancipation*, published in September 1882, Pinsker laid the theoretical basis for political Zionism and devised a program which anticipated many of Herzl's ideas.[4]

Pinsker was born in a small town in Poland, the son of a well-known Jewish scholar who had published a comprehensive work on Karaism and its literature. Until the pogroms of 1881, Pinsker was a member of the liberal intelligentsia who advocated enlightenment of the Jews through a study of the Russian language and culture. When the Society for Enlightenment of the Jews was founded in 1863, he took a prominent part, urging at its meetings the translation of the Bible and the prayer book into Russian.

The pogroms, however, convinced him that emancipation had failed and that there was need for a new solution to the Jewish problem. Embracing the idea of Jewish nationalism with prophetic fervor, Pinsker travelled through Central and Western Europe and attempted to convince Western Jewish leaders that the return to Palestine was the only way to insure security for the Jew. To his great disappointment his ideas met with a very cool reception. Adolph Jellinek, Chief Rabbi of Vienna, a close friend of his father, insisted that Pinsker was exaggerating the importance of anti-Semitism and suggested he must be ill to put forward such ideas. In London, however, Arthur Cohen, a Jewish member of Parliament, was sympathetic and urged him to put his ideas on paper. On his return, Pinsker wrote a small thirty-six page brochure entitled *Auto-Emancipation*, undoubtably one of the great Jewish documents of modern times.

The pamphlet was a call to Jews not to rely on civil emancipation but to rise and liberate themselves. The Jewish problem, as Pinsker saw it, lay in the fact that Jews formed a distinctive, unassimilable element in the midst of the nations among whom they lived. Everywhere they were regarded as aliens, a "ghostlike apparition of a people without unity or organization, without land or other bond of union." Hatred of the Jews ("Judeophobia") is a hereditary incurable disease, he wrote, a "psychic aberration," which after twenty centuries is so deep-rooted that it cannot be eliminated by polemics or rational arguments. What was needed was to transform Jews into an independent nation living a normal life like other peoples on its own soil. This would require the purchase of a carefully chosen tract of land, uniform and continuous in extent, in North America or in Asiatic Turkey, upon which in the course of time several million Jews could settle. Neither Pinsker nor Herzl after him were at the outset committed to Palestine as the Jewish homeland, though Pinsker wrote wistfully: "Perhaps the Holy Land will again be ours. If so, all the better."

His appeal, however, did not have the effect for which he hoped. Western Jewish leaders were indignant because he lacked faith in the ultimate victory of humanity over prejudice; and Orthodox Jewry in Russia condemned him for his indifference to religion.

It was only among the recently organized *Hibbat Zion* groups, whose goal was the establishment of colonies in Palestine, that he found encouragement. The "national resoluteness" he called for in his pamphlet could only be found, he thought, among them.

These circles sprang up soon after the pogroms, particularly among middle-class intellectuals and students at the universities. They began to engage in fund-raising activities, organized glee clubs, conducted Hebrew courses, and prepared *halutzim* for settlement in Palestine. For several years they met in secret at the risk of arrest, since Zionist activities were illegal in Russia. The movement soon spread to other countries, developing considerable strength in Rumania, where thirty-two societies existed before the end of 1882. Under the inspiration of Smolenskin several groups were formed in Vienna by students from Eastern Europe, the most famous of which was *Kadimah*, meaning "forward and eastward." In 1885 Nathan Birnbaum founded the journal *Selbst Emancipation*, which became the rallying point in Central Europe for all interested in the idea of a Jewish renaissance and resettlement of Palestine. It was Birnbaum who first used the word "Zionism" in May 1890, to emphasize the Palestine tendency of the *Hibbat Zion* movement in contrast to the efforts to settle Jews in other countries.[5]

In Berlin the national idea found enthusiastic support in the Russian Jewish student colony. Although some of these young people, forced by the *numerus clausus* to seek their education abroad, were rebels who tried to deny their cultural relationship with their people, the hostility of their German fellow students and the nationalist agitations they observed in various European countries heightened their national consciousness. Several members of these *Hibbat Zion* groups such as Chaim Weizmann, Shemaryahu Levin, Leo Motzkin, and Nahman Syrkin were later to become distinguished leaders of world Zionism.[6]

In England and Ireland there were several branches under the leadership of the picturesque and influential Colonel Albert Goldsmid (1846-1904). Though brought up as a Christian, Goldsmid openly accepted Judaism at the age of twenty-four. After a trip to Palestine in 1882 he suggested the formation of an organization among the Jews of Western Europe to insure the security of the colonies in Palestine. The English *Hovevei Zion* bore the stamp of Colonel Goldsmid's military background in their organization and outlook.[7]

In the United States also societies were established as early as 1882 and supported not only by immigrants from Russia but by outstanding rabbis such as Pereira Mendes and Aaron Wise and by Professor Richard Gottheil.

In 1884 an international conference on *hovevei Zion* societies —the first pro-Palestine gathering in modern Jewish history—took place in Kattowitz, Upper Silesia, then a part of Russia. Although the aim of the organization was much more limited than his own national political ideas, Pinsker agreed to serve as president, while Lilienblum was elected secretary. Rabbi Samuel Mohilever (1824-1898) of Bialystok, who had formed the first group of *Hibbat Zion* in Warsaw, was chosen honorary president by the thirty-four delegates present. He undertook to win support for the new movement among the Orthodox, urging cooperation with unobservant Jews on the basis that all who came to rescue Jews should be received gladly and with love.[8]

During the fifteen years preceding the advent of Herzl, *Hovevei Zion* gave the impetus to the migration of between twenty and thirty thousand Jews to Palestine. Most of this first wave or *Aliyah*, however, flocked to the cities of Jerusalem, Jaffa, Haifa, and Hebron. Like the thirty thousand Jews already in the land, many of them became dependent on the system of charity known as *Halukkah*.

Early in 1882 one small group of Russianized students from the University of Kharkov, however, stirred by the pogroms, renounced their careers and decided to emigrate to Palestine and establish there model colonies built on cooperative principles. They were known as *Bilu*, from the initial letters of their motto which was taken from the book of Isaiah *"Bet Yaakov lekhu ve-nelkhah,"* "O house of Jacob, come and let us go." Over five hundred young people in various cities joined the *Bilu* movement, and negotiations got underway with influential leaders abroad for financial help. Unfortunately this help did not materialize, and only twenty—nineteen young men and one girl—all completely untrained for agricultural labor—actually succeeded after many unpleasant adventures in reaching Palestine in August, 1882. They suffered hunger and neglect and had to hire themselves out as farm hands. Before long six of the group became disheartened and returned to Russia. Four left the soil and went into the cities, but the others stuck it out. They grew to thirty, and after two years of hardship found a patron who helped them acquire a parcel of land on the coast between Jaffa and Gaza, where the first attempt at a Jewish cooperative colony was founded at Gederah.[9]

For the most part the members of the First *Aliyah*, unlike the *Bilu*, were middle class in outlook and less idealistic than the student group. They laid the foundations for the colonies of Petah Tikvah (which had been temporarily established a few years previously by Jews from Jerusalem), Rishon Le-Zion, southeast of Jaffa, Zikhron Yaakov in Samaria and Rosh Pinnah east of Safed. Conditions were hard, the settlers inexperienced in farming, and raids by marauding neighbors caused much suffering to the first settlers. In spite of sacrifices and toil, it was only through the assistance of Baron Edmond de Rothschild of Paris that the colonies were put on a stable foundation. He reorganized the *Hovevei Zion* colonies, converted them into grape-growing settlements, and established at Rishon Le-Zion the famous wine cellars bearing his name. During the next half century Rothschild expended over fifty million dollars in behalf of the colonies. Unfortunately, however, though instinctively sympathetic with the efforts in Palestine, he relied on administrators whose autocratic methods and lack of sympathy for the larger goals of the movement gave rise to resentments and dissension.

In spite of Baron Rothschild's help the situation of the early colonies remained precarious. They were constantly at the mercy of the whims of the Turkish government and the chicanery of Turkish officials. Most of the settlements were based upon wine making, and when the harvests were bad or the markets failed, the settlers required further relief.

The *Hibbat Zion* movement, though it was legalized in 1890 under the name of the "Society for Support of Jewish Agriculturists and Artisans in Palestine and Syria," was unable to be of much help. The wealthy Jews were opposed to the movement and it was difficult to arouse the masses from their torpidity. It proved impossible to raise funds of any significant size. The methods of *Hovevei Zion* were slow and haphazard, its organization too small and unrepresentative to undertake major projects. Progress seemed to depend on the benevolence of a single philanthropist rather than on the contributions of the Jewish people as a whole. Clearly, conditions demanded some new approach.

The thinker who set forth the clearest criticisms and who presented the boldest program for such a revitalization was Asher Ginzberg (1856-1927), better known by his pen name of Ahad Ha-am.[10] In a series of penetrating essays, many of which have become classics of modern Jewish thought, he analyzed the crisis confronting the *Hibbat Zion* movement and tried to furnish a rationale for those interested in the national revival.

Asher Ginzberg was born in the small town of Skivira in "one of the darkest corners of the *Hasidic* district in the Russian Ukraine." He spent his twelfth to thirtieth years without benefit of companionship or continuing cultural contacts in a small village where his father managed the estate of a large landowner. In the virtual isolation of the village he nevertheless acquired through self-study a deep knowledge of both Jewish tradition and secular philosophy and literature. Breaking with the *Hasidism* of his father at an early age, he became for a time a follower of *Haskalah*. On a trip to Warsaw, however, he met some of the leaders of the *Haskalah* movement and became disillusioned with their negative approach to Judaism. Gradually he arrived at the philosophy of cultural or spiritual Zionism with which his name is associated. Moving to Odessa in 1886, Asher Ginzberg joined with Pinsker, Lilienblum and the other Jewish leaders of *Hibbat Zion* in working for the resettlement of Palestine. In his first essay, written in 1889, *This Is Not the Way*, Asher Ginzberg presented his central idea that Palestine was not a solution for the economic needs of the individual Jew nor an answer to the growing anti-Semitism of the age, but was rather to be a "spiritual center" which would overcome the modern "plight of Judaism." The cause of the crisis in. the *Hibbat Zion* movement lay not with the *Halukkah* system, which doled out charity to many of the settlers, or with Baron Rothschild's agents and their autocratic methods of administering the colonies, but rather with its narrow appeal to economic interest rather than to the national sentiments of the group. The task of *Hibbat Zion* was to work toward "the revival of the spirit," to enlarge the love of the collective life and to glorify the desire for its success." Ahad Ha-am was opposed to Lilienblum's "practical Zionism," which regarded every Jew and every goat added to the land as an achievement. More important to him than the quantitative growth of the colonies was the slow and careful preparation of a generation for national redemption.

This essay and those that followed created a storm in *Hovevei Zion* circles as did his realistic and candid reports on conditions in the colonies after his visits to Palestine in 1891 and 1893. Gradually Ahad Ha-am became the teacher of his generation. Solomon Schechter described him as "one of the finest intellects and most original thinkers." Bialik looked to him as his mentor, and Chaim Weizmann pays tribute to him again and again in his autobiography.

For a time Ahad Ha-am stood at the head of the *Bene Mosheh* society which had been organized to implement his ideas. It established the great publishing house Ahiaseph as well as the first modern Hebrew school in Palestine, and it helped found the colony of Rehovot. Most important of all, it contributed a number of gifted leaders and teachers to the Zionist movement. But Asher Ginzberg did not have the temperament to serve as the leader who could revitalize the nationalistic movement. After eight years, the organization disbanded, and Ahad Ha-am was afterwards to describe it as "an experiment that did not succeed."

Thus, there was need in the mid-1890's for a leader as well as a thinker, one concerned with political as well as cultural problems, if Jewish nationalism was to become more than a philanthropic enterprise. It was Theodor Herzl who arose to meet this need, in a bold and dramatic fashion. He and, later, Weizmann, Brandeis, and Henrietta Szold became the builders who helped bring the dream of a national rebirth into reality.

8 . *Theodor Herzl*
[1860–1904]

MARVIN LOWENTHAL

M o r e than any other one man, Theodor Herzl changed the course of modern Jewish history. The Jews, he proclaimed in a clear, measured voice that caught the world's ear, were a people and not a sect or a race, and they were one people and not a collection of miscellaneous communities. It followed—so he insisted—that the nations of the world and the Jews themselves must be brought to act in the light of this reality. By speech and deed Herzl elevated a local sore spot, a domestic misery usually met by stopgap measures, into a challenging international issue. He removed the Jewish problem from the waiting rooms of philanthropists and laid it before the chancelleries of European statesmanship. He turned a religious, racial, or parochial set of troubles into a single broad political question to be settled on the highest level of diplomatic negotiation.

Thus Herzl became, in Israel Zangwill's phrase, "the first Jewish statesman since the destruction of Jerusalem." He represented and presented not the cause of the Russian Jews, Galician Jews, or any other segment of Jewry, but the cause of the Jewish people as a whole—a people with a common past and the aspiration toward a common future. He put Zionism, the program of the indivisible people, on the map; and in creating the Zionist organization, he gave the Jewish people an address.

Herzl was a remarkable sort of statesman. To begin with, he was to all intents a man of letters: a journalist, playwright, feuilletonist, and short story writer. He aspired to become a novelist. Then in 1895, while serving as Paris correspondent of the Vienna *Neue Freie Presse*, he conceived the plan of a Jewish state not merely as the reaffirmation of a traditional ideal and not only as the solution to a world-vexing problem, but as something to be created forthwith through the collaboration of the leading European powers. Virtually overnight he found that his idea had catapulted him into statesmanship on an international scale.

After his premature death, Herzl's dream of a Jewish state eventually came true, thanks to the path he cleared, the implements he fashioned, the procedure he developed, and the will he infused into his people. "He who wills something great," Herzl once wrote in perhaps unconscious echo of Montaigne, "is in my eyes a great man—not he who achieves it. For in achievement luck plays a part."

The present State of Israel owes its origin to Herzl—at least in the sense that he was the catalyst who precipitated the modern forces that brought it to birth. Since Moses no single man, no Washington or Bismarck, has been in equal degree the father of a country. Theodor Herzl was in the noblest sense a man who willed something great.

From Budapest to Vienna

Theodor Herzl was born May 2, 1860, in Budapest, where he was reared during an era when things went well with the Hungarian Jews. During his boyhood the essential Jewish customs were observed in the Herzl household, the festivals were celebrated in the traditional manner, particularly Passover and *Hanukkah,* and little Theodor accompanied his father to the Tabakgasse synagogue every Friday evening and Sabbath morning. From the age of six to ten he attended the local Jewish community school—there were no normal public schools—and the reports show that in "Religion" and "Hebrew Subjects" his marks ranged from good to excellent. At eight his father enrolled him as a contributing member of the Chevra Kadishah,* and at thirteen he was confirmed in accordance with time-

---

* The society found in most Jewish communities which cares for the sick and buries the dead. It was customary for wealthier members of a community to enroll their male children, as contributing members, at an early age.

honored usage, learning enough Hebrew, even if by rote, to read the appropriate "portion" of the Torah and recite the blessings. Later in life, when entering upon a critical new venture, he never failed to ask for the parental blessing—a Biblical observance that weathered Johann Strauss' Vienna. The home ceremonies and regular synagogue attendance, with their inevitable exposure to something of the Hebrew language and Jewish spirit, were bound to leave on a sensitive nature impressions which the outer world would blanket but never could efface.

Then there was Grandfather Herzl. He lived a conscientiously Orthodox life in the old Orthodox community of Semlin (now in Yugoslavia); his standing and piety, as well as the requisite art, were such that it fell upon him to blow the *shofar* on New Year's and chant the *Kol Nidre* prayer on the Day of Atonement; he paid an annual visit to Budapest, where he died when Theodor was past nineteen, and held a tender place in the affection of his grandson. He, too, left an impression. When, nearly twenty years afterwards, Herzl remarked a bearded, fur-capped figure in Sofia, he did not comment as a Westerner might on his exotic looks. He took him to be something familiar: "He resembled," Herzl's diaries record, "my grandfather Simon Herzl." Similarly, when he visited the main Paris synagogue for the first time, in 1895, he found the services "once again" solemn and moving. "Much," he noted, "reminded me of my youth and the Tabakgasse synagogue in Pest."

But, on the whole, there was little in his training, interests, or outward circumstances to inspire him with any particular devotion to things Jewish beyond a deep sense of loyalty grounded in self-respect. His immediate family, Central European in origin with a Sephardic strain on his father's side, was sufficiently well-to-do and world-minded to supply him with a German environment, education, and cultural outlook. But, while there was small evidence of any significant Jewish interest, he soon began to evince a pronounced taste for magnificent scheming. At ten, when most boys were content to dream of becoming the engineer of an express train, he planned to be a second De Lesseps and hew out the Panama Canal. He scribbled stories, plays, and verse at an early age, but, later, on the practical advice of his elders, he took up the study of law. His family moved to Vienna when he was eighteen, became decently rich, and lived as part of the "up-town" Jewish community in the Währing quarter.

The Writer in the Making

Soon after Herzl obtained his law degree in 1884, he gave up the law for his earlier love: literature and the theater. He traveled and wrote. By the time he was thirty he had seen something of Germany, Switzerland, France, the Lowlands, England, and Italy, and had on his own reckoning turned out seventeen plays, besides inumerable articles, travel sketches, and short stories.

Herzl's first play to be produced, a one-act drama called *Tabarin*, enjoyed its premiere at the hands of a German troupe in the Star Theater, Broadway and 13th Street, New York, on November 23, 1885. Five other plays saw the boards in Austria, Bohemia, and Germany, with varying success. Vienna and Berlin newspapers opened their columns to his colorful, not very substantial, but scrupulously composed articles, and in 1887, the *Wiener Allgemeine Zeitung* appointed Herzl, for a spell, its literary editor; he had "arrived" as a journalist. He published two volumes of his essays and sketches, the pick of his feuilletons —*Neues von der Venus* (1887) and *Das Buch der Narrheit* (1888)—and earned himself critical esteem if little else. He had become a master of that fragile and evanescent form of journalism, the feuilleton, especially beloved on the continent. He was not yet, to be sure, a young Heine or Schnitzler, and fate determined that he should never become one.

In 1889, confident of his career as a playwright and man of letters, though still impatient at its slow progress—he was already twenty-nine!—he married a bright, golden-haired, blue-eyed young woman, Julie Naschauer, whose family had much the same background as his own, but more wealth. Three children came in rapid succession, two girls and a boy: Pauline, Hans, Margarete.

Almost from the start, however, the marriage ran into heavy seas. Temperamentally, the young couple were not in accord. Julie loved a gay social life, she wanted her husband to succeed and she wanted to enjoy his success, but she was apparently unable to help him earn it by self-effacing sympathy and devotion; and the efforts she made were rendered harder by a mother-in-law problem. Herzl's mother was intelligent and warm-hearted, but, like Herzl's father, she doted on her son jealously and obsessively—the more so in that her only other child, Pauline, a year older than Theodor, had died before reaching twenty. Herzl, in turn, doted on his parents, partly also because he was led to fill the role of son and daughter. When the Zionist cause, along with journalistic obligations, came to monopolize Herzl's life, the estrangement with his wife widened; Julie had no emotional identification with the destiny of the Jews, and she looked on Zion, rightly enough, in her eyes, as a husband-snatcher and home-breaker. Only the children, to whom they were both passionately devoted, held them together.

Paris Correspondent

In August of 1891 Herzl set out on a conjugal vacation—an experimental separation from his wife and their troubled domestic existence. He wandered for two months in the Pyrenees, recovering his composure and power of decision, and writing travel sketches of more than customary substance. One of them, describing the village of Luz, "a fine abode for convalescents of all sorts," elicited an invitation from the *Neue Freie Presse* to become its Paris correspondent. This leading Vienna newspaper was one of Europe's most influential liberal organs, and Paris was the prize post for all European journalists. Naturally, Herzl accepted the position—at twelve hundred francs a month, plus expenses and one hundred francs per feuilleton—and, without returning home, settled in the French capital toward the end of October. His wife and children joined him there the following February.

Paris put an end to Herzl's career as an independent man of letters, at liberty to indulge his personal inclinations, and to a free lance's search for a public. He apprenticed himself to the affairs of the world as a responsible newspaperman. He learned politics and politicians at close range in the Chamber of Deputies; he studied statesmen and statecraft at the Quai d'Orsay; he milled about in the election campaigns in town and village; he reported firsthand the investigations, trials, and mad parliamentary debates attendant upon the Panama fiasco. He wrote up anarchist bombings, cabinet rumpuses, and the stabbing of President Sadi-Carnot. Notebook in hand, he "stared at the phenomenon of the crowd," as he later said, "without for a long time understanding it"—not only election crowds, but unemployment riots, anti-Italian riots, and pro-Russian demonstrations (the latter at Toulon, where he suffered a severe attack of malaria and probably began the history of his heart ailment). He turned out dramatic and literary criticism as well as feuilletons on the many sides of life that do not make spot news. Applying his dramatist's talent to the stage of reality, he fascinated his readers and won a wide reputation by writing politics in terms of personalities and by going behind both to the social and economic forces of which they were lime-lighted protagonists. At the end of his Paris experience he incorporated the best of these human yet broadly analytical articles in a volume entitled *Das Palais Bourbon* (1895).

Herzl's journalism brought him inevitably into frequent contact with newsworthy events and experiences related to anti-Semitism. A libel suit against the anti-Semitic Drumont (in 1892), which Herzl later characterized as a prologue to the Panama affair, ended with Drumont crying out before the court, "Down with the German Jews! France for Frenchmen!" and his adherents shouting, without such nice distinction, "Down with the Jews!" The Panama scandals, though they involved virtually no Jews, provoked the introduction of a bill to disbar all Jews from holding public office and won for it 160 votes in the Chamber of Deputies. A series of duels between anti-Semites and Jews who defended the honor of their people reached a climax when a French-Jewish army captain was mortally stabbed. Disorders broke out during the funeral procession, in which fifty thousand sympathizers followed the hearse. Stock market scandals and other incidents brought a constant recurrence of the Jewish theme. Dramas dealt with it frankly, such as Dumas' *La Femme de Claude* and Lavedan's *Prince Aurec*, and led Herzl, in his reviews, to further cogitations on what it was all about.

The Dreyfus Affair

An army captain, Alfred Dreyfus, was arrested October 15, 1894, on the charge of high treason. His military trial, behind closed doors, took place in December, and he was pronounced guilty and sentenced for life to a penal colony in French Guiana; and on January 5, 1895 he was publicly degraded on the parade ground of the Ecole Militaire. Herzl heard as much of the preliminaries to the court-martial as a reporter could, he witnessed the public degradation, and his ears rang with the howl of the mob, "Death to the traitor!"—or, as he remembered it three years later, "Death to the Jews!" He telegraphed long dispatches on the events when they occurred, but no word about Dreyfus appears in the account of how he came to the Zionist idea which he confided to his diary but a few months afterwards.

In truth, there was no Dreyfus Affair to impress him in 1895; there was only the arrest and condemnation of an officer who chanced to be a Jew. It was not until 1896, well after *The Jewish State* had been written, that evidence of foul play began to come to light and the anti-Semitic implications unfold. Even though Herzl expressly stated in 1899 that the Dreyfus case had made him a Zionist, it was at best an appropriate myth, a dramatic foreshortening of the facts.

In other terms, the Dreyfus Affair, which did not yet exist, fairly epitomized the Jewish aspects of Herzl's experiences in Paris and condensed into one salient example his views on anti-Semitism and the Jewish future. If such things could happen, to use his words, "in republican, modern, civilized France, a century after the Declaration of Human Rights," the Jews as a whole had better look to themselves for salvation in a land of their own making.

The Jewish State

An old idea of writing a novel on the Jewish problem which Herzl had long had in mind now came to new life. So he records in the very opening of his *Diary:*

I have been pounding away for some time at a work of tremendous magnitude. I don't know even now if I will be able to carry it through. It bears the aspects of a mighty dream. For days and weeks it has saturated me to the limits of my consciousness; it goes with me everywhere, hovers behind my ordinary talk, peers at me over the shoulders of my funny little journalistic work, overwhelms and intoxicates me.

What will come of it is still too early to say. However, I have had experience enough to tell me that even as a dream it is remarkable and should be written down—if not as a memorial for mankind, then for my own pleasure and meditation in years to come. Or perhaps as something between these two possibilities —that is, as something for literature. If no action comes out of this romancing, a romance at least will come out of this activity. Title: The Promised Land.

Herzl also embarked at this time on an attempt to win over Baron Maurice de Hirsch, who was, along with the Rothschilds, one of the great multi-millionaires of the nineteenth century, to a constructive, daring plan for founding a Jewish state. He made a series of notes for his conference with Hirsch, but the latter, without hearing him through, summarily rejected the idea. Both men as good as lost their tempers. "Perhaps," Herzl later confessed, "I did not know the right way of handling him."

After that bad half-hour with Baron de Hirsch, Herzl "plunged" to his desk and indulged in a frenzy of note-making. Day in and day out, for weeks, he committed to slips of paper a torrent of ideas, which were inserted a year later into his diary. In all, these notes run to some fifty thousand words— about two hundred pages in the German edition. They were earmarked partly for an "Address" (itself twenty thousand words) which he intended to read before the Rothschilds assembled in family council; partly for a memorandum to be laid before two competent advisors—Chief Rabbi Gudemann of Vienna, and an experienced businessman—both of whom were to tell him how to gather the Rothschilds together; and partly for the eventual book, whether a treatise or novel he was not sure, if, all else failing, the plan had to be made public. In the end, pruned, tamed, and organized, the notes became *The Jewish State*, a booklet which heralded a turning point in modern Jewish history.

It is significant that, even in the first flush of Herzl's imagination, the details of the new society he envisioned, however extravagant (as he admits), were not utopian. He proposed nothing unknown, untoward, or impossible. He merely drafted a perfected *fin de siècle* commonwealth—1895 model. It was a liberal-spirited Viennese version of a decent, righteous order of things, with time out for light opera and pretty women in stylish gowns. Everything in it was plausible, technically feasible, and consonant with the average run of human nature. "Observe," he wrote for his imaginary audience, but with an eye to reassuring himself, "I do not make up fantasies; I deal entirely with real factors—which you can check up for yourselves; the fantasy lies only in the combination."

It is also significant to observe the comparatively minor role played by anti-Semitism in the original stream of notes and in the mood that dictated them. The psychological distress of Western Jews, which Herzl knew firsthand, and the physical misery of the East European Jews, which was common knowledge, haunt the background. Indeed, the *Elend*—the suffering and plight—of Jewry was to supply in Herzl's view, as alas it did in eventual fact, the motive power which would turn the vision into reality. But the dominant mood, a mood Herzl never abandoned, was positive and creative, an exhilaration in planning a new world where men shall lead finer and truer lives. It was akin to the mood of an Amos or an Isaiah. The "burden of the Lord" had fallen on Herzl to announce not so much the curses as the blessings of Jewish destiny.

The restoration of Zion was an age-old religious theme integral to Judaism; it had its source and divine sanction in the Hebrew prophets—beginning with Moses, who led his people from bondage to freedom. In the mid-nineteenth century a German Jew, Moses Hess, gave the ideal a contemporary nationalistic expression; and while he was a voice crying in the wilderness he did not long remain the only voice. In 1882, Leon Pinsker, a Russian Jew, not only restated the ideal but set forth the instruments for its realization in substantially the same terms that Herzl, who knew nothing of Pinsker's brochure called *Auto-Emancipation*, employed over a decade later. Throughout the eighties and early nineties Zionist essays and tracts abounded. The major novelty and force of Herzl's pamphlet lay not in its contents but in its tone—and, as will be seen, in the character of its author.

Pinsker, and many like him, wrote primarily as a Jew addressing himself to other Jews on a subject of intramural concern. Herzl, in contrast, wrote as a Jew who was a man of the world, an experienced political observer, a ranking journalist with international horizons; and his *Jewish State* was directed as much to the Bismarcks and Rothschilds as to the common reader. It had epigrams and eloquence, but in tenor it was the cool exposition of a trained publicist. Bismarck and Rothschild dismissed it, while Bülow and Plehve did not; neither of these reactions mattered so much as the fact that the common reader, who included editors, university men, and other makers of public opinion, heard about Zionism for the first time in language he was accustomed to understand.

But Herzl's *Jewish State* would have remained one more Zionist tract, even if better known than its predecessors, had he been a man content with words. He was, in fact, over and beyond his literary bent, intrinsically a man of action, and action on a grand scale; he was the boy, grown up, who had wanted to build the Panama Canal. He conceived of the Jewish state not as a subject for discourse, but as something to be acted upon by others and first of all by himself. When the idea first coalesced in his mind, he leaped beyond the thought of a novel or a pamphlet, and his almost instantaneous reaction was to exclaim to himself: "What correspondence, meetings, activities I shall have to encompass—what disappointments if I fail, what grim struggles if I succeed!"

No one better foresaw the unceasingly strenuous life that was to be his than Herzl himself. In a compartment of the Orient Express, on the way to lay his scheme before the Grand Duke of Baden—the first of a long series of princes, sultans, emperors, and influential statesmen he was to entreat on behalf of the projected Jewish state, he jotted in his ever-ready diary: "If I had trouble enough keeping a record of things when the Jewish matter began, what will it be like in the future as we pass from the dream into the reality! For it may be expected that every day now will bring its store of interesting experiences, even if I should never get so far as to found the State."

That was in April 1896, and a few weeks later Herzl was on his way to Constantinople, hoping to win over Sultan Abdul Hamid, the suzerain of Palestine. He was simultaneously occupied with putting a dozen irons into as many fires. Max Nordau, Baron Rothschild, newly-made English connections, the old-fashioned "Lovers of Zion" societies with their emphasis on slow, piecemeal settlement in the Holy Land and their incomprehension of political action, the insurgent Zionistic-minded youth champing at the bit, the Armenians in England, the *Hasidim* in Galicia, Prime Minister Salisbury, Papal Nuncio Agliardi, all received attention in the hope of using them for the acquisition of Palestine. These multiple activities were motivated by a single-minded goal: "to concentrate all our strength upon an internationally sanctioned acquisition of Palestine. To achieve this, we require diplomatic negotiations, which I have already begun, and propaganda on the largest scale."

Much of Herzl's efforts went into trying to win over the great bankers of France and England. But when the Rothschilds, Montagues, and their like turned a cold or lukewarm shoulder on anything that smacked of a political recognition of the Jewish people, he resolved to appeal directly to the masses and, what was more original, organize them for political action. Nothing quite like this had ever been attempted among the Jews since ancient times.

Swaying the Multitude

The instrument for political and financial action, as Herzl conceived it, was to be a world-wide Zionist organization, to be inaugurated by a congress—itself a novel and untried experiment in Jewish life. It was a sound idea, but the road from idea to reality—to the Congress finally convened at Basel—was long, complicated, and arduous. Almost anyone but Herzl, a man with a peculiar talent for not giving up, would have despaired.

During the year and more of preparatory labor, Herzl continued his efforts in a score of complementary directions. He interested Ferdinand of Bulgaria in trying to interest the Czar. He sent medical aid to the Turks in their war against the Greeks. He sounded out King Milan of Serbia and sought to gain the ear of Cardinal Rampolla and the Pope. He fought a continuous round of battles with his employers at the *Neue Freie Presse*. The latter were particularly furious when he founded the Zionist weekly, *Die Welt*, and it did not soothe them to learn that a number of leading *Welt* writers were members of their own staff.

Herzl was attacked on all sides, and he was often despondent: "This business takes a strong stomach," he wrote. A little later, when he discovered that he was the victim of a slander campaign conducted by prosperous Jews, he confessed that he was "beginning to have the right to become the world's worst anti-Semite. I often think of Levysohn's prediction: 'Those whom you want to help will start by nailing you rather painfully to the cross.' " And yet the movement continued to gather momentum. In January, 1897, he wrote: "I receive visitors from every corner of the world. The road from Palestine to Paris is beginning to pass through my door. In these past few weeks there were some interesting figures . . . I gave instructions to each of them . . . unless I am mistaken, Zionism is gradually winning the esteem of ordinary men in all sorts of countries. People are beginning to take us seriously."

First Zionist Congress

The First Zionist Congress met at Basel, August 29-31, 1897. It convened in the Stadt Casino, a concert and dance hall on the Steinenberg, adjacent to the Historical Museum. Besides a throng of spectators, the sessions were attended by 197 "delegates" from fifteen countries: Russia, Germany, Austria-Hungary, Rumania, Bulgaria, Holland, Belgium, France, Switzerland, Sweden, England, the United States, Algeria, and Palestine. They represented old Lovers of Zion societies, newly-formed political Zionist groups, and in some cases only themselves; they came from every stratum of society and embodied every shade of contemporary thought: Orthodox, liberal, atheist, culturalist, nationalist, anarchist, socialist, and capitalist minded Jews. "This was not a mere gathering of practical men," Jacob de Haas reported at the time, "nor yet a mere assembly of dreamers; the inward note was that of a gathering of brothers meeting after the long Diaspora."

Congratulatory greetings and endorsements with approximately six thousand signatures of individuals or organizations, as well as 550 telegrams, poured into the Congress office on Freie Strasse. Petitions, which had been circulated at Herzl's suggestion, brought fifty thousand signatures from Rumania alone, and ten thousand from Galicia; the signers declared their readiness to emigrate, and besought the Congress to create the necessary political and economic conditions for a return to Zion.

Almost the first words of Herzl's opening address set forth the purpose of the assembly: "We want to lay the foundation stone of the house which is to shelter the Jewish nation." It received a precise formulation in the Basel Program (largely drafted by Nordau), which became the official platform of the Zionist movement: "Zionism seeks to obtain for the Jewish people a publicly recognized, legally secured homeland in Palestine." Another memorable phrase from Herzl's opening address —"Zionism is a return to the Jewish fold even before it is a return to the Jewish land"—reappeared in the official platform under more abstract guise as one of the methods by which Zionism was to achieve its aim, that is, by "strengthening the Jewish national sentiment and national consciousness."

In addition to formulating its program, the Congress drafted the main lines of a constitution for the newly-born World Zionist Organization, and recommended the creation of a bank and a national fund, the latter specifically for the purchase of land in Palestine.

An exalted mood pervaded the Congress and rendered its sessions an unforgettable experience. One memorable feature was the impression Herzl made upon the delegates and spectators—who saw for the first time a figure that was already becoming a legend.

"A great eagle had suddenly spread its wings and threshed the air about him," recalled Joseph Klausner, the eminent historian who attended the Congress while a university student. In Martin Buber's memory Herzl had "a countenance lit with the glance of the Messiah." Or more soberly, Mordecai Braude recalls Herzl mounting to the dais at the First Congress: "Suddenly a compelling force had arisen, and he dominated us with his extraordinary personality, with his gestures, manner of speech, his ardor and vision."

"A majestic Oriental figure," observed Israel Zangwill, who had come prepared to scoff and remained to pray and cheer,

> not so tall as it appears when he draws himself up and stands dominating the assembly with eyes that brood and glow—you would say one of the Assyrian kings, whose sculptured heads adorn our museums, the very profile of Tiglath Pileser . . . In a congress of impassioned rhetoricians he remains serene, moderate; his voice is for the most part subdued; in its most emotional abandonment there is a dry undertone, almost harsh . . . And yet beneath all this statesman-like prose, touched with the special dryness of a jurist, lurk the romance of the poet and the purposeful vagueness of the modern evolutionist; the fantasy of the Hungarian, the dramatic self-consciousness of the literary artist, the heart of the Jew.

As for Herzl himself, he too found that "the Congress was magnificent." While he confessed, "I felt as though I were being obliged to play thirty-two games of chess simultaneously," he was sure of the ultimate outcome: "If I were to sum up the Congress in a word—which I shall take care not to publish—it would be this: At Basel I founded the Jewish State. If I said this out loud today I would be greeted by universal laughter. In five years perhaps, and certainly in fifty years, everyone will perceive it." He wrote these words in his diary on September 3—almost fifty years to the month before the 1947 decision of the United Nations to sanction the State of Israel.

Building the Zionist Organization

Meanwhile the Zionist revolution—action and not pamphlets, a political and not a philanthropic goal—was working powerfully upon the popular Jewish imagination. The Congress and a world organization, both the creatures of Herzl's mind and boundless energy, were conceived as practical instruments for creating a Jewish state, but their moral effects were more immediate. In the nature of things, only a small minority of Jews formally joined the organization; but a large, perhaps a vast majority thrilled to Herzl's championship of the solidarity and mutual responsibility of all Jews. Through the spirit of these Zionist institutions he rallied and transformed them from a miscellany of individuals and communities into a cohesive, articulate community. Herzl restored their self-confidence and self-respect. He gave them, as he had told Baron de Hirsch he would do, a flag—"and with a flag you can lead people where you will, even into the Promised Land."

The pressing need, naturally, was for funds—to inspire confidence among government circles, to win concessions from Turkey, and, when won, to lay the foundations for large-scale settlement. But funds were hard to come by; as an old banker friend told Herzl, "men only lend money to the rich." At a preliminary conference in Vienna, which laid plans for the Second Congress, Herzl urged that a sales campaign for the contemplated Zionist bank be carried straight to the people: "As it is, we are like the soldiers of the French Revolution who had to take to the field without shoes or stockings."

The Second Zionist Congress was held again at Basel, on August 28-30, 1898. Herzl had no time, according to his diaries, for depicting moods—"everything was action." Among other decisions, the Congress established the bank Herzl had desired—the Jewish Colonial Trust—but left it mainly for him to turn a parliamentary resolution into a reality. On the diplomatic side, a message of greetings to the Sultan elicited a telegraphic acknowledgment, "which," Herzl confessed, "I never counted on." But meanwhile, more promising prospects were in the offing.

Interviews with the Kaiser

Immediately after the Congress sessions, Herzl went to the Lake Constance island of Mainau, where he had a long and fruitful talk with the old Grand Duke of Baden—"a truly magnificent conversation and on a high political plane." The Grand Duke, he learned, had submitted an "exhaustive account" of the Zionist movement to the German Kaiser, who had in turn "thereupon instructed Count Eulenberg to study the matter and report on it." The German government, moreover, had ascertained through its ambassador at Constantinople, that the Sultan viewed the Zionist cause "with favor." Since the Kaiser was to make his famous visit to Constantinople and the Holy Land in October—a visit inspired by political as well as pious motives—Herzl maneuvered successfully to get a rendezvous with him in both places.

On the occasion of his first audience with Wilhelm II, October 18, 1898, Herzl found that his attention wandered somewhat when the Kaiser launched upon the subject—"for I could not help noting the effect of my three years' work in making the obscure word 'Zionism' a *terme reçu* and one that fell naturally from the lips of the German emperor." When less than six years later, death cut short his pioneer negotiations in the foreign ministries and royal audience-chambers of Europe, Zionism had become not only a current expression in the world's forum but an item on the agenda of premiers and princes. Meanwhile, at the moment—and only for the moment—the Kaiser virtually gave his word to urge upon the Sultan a German protectorate for an autonomous Jewish territory in the Holy Land.

The Kaiser's journey to Palestine began as a religious pilgrimage, centering on the dedication of the German-built Church of the Redeemer in Jerusalem; but it turned into a political demonstration. It played a studied role in Germany's strategy to penetrate the Near East—via the proposed Berlin-Baghdad railroad and similar concessions. Herzl was therefore fairly justified, before the event, in believing the Grand Duke and Philip zu Eulenburg, the Kaiser's intimate friend, when they implied that a large Jewish settlement in Palestine under German protection was consonant with German interests and ambitions; and, after the event, that the Kaiser meant what he said.

In 1898 Palestine was a thinly inhabited land. Only eight per cent of its soil was cultivated; its total population probably did not reach five hundred thousand. It contained eighteen Jewish rural settlements, called "colonies," none of them over twenty years old, and only three or four large enough to warrant the name of village. Perhaps forty-five hundred Jews, all told, lived on the land. None of these settlements, moreover, had a legal basis for its existence; permission to reside in Palestine, buy land, or build was obtainable only through bribery or outwitting the laws. About forty-five thousand Jews lived in the cities, chiefly Jerusalem and Jaffa, and the majority of these urban Jews depended for a miserable existence on a world-wide collection of religious alms.

Of the settlements visited by Herzl, Rishon le-Zion (founded in 1882), like most of the others, owed its living and administration to Baron de Rothschild. Rehovot (founded in 1890) was one of the rare Jewish villages that maintained itself without patrons, supervisors, or subsidies. The Mikveh Israel agricultural school had been established in 1870 by the Alliance Israélite Universelle and was gradually training a generation of capable farmers.

As for the second interview with the Kaiser, at Jerusalem, Herzl came away dubious: "he said neither yes nor no." In the months following his return from Palestine, Herzl gradually came to realize that the Kaiser had bowed out of the picture.

The Unceasing Quest

Founding the land company as well as the bank, or Jewish Colonial Trust, Herzl suffered endless difficulties and postponements. Without the backing of capital, political concessions were impossible, and without political concessions, capital was unavailable. "Days of despondency," Herzl wrote on February 11. "The tempo of the movement is slowing down. The catchwords are wearing out. The ideas are becoming themes for declamation, and the declamation is losing its edge."

The Jewish Colonial Trust, though already established, could not begin operations until it had a paid-up capital of two hundred and fifty thousand pounds—which, in fact, it was not able to secure until 1901. Meanwhile, the condition of Russian Jews grew worse, and, in Rumania, a wave of persecution was driving thousands of Jews into a frantic, disorganized emigration. The morale of East European Jewry, together with the Zionist financial instrument which might bring relief, stood in desperate need of some hope or sign of a concession in Palestine, and spurred on Herzl's efforts to reach the Sultan. Several round-about approaches via Great Britain and Russia had so far led nowhere: Lord Salisbury, then Prime Minister of England, remained as inaccessible as the Czar. Germany was engaged upon a deal with Turkey in which Zionism apparently had no role. The Turkish minions of the Sultan, whom Herzl had enlisted at considerable expense, did nothing.

Herzl finally got to see the Sultan, in 1901, and concessions were offered him for the exploitation of mines, the establishment of a pro-government bank, and the creation of a land company for settling Jewish immigrants—but, as expressly stipulated, not in Palestine. He soon had convincing proof that the whole performance was staged in order to play him off against a French financial and political combine, headed by the French Minister of Finance—who also got nowhere, but not quite so fast as Herzl.

Meanwhile, Herzl had made fruitless efforts in Paris and London to secure financial backing for the concessions. For this as well as for political support, contacts were vainly sought with the Péreires, Rothschilds, Carnegie, Cecil Rhodes, Sir Thomas Lipton, Edward VII, President Theodore Roosevelt, and of course the Czar. Max Nordau and others of Herzl's most faithful colleagues deplored the recklessness and nebulous character of his ventures, and he was led to confide his own estimate of himself to the pages of his diary:

> When once the Jewish State exists, all of this will of course look trivial. Perhaps a juster historian will discover that it was still something after all for a Jewish journalist without means, during an era of the most abominable anti-Semitism and when the Jewish people had sunk into the depths, to have converted a rag into a flag, and a degraded multitude into a nation, which rallied, heads erect, around that flag.

The middle of 1902 opened new vistas and ventures. Alarmed by the influx of Jewish refugees from Russia and Rumania, with their presumed threat to the standard of living among English workers, the British government, of which the Prime Minister was Arthur James Balfour, appointed a royal commission to examine the question of alien immigration. A popular demand for restricted immigration was about to prevail over the tradition of free asylum which had been Great Britain's pride. Herzl's friends persuaded the Royal Commission to invite him to appear as an expert witness before the hearings—in spite of the strong opposition of Lord Rothschild, who looked upon Herzl as a demagogue and who had hitherto refused to see him or answer his letters.

Meanwhile, Herzl's novel, *Altneuland*, had appeared. Under the motto, "If you will it, it is no fable," the book depicted life in a flourishing Jewish state, in Palestine, twenty years hence. He sent copies to the Kaiser, Eulenburg, Bülow, Rothschild, and other important personages. What, in large, Herzl thought of the book may be seen in the note he wrote the Grand Duke of Baden when sending him a copy: "It is a story which, as it were, I am telling by the camp-fires to keep up the spirits of my poor people while they are on the march. To hold out is everything."

While in London for the purpose of testifying before the Royal Commission, Herzl managed to lunch with Lord Rothschild, and win from him flattering personal tributes, vague assurances, and little more. But he did better with the British government. Through other English friends, and to Rothschild's astonishment, he persuaded Joseph Chamberlain, the most talked-of as well as one of the most influential figures in the British cabinet, to support a large-scale Jewish settlement in the El Arish region, just south of Palestine. When nothing came of this—ostensibly because of the Egyptian government's refusal to supply water from the Nile—Chamberlain, the following year, procured from the British government an offer of a large area in Uganda, with an arrangement for local autonomous government which recognized the political existence of the Jewish people.

Russia and the "Uganda" Congress

That same year, 1903, a Russian atrocity horrified the world. The Kishinev massacre, during the opening days of Easter week, wreaked murder, pillage, and rape upon a defenseless and unresistant Jewish community while the police stood by with folded arms: this threw a ghastly light on the character of the Jewish problem and the need for a speedy, radical solution.

Herzl bent his efforts in every possible direction. He tried to weave "combinations"—with Portugal for territory in Mozambique, with Belgium for Congo lands, and with Italy for tracts in Tripoli. He reinvigorated his connections at Constantinople.

He also turned to Russia itself, the archenemy, for a number of compelling reasons. His long-cherished plan of persuading Russia to exert influence on Turkey seemed more timely and feasible than ever, now that the Czarist government stood on the defensive before the bar of world opinion. If Russia would do nothing to relax the persecution of Jews at home, it might conceivably be willing to appease the indignation of an outraged humanity by helping secure for them an asylum abroad —which meant Palestine. In addition, the Zionist movement in Russia was threatened with suppression, and his colleagues there sought his intercession.

After several futile efforts to establish contact with the Czar or other influential authorities, Herzl succeeded in obtaining an appointment for an audience with Vyacheslav Plehve, the Minister of the Interior, and therefore answerable for the Kishinev massacre and, by common report, the sponsor of it. Herzl chose to ignore the record of Plehve and Russia. He was not undertaking to act as an historian, a moralist, or an indignant tribune. As a statesman he considered it his duty to negotiate for a solution of the Jewish problem with anyone in whose hands a solution might lay. There must be, he felt, some answer to Kishinev.

"Alas, what I saw in Vilna!" Herzl kept repeating after his journey to Russia. The cry was not merely the reaction to a personal experience; it voiced a sense of the Russian tragedy which had gripped the whole Jewish people and aroused the concern of civilized men everywhere. It gave a precious though illusory value to the letter he bore from Plehve—with its assurance of Russian aid in securing Palestine—and which he was carrying to the forthcoming Zionist Congress (August 22-28).

The Russian tragedy also gave immediate and poignant urgency to a spacious offer on the part of Great Britain to create the Jewish state in Uganda—which turned out to be not Uganda at all, but a district east of the Mau Mau escarpment in what is now Kenya.

The British offer evoked debates and demonstrations which made the Sixth Congress memorable in Zionist history. At the outset, Herzl stressed that the East Africa project was emphatically not Zion: "It is only an auxiliary colonization—but, be it noted, on a national and state foundation." Palestine, he declared, remained the unalterable goal. The vote was proportionally five to three in favor of an investigation. At once the entire body of nay-voters walked out of the Congress hall. For them the mere examination of a tract in East Africa meant the abandonment of Zion; gathering in another room, they argued, fumed, and wept—some of them sat on the floor mourning as people mourn for the dead.

Herzl went to them with pleas and reassurances. Also with reproaches: the Congresses which were generous with sentiments, tears, and pledges, gave him neither the money nor the disciplined political support to carry out the Basel program on which the movement was founded and to which they all remained true. Eventually, the dissidents were won back to the sessions, though not to a change in their vote.

The aftermath—conclaves of rebels in Russia and Austria, painful scenes of protest, threat, rebellion, and negotiation—continued many months. In December, during a Zionist ball in Paris, a half-crazed Russian Zionist fired a revolver at Nordau. And a bitter irony enveloped the entire affair when it became apparent, by the end of the year, that no suitable territory could be found in East Africa.

The only real victim was Herzl. Although the mass of Zionists, in Russia no less than elsewhere, never wavered in their support of him, the six months of strain and wrangling depleted his physical reserves and hastened his untimely death. Years before, Herzl had written apropos of a play by Björnson: "Why is it that the best men fall? Because the reason that they are the best is that they exceed their strength."

Last Days

Shortly after the middle of January 1904, Herzl set out for Italy, with Venice as his first stop. Within the space of a few days he met and sought to win the regnant figures in the Vatican and Italian governments. It is fairly safe to say that Herzl's buoyant humor throughout the Italian journey, and the sparkle it left in his diary, was due not only to the charms of

Italy, but also to a sense of respite from the Russian Zionist leaders, with whom he had been tussling these many months. It soon became apparent that Italy, like Germany and Russia, had joined the list of major powers which at the start were willing and in the end inactive.

Herzl kept on negotiating, writing letters, and trying to win over statesmen and bankers: the Foreign Minister of Austria, Jacob Schiff, and others. But his health rapidly worsened. He returned home, and then on June 3, 1904 he left for Edlach in the Semmering mountains. Behind, on the desk in his study, lay a sheet of paper on which he had written in English: "In the midst of life there is death."

On July 1 Herzl's heart began to function with marked irregularity, breathing became hard and painful, and a bronchial catarrh set in bringing violent and bloody coughing fits. "Give them all my greetings," he told a friend who had journeyed to his bedside, "and tell them that I gave my blood for my people."

During spells of semi-delirium he presided again at the Congress he had created, beating the bed-quilt with a phantom gavel and calling out, "*Ad loca! Ad loca!*" Or, at another moment, he was executing his vision of a redeemed Palestine: "These three tracts of land must be bought. Did you make a note of it? These three tracts!"

Pneumonia settled in his left lung. His mother and children were summoned. Shortly after their arrival, on the afternoon of July 3, 1904, he died—at the age of forty-four years and two months.

In his will Herzl asked that his body be buried in Vienna, next to that of his father, "to remain there until the Jewish people will carry my remains to Palestine." On August 16, 1949, his coffin was flown to the State of Israel and, the next day, laid to rest on a ridge facing Jerusalem from the west and honored with the name of Mount Herzl.

The Man and the Legend

The posture of world affairs prevented Herzl from achieving his ends while he lived; his heirs, working under more propitious circumstances, finished the task; and though they merit the fullest appreciation for their consummate skill, they are comparable to the architects who brought Michelangelo's great church to completion.

The men whom Herzl attracted to the executive body of the Zionist movement, some of them young enough to be nearly lifelong Lovers of Zion, learned from him the techniques of statesmanship, without which Zion was doomed to remain only an intangible object of emotion and belief. Above all, they learned from him the possibility of statesmanship and the self-assurance to avail themselves of it.

"To all of us," said Chaim Weizmann,* the coming leader among Herzl's successors, an habitual critic of Herzl's policy, and the first president of the State of Israel, "he was first and foremost a great teacher of organization and politics . . . we hearkened to his maxims and teaching with joy."

Herzl went further than providing young Weizmann and other Zionist leaders with precept and lesson. He broke open the roads they followed to success; it was almost literally in his footsteps that they walked into the Quai d'Orsay, the Quirinal, and No. 10 Downing Street.

The same Balfour who as Foreign Secretary signed the famous Declaration in 1917 was Prime Minister in 1903, when Herzl secured the British offer of territory in East Africa—an offer couched in terms which, to quote Weizmann, re-established "the identity, the legal personality of the Jewish people." And in 1906, when he first met Weizmann, Balfour was still arguing on behalf of the East Africa scheme. Lloyd George, who headed the cabinet which issued the Balfour Declaration, had drawn up for Herzl the draft charter for a quasi-autonomous regime in East Africa and had advocated the Zionist standpoint during the Parliamentary debate on the offer in 1904. Lord Cromer, Sir Edward Grey, and Lord Milner, all of whom proved helpful to Weizmann in procuring the 1917 Declaration, had been politically inclined toward Zionism by Herzl and his agents in the course of the El Arish and East Africa negotiation. "Our negotiations with the British government," Weizmann cheerfully attested in 1923, "were simple compared with the unending, intense, tiresome, heartrending negotiations which he [Herzl] conducted." Weizmann's labors

* See Chapter 10.

were far from easy, but they were rendered simpler because of Herzl.

Under Herzl's leadership, the anomalous denizens of the ghetto together with the drifting Jews of the West, above all the youth, set forth on their march to the rank of a nation, conscious of its destiny. A new literature and art, a revival of the Hebrew language, received fresh encouragement and gave fresh stimulation in its wake. Herzl once described what he was doing in a homely comparison: "I am a good cooper and I understand how to make one whole cask out of many different staves. . . . I shall bind the cask with the hoops of our common past and future, and I shall fill it with our national ideals of right and justice."

Energy and a genius for organization go far toward accounting for these achievements. It was characteristic of Herzl to awake at dawn and "as customary plan out everything beforehand," and by the day's end do what he had planned.

But this was not the whole secret. Herzl's advent on the scene struck his contemporaries as something unfamiliar and indefinable that embodied a new spirit. There was in his deep, lambent, magnetic eyes, his imperial nose, his stature and bearing, a blend of the Hebrew prophet and the Assyrian monarch, beside which the Hirsches, Rothschilds, Bülows, Chamberlains, Grand Dukes, and Sultans looked like nonentities, plain or fancy. The contrast must have unconsciously contributed to his self-assurance. Physically, he imposed.

But his world was not succumbing to the looks of a man. Perhaps it was his innate knightliness that made him, as well it might, seem mysterious and extraordinary. Genuine knights are rare in any age and among any people. Of course, Chaucer notwithstanding, no knight has ever been perfect. The flaws in Herzl's character—his petty jealousies, undue suspicions, and over-sensitive *amour-propre*—are obvious, even today, because in his writings he had the honesty not to cloak them. His "legend" in fact grew so rapidly and "the cloud in which he walked" became so dense with incense and pious adulation that it is a happy relief to discover in his portrait of himself in his diaries a palpable man with common follies and shortcomings.

Yet the same confessions unconsciously disclose Herzl's

knightliness. It was this that enabled him to surmount with a touch of the magnificent and a flourish of *panache* obstacles enough to daunt the stoutest heart: the recurrent failure of his fellow-workers to understand what statesmanship meant, the purblind opposition of the Lovers of Zion to the actual re-establishment of Zion, the discovery that the kind of money which talks was deaf, the impotence of the masses, the hostility of the publishers upon whom his livelihood depended, the mockery or indifference of his own social and intellectual world, and at almost every turn the refusal to lift a finger on the part of men whose help would have counted most.

Zion ruled Herzl as fate governed a Greek hero or as the burden of the Lord weighed on a Hebrew prophet, and kept him fighting when he knew that the opposing odds were over-whelming and, worse, when he knew that the tactics and human figures in the battle were on occasion tawdry. He was tragic not because he was a Don Quixote winning our indulgent sym-pathies, but because he was a Don Quixote who recognized his own Quixotism and yet, in obedience to the ideal, never low-ered his lance—and drove himself to an untimely grave.

This same knightliness had led Herzl, against the grain of his times, to the sacrifice of his own and his family's fortune to an enterprise which could earn them only moral returns. It imbued his vision of the future Jewish state, the old-new land, with something beyond the embodiment of righteous social princi-ples, or even, when he came to know them, traditional Jewish values; he strove for a state and a people that would become in the truest sense noble. For he could have said of himself, as Heine did, *ich selber bin ein solcher Ritter von dem heil'gen Geist*—"I too am a knight of the Holy Spirit."

He liked to recall the remark an old fisherman once made to him: "The most remarkable of all things is when a man never gives up." The words could have been the emblazoned motto, as they were the perfect expression, of Herzl's life.

FOR FURTHER READING
Books by Theodor Herzl

The Diaries of Theodor Herzl, abridged, edited and translated by Marvin Lowenthal (New York: Dial Press, 1956). This is the best entryway into the mind and vision of Herzl.

The Jewish State (New York: American Zionist Emergency Council, 1946). One of the most widely printed editions of Herzl's seminal work.

Old-New Land, (New York: Bloch, 1960). A utopian novel whose purpose was to prove that the vision of a Jewish State need not be a dream. Heavily autobiographical, the plot is thin, often melodramatic, but it conveys essential elements of Herzl's vision.

A Herzl Reader, Benjamin Jaffe, compiler (Jerusalem: The Jewish Agency, 1960). A useful compendium of Zionist writings by Herzl and some of his close associates.

Books About Theodor Herzl

BEIN, Alex, *Theodor Herzl: A Biography,* translated by Maurice Samuel (New York: Atheneum, 1970). Originally published in English in 1941 by The Jewish Publication Society, this is the classic biography, and still the best.

RABINOWICZ, Oscar K., *Herzl: Architect of the Balfour Declaration* (New York: Herzl Press, 1958). Rabinowicz is an irascible historian whos original and provocative opinions are not always sustained by the evidence.

ELON, Amos, *Herzl,* (New York: Holt, Rinehart and Winston, 1975). Using a wider range of sources than was available to Bein a generation earlier, this biography has an insightful study of Herzl's life in Vienna, the city where Elon himself was born.

AVINERI, Shlomo, "Herzl: The Breakthrough" in *The Making of Modern Zionism,* (New York: Basic Books, 1981). An excellent essay in an important volume about the intellectual origins of Zionism.

VITAL, David, *The Origins of Zionism* (Oxford: Clarendon Press, 1975), *Zionism, The Formative Years* (Oxford: Clarendon Press, 1982). This is brilliant history. The finest history of Zionism yet written. Moreover Vital has a beautiful prose style.

9 . *Chaim Weizmann*

[1874–1952]

NORMAN BENTWICH

C H A I M Weizmann was the first president of the State of Israel, the head of the first independent sovereign Jewish community since the destruction of the Temple and the state by the Roman, Titus, in the first century. He was statesman, scientist, and man of action. While he was not an original thinker either in his scientific research or in his Zionist leadership, his genius lay in applying the theories of others, and giving them an exceptionally clear, concrete content. Sir Isaiah Berlin has pointed out that he was essentially an empiricist who looked on ideas as the tools of political judgment. He had a strong and vivid sense of reality, and illustrated the maxim that politics is the art of the possible. He was born to the leadership of his people and devoted his whole life to it. To quote Sir Isaiah: "Such men—from Moses to Nehru—create or lead movements primarily because, finding themselves naturally bound up with the aspirations of their society, and passionately convinced of the injustice of the order by which they are kept down, they know themselves to be stronger, more imaginative, more effective fighters against it than the majority of its victims."

Among the Jews of his generation who were creators of Zionism and founding fathers of the State of Israel, Weizmann stood out for his combination of three qualities: intellectual power, concentration of purpose on the practical fulfillment of ideas, and an incomparable personal charm. He represented most fully the ideals and aspirations of the Jewish masses in Russia and Eastern Europe. His distinction as scientist and statesman never impaired his contact with the simple Jew. He was one of them, not a brilliant, heroic outsider like Theodor Herzl or Max Nordau, or a partially assimilated Jew from a Western country like Herbert Samuel or Justice Louis Brandeis. At the same time Weizmann was recognized as one of the great men of his age. Winston Churchill said of him in the English House of Commons: "He was a man whose force and fidelity were respected throughout the free world, and who led his people back to the Promised Land, where we have seen them invincibly established as a free and sovereign State." And Jan Christian Smuts stated: "I love to think of that boy from the Russian ghetto rising to his destined place among the great men of his time."

An Age of Revolution

Weizmann lived in an age of revolutionary transformation of the conditions of the Jewish people. During his childhood Russian Jewry began to move from East to West. The May Laws, enacted in 1881, after the assassination of the liberal Czar Alexander I, imposed the harshest discrimination against them, narrowly limiting both their residence and activities. Seeking emancipation and freedom of opportunity, a mass began to emigrate to Western Europe and North and South America, with the assistance of philanthropic societies of Western Jews and Baron de Hirsch's Jewish Colonization Association.

The more idealistic elements, however, stirred by the national revival which was part of the spirit of the age, organized societies of Lovers of Zion, and began to migrate in small groups to Palestine. Among Western Jews Moses Hess, the German Socialist pioneer, in a previous generation had called for the re-establishment of the Jewish nation. Leon Pinsker, a Russian-Jewish physician, proclaimed that the solution of the Jewish problem lay in "auto-emancipation," that is, the Jews' own efforts to achieve national independence. In England, Moses Montefiore, the Anglo-Jewish philanthropist, had taken the first steps to get Jews in the towns of Palestine to settle in garden suburbs and work the soil. The Alliance Israélite in France, the first modern Jewish international organization, had founded an agricultural school near Jaffa; and in 1884 a famous conference was held at Kattowitz, with delegates from all bodies concerned with Jewish colonization in Palestine.

This was the atmosphere in which Chaim Weizmann grew up. The ideal of building a national home for the Jewish people, where they could be independent and free to live a Jewish life, was part of the air he breathed—during his childhood in a small Russian village, in his student days in Germany, and later as an eminent scientist in England. Belonging to the group whom in those days Westerners, with a touch of deprecation, called *Ostjüden*, East European Jews, he was completely free from any sense of inferiority or superiority. He was a fully conscious Jew, proud of his heritage and devoted to one purpose: to give his people freedom and security in a national home in which they would be equal members of a world society. He emerged as the head of the nation before he had any country or even an organized people to back him.

Formative Influences

Chaim Weizmann was born in 1874, in the little town (*shtetl*) of Motol, in White Russia, in one of the most forlorn corners of the Pale of Settlement. A few hundred Jewish and a few hundred non-Jewish families inhabited it, living on friendly terms, but separately. Chaim was the third of a family of fifteen children born to Oser and Rahel Weizmann; twelve lived to a full age, and most of them eventually made their homes in Palestine. His father was a small timber-merchant, engaged in the skilled work of cutting and hauling lumber, and floating it down the river. Like many Russian Jews engaged in trade and industry, he was a scholar, an intellectual, a *maskil*, a lover of Hebrew and enlightenment. His son wrote of him: "He was a natural aristocrat and something of a leader, the only Jew ever chosen to be the headman of the township of Motol." His mother was a pious woman, the homebuilder, concerned, like the father, that each of her children should develop his or her talents. It was a remarkable record that nine of the children, boys and girls, studied at universities. Yiddish was the language of the mother and of the home, but they all learned modern Hebrew from their infancy. "I never corresponded with my father in any other language except Hebrew, though to my mother I wrote Yiddish," Chaim relates. "I sent my father one Yiddish letter. He returned it without an answer."

Chaim went first to the elementary Jewish school, the *heder*, and then to Talmud Torah. He showed early promise, and he and an elder brother, Feiwel, were sent to the Russian technical school (*Realgymnasia*) in the neighboring town of Pinsk, which had a good sized Jewish community. He earned his maintenance by working as a tutor in the household of a well-to-do Jew. The glory of the school was Korneyekos, a teacher who fostered the pupil's aptitude in chemistry. Chaim later credited that instructor with having been a decisive influence in his own later scientific career.

While in Pinsk, Weizmann came in contact with a group of ardent Lovers of Zion, predecessors of the Zionists. The principal rabbi of the community had been a delegate to the Kattowitz Conference, held the year before Weizmann arrived in Pinsk. Among the youth, Aaron Eisenberg subsequently migrated to Palestine, and became a founder of the village of Rehovot, where Chaim was later to make his home. Another pioneer emigrant from Pinsk was the father of Moshe Shertok (Sharett), later to serve as Foreign Minister of Israel. In those early days, there was no organized, ordered movement for Palestine. Chaim's first activity was to go around from house to house collecting money for the small settlements of the "Lovers" in Palestine.

The great teacher of Russian Zionists at this time was Asher Ginzberg, the Hebrew philosophical writer known under his pen name Ahad Ha-am ("one of the people"); he conceived of the homeland as a spiritual center, i.e., a source of spiritual influence for the Jewish people. He was concerned with the plight of Judaism rather than with the plight of individual Jews; the love of Zion must be a state of feeling, the effort of the Jew to regain a national and normal life. Weizmann was in his seventeenth year when Ahad Ha-am's famous article "Truth from Palestine" appeared in a Hebrew monthly. He read and reread his words, and discussed them endlessly. Ahad Ha-am was what Gandhi was to the masses of India, and what Mazzini, the prophet of Italian nationalism, was to young Italy a century ago, teaching that every nation has its mission to humanity.

When Chaim finished the technical school, the next step was to go abroad to a university. Only a tiny proportion of the Russian-Jewish youth who embarked on a profession could be admitted to Russian universities, and it required wealth to obtain a place. When Chaim was offered the opportunity to study at the University of Darmstadt in Germany, therefore, he accepted because he could support himself by tutoring the son of a wealthy assimilated Jew in the neighboring town of Pflogstadt, about an hour's journey away.

Young Weizmann's first year in Germany was unhappy. He hated the atmosphere of Orthodox but assimilated Jews which he found both in his pupil's home and at the university. It seemed to him an example of what Ahad Ha-am had called "slavery in freedom," the term he used to describe the condition of Jews who had bartered their self-respect and culture for civil and political emancipation. Further, the strain of combining university studies with tutoring and the long journey each way undermined his health. After a year he returned to his home in Russia; a year later his father's economic situation improved, and Chaim was able to resume his studies, this time in Berlin where there was a large Russian-Jewish student population. He was admitted in 1895 to the Polytechnikum, one of the best high schools for science. The Russian and Polish-Jewish students, living under the most austere conditions, were organized into ardent nationalist brotherhoods, the most important of which was the Russian-Jewish Scientific Society, whose leaders included such famous Zionists of the future as Shemaryahu Levin, Leo Motzkin, and Nahman Syrkin. Levin was later a member of the Russian Duma, and the Zionist apostle to the United States before and during World War I; Motzkin became head of the permanent committee fighting for national rights for Jewish minorities; Syrkin was a founder of the Zionist Socialist Party. Ahad Ha-am, too, was at that time living in Berlin, and the young Zionists often visited him in his home and were inspired. These were the formative years of Chaim's Jewish nationalism.

First Zionist Congress

It was during Weizmann's second year in Berlin, in 1896, that Theodor Herzl published his dramatic book on the solution of the Jewish question, *Der Judenstaat*. Weizmann was later to describe this event in his autobiography: "It was an utterance which came like a bolt from the blue . . . its effect was profound. Not the ideas, but the personality which stood behind them, appealed to us. Here was daring, clarity and knowledge." The convening in 1897 at Basel of the first world Jewish parliament, the Zionist Congress, also made a profound impact. Weizmann had a mandate to it from the Pinsk Zionists, but missed the Congress because of a family crisis. He attended the second Congress, again at Basel, in 1898, and met Herzl for the first time. "Though he was impressive, I cannot pretend that I was swept off my feet."

The young man immediately became a Congress personality. His intellectual stature and innate power of leadership would have brought him to the front in any society. He was politically active. With a number of fellow students from Eastern Europe, including Berthold Feiwel and Martin Buber, he formed what was called the Democratic Fraction. They were a kind of opposition of young Eastern Jews to the ruling class of the Congress, which was made up of Western Jews of established position like Herzl, Max Nordau, Max Mandelstamm, and Leopold Greenberg of England. Democratic Fraction members felt that these leaders were remote from the deeper feeling of the Jewish masses, that Herzl's diplomatic negotiations for a charter with emperor and sultan, princes, and premiers were futile. Spokesmen for the Russian-Jewish masses, they sought in Zionism not merely rescue but self-expression. For them the movement had to respond to the needs and aspirations of the millions. It was the whole of Jewishness, a unifying spiritual force, not a movement to find a home for oppressed Jews. The Jews must return to the land of their fathers, free intellectually as well as physically, speak their own language, renew their culture, and develop their spiritual heritage.

At first the group was regarded as subversive, but they early had a positive cause, one to which Herzl was eventually won.

Inspired by Ahad Ha-am, they put among their first objectives the establishment in Jerusalem of a Jewish *Hochschule,* an embryo of a university, where Jews could pursue higher studies in the sciences, arts, and Jewish culture. That was to be the beginning of a spiritual center in Palestine. Herzl submitted a memorandum to the Sultan about a university in Jerusalem which would be open to Muslims as well as Jews. But there was no response.

Opposition to Uganda

When Herzl in 1903 obtained from the British government an offer of Uganda, a territory in East Africa, as an autonomous if temporary Jewish home until Palestine should become available, a schism rent the movement. Almost all members of the Russian delegation were uncompromisingly opposed even to sending a commission of inquiry to the territory, and they left the Congress hall in protest. The Western Zionists approved the plan. Weizmann led the debate for the *"Neinsagers"* against Uganda, though his father, who was also a delegate, voted for it. To him and to most of the Russians it was impossible to transfer the longing for the land of Israel to any other territory. There was, then, no immediate solution for the Jewish problem. Zionism was an organic movement and had to grow slowly. Years later, when Weizmann was in England, he explained the reason for the rejection to Arthur Balfour, whose government had made the original offer of the territory: " 'Mr. Balfour,' I said, 'supposing I were to offer you Paris instead of London. Would you take it?' He sat up and answered, 'But, Dr. Weizmann, we have London.' 'That is true,' I said, 'but we had Jerusalem when London was a marsh.' "

Weizmann had moved in 1898 from Berlin to Freiburg (in Switzerland) to complete his doctorate in science, his chemistry professor in Berlin having been appointed to the chair at the university there. He took his degree with the highest distinction, having already shown his competence in applied chemistry with relation to dyestuffs. By selling scientific inventions, he became financially independent. It was an important factor in Weizmann's public life that he never accepted a salary for his Zionist activities.

Geneva

Weizmann found his first academic position as a *privatdozent* in chemistry at Geneva University; and in that mecca of revolutionary students, at the crossroads of Western and Eastern Europe, he plunged into the ideological battle for the souls of Jewish youth. The Russian socialist exiles, Plekhanov, Lenin himself, and among the Jews, Leon Trotsky (then called Leon Bronstein), upheld the Marxist solution for all problems, including that of the Jews. Weizmann and a small group of Zionists took up their challenge, and debated with them in stuffy halls in Berne and Geneva. On one occasion he, Feiwel, and Buber conducted a three-day debate before the Jewish students, most of whom were revolutionaries, and at the end of the debate a Zionist society was formed, with 180 members. That was a triumph!

Weizmann had already mastered the art of both refuting and convincing opponents. He also gave a great part of his time to Zionist spadework, and each year enhanced his reputation at the Congress. What singled him out from other Russian-Jewish academic enthusiasts was his pertinacity and his capacity for giving practical form and direction to long-range goals. And he always took an empirical approach, content to go step by step. There was no shortcut. He set himself against demagogy and the painting of too bright hopes. "Miracles may happen," he said, "but you have to work very hard for them." He brought to Zionism the scientist's mind, seeking the truth, realistically facing the facts, believing in organic growth and development, and prepared to revise ideas and alter methods which did not succeed. Throughout his life he struggled with the desire to devote himself entirely to science, the discovery of fresh knowledge. But the call of his people prevailed, and he found time to engage in politics.

While in Geneva, Weizmann was betrothed to a beautiful and talented Russian Jewess, Vera Chatsman, who was completing her scientific and medical studies. She came from Rostov-on-Don, where the small Jewish community of relatively well-to-do families were free from the persecution of the masses in the

Pale of Settlement. Though she was not then a Zionist, Weizmann gradually exercised over her the same spell that he was to exercise over countless men and women, Jews and non-Jews, in his efforts for the Jewish national home. They shared an almost fastidious discrimination in the choice of friends. Though Weizmann had led the Democratic Fraction in opposition to Herzl partly on the ground of the aloofness of the inner circle, and although he himself was "one of the people" in aspiration and outlook, and his manner of speech, his humor, and his language were rooted in Jewish tradition, he did not conceal a consciousness of his own aristocracy of mind and his scientific prowess.

Chemist at Manchester University

In 1904, before his marriage, Weizmann accepted an appointment as lecturer in applied chemistry at Manchester University. Like Solomon Schechter,* he felt that England was more free of anti-Semitism than any other country, and offered a good field for his scientific work. While still a schoolboy, he had written to his master in Hebrew: "England is a free country which helps the Jews to establish their state." And he believed in the affinity of the English and the Jews. The Bible-loving English people had, from the early part of the nineteenth century, shown a deep interest in a practical form in the return of Jews to Palestine. Indeed, to the end of that century, English Christians were stronger Zionists than were English Jews.

The choice of Manchester proved fortunate since the "Cotton City" was, by tradition, ahead of London in welcoming new ideas. As the popular saying went, "What Manchester thinks today, England thinks tomorrow." The university at that time had eminent teachers: the physicist Lord Rutherford, the chemists Sir Robert Robinson and Sir Arthur Schuster—the latter descended from a Jewish banking family of Hamburg—and, in a different discipline, Samuel Alexander, a Jew and the most distinguished philosopher in the country. Another outstanding citizen was the foremost Liberal Party journalist in

* See Chapter 5.

the United Kingdom, C. P. Scott, proprietor and editor of the *Manchester Guardian*, which next to the *London Times* was the most important daily paper in Britain. Years later, Scott proved to be a powerful ally for the cause of Zionism.

Weizmann played little part either in the Jewish communal life of Manchester, apart from the Zionist societies, or in the central Zionist organization of Britain, the English Federation, which was then rent with dissension between the "politicals," who wanted diplomatic action, and the "practicals," who believed in more modest and systematic efforts to extend agricultural and industrial enterprises and Hebrew cultural institutions in Palestine. He went occasionally to London to address Zionist groups, bringing to his hearers a depth of conviction and a refreshing freedom from fine phrases and rhetoric.

In Manchester he came in close contact with a less polemic group of young Zionists, enthusiasts who had the rare quality of being both idealists and enterprising, prosperous men of business. Two families particularly, those of (Sir) Simon Marks and Israel Sieff, which included young women of talent and devotion, sat at his feet, and put their dynamic energy and wealth at the disposal of the Zionist cause for the rest of Weizmann's life. They were for him a "happy breed of men," uninvolved in the wearisome bickerings of contending official Zionist chiefs.

In his early years in Manchester, Weizmann also met Arthur Balfour, who was then Prime Minister of the Conservative government, and discussed Palestine with him. Balfour, a philosophical statesman, and a member of the Scottish aristocracy, was, as it happened, interested in the Jewish problem. He was a friend of the Rothschilds, who were strongly anti-Zionist. During his premiership the Conservative government had passed the Aliens Act, restricting the admission of poor aliens even if they were seeking asylum from persecution. That was a break in English tradition, and Herzl had come to London in 1901 to give evidence before the Royal Commission, which recommended the legislation, and to propose as a solution the establishment of a Jewish home or state. Weizmann made a deep and permanent impression on Balfour, who was defeated in the general election of 1905 in which Winston Churchill, Lloyd George, and Herbert Samuel were bright hopes of the

Liberals: Weizmann was not to meet Balfour again until 1915, after the outbreak of the war, and under very different circumstances.

First Visit to Palestine

Weizmann paid his first visit to Palestine in 1907, after attending a Zionist congress at The Hague, where he had urged a policy of "synthetic Zionism" which could combine political and practical work. While in Palestine, he called for more settlements, agricultural and industrial, and more cultural activity in the ancient land. A charter for colonization would be useless unless Jews were already rooted in the soil. Like Judah Magnes, who had preceded him, he was more convinced than ever of the need to make the founding of a university a principal aim. With his infallible purposiveness, he set about winning the support of the French Baron Edmond de Rothschild, the munificent founder of agricultural settlements, hospitals, and schools in Palestine, and of Paul Ehrlich, the world-famous scientist who had discovered a treatment for syphilis. Simultaneously, in America, Judah Magnes was enlisting the interest of Jewish academic men and of Nathan Straus, the philanthropist. The university they contemplated was to start with small research institutes for chemistry, medical science, Jewish studies, and archeology.

In 1913 the Zionist Congress passed with acclamation a resolution urging that steps be taken to secure the university site and initiate practical measures. A committee was set up, and its first meeting convened in Paris under the presidency of James de Rothschild, son of Edmond, on August 4, 1915, the very day of the declaration of World War I. Weizmann wrote to Magnes in America: "It breaks my heart. All our work is thrown away for years."

World War I

The war, in point of fact, however, gave him providentially the chance of leadership. He was quick to seize the positive opportunity in any crisis. Realizing that the entry of the Ottoman Empire on the German side might win full support of the

British government for a Jewish national home in Palestine under British protection, he sought an interview first with Herbert Samuel, the first professing Jew to have become a member of a British Cabinet. Though hitherto Samuel had taken no part in Zionist efforts, and little in those of the Jewish community, being concentrated on English Liberal politics, he now saw the possibility of England's promoting the cause of a Jewish national home, and had actually addressed a memorandum to the Cabinet on this subject. Together Weizmann and Samuel approached Lloyd George, who was quick to catch their vision.

A little later Weizmann had another opportunity to increase his public stature. In 1915 a grave crisis loomed in the manufacture of munitions. England lacked acetone, an essential ingredient in the making of high explosive shells. In his special studies in fermentation chemistry he had worked out a process by which the necessary material could be produced from acorns. He offered his services to the government, convinced the experts, and was established in a laboratory under the Admiralty. The First Lord of that ministry, Arthur Balfour, who had been brought into the coalition government for the conduct of the war, remembered his earlier Manchester talk with Weizmann about Zionism. And he, too, realized that the vision might now become a reality. "I was thinking of that conversation of ours, and I believe that, when the guns stop firing, you may get your Jerusalem," Balfour told the Zionist leader.

Weizmann had a magical gift for convincing British statesmen. Besides Balfour and Lloyd George, he won the wholehearted support of Jan Christian Smuts, who was then a member of the War Cabinet. "An almost feminine charm . . . to gether with burning enthusiasm, and the prophetic vision of what negotiation may win" was how an English officer, Ronald Storrs (Governor of Jerusalem when the Zionist Commission came to Palestine in 1918) described Weizmann's persuasive powers.

Meanwhile, Weizmann had almost severed his connections with the central Zionist organization, which had set up provisional headquarters in Copenhagen, where it maintained a neutral attitude in the war. He refused to participate in what seemed to him a strange correctness, and was convinced that Zionism must be linked with the Allied cause. In this, he had the support of Nahum Sokolow, the Polish Hebrew writer and some Russian Zionists, notably Vladimir Jabotinsky, Pinhas Rutenberg, the engineer, and Shemaryahu Levin, who was in the United States. And he had the moral backing of Ahad Ha-am, who remained in London.

With Herbert Samuel's help, the English Zionists made a sustained effort to obtain from the British government a declaration recognizing the historic right of the Jewish people to make Palestine its national home, and pledging official support for that purpose. There were many hurdles in the way, however. The presidents of the two representative Anglo-Jewish bodies, the Board of Deputies of British Jews and the Anglo-Jewish Association, still strongly opposed to the political restoration of the Jewish nation, used their influence to prevent such a declaration. Moreover, certain assimilated Jews powerful in political life, most conspicuously Edwin Montagu, a Cabinet minister in Lloyd George's coalition government, denounced the proposal to the Cabinet, protesting that it would imperil the British position among the millions of Muslim subjects in the Empire.

The Balfour Declaration

Weizmann and his friends, marshalling to their cause prominent English statesmen as well as the President of the United States, convinced the Cabinet to stick to its original promise. With some significant changes of wording, the declaration was issued on November 2, 1917, on the very day the Bolsheviks seized power in Russia, and at a most critical moment of the campaign in Palestine against the Turks. Signed by Arthur Balfour, who was then Foreign Secretary, it was addressed to Lord Rothschild, a representative English Jew who was a Zionist.

The Balfour Declaration, promising help for the establishment of a Jewish national home in Palestine, electrified the Jewish world and much of the Gentile. Weizmann realized that it was only the first step, and to have practical effect should be followed immediately by dramatic action. He skillfully secured the agreement of the government to his going out to Palestine as the head of a small commission of Zionists from England

and the Allied countries to take the first steps to implement the declaration. They were accompanied by a member of the War Secretariat of the government, the Honorable Ormsby-Gore. The chemist from a small Russian village was suddenly recognized by the Allied Powers as the head of the Jewish nation. With his sincerity and dignity he created the illusion among statesmen that he represented not only a people but a government in exile, and behind him stood a large, coherent, articulate community.

Weizmann's welcome by the Allied Commander-in-Chief, General Edmund Allenby, and his military staff, was far from cordial. These officers were baffled by what seemed to them an unusual political act in the midst of a stern campaign. Care and responsibility for the surviving Jewish population in Palestine as it came under British military administration was a difficult task, since the *Yishuv* had been reduced by forced emigration, disease, and privations of war.

Weizmann, with his unerring persuasiveness, was able to break down the opposition, and inspire confidence by his own sincerity and candor. He won the devoted support of a few members of the higher staff, notably Brigadier Wyndham Deedes, a religious Christian, one of the heads of Army Intelligence and a future Secretary of mandated Palestine. Realizing that it was essential to win the good will of the Arabs, Weizmann made an adventurous journey to Aqaba to meet the Emir Feisal, commander of the Arab revolt in the desert, and T. E. Lawrence, his adviser. His account of that journey reflects his deep feeling of mission. "To get to Aqaba . . . I had to travel south to Egypt, cross the Red Sea, and go back to Transjordan, 12 days, 5 days through scorching desert, the Sinai, and then right across the waters of the sea. I then turned north-east through Moab. On the last day of my journey a magic feeling of the miracle of it came over me. Like Abraham of old, I approached the country God has promised to His chosen people. And like him, I came through Moab to take possession of the land. . . ." The conversations with the Emir were friendly, and Weizmann won his good will.

Weizmann's commission had as one of its tasks the laying of the foundation stones of the university on Mt. Scopus, a site acquired during the war. This was done in July, 1918, in the presence of Allenby, his chief staff officers, the heads of the Jewish, Muslim, and Christian religious communities, and a large congregation of the *Yishuv*. Weizmann declared that this dedication in the midst of war showed the Jewish people's determination to go beyond its own restoration, and to make a contribution to humanity. It made a deep impression on the Jewish people and also on the British army in Palestine and the world at large.

It was Weizmann's difficult but self-chosen lot as the statesman of the Jewish people to travel from country to country, between Palestine, London, and Paris, in order to assure the next steps in the achievement of the Jewish national home. There were those who thought that he held too much power in his own hands, but he felt that nobody else carried the authority or necessary conviction. He identified himself with the national Zionist movement to the extent that he was unwilling to share or delegate authority, and at times was disturbed by independent action on the part of those working with him.

After the Turks and Germans surrendered in November, 1918, Weizmann attended the Peace Conference in Paris, where, through the skilful negotiations of Felix Frankfurter (a member of the American Jewish delegation), Emir Feisal was induced to support in a letter the case for Jewish immigration, autonomous settlement in the land, and development of Palestine under the benevolent administration of a trustee power, provided that the interests of the Arab inhabitants were safeguarded. The Arab leader's acceptance was conditional on the fulfillment of the legitimate aspirations of the Arab people in other countries delivered from the Turks. In spite of the fact that that stipulation was not satisfied because of French claims in Syria and Lebanon, a favorable verdict was rendered by the Council of Ten representing the Big Five powers, and including Woodrow Wilson, Lloyd George, and Georges Clemenceau.

The British Mandate

By decision of the Conference of the Principal Allied Powers held at San Remo in May, 1920, England was to be the trustee or mandatory power for all Palestine, including Transjordan. The terms of the Mandate were still to be worked out in consultation with the British government, and were to be confirmed by the Council of the League of Nations, the new world authority which emerged out of the peace treaties. In 1920 Weizmann's position in the international Zionist organization was at last regularized constitutionally. The Zionist Congress elected him president, and the Executive Council was to have its seat in London.

The Zionist commission remained in Palestine, and in the spring of 1920 was faced with an ugly situation. Arab nationalists incited the Arab populace thronging Jerusalem for a Muslim holiday to attack the Jewish quarters. There were many casualties, and Jewish self-defense bands, organized by Vladimir Jabotinsky, were arrested and condemned to heavy sentences by military courts. Weizmann, suspecting that many members of the military administration were hostile to the Balfour Declaration, used all his friends and influence to bring about a radical change. Lloyd George, still Prime Minister in 1920, immediately after the San Remo decision on the Mandate, announced that the British High Commissioner for Palestine was to be Herbert Samuel.

Though the five years in which Samuel held office (1920-1925) were marked by extraordinary systematic development and progress in Palestine, this was a period of great trial and stress for Weizmann. Jewish immigration, though encouraged, remained small because of the lack of means for settlement. Russian Jewry, which before the war was the principal source of immigrants, was cut off almost entirely by the Soviet refusal to let its Jews go. Weizmann had to assume another large burden, the annual collection of funds for the Palestine work from Jewish communities throughout the world; and every year he had to travel the "Via dolorosa" on the American continent on behalf of the Foundation Fund (Keren Hayesod). Because of his failure, when he visited the United States for the first time in 1921, to come to an agreement with leaders of the American Zionists, Justice Louis Brandeis and Judge Julian Mack, he had to create and build up the Zionist instrument in the United States by his own efforts.

The break with American leaders resulted from a clash of fundamental attitudes and temperaments, which was compared by Weizmann to the clash between President Wilson and his

European colleagues at the Paris Peace Conference. Brandeis and his group held that after the Balfour Declaration the work of the World Zionist Organization was essentially economic, and it should abandon political activity. They were opposed also to the inclusion in The Jewish Agency of those who were not Zionists. There was, too, a serious disagreement over the American contribution to the budget of the Foundation Fund, which Weizmann was to launch. They believed in private investment in Palestine rather than in national funds. Weizmann and most of the rank and file among American Zionists were convinced that the settlement must be based first on a national contribution. The gap between Washington and Pinsk could not be bridged. At the Cleveland conference of American Zionists, where the issues were fought out, a large majority, led by Louis Lipsky and Morris Rothenberg, favored Weizmann: Brandeis and his group for a time formed their own organization.

The White Paper: 1921

In 1921 serious Arab rioting in Palestine led the British government, in consultation with Herbert Samuel, to define more precisely, and with greater limitation, the principles of the trust for the Jewish home. This document, the Churchill White Paper, bears the name of the Colonial Secretary, Winston Churchill, who had visited the country a few weeks before the trouble erupted. Though it caused grave disappointment to the Zionist Organization by restricting immigration to the economic absorptive capacity of the country, it was accepted by Weizmann, who remained faithful, in spite of many setbacks, to the principle of Anglo-Jewish partnership. He accepted, too, the exclusion of the country across Jordan from the area of Jewish settlement, and thereby antagonized Jabotinsky and other extreme nationalists who demanded spectacular concessions under the name of Revisionism, and without regard to Arab feeling and opposition.

Weizmann, however, was able to control the biannual Congress by his personal authority. His speech was quiet, closely reasoned, without any rhetoric or oratorical art, but relieved by Jewish wit and humor. Above all, he gave the conviction of utter sincerity and of deep feeling and compassion, even when he dashed the hopes of his audience. Balfour once remarked that "his speech was the swish of a sword." For example, in 1914, Weizmann remarked: "It is the Zionist good fortune that they (the Jews) are considered mad; if we were normal, we should not think of going to Palestine, but stay put, like normal people." At Oxford in 1922, he quipped: "The pioneers did not walk in and expect it to be a walk-over." At a Zionist conference in 1922, he stated that "the redemption cannot be accelerated by resolutions. We must believe in it, as we believe in the indestructible life and will of the Jewish people, but we must not make it trivial by political resolutions." He confessed in 1927: "When I had the Balfour Declaration in my hand, I felt as if a sun-ray had struck me, and I thought I heard the steps of the Messiah. But I remembered that the true Redeemer comes silently like a thief in the night. I had to hold myself back, and to fulfill the bitter task of bringing back to reality the Jewish masses struck by a sun-ray." Weizmann was famed for his many pithy remarks: "Practical politics, like mechanics, are governed by a golden rule: you can only get out of them what you put into them." "What is tradition? It is telescoped memory; we remember." "I believe that in this tormented Jewish people there resides that ancient and elemental will which has carried it across many crises in human history, and still demands a creative, and not merely a curative, outlet."

During the first years of the Mandate the Hebrew University remained close to Weizmann's heart. In 1921, with Albert Einstein, another enthusiast, he obtained enough support in the United States to initiate medical and chemical research on a small scale. Judah Magnes in 1922 headed a committee in Jerusalem for bringing the university into being, and in 1925 was appointed Chancellor, a post he held for the following ten years. In 1925 Weizmann organized an impressive ceremony for the formal opening of the university, to which he invited Arthur Balfour, who was then Chancellor of the University of Cambridge. Balfour's visit with members of his family was a triumph. The opening ceremony was held in a natural amphitheater on the grounds of Mt. Scopus, in the presence of distinguished guests from all parts of the world, including representatives of great universities and academies, and seven thousand Jews from all the communities. The university was Weizmann's first

Zionist child, but in the years to come he was sorely disappointed in it. The child did not grow up in the way he wished, and, as usual, he found it difficult to share responsibility. He began to think of a separate scientific institute for his own research; the Daniel Sieff Institute was founded for him at Rehovot by friends in 1932.

Palestine was blissfully peaceful from 1922 to 1929. Once the Council of the League of Nations had adopted the Mandate instrument, after many postponements and rumblings, Weizmann was able to turn to strengthening the country's economic and financial base. He established personal contacts with members of the Permanent Mandates Commission of the League of Nations in Geneva, to which the Palestine administration had to account annually for the way in which it was carrying out its trust. His main concern, however, was to enlarge The Jewish Agency to include persons nominated by non-Zionist and philanthropic bodies, which would take full part in the settlement. He won for support of the enlarged Agency such men as Louis Marshall and Felix Warburg of America, Leon Blum of France, and Lord Samuel and Alfred Mond (Lord Melchett) of England.

Arab Riots—1929

An imposing gathering of eminent Jews from many countries met at Zurich immediately after the 1929 Zionist Congress, and affirmed the constitution of the Agency. Barely had they parted when new Arab riots broke out, incited, as in 1920 and 1921, by inflammatory orators on the pretext that the Jews were seeking to take the Muslim holy places in Old Jerusalem, on the site of the Hebrew Temple. For a week the position in Palestine was critical, and the riots were followed by a prolonged inquest, lasting over a year, by the British government and expert commissions. The Labor government in power, with Sidney Webb (Lord Passfield) as Colonial Secretary, was not sympathetic; Weizmann had no close personal contacts except with the Premier, James Ramsay MacDonald. The White Paper that was finally issued after the enquiries was a niggling criticism of the whole policy, proposing drastic restrictions on further growth. This shook Weizmann's long-suffering faith in British sincerity; he resigned his office as president of The Jewish Agency, and was followed by other heads of the Agency. After a painful period of negotiation, the Prime Minister wrote a letter explaining away or negating the harsh criticism, and Weizmann withdrew his resignation. But permanent harm was done to his position and his trust in England.

Weizmann had to face an angry Zionist Congress in 1931. The opponents of his policy of trust in Britain made the most of their opportunity, while ambitious rivals thought they could grasp power. He was not re-elected president, and for four years thereafter was unwilling to resume office. In his place Nahum Sokolow, who shared his views for the most part, was chosen.

Rise of Hitler

When Hitler's persecution of the Jews began in 1933, Weizmann was pressed by acclamation to direct a central bureau for the settlement of German Jews mainly, but not exclusively, in Palestine. It was clear that he was not only the leader of Zionism but the representative statesman for the whole Jewish people. Once again grasping opportunity out of crisis, he contrived to get Jewish communities in Germany and throughout the world to recognize Palestine as the principal country of refuge; and the immigration figures leaped up in 1934 and 1935. He was less successful in his effort to persuade some of the famous exiled scientists and scholars to look to Palestine for their haven. Yet something was done to secure talents for the university and the Technion, and he personally rescued several scientists and brought them to the Institute at Rehovot.

Partition Proposal

At the Lucerne Zionist Congress in 1925, he was called back to the presidency, a post he held, though with declining authority and mastery, for another ten years. Arab rioting in April, 1936 quickly turned to Arab revolt against the British administration and the Jewish homeland. A large force of regular troops was required to put it down, and Jewish immigration was cut down by the administration. At the end of that year the British government appointed a Royal Commission to inquire into the causes of the trouble and make recommendations to prevent a recurrence. This turned out to be the most impressive and understanding of the many official bodies which had conducted inquests. Their broad conclusion was that the principle of the Mandate as hitherto interpreted, to foster a binational commonwealth, would no longer work. Nationalist feelings on either side were too strong. The remedy was to divide the "least of lands" into two states, Jewish and Arab, with a third section, including Jerusalem, remaining under the British Mandate. Weizmann, empirical realist and spokesman for the Jews, was in favor of accepting the idea in principle; it could give what they most urgently needed, freedom of immigration and development, even if only in the smaller part of the country. But the Zionist Congress and the Council of The Jewish Agency, meeting during the summer of 1937, were not easily persuaded. The tables were turned. In a reversal of his early position on the Uganda scheme, Weizmann now favored practical gains, while the old Zionist guard wanted the whole or nothing. In the end the British government withdrew the offer in the face of renewed Arab revolt.

The two years that preceded World War II were a humiliating period, during which British policy appeased Hitler and Mussolini. The culmination of conferences by the British government, under Neville Chamberlain, with Jews and Arabs separately, in London 1939, was a new statement of Palestine policy, which whittled away the promises of the Balfour Declaration and the Mandate without substituting partition. This came at the moment when the need for saving Jewish lives from Hitler's massacre was at its greatest.

Weizmann, struggling to keep his faith in England, was heartened by Churchill's denunciation of the White Paper of 1939 and the opposition Labor Party's declaration that they would not be bound by it. He continued to uphold the principle of Jewish self-restraint and the avoidance of reprisals against Arab terrorism, and he would not condone the violent actions of the Jewish extremists, the *Irgun Tzevai Leumi* (in English, "National Military Organization"), or their American backers. The Zionist Congress held in August, 1929 passed passionate resolutions impugning the validity of the new British policy.

Before the delegates parted, the thunderclap of the Nazi-Soviet pact broke over their heads. Weizmann made it clear where Jews must stand, regardless of the White Paper. He won the assent of the Congress to offer the Western Allies the Jewish manpower of Palestine, but this generous gesture was spurned for four years by the British administration.

World War II

The war years (1939-1945) brought Weizmann more tribulations. He offered his scientific services unconditionally to the British government, and believed that he could give valuable help with munitions and synthetic rubber. But his friends in high places, with the exception of Winston Churchill, had gone, and lesser men were not sorry to snub him. Churchill has recorded that on one occasion he would not give Weizmann an audience because he knew that he would be convinced, and he was not in a position to grant what Weizmann wanted. In 1941 the Zionist leader was advised to go to America, where better use might be made of his talents. As he and Mrs. Weizmann were about to embark, an overwhelming personal tragedy struck. Their second son, Michael, a pilot in the Royal Air Force, was lost in an attack on German warships. Though Weizmann later crossed the Atlantic to carry on his experiments on behalf of the war effort, vested American oil interests prevented the full use of his inventions in the United States.

Weizmann was finding it increasingly difficult to carry on his struggle, especially since he was cut off from the *Yishuv* during most of the war. In 1945 he decided to celebrate his seventieth birthday in Palestine, and to renew his direction of its cultural and scientific institutions. If he had lost some authority, he had lost no affection; and if he could not be the tireless political spokesman, he could and would be the man of science setting his people an example of the search for knowledge which must be the foundation of well-being and progress. Generous friends in many countries provided the means of endowing at Rehovot an enlarged Institute of Science, which was to become famous throughout the world, even during his lifetime.

Post-War Frustration

More disappointment was in store, however. In the summer of
1945 the English Labor Party won a suprisingly large victory
in the general election, defeating his trusted friend Churchill.
The new Foreign Secretary, Ernest Bevin, a former trade union
leader, had little understanding of the desperate Jewish need—
and less sympathy. For once, Weizmann, now weary, was unable to persuade or make the man who mattered listen and pay
attention. Another period of commissions of inquiry was substituted for positive action. The first was an Anglo-American
body, six men of standing in public life from each country, who
examined the whole Jewish problem in America, Europe, Palestine, and the Middle East. Weizmann, stricken with failing
vision, was again the spokesman of the Jewish people when the
delegation took evidence in Palestine, and he put forward
practical plans. The committee issued a unanimous report
recommending the immediate entry of a hundred thousand
Jews, continuing substantial immigration, and the cancellation
of restrictions against Jewish settlement on the land. While
the British government dallied, groups of Palestine Jews resorted
to systematic terrorism against British civil officials and soldiers
as well as Arabs. Repression provoked retaliation and more
repression. Though nothing could shake Weizmann's profound
rejection of any unethical short cut, he was almost impotent to
keep the situation in check. He was an invincible humanist,
opposed to the killing of innocent persons, whatever the provo-
cation. "Anything savouring of domination by physical force,
whatever that force may assume, would be intolerable and
belie our history," he affirmed.

When the Zionist Congress met under Weizmann's presidency in Geneva in the critical months of 1946, the aged leader
took his stand against the outrages and pleaded that negotiations
with the British government, however frustrating, should not
be broken off. The majority of the delegates, however, were
impatient and aggressive. The Americans, led by Abba Hillel
Silver, and now the most powerful delegation, had no tradition
of trusting England. David Ben-Gurion and a large section of

Mapai, the labor party, believed that the Jews must fight the English as well as the Arabs in order to obtain the State, and that Weizmann's moderation and his trust in England were detrimental to the Zionist purpose. In the ensuing struggle, Weizmann lost a vote of confidence and ceased to be president of The Jewish Agency and the Zionist Organization. Significantly, nobody was chosen in his stead. His opponents, marshalled to defeat him, knew that nobody could take his place in the larger world as the spokesman of the Jewish people fighting for its existence. But Ben-Gurion was now the unquestioned leader in Palestine.

Negotiating the State

Weizmann returned to his laboratory. But in 1947, when the Assembly of the United Nations, asked by the British government in sheer desperation to advise a solution for the end of the Mandate, appointed a special committee composed of representatives of the states not directly involved, Weizmann was called to expound the history and spiritual ideals of Jews and Zionism. Again he responded, realistically suggesting partition instead of asking for the whole country, which the Zionist Congress majority would have demanded. Again he made a deep impression, as the committee report proved. He repeated his plea before the members of the ad hoc committee at Lake Success, appointed by the General Assembly the following autumn to consider the report.

There was heroism in this aging half-blind prophet crossing continents and oceans to convince world statesmen of the truth and justice of the Jewish cause. His colleagues might reject him as their president, but they knew that he alone could present their case with persuasive moral authority. He alone could say to the United Nations Committee: "The White Paper released certain phenomena in Jewish life which are un-Jewish, and contrary to Jewish ethics and Jewish tradition. 'Thou shalt not kill' has been ingrained in us since Mount Sinai. It was inconceivable ten years ago that the Jews should break this Commandment. Unfortunately they are breaking it today. . . . I hang my head in shame when I have to speak of this fact before you." Against the view of many leaders in Israel and America, he insisted that Jewish terrorism did harm to the Jewish cause.

A few months later, while the debate on the partition of the territory was hotly proceeding, and it was feared that the American delegation was supporting the proposal to allot to the Arabs the greater part of the Negev, with the strip of shore on the Gulf of Aqaba, Weizmann was once again asked to be the savior. In an interview, obtained through the personal intervention of Eddie Jacobson, formerly the business partner of President Truman, he convinced the latter that that desert area was vital to the Jewish state. As a result, the American delegation supported the Jewish claim and swayed the majority. He could win the confidence of the American President, as he had of Balfour, Lloyd George, and Smuts, because he appeared to them as a Hebrew prophet. Weizmann's task before the Assembly and the Committee completed, and the decision of November 29, 1947 for partition and a Jewish state having thrilled the surviving twelve million Jews of the world, he intended to return to Palestine to resume his scientific research. On the way he stopped in England to arrange his affairs—he was still a naturalized British subject—and was to fly to Rehovot the following January.

Weizmann was at this period writing his memoirs, which, with a scientist's modesty and a characteristic approach to human affairs, he called *Trial and Error*. But irresistible pressure from America demanded his return. Measures for implementing the Assembly's decision were not going well: civil war was raging in Palestine between Jews and Arabs; the British administration in the name of neutrality obstructed any systematic preparations prescribed by the Assembly's resolution; chaos loomed when the Mandate was to end in May, 1948. Because of this, the American delegate to the Special Committee was favoring a period of United Nations Trusteeship for the government of the country and the postponement of Jewish and Arab statehood.

Weizmann was asked to avert such a development by using once again his personal influence with President Truman. Early in May it was known that the Jewish Council in Palestine would proclaim the independent State of Israel on the last day of the Mandate, and that the territory allotted to the Jewish state would at once be invaded by Arab armies. It was of supreme importance that without delay Israel should be provisionally recognized as a legitimate state by one of the Great Powers. This time Weizmann wrote to the President, and pleaded the case moderately, ethically, and successfully. Truman granted recognition *de facto* within a few hours of Israel's proclamation of independence at Tel Aviv. That act, followed quickly by recognition by the Soviet Union, gave immense moral encouragement to the hard-pressed nation, fighting against what seemed hopeless odds from the day of its birth.

President of the New State

A few days later Weizmann was named by the Provisional Council of the government of Israel, headed by Ben-Gurion, as the Provisional President of the Republic. Ben-Gurion, after speaking of the differences of opinion which had divided the two leaders in recent years, said: "I doubt whether the Presidency is necessary to Dr. Weizmann, but the Presidency of Weizmann is a moral necessity to the State of Israel." Weizmann's first official act was to accept the invitation of President Truman to be the latter's guest in Washington as president of the youngest democratic state.

After a few days he left America for the last time. He rested a few months at the Lake of Geneva completing his autobiography, until he was strong enough to proceed to Israel to take up his duties, which were mainly formal and honorific. The Prime Minister was the head of the State and the Executive, while the President had more the functions of an English king than of an American president. He could only influence policy indirectly. It is notable that in the last chapters of his book, and in his addresses and messages on formal occasions in Israel, Weizmann constantly emphasized the moral and spiritual aspects of the nation.* He was the sage counselor of He also dwelt almost lovingly on the lessons which the Jews

---

* Lord Halifax, who had been Foreign Secretary and English Ambassador in the United States during the war, records in his *Memoirs* that during the German air attacks on London in 1940, when he and Weizmann were together in the air raid shelter of the Dorchester Hotel, Weizmann spent the time reading the Hebrew Bible.

had learned, and which Israel should go on learning from England.

Weizmann's home in Rehovot, commanding a serene and enchanting view over Judea and Sharon, was his official residence. He was happier there than in Jerusalem or Tel Aviv, and his beloved laboratory in the Institute of Science was but a few hundred yards away. In his last as in his first years, he believed in the importance of science. "The creation of scientific institutions in Israel is essential if we are to secure the intellectual survival of the Jewish people." He felt strongly that Israel must make up for her tiny territory and her modest material resources by excellence in the basic and applied sciences. In that way, too, she could make her worthy contribution to humanity. He was happy that he could attract to Israel some of the eminent Jewish scientists of the world.

Weizmann's scientific legacy to his people and to the world is the constantly expanding Institute of Science at Rehovot which now bears his name. The Weizmann Institute has already made significant contributions in the fundamental sciences of physics, chemistry, and biology; and its workers are engaged in the constant investigation of chemical processes which may help to make Israel economically able to integrate all Jews who wish to live there. They carry on Weizmann's precepts: the constant application of science to the needs of life.

In January, 1949 the Constituent Assembly of Israel, elected by universal adult suffrage, chose Weizmann as president of what was now not a provisional government but a constitutional state. He entered the Assembly Hall of The Jewish Agency in Jerusalem, the temporary chamber for the occasion, to the blowing of the ram's horn, took the oath, and delivered an address stressing Israel's ethical foundations and her hopes and yearnings for peace with the Arabs.

"Today we stand on the threshold of a new era. We leave the dawn of provisional authority, and enter the sunshine of orderly democratic rule. A just struggle is of avail if we, the people of sorrow and affliction, have been vouchsafed today's event, and there is hope in the end for all who long for justice. We stretch out the hand of hope to our neighbors, and of friendship to all peace-loving peoples." Weizmann was president till his death in 1952, but most of the time he was a sick man.

Yet he had cause enough for joy. Israel was now a conscious independent nation, a vibrant reality, a full member of the brotherhood of nations. The ideal that the Jews, once scattered, insecure, disintegrated, should live not on sufferance but as of right in the Land of Israel was accomplished.

Weizmann's Essential Greatness

The essential greatness of Weizmann was his combination of intense Jewish feeling and profound faith in the Jewish future with the imagination and trained mind of the scientist. He applied the methodical logic of the laboratory to political problems. At the same time, he was a living cell from the body of his people, and his face and eyes reflected the suffering of Israel through the ages. He gave his heart and mind to the purposes of restoring the Jewish nation and creating a renaissance of Jewish culture in its old home. He was at once humble and proud, without self-seeking or conceit, but convinced that he must be the leader of people. As a colleague he was difficult, unwilling to exchange counsel, intolerant of criticism, inclined to be authoritarian. Yet he was loved by the scattered Jewish people and the people of Israel, who could all feel that he was one of them. And he attracted eager young men of brilliant mind: for example, in Manchester, Harry Sacher and Leon Simon; in London Professor Brodetsky (later president of the Hebrew University), and Colonel Fred Kisch, the English staff officer who gave up his military career to be a link of the Zionist Executive in Palestine with the mandatory administration. In later years Weizmann commanded the devotion of Abba Eban, Israel's former Ambassador to the United States, Eliahu Elath, Israel's Ambassador to England, and Sir Isaiah Berlin, professor at Oxford Unixersity. His circle of intimate friends was small, but included statesmen and scientists of world renown, and Jewish men of business and affairs. In his wife he had the ideal mate, beautiful and talented. In his Manchester days she was a skillful doctor; in London and Rehovot a most gracious hostess, and devoted to the cause of children and youth immigration.

More than any single person, Chaim Weizmann was responsible for the creation of the physical, mental, and spiritual home for the Jews. He changed world history, and that without ever

practicing or counselling violence. A liberal humanity determined his conduct and his outlook to the end, and he believed
in divine guidance. His legacy is nothing less than the State of
Israel, the fruit of his achievement; and he gave the nation its
pattern of tradition and science. As he embodied the thought
and aspirations of Jews of many ages, so Israel of our age has
been created in his image. The time called for a Jewish leader
who could measure up to the challenge of a Messianic age.
Weizmann was that man.

FOR FURTHER READING

Books by Chaim Weizmann

Trial and Error: The Autobiography of Chaim Weizmann (New York: Harper &
Brothers, 1949). While not always reliable, the author forgets the unpleasant and unflattering. Few individuals have written as well about
their life and times.

The Letters and Papers of Chaim Weizmann, Meyer W. Weisgal and
Barnet Litvinoff, general editors, Series A: Letters, 23 volumes;
Series B: papers, 2 volumes. (Jerusalem, Israel Universities Press,
New Brunswick, New Jersey: Rutgers University Press, 1968–1980,
1985.) A definitive collection, well presented with ample explanatory
notes.

The Essential Chaim Weizmann, compiled and edited by Barnet Litvinoff
(New York; Holmes and Meier, 1982). A one-volume distillation from
the massive 25 volumes cited above. The editing has been careful with
the happy result that there is good value on every page.

Books about Chaim Weizmann

WEISGAL, Meyer W., editor, *Chaim Weizmann* (New York: Dial
Press, 1944). Here are thirty essays by political, literary and scientific
leaders of the day that were presented to Weizmann on the occasion of
his seventieth birthday. The stature of the writers reflects the prestige
of the honoree, and each essay makes a special contribution to
understanding Weizmann.

WEISGAL, Meyer W. and CARMICHAEL, Joel, editor, *Chaim
Weizmann, A Biography By Many Hands* (New York: Atheneum, 1963).
Weisgal's second effort to capture other people's view of Weizmann is
only a little less successful than the first. Isaiah Berlin, Abba Eban, Jon
Kimche, and Richard Crossman are among the contributors.

LITVINOFF, Barnet, *Weizmann: Last of the Patriarchs* (New York: G.P. Putnam, 1976) A brief biography, too brief and thin, but useful for some purposes.

RABINOWITZ, Oskar K., *Fifty Years of Zionism: A Critique of Trial and Error,* (London: Anscome, 1952). A spirited examination of Weizmann's lapses as an autobiographer and historian of his times.

REINHARZ, Jehuda, *Chaim Weizmann: The Making of a Zionist Leader* (New York: Oxford University Press, 1985). The first volume of a long awaited scholarly biography by a professor of modern Jewish history at Brandeis University. The volume concludes with the outbreak of World War I. Reinharz is respectful, but not adulatory, his scholarship is first-rate, and he writes very well.

10 . Louis D. Brandeis
[1856–1941]

MILTON R. KONVITZ

A M O N G the personalities considered in this book, Brandeis is unique in that his fame rests primarily on his contributions to society in general. Had he achieved no position of leadership among Jews, he would still be famous. Of course, some of the other personalities have been recognized as great men by the non-Jewish world, but in every instance they have become famous primarily as Jewish thinkers or leaders. Moses Mendelssohn,* for example, held an important position as philosopher among his contemporaries, but his chief importance was as a leader in the movement to advance the culture of the Jews without lessening their devotion to Judaism. Moses Montefiore** was one of the few Jewish brokers permitted in London in the nineteenth century, but it was his work on behalf of civil equality of English Jews and Jews in Turkey and Russia that brought him esteem. Chaim Weizmann*** discovered a process for the manufacture of acetone and was director of the Admiralty laboratories in World War I, but it was as a Zionist leader that he won world fame.

Another way of seeing the uniqueness of Brandeis is to observe that to most of the other personalities the non-Jewish world became important mainly as it affected Jews and Judaism. Not so Brandeis. He did not begin to think of himself in any significant way as a Jew until he was fifty-four years of age, and by

* Chapter 1.
** Chapter 3.
*** Chapter 9.

that time he had already achieved fame as a lawyer, social scientist, and social reformer. He was at home in different disciplines and different cultures. He had many interests and played many roles. He was an American. He was a humanist. The time came when he was also a Jew. As an American he found that he could give to his Jewish and humanistic values "a local habitation and a name." Brandeis found his world to be a oneness and a manyness: a world big enough for many nations, many religions, many groups, many loyalties, many systems of values—and yet one world where there was interdependence, and need for cross-fertilization, common respect, and understanding.

Brandeis, then, was a great Jewish personality in a unique way. He was not representative of Jewish leaders of the past. He was the product and expression of a free democratic society —in which a man was free to be a Jew, and a Jew was free to be a man and citizen. His life and work were those of a civilized man who came to cherish Judaism, and those of a Jew who cherished humanity. Brandeis was thus a symbol of the adventure of a free spirit; of an intelligence that rejected all that was parochial, narrow, confining; of a courage that identified itself with all that was vital and creative in man and society. What the poet Keats wrote in a letter would have been acceptable to Brandeis: "I do not live in this world alone, but in a thousand worlds."

Background and Beginnings

In 1654 a tiny vessel, the St. Charles, deposited twenty-three Jews at New York, the Dutch colony on the Hudson. While individual Jews had probably arrived earlier, the landing of this group marked the beginning of Jewish immigration to the United States. By 1848 the Jewish population was about twenty thousand, most of them immigrants from Western Europe. Some of these men and women, touched by the Emancipation and the Enlightenment, came because the failure of the 1848 revolution in Central Europe had convinced them that only in the United States would they find freedom and equality of opportunity.

Among the "Forty-Eighters" was Adolph Brandeis, a native

of Prague, who would have fought in the 1848 revolution had he not been stricken by typhoid fever. Instead, in the fall of that year, he migrated to the United States. Adolph, fascinated by America, promptly applied for naturalization. "I already love our country so much," he wrote to Frederika Dembitz, his fiancee, "that I rejoice when I can sing its praises." In 1849 the steamship Washington brought twenty-six members of the Brandeis, Dembitz, and Wehle families. Adolph and Frederika were soon married, and settled in Madison, Indiana; after two years they moved to Louisville, Kentucky, where their son Louis Dembitz was born on November 13, 1856.

Adolph Brandeis prospered as a grain merchant. After Louis was graduated from high school, the family went to Europe for three years, part of which time Louis spent at school in Dresden. When they returned to the United States, Louis, then nineteen, entered Harvard Law School, and achieved a scholastic record for excellence that became a legend—a record that no student has since equalled. On graduation Brandeis went to St. Louis, but two years later he opened a law office in Boston in partnership with Samuel D. Warren, Jr., a former classmate at Harvard. The firm did well. At the age of twenty-six Brandeis was successful in raising a fund sufficient to install Oliver Wendell Holmes, Jr., in a law professorship at Harvard Law School. At about the same time he himself accepted an invitation to teach a course in legal evidence at Harvard, but the next year refused the offer of an assistant professorship—he preferred to remain in active law practice. He organized the Harvard Law School Association, and for this as well as other notable contributions to his alma mater, Harvard awarded him an M.A. degree in 1891. By this time he enjoyed an annual income of fifty thousand dollars—a fabulous amount at that time (by 1907 Brandeis had earned a million dollars, and ten years later was a millionaire twice over). His reputation as a leading corporation lawyer was firmly established.

Brandeis' financial independence enabled him to work without compensation for public causes that interested him. Early in life he had begun to seek out such causes, and soon many such causes sought him. He was a rare phenomenon: a successful corporation lawyer with a keen social conscience and an irrepressible desire to work for a better world. Although never opposed to capitalism, Brandeis was one of the first successful Americans to propose measures against the social and moral abuses of aggressive capitalism. He was among the first also to insist on representation of the public interest at legislative hearings. He wanted government to stay out of business, but even more he wanted business to stay out of government.

Early Concern with Social Problems

Brandeis pioneered for the idea of collective bargaining between employers and labor unions. He maintained that unions should not be branded and persecuted as criminal conspiracies; big business made big unions necessary. If unions acted arbitrarily, unreasonably, or criminally, their evil acts or tendencies should be repressed, but their existence and legitimate interests should be encouraged and protected. As early as 1911 he favored legislation restricting the use of the injunction in labor disputes. Earlier in 1904, he had urged stabilization and full employment policies. He had advised management to open its books for inspection by unions so that a proper factual basis for collective bargaining with respect to wages could be established, thus anticipating a decision of the Supreme Court made in 1956. He saw the labor unions as a great conservative force, a bulwark against radicalism and socialism. Though he opposed the closed shop as a restriction on the rights of workers, he favored a union in every shop. The right to combine, he maintained, was absolute, even among public employees; the right to strike, however, was not absolute. In sum, Brandeis was a pathfinder: he projected social policies that later were embodied in the Norris-LaGuardia Act of 1932, the Wagner Act of 1935, the Employment Act of 1946, and the Taft-Hartley Act of 1947.

According to Brandeis himself, it was the Homestead Strike of 1892 that set him to thinking seriously about the labor problem. At Homestead, Pennsylvania, the scene of one of the most bitterly fought labor disputes in American history, the manager of one of the largest steel plants in the United States had hired about three hundred men of the Pinkerton private detective agency to protect company property as well as the non-union men who had been hired during the strike. An armed battle broke out between the Pinkerton men and the strikers in which sixty men were wounded and ten killed. The governor of Pennsylvania called out the National Guard, under whose protection the company kept the non-union employees at work and broke the strike. It took the shock of that battle, said Brandeis, "to turn my mind definitely toward a searching study of the relations of labor to industry." While other American leaders were also shocked by the happenings at Homestead, Brandeis was one of the very few who proceeded to study the causes of the evil and search for remedies.

Brandeis also tackled other pressing social problems. He exposed the industrial life insurance racket and agitated on behalf of insurance by savings banks instead of by insurance companies. (Three states—Massachusetts, Connecticut, and New York—have since enacted laws that permit the Brandeis form of insurance.) Indeed, whenever he had an opportunity, Brandeis fought against monopolies. He saw a threat to the average person in the large trusts, holding companies, cartels, interlocking corporate directorships—in big business in general. Without economic opportunity and economic democracy for individuals, Brandeis argued, political democracy would be ineffective. He therefore raised his voice against every form of absolutism, whether in government, business, or organized labor. He did not consider monopolies a necessary evil that should or could be regulated by government, and opposed regulated monopoly; he wanted instead regulated competition among business and industrial units that would not engage in monopolistic practices.

Contribution to American Labor History

In the first several decades of the twentieth century both the employers and workers in the garment industry in New York City were predominantly Jewish immigrants. The International Ladies' Garment Workers' Union was demanding the closed shop while the employers attacked the union as a Marxist conspiracy. A state of anarchy existed. In 1910 there was a general strike that engendered much bitterness on both sides. Neither party was willing to make concessions or consider compromises. Following the intervention of certain civic leaders, all agreed that the only hope of bringing the dispute to an end lay in empowering Brandeis to confer with both labor and management and submit a plan of negotiation.

This was done; and it is related that in the course of the bitter arguments between garment workers and their "bosses," Brandeis at times heard a man shout in Yiddish: *"Ihr darft sich shemen! Passt dos far a Idn?"* ("Shame! Is this worthy of a Jew?") On one occasion he heard a shopworker confront his employer with a quotation in Hebrew from the prophet Isaiah (3:14-15):

> It is you who have devoured the vineyard, the spoil of the poor is in your houses.
> What do you mean by crushing My people, by grinding the face of the poor? says the Lord God of hosts.

Brandeis was deeply moved by such incidents.

At Brandeis' insistence, the union waived the closed shop, which led to a temporary split in the ranks of the workers. At a peace conference of union representatives and employers, Brandeis stated that his interest was not only in getting them to reach an accord that would end the strike, but also, and of greater significance, to create a relationship that would make future strikes unnecessary. As the basis for industrial peace, Brandeis proposed the preferential union shop, whereby the employer would have the right to select employees on the basis of their qualifications, but with preference for qualified union members. Union shop standards were to prevail in the industry. This proposal was attacked by extremists as a sell-out to the other side; and Jacob Schiff* and Louis Marshall** tried to placate both parties. After months of wrangling and negotiations, the protocol, as Brandeis called it, was accepted and signed by all concerned.

This agreement has played a notable role in American labor history as one of the first important collective bargaining agreements. It marked, on the one hand, a departure by organized labor from its persistent demand for total union security, that

---

* Financier and philanthropist (1847-1920), and virtual lay head of American Jewry.

** Jurist and Jewish communal leader (1856-1929), eminent as an appellate lawyer and defender of civil liberties as well as in Jewish affairs.

is, the closed shop, and, on the other hand, a departure by employers from their obstinate refusal to concede recognition to labor unions. The protocol also introduced into a disorganized industry a form of self-policing and self-government by setting up an inspection board to standardize and maintain proper working conditions. The protocol also proceeded on the principle, now universally followed, that the agreement is only the initial step in achieving and maintaining industrial peace and democracy; accordingly, it provided for a grievance board with authority to settle disputes arising out of the agreement; if this agency failed to achieve a dispute settlement, the grievance was to be submitted to a board of arbitrators. Lockouts and strikes were not to take place. For its day, the introduction of arbitration for the settlement of grievances was a pioneering step—one which set the pattern for the future.

Efforts for Scientific Management

Shortly after the protocol was signed, Brandeis turned his attention to scientific management, which attracted national attention to the inefficient methods prevailing in American industry. At the end of 1910 the Interstate Commerce Commission conducted public hearings on proposed increases in railroad freight charges. Brandeis, testifying on behalf of the public interest, opposed the increases on the ground that the public should not be compelled to subsidize the inefficient operation of the carriers. Brandeis charged the railroads with engaging in practices that victimized the consumer and the small businessman—particularly, increasing rates constantly in order to meet higher costs. With scientific management, Brandeis maintained, the carriers could pay higher wages without raising rates. By introducing efficiency methods, he argued, they could add a million dollars a day to their income.

These statements by Brandeis created a sensation, and the subjects of business efficiency and scientific management were widely discussed by the public for the first time. Though the railroads attacked Brandeis, within a decade industrialists, including railroad executives, admitted the legitimacy of his claims on behalf of the application of scientific methods to industrial management.

What seemed radical in the first decade of the twentieth century has since become an accepted truth. Just as he worked to make industrial management scientific, Brandeis also sought for ways to make business a profession. In this effort, too, he was a pioneer: today schools of business administration are integral divisions of many universities throughout the country.

In these various ways, Brandeis contributed greatly to an awareness and understanding of social problems. One can easily see his influence in the policies of Samuel Gompers, Sidney Hillman, David Dubinsky, Walter Reuther, and other leaders of American organized labor. Brandeis helped direct American thought and institutions away from the class-struggle ideologies and toward union-employer cooperation, expressed in thousands of collective bargaining agreements and in basic social legislation. Not utopianism, but constant improvement through practical measures was the aim of Brandeis' reformism—a philosophy he derived from Benjamin Franklin, Jefferson, Emerson, and William James, which eventually linked itself with the New Freedom, the New Deal, and the Fair Deal.

Contribution to American Law

Notable and enduring as was Brandeis' impact on American liberal thought and the country's social and economic institutions, his contribution to American law and legal institutions was even greater. In his work as a legal reformer he was, on the whole, a solitary pathfinder: his work was daring and original. And here, too, his effort was not to destroy but to preserve and to give new direction and new life.

In 1908 Brandeis introduced the economic or "Brandeis" brief into the Supreme Court, an act of adventurous courage which alone would have won him distinction in American jurisprudence. In *Muller v. Oregon* the Supreme Court had before it a state statute that limited to ten the number of hours for women workers. At the request of the State of Oregon, Brandeis wrote the brief in defense of the statute, devoting most of it to economic and statistical data and to arguments drawn from official reports which showed that long hours of work were dangerous to women's health, morals, and welfare. This approach—putting the main weight of the argument on economic and sociological factual studies, rather than on dry logic or *a priori* arguments—was bold and new. No lawyer had ever before dared to argue a law case in this way. The Supreme Court was won over by Brandeis and his brief: the Oregon statute was held to be constitutional, and the Court openly complimented Brandeis for bringing before it facts and opinions showing that the act was not unreasonable.

After this sensational success, Brandeis continued to file similar briefs in state and federal cases; a pattern was thus established that lawyers and judges no longer question. The later struggle to validate, constitutionally, social legislation enacted by Congress and by the state legislatures, which was won in 1937, when the Supreme Court began to uphold New Deal legislation, could never have been resolved were it not for the deep and pervasive influence of the Brandeis approach to constitutional questions affecting social legislation. The American people enjoy today the fruit of ideas planted by Brandeis as far back as 1908.

Justice of the Supreme Court

It was against the background of such monumental achievements that Brandeis was nominated for the United States Supreme Court by President Woodrow Wilson early in 1916. Since he was the first Jew to receive this honor, the conservative forces in the country were aroused: seven former presidents of the American Bar Association, including William Howard Taft, opposed confirmation; so, too, did A. Lawrence Lowell, President of Harvard University (although Brandeis was a Harvard Law School Overseer at the time). But Charles W. Eliot, Harvard's President Emeritus, favored Brandeis; so did Newton D. Baker, who became Secretary of War in March 1916, and Frances Perkins, who was to become Franklin D. Roosevelt's Secretary of Labor. In the Senate committee named to consider the nomination, ten Democrats voted for and eight Republicans voted against confirmation. After five months of public controversy, the appointment was approved in the Senate by a vote of forty-seven to twenty-two.

Brandeis was sixty years of age when he took his place on the Supreme Court. He retired in 1939 after twenty-three years of distinguished service. His name and his record stand with those of John Marshall, Joseph Story, Roger B. Taney, Stephen J. Field, and Oliver Wendell Holmes.

A major contribution of Justice Brandeis was to deepen public consciousness of the significance of civil liberties. With Justice Holmes, Brandeis worked incessantly to teach his colleagues and the American people that unless basic human freedoms were respected, protected, and strengthened, American society and institutions would hardly be worthy of a notable place in the history of mankind. This conviction was expressed by Holmes and Brandeis consistently and repeatedly, most of the time in dissenting opinions, some of which have become important historic documents.

In a case before the Court in 1919, Justice Holmes first formulated the clear and present danger doctrine; it remained, however, for Justice Brandeis to give the clearest articulation of this doctrine in an opinion he wrote in 1927. The fundamental freedoms enumerated in the First Amendment, he said, may not be denied or abridged; yet the freedoms of speech and assembly that were involved in the case are not absolutes. They may be restricted by necessity, but constitutionally the necessity does not exist "unless speech would produce, or is intended to produce, a clear and imminent danger of some substantive evil which the state constitutionally may seek to prevent." When a state enacts a law to meet an evil, and the law limits the exercise of a fundamental liberty, it is the duty of the Court to determine for itself whether the enactment was in fact necessary; the Court is not bound by the fact that the vast majority of a state's citizens believe that the dissemination of certain doctrines is fraught with evil consequences. At one time, said Brandeis, "man feared witches and burned women. It is the function of speech to free men from the bondage of irrational fears." To justify, constitutionally, restrictions on free speech, said Brandeis, there must be "reasonable ground to fear that serious evil will result if free speech is practiced; reasonable ground to believe that the danger apprehended is imminent; reasonable ground to believe that the evil to be prevented is a serious one."

The clear and present danger doctrine, as stated by Holmes and Brandeis in numerous opinions, has become an accepted constitutional interpretation. Though it has not always been followed, even those who attack or question its force do not disregard it. The doctrine stands as a "fence" to protect the First Amendment freedoms against attempts to whittle them down in the name of alleged national security or state emergencies. To all persons who would play fast and loose with these freedoms, the words of Brandeis stand as a reminder and a warning: "Those who won our independence by revolution were not cowards. They did not fear political change. They did not exalt order at the cost of liberty."

Brandeis' second most notable contribution as a Justice of the Supreme Court was his insistence that Congress and the states have constitutionally the discretion to experiment with economic and social institutions in the light of facts that show a need for action. While a clear and present danger—and only such a danger—may justify an abridgment of a fundamental liberty, much more freedom is vested in the legislative judgment as it is brought to bear on economic and social problems. There is no right to experiment with human rights, but there is a right to experiment with economic and social institutions. It is, said Brandeis, "one of the happy incidents of the federal system that a single courageous state may, if its citizens choose, serve as a laboratory, and try novel social and economic experiments without risk to the rest of the country." As long as the statute setting up the social experiment is not arbitrary, capricious, or unreasonable, the United States Constitution should not be interpreted to stand in the way.

The same open-mindedness for which Brandeis pleaded in his economic brief submitted to the Court in *Muller v. Oregon* appears in his work as a Supreme Court Justice, mainly, however, in his dissenting opinions (with which Justice Holmes generally agreed). The scientific attitude, he argued, must be permitted application to social and economic problems faced by the nation and the states. The advances in science have shown that what seems to be impossible sometimes happens. The progress made in science and technology attests to the value of the trial-and-error method, the method of experimentation. The Due Process Clause of the Fourteenth Amendment, Brandeis contended, must not be used to stand in the way of efforts to improve our social institutions—and improvements can be brought about only through experiments, some of which may fail and some of which may succeed. In 1931, in a dissenting opinion, Brandeis told his colleagues on the Court that to stand in the way of experimentation in social and economic matters was a grave responsibility; the denial of this right may bring about serious consequences; the right should not be denied unless the legislative measure is clearly arbitrary. The Court should not strike down a statute that seeks a solution to a difficult social problem by interjecting prejudices into legal principles. "If we would guide by the light of reason," said Brandeis, "we must let our minds be bold."

The intellectual boldness to which Brandeis challenged the Court often involved the necessity to overcome prior decisions. On this point, too, Brandeis insisted that the Court must follow not precedents, but the light of reason. In constitutional cases the Court should decide either to follow a precedent or to overrule it. In overruling earlier decisions that involve constitutional provisions, said Brandeis in a dissenting opinion in 1932, the Court merely bows to the lessons of experience and to the force of better reasoning and recognizes that the process of trial and error, so fruitful in the physical sciences, is also appropriate in the judicial process. In other words, just as the legislatures may resort to the scientific method in conducting social experiments, so, too, may the courts conduct judicial experiments which entail the rejection of precedents that have not stood the test of time.

The Constitution, if it is to be a living force in the affairs of men, must not be worshipped or venerated but used as an instrument that encourages the exercise of the free intelligence as it struggles with the complex problems of American society. It was not until 1937 that the Supreme Court was won over to the Brandeis logic and method. It was the dissenting opinions of Brandeis—and Holmes—that prepared the ground for the New Deal changes in the Supreme Court—and for the school desegregation decision in *Brown v. Topeka* in 1954.

Brandeis Joins Zionist Movement

It was characteristic of Brandeis, who demonstrated in every aspect of his legal career a passion for social justice, that, once won to the cause of Zionism, he would approach it on the prac-

tical, pragmatic level, and give it the fullest measure of his devotion. In 1912, two years after Brandeis' mediation of the
ILGWU strike, Jacob de Haas, who had been London secretary to Theodor Herzl, and was now editor of the *Jewish
Advocate* in Boston, called on Brandeis for his views on certain
aspects of savings bank insurance that might be of special
interest to Jewish parents. At one point De Haas spoke of
Louis N. Dembitz, Brandeis' uncle, as a "noble Jew" and an
early Zionist. De Haas spoke also of Herzl and the Zionist
movement. Brandeis was greatly interested. Other discussions
followed, which led Brandeis to study published materials on
Zionism. When he joined the Federation of American Zionists,
this fact was publicly announced at the Zionist convention in
Cleveland. In 1913 Brandeis presided at a meeting in Boston to
welcome Nahum Sokolow, Zionist intellectual and leader from
Europe, and he made other appearances at Zionist meetings in
different parts of the country. At the national Zionist convention in Cincinnati in 1913, Brandeis advocated the diversion of
Jewish immigration to Palestine, negotiation with the Turkish
government (then in control of Palestine) for large concessions,
and the industrialization of Palestine through capital investment.

After the outbreak of World War I in 1914, it seemed de-
sirable to move the world center of Zionist activities from
Europe to the United States. On August 30 of that year a New
York conference of one hundred and fifty Zionists was held,
at which a provisional executive Committee for General Zionist
Affairs was organized. Brandeis became chairman and thus
leader of the Zionist movement in the United States at a time of
international crisis.

Chairman of Zionist Provisional Committee

At the close of the New York meeting which elected Brandeis, the administrative committee which he headed worked
almost all night and the next day. Characteristically, Brandeis
injected into the new task his tremendous drive, capacity for
hard work, and an eagerness for facts and practical results.

In accepting the chairmanship Brandeis had told the conferees
that he considered it his duty to aid the cause "so far as it is in

my power to do so." He was aware of his own "disqualifications" for the important task:

> Throughout long years which represent my life [he was then fifty-eight], I have been to a great extent separated from Jews. I am very ignorant in things Jewish. But recent experiences, public and professional, have taught me this: I find Jews possessed of those very qualities which we of the twentieth century seek to develop in our struggle for justice and democracy: a deep moral feeling which makes them capable of noble acts; a deep sense of the brotherhood of man; and a high intelligence, the fruit of three thousand years of civilization.
>
> These experiences have made me feel that the Jewish people have something which should be saved for the world; that the Jewish people should be preserved; and that it is our duty to pursue that method of saving which most promises success.

In his position as leader of Zionism in the United States, Brandeis subsequently traveled to many cities, where he delivered lectures which were heard by thousands of persons and were read in printed form by many additional thousands. He made a special point of answering the charge of some anti-Zionists that Zionism was disloyalty to America. Zionism "is not a movement to remove all the Jews compulsorily to Palestine," Brandeis pointed out. Zionism was a movement to enlarge—and not to contract—the freedom of the Jew so that, like the Greek, the Irish, or the German, he might exercise an option to live in the land of his fathers or in another country of his choice. By supporting Zionism, an American Jew was not necessarily seeking to change his own home, but rather to win for Jews everywhere the freedom to make their home in Palestine or elsewhere. For Jews who did not wish to leave the United States, a Jewish state in Palestine would serve as a center from which Jewish values radiate and as a spiritual force to preserve Jews from assimilation; it would give Jews everywhere "that inspiration which springs from memories of a great past and the hope of a great future."

Brandeis brought this same message to audiences of young people at Harvard, Columbia, and other universities. In 1915 he wrote that "Zionist affairs are really the important things in life now." Not a day went by that he did not do some work on behalf of the cause. He insisted on frequent and detailed reports from the Zionist organization staff—no detail was too small for his interest. He sought opportunities to address groups hostile to Zionism so that he might win them over. He was deeply moved by the disclosures of wholesale miseries suffered by Jews in Russia and Poland, and in his speeches he appealed for funds, linking relief and Zionism, the immediate needs and the future hopes of the Jewish people.

Anticipating the end of the war and settlement of international political questions, Zionist leaders in Europe and the United States prepared themselves to place before the Allied Powers definite demands with respect to Palestine as well as for equal rights for all European Jews. Since Brandeis thought it essential to unite American Jewry, early in 1916 he joined in a call for a democratically constituted American Jewish congress, to help win Jewish rights in Palestine and the rights of Jews in other countries. Twenty-six organizations agreed to establish this congress. Brandeis was temporary chairman and honorary president. Just at that time he was confirmed as Associate Justice of the Supreme Court, and he felt it necessary to resign from these positions. Though he cut all his other ties with social causes and organizations, his Zionist work, however, did not cease.

Balfour Declaration

As a Justice of the Supreme Court, Brandeis enjoyed even more prestige than he had in the past; and this increased his usefulness for Zionist ends. Zionist leaders everywhere were intent on winning a settlement of the Palestine question as part of the over-all peace settlement that was to follow the end of World War I. In 1914 Brandeis had discussed the Palestine question with President Wilson and later with the British and French ambassadors to the United States, and in the next few years he continued discussions and negotiations with the Department of State and Allied officials. On April 6, 1917, the United States entered the war, which facilitated negotiations with regard to Palestine. In May, 1917, Brandeis met Lord Balfour, Foreign Secretary in Lloyd George's coalition ministry, at the White House, where the latter had come as head of

Britain's war mission. Balfour had expressed his eagerness to see Brandeis, and later Brandeis conferred with both Wilson and Balfour. He was also in close contact with Zionist leaders in Britain, notably Chaim Weizmann and James Rothschild.

On November 2, 1917, the Balfour Declaration was issued, pledging British support to the establishment in Palestine of a national home for the Jewish people. At the 1918 Zionist Convention, held in Pittsburgh, Brandeis offered a five-point social justice code for Palestine, which was adopted and became known as the Pittsburgh program. It called for political and civil equality of all inhabitants without regard to creed, race, or sex; public ownership and control of the land and its natural resources and all public utilities; the leasing of land on conditions that would insure fullest opportunity for development and continuity of possession; the setting up of all economic institutions on the cooperative principle; and a system of free public schools. Since American Zionists supported these principles, but European Zionists resisted making them part of the Zionist policy for and in Palestine, the two groups began to drift apart.

Brandeis and Weizmann

On November 11, 1918, the war came to an end. The following year Brandeis travelled to London, where he met Weizmann* for the first time. In his autobiography, *Trial and Error*, Weizmann described his impression of Brandeis as follows:

Justice Brandeis has often been compared with Abraham Lincoln, and indeed they had much in common besides clean-chiseled features and lofty brows. Brandeis, too, was a Puritan: upright, austere, of a scrupulous honesty and implacable logic. These qualities sometimes made him hard to work with; like Wilson, he was apt to evolve theories, based on the highest principles, from his inner consciousness, and then expect the facts to fit in with them. If the facts failed to oblige, so much the worse for the facts. Indeed, the conflicts which developed between Brandeis and ourselves were not unlike those which disturbed Wilson's relations with his European colleagues when he first had to work closely with them.

* See Chapter 9.

Weizmann thought of Brandeis as a doctrinaire theoretician whose mind worked from premise to fact; this was, however, a complete misconception because actually the mind of Brandeis worked in just the opposite way, from fact to concept. In truth, Brandeis was the least doctrinaire of men: his hunger for facts was insatiable, and he searched them out without fixed preconceptions.

After Brandeis left London, he went to Paris to confer with Wilson, Balfour, and others; he then travelled to Palestine, where he visited all the cities and most of the colonies. This trip confirmed his belief that Palestine must become the Jewish homeland.

The following year (1920), a World Zionist Conference was held in London. Weizmann was elected president; Brandeis, head of the American delegation, was named honorary president. But it was apparent that these two men did not agree on fundamental policies, and that a break between them was inevitable. In Brandeis' view, the future called for practical work in Palestine: acquisition of more land, reforestation, public health, immigration, capital investments. He wanted men with business and executive abilities to take over the main portion of the work, and he was prepared to welcome the cooperation of non-Zionists in the practical work of upbuilding the land. To Weizmann, however, political Zionism still had important functions to perform; the Balfour Declaration and the acceptance by Great Britain of the mandate over Palestine in April 1920 were only the start of a new era of Zionist political work and political action. Weizmann did not want to see Zionist forces compromised in any way by non-Zionists working within the organization. When Weizmann's views prevailed at the London conference, Brandeis resigned as honorary president.

The Cleveland Convention

In time Brandeis also lost the support of most American Zionists. In 1921 the Zionist Organization of America met in Cleveland, and Weizmann came over to attend the convention. Brandeis' administration lost on a vote of confidence; he resigned as leader but refused to lead a secessionist movement or leave the organization. Thereafter he devoted much time and energy to those Palestine agencies that had undertaken practical tasks in the rebuilding of the land.

As later years demonstrated, Weizmann had been right in thinking that the political activities of Zionist organizations had much work to accomplish before Palestine would in fact become the national homeland. But Brandeis had also been correct in stressing the practical work that needed to be done. Perhaps if each had accepted the other's point of view without relinquishing his own, Zionism would have made much faster strides, both practically and politically, during the period from 1921 to 1948.

Even after Brandeis had ceased to be an official leader of the Zionist forces, he continued until the end of his life to give the movement his moral and financial support. At the time of his death, the residue of his large estate, beyond what was willed to his immediate family, was divided as follows: one-fourth to Survey Associates for the maintenance of civil liberty and the promotion of workers' education, one-fourth for the library and law school of the University of Louisville, and the remaining one-half for "the upbuilding of Palestine as a national home for the Jewish people."

Brandeis' Zionist Philosophy

What did Zionism mean to Brandeis? Why did "the upbuilding of Palestine as a national home for the Jewish people" have such a profound hold on his mind and heart?

First, he saw the Jewish homeland as a small country, free of the curse of bigness. Being small, it could conduct daring experiments in social living and social justice, and the citizens would be able quickly and effectively to judge of the success or failure of their new ventures.

Second, Brandeis felt that given the character of the Jewish pioneers in Palestine, the new settlement would be an almost pure democracy, with women and men equal partners in economic and political rights and activities. In the colonies, economic differences, if they existed, were not to serve as a basis for the enjoyment or denial of political and economic democracy or the rights and duties flowing from democracy. Brandeis was certain that the ideals of freedom and equality would flourish in the Jewish homeland, and lead to extraordinary spiritual and social developments.

Third, Brandeis sensed that in the Jewish homeland the settlers would enjoy the fundamental right to be different, to be themselves. A people, no less than a person, he felt, has the right to mold and order its life in its own way, expressing its own genius, ideals, history, and traditions. The Jews collectively should enjoy the rights and freedoms to develop as do other groups of people. In Palestine, Brandeis stated, Jews would enjoy not only the personal rights and freedoms they should have as citizens of any democratic state, but, in addition, they would also enjoy group rights and freedoms, to develop their own language, ways of thought and living.

By achieving these group rights and freedoms in their own homeland, Jews could make an important contribution to their coreligionists living elsewhere. The American Jew would thus benefit from the development of Jewish culture in the homeland. Furthermore, like all other peoples, American Jews should have the option to remain in the United States or go to Palestine. The establishment of a Jewish homeland would thus give Jews everywhere freedoms hitherto denied them by the tragedies of their history—freedom of choice, freedom to be different, and freedom to enjoy spiritual ties with their own people.

The Jewish nation in Palestine would be different, for the Jewish settlers there would bring to a common center qualities of character and moral and social ideals that were the fruit of their history, tradition, and experience. Brandeis put high among those qualities and ideals the reverence for law and the concept of morality. He also included commitments to brotherhood and righteousness, democratic and cooperative living, social justice, and peace. Further characteristics were, in his view, a strong sense of duty and right, high intellectual attainments based on the belief in universal education, and a strong sense of community responsibility.

"Such is our inheritance," said Justice Brandeis; "such the estate which we hold in trust." What obligations are imposed by this trust?

. . . The short answer is *noblesse oblige;* and its command is twofold. It imposes duties upon us in respect to our own conduct as individuals; it imposes no less important duties upon us as part of the Jewish community or people. Self-respect demands that each of us lead individually a life worthy of our great inheritance and of the glorious traditions of the people. But this is demanded also by respect for the rights of others. The Jews have not only been ever known as a "peculiar people"; they were and remain a distinctive and minority people. Now it is one of the necessary incidents of a distinctive and minority people that the act of any one is in some degree attributed to the whole group. A single though inconspicuous instance of dishonorable conduct on the part of a Jew in any trade or profession has far-reaching evil effects extending to the many innocent members of the race. Large as this country is, no Jew can behave badly without injuring each of us in the end. . . . Since the act of each becomes thus the concern of all, we are perforce our brothers' keepers, exacting even from the lowliest the avoidance of things dishonorable; and we may properly brand the guilty as disloyal to the people. . . .

And yet, though the Jew makes his individual life the loftiest, that alone will not fulfill the obligations of his trust. We are bound not only to use worthily our great inheritance, but to preserve, and if possible, augment it; and then transmit it to coming generations. The fruit of three thousand years of civilization and a hundred generations of suffering may not be sacrificed by us. It will be sacrificed if dissipated. Assimilation is national suicide. And assimilation can be prevented only by preserving national characteristics and life as other peoples, large and small, are preserving and developing their national life. Shall we with our inheritance do less than the Irish? . . . And must we not, like them, have a land where the Jewish life may be naturally led, the Jewish language spoken, and the Jewish spirit prevail? Surely we must, and that land is our fathers' land; it is Palestine.

Adapting a phrase of Mazzini, Justice Brandeis said that no Jew may be a moral mediocrity. And that, he added, was precisely how the Jewish pioneers in Palestine felt because they were conscious of their inheritance. "It is the Jewish tradition," Brandeis said, "and the Jewish law, and the Jewish spirit which prepare us for the lessons of life. In Palestine the younger generation is taught that heritage and as a result they live for the highest and the best of what life is and what it may be."

Finally, Brandeis saw in Zionism the possibility for the American Jew of living and thinking in a pluralistic world. A free man who seeks spiritual riches must have many loyalties. "Multiple loyalties," said Brandeis, "are objectionable only if they are inconsistent. . . . Every American Jew who aids in advancing the Jewish settlement in Palestine, though he feels that neither he nor his descendants will ever live there, will . . . be a better American for doing so."

Zionism and Americanism Compatible

Since "the twentieth-century ideals of America have been the ideals of the Jew for more than twenty centuries," and Zionism is committed to the preservation and strengthening of these ideals in Jewish living in a Jewish homeland, it followed for Brandeis that "to be good Americans, we must become Zionists." The Jewish rebuilding in Palestine, furthermore, would enable American Jews better to perform their duty to the United States, for it would help them to make "toward the attainment of the American ideals of democracy and social justice that large contribution for which religion and life have peculiarly fitted the Jew." The "Zionist ideals, the highest Jewish ideals," Brandeis said, "are essentially the American ideals."

Thus, with a logic that is unanswerable and with a conviction that went to the deep recesses of his heart and soul, Brandeis found in Zionism a home for all his important values and ideals, both Jewish and American—for his faith in freedom and democracy, his love of experimentation, his pluralistic philosophy, his social conscience, his prophetic commitment to righteousness and justice, his strong sense of group loyalty, his belief in equality and in the right of the person and the group to be different.

In an opinion he wrote in 1927, Brandeis said that "the greatest menace to freedom is an inert people." While in saying this he had in mind the American people and American civil liberties, Brandeis could have applied the same thought to the Jewish people. In Zionism, Brandeis saw a way to maximize the living forces in Judaism and in the Jewish people: free acts on behalf of freedom.

FOR FURTHER READING
Books by Louis Brandeis

Letters of Louis D. Brandeis, edited by Melvin I. Urofsky and David W. Levy (Albany: State University of New York Press, 1971–1975). To trace Brandeis' espousal of Zionism the reader should begin with Volume 3.

Brandeis On Zionism, edited by Solomon Goldman (Washington: Zionist Organization of America, 1942). This important collection of Brandeis' Zionist writings is hard to obtain, but well worth the effort.

Books about Louis Brandeis

DE HAAS, Jacob, *Louis D. Brandeis, A Biographical Sketch* (New York: Bloch, 1929). A panegyric that contains much of value about Brandeis and his Zionist work.

MASON, Alpheus T., *Brandeis, A Free Man's Life* (New York: Viking, 1946). The most thorough, balanced biography. It lacks only the richer archival sources of later studies.

UROFSKY, Melvin I., *A Mind of One Piece: Brandeis and American Reform* (New York: Scribners, 1971). A useful supplement to the Mason biography by a leading historian of Zionism in America.

UROFSKY, Melvin I., *American Zionism From Herzl to the Holocaust* (New York: Doubleday, 1975). This major study will allow the reader to place Brandeis' contribution to American Zionism in its proper context.

11 . Henrietta Szold

[1860–1945]

TAMAR DE SOLA POOL

ON FEBRUARY 13, 1945, Henrietta Szold succumbed, at the age of eighty-four, after a year's struggle with pain. "I have not lived one life, but several, each one bearing its own character and insignia," Miss Szold had written from her hospital bed in Jerusalem.

It would have been no easy task even for her to trace her many careers, starting in her teens when she became a teacher of German, French, English, algebra, and botany in a fashionable school in Baltimore, Maryland. Her literary inclination and compelling humanitarianism, which later lifted her to dynamic and creative heights, emerged during her teaching experience. A journalist at seventeen, she entered the wider field of publication in her twenties. Her far-visioned Americanization work preceded her Zionist interests, which reached their climax when, at fifty-two, she founded Hadassah, the organization through which she set her healing hands upon her people.

As the years passed, Henrietta Szold entered many other avenues of service. She was the health pioneer of Palestine, and later set the pattern for a lasting system for youth rehabilitation in the new state through an inspired program of labor, study, and social integration. In her direction of Youth Aliyah she helped to rescue thousands of children, victims of Hitler, whom she called "brands plucked from the burning." By any test or measure, Henrietta Szold was the mother of social service in Palestine. She viewed social work as one of the great human achievements of her era.

Early Influences

The eldest of eight children (five survived to maturity) of Rabbi Benjamin and Sophie Schaar Szold, Henrietta was born in Baltimore on December 21, 1860—*Kislev* 26, 5620, the second day of *Hanukkah* in that year. The influence of the Szold home never left Henrietta.

She was a bright child and accepted early the prerogatives and responsibilities of primogeniture that tradition usually conferred on a son. At the family table she had an assigned seat at the right of her father, her teacher and counselor. From him she learned Hebrew, the Scriptures, and elements of rabbinic literature. He discussed with her questions of right and wrong in the social order. There in the Lombard Street home, her humanitarian fire was kindled. "It is Lombard Street," she later wrote from Jerusalem, "that makes for sympathy and understanding; the rest may do its worst." It was there too that her social service career really began.

Henrietta's father was an active and vocal abolitionist. One of her earliest recollections centered on April 21, 1865, when at the age of four she was taken to see the funeral cortege of Abraham Lincoln, in which her father marched.

A friend of the immigrant in the 1880's, Rabbi Szold also made his home a welcoming center when Jewish refugees streaming from Czarist Russia found a port of entry in Baltimore. Miss Henrietta, as she was called, played an active part in the home hospitality. "I feel very much . . . drawn to these Russian Jews. . . . There is something ideal about them. Or has the suffering through which they have passed idealized them in my eyes? At all events I have no greater wish than to be able to give my whole strength, time and ability to them. . . ."

Night School for Immigrants

Out of Henrietta Szold's desire to help the immigrants and her concrete practical idealism, a project evolved that made history. She established the first "Night School" in Baltimore, and one of the first in the country. Knowledge of English, skilled trades, the dignity of self-help, she felt, were imperatives in effecting the integration of the immigrant into the fabric of American democracy. Her project seemed visionary and found little general appeal, but the Jewish community rallied to its support.

The night school overshadowed all the young girl's other interests, and it was a great success. "As was predicted," she wrote, "a tremendous rush of pupils came in on Monday after the holidays. Three hundred and forty have been enrolled. Of course as we can with difficulty shelter three hundred, a great many were turned away. But the rush has been so great that we have determined to rent two rooms elsewhere and open two new classes. We shall have seven English classes, a bookkeeping, an arithmetic, a Hebrew and a dressmaking class running." As far as possible all subjects were a vehicle for added knowledge of what America means, and United States history was basic to the entire curriculum.

The school was more than a classroom. From the beginning, Miss Szold insisted on making it a cooperative, self-help venture on the part of the newcomers. She scrupulously avoided making the instruction a handout, insisting that the school be managed by the immigrants, with herself but another participant. "Whenever I go to a board meeting, I carefully refrain from influencing my Russian friends directly on any subject under discussion. This is their school and they must run it." Miss Szold accepted student decisions as a mandate she had to execute, a pattern of work which marked her long leadership. After more than five thousand graduates had proved the worth of her pioneering educational mission, the municipality of Baltimore took over the evening school. It was a key contribution to the concept of American education for new immigrants and other adults. Many years later, in 1935, at a reception given in honor of her seventy-fifth birthday in New York's City Hall, Mayor Fiorello LaGuardia paid special tribute to her pioneer work in this area: "If I, the child of poor immigrant parents, am today Mayor of New York, giving you the freedom of our city, it is because of you. Half a century ago you initiated that instrument of American democracy, the evening school for the immigrant. . . . Were it not for such programs of education and Americanization at the time of our largest immigration waves, a new slavery would have arisen in American society perhaps worse than the first. . . ."

Henrietta Szold at seventeen also became the "fair correspondent . . . from the Monumental City" for the *New York Jewish Messenger*. Her comments, under the pen name of Sulamith, on current Jewish questions revealed an early maturity and insight.

In 1881 she went abroad for the first time and in the company of her father visited the ghettos of Eastern Europe. She saw the darkness and distress of her people's living and never ceased to hear their cry. When she returned to Baltimore she joined the *Hovevei Zion*, "Lovers of Zion," precursors of Herzlian Zionism, who laid the foundation on which Herzl was later to erect the political structure of Zionism. "Their ideal, the ideal of Zion rebuilt, supplies my bruised, torn and bloody, distracted people with an answer to its woes through its own efforts," Miss Szold said at that time.

Jewish Publication Society

In 1888 Henrietta Szold was drawn into an undertaking for which her father's instruction and her own predilections well fitted her. She was one of a small company of leaders who saw that the rising and prospering Jewry of America required a parallel spiritual development, an effort to enlarge and spread Jewish knowledge and create a sound cultural climate. In the belief that Jewish learning, which had existed heretofore only as an imported plant, could take root and grow in American soil, this group founded the Jewish Publication Society of America. Its task was to make Jewish classics accessible to English readers, and to foster the talents of contemporary writers and lay the sound foundations of a worthy and creative cultural future.

Henrietta Szold plunged into the work of the Society with her usual thoroughness, and soon became a specialist in the new field. She knew no halfway responsibility. Increasingly, administrative and editorial tasks took her away from her old home, and by 1892 her life had ceased to center around Baltimore. A year later she became formally the executive secretary of the

Society and moved to Philadelphia. She served simultaneously as editor, translator, talent scout, and public relations counselor. A quiet modest demeanor concealed her great drive and vigor. She was editor or co-editor of all the early volumes of the *American Jewish Yearbook* published under the joint auspices of the Society and the American Jewish Committee. She wrote some fifteen articles for the *Jewish Encyclopedia*.

Great emphasis was placed on historical works, and it is significant that the Society's first volume was *Outlines of Jewish History* by Lady Katie Magnus. That little book (republished in 1959) was followed by Graetz' monumental five-volume *History of the Jews* in a translation revised by Henrietta Szold, with an index volume that she meticulously prepared. She also assumed the burden of indexing the papers of the Reverend Jacques Lyons, the minister of the Spanish-Portuguese Synagogue, which were in the possession of the American Jewish Historical Society.

There were also scholarly publications by Solomon Schechter* and by Nahum Slouschz, author of the first history of modern Hebrew literature. There were philosophic works of Ahad Ha-am in English translation, and Israel Zangwill's *Children of the Ghetto*. Miss Szold collaborated with Louis Ginzberg in the research and organization of his encyclopedic study *Legends of the Jews*, and also assisted that scholar in the preparation of his lectures at the time that English was still a new language for him.

In 1902 Rabbi Szold passed away. He remained an inspiring force throughout his daughter's life. When a speaker in Berlin during the Hitler days recalled an address delivered by her father fifty-three years earlier, Miss Szold was profoundly moved. "He continued to quote from our father's sermon striking passages, many of which I remember. . . . Can you imagine my consternation and embarrassment and pride. . . . I confess I felt solemn and touched." On her eighty-fourth birthday, she heard students of the Hebrew University in Jerusalem expound the writings of Rabbi Szold, a tribute to him but even more to his daughter's filial devotion.

* See Chapter 5.

Move to New York

After her father's death Miss Szold moved to New York with her mother, in whose humanity too "lay a root" of Henrietta's being. They made their home across the street from the Jewish Theological Seminary of America, where Miss Szold enrolled in classes. She was the first woman student there, and became a center of admiration and affection among faculty and student body alike. President Solomon Schechter would read her his manuscripts and discuss with her the spiritual problems with which he struggled. She enjoyed the companionship of intellectual peers and developed many lasting friendships.

In all this time and in the midst of all these labors, though Miss Szold enjoyed the attentions of many distinguished admirers with whom she was to maintain lifelong friendships, she apparently gave little thought to the more traditional affairs of the heart. For her father, toward whom she retained a worshipful attitude, she had been as good as the son she had wished to be. Yet she was essentially feminine and had learned from her mother to be an excellent housekeeper. She carried a little tatting spool to salvage time during long conversations. She was gaily proud of her pretty ankles. Her room was always adorned with flowers. She had a quiet sense of humor. She adored children: "I should have had children, many children," she once confessed. A career, whatsoever it was, could not in her view compete for primacy with motherhood in a woman's life.

Yet only belatedly, and at first unrecognized, love entered her life. When she met a man who was for her the scholar par excellence, a force very different from Platonic friendship possessed her. In her great physical vitality, she forgot she had passed her fortieth birthday, and she dared dream. Suddenly, without prior intimation to her, the man she loved, who was somewhat younger than she, married while he was abroad and returned with a mate nearer his own age. She broke down in her agony. Her health, her will to live were shattered. Her eyesight was threatened. The care and solicitude of Harry Friedenwald, physician and Zionist leader, and of other friends helped to counter her despair. Her spirit finally triumphed and emerged whole. Her desire to serve others renewed itself and brought healing.

As for many others in flight from sorrow, surcease also came from new surroundings. Henrietta Szold went abroad with her mother. For the second time she saw Europe, this time the Europe of history, architecture, and art, to which she reacted enthusiastically. Following the European tour came her first pilgrimage to the Land of Israel. A gift of money in recognition of her services to the Jewish Publication Society made that journey possible as a sequel to the European vacation. The appreciation expressed by Cyrus Adler of her "loyal, intelligent, conscientious and effective . . . service to the Society, would be," Miss Szold wrote, "as potent as the vacation itself in restoring me to a normal degree of self-confidence and joy in living and working."

Henrietta Szold looked upon this gift as "a thing apart," labelling it her Palestine fund. "Never," she said, "did it enter my mind remotely that the privilege of beholding the Holy Land could fall to my share . . . with all it implies of Jewish emotion and education. . . ." Her heart was lifted at that first vision of Palestine. The mountains and valleys resounded with echoes of the past and the call of the future. The *Yishuv* was small, but already all the marks of the surging renaissance were there. Having seen with her own eyes the validity and promise of the dreamers of Zion, she now made Zionism her way of life.

Worker for Zionism

Miss Szold later pointed out that her Zionist conviction antedated the first Zionist Congress. In 1896, addressing the National Council of Jewish Women in Baltimore, she said: "To meet a people's need through a people's own efforts . . . this ideal of self-emancipation was Zionism—a movement that epitomizes the finest Jewish impulses of the day."

Henrietta Szold found it possible to take her place in the nascent movement in spite of the concentrated work which her position with the Jewish Publication Society imposed. Overlapping responsibility was not new to her. During her years of service in the publishing field, from 1888 to 1916, she was simultaneously involved in the education of immigrants in Baltimore and later with the creation of Hadassah in New York.

There were also subsidiary Zionist activities that absorbed Miss Szold. In 1910 she became the honorary secretary of the Jewish Agricultural Experiment Station of Palestine, and the same year was elected secretary of the Federation of American Zionists. "They call it honorary secretary," she wrote. "The Zionist dictionary, however, defines honor as work." She tackled an "appalling desk of neglected, jumbled organization problems" at night, while conducting the business of the Jewish Publication Society as editor, secretary, and general factotum.

Hadassah Is Founded

Before her Palestine journey, and in response to an invitation from Judah Magnes, Miss Szold had joined the "Hadassah Study Circle," banded together for Zionist study. Upon her return, aroused as she had been by the disease and misery she had witnessed on her journey, she communicated to this group her sense of need for practical health work in Zion as well as study at home. She thus projected for Hadassah the concept of a concrete Zionist program. On *Purim*, February 24, 1912, in the vestry rooms of Temple Emanuel of New York, the group that had been the Hadassah Study Circle constituted itself as Hadassah, New York Chapter of the Daughters of Zion. Henrietta Szold was elected chairman of the new unit.

The guiding idea of service, which she launched with the founding of Hadassah, assumed growing meaning with the years. Miss Szold never ceased to proclaim and enjoin the command of study. A school of Zionism headed by one of her most remarkable colleagues, Jessie Sampter, was the cradle of many of Hadassah's leaders. But Zionism could not stop in the classroom or on the platform. She considered deeds more important than words. Lip service had no place in the Szold vocabulary: espousal of an idea meant acceptance of responsibility. She looked upon study and knowledge as the bases of action, the underpinning of her philosophy of Zionism. And dedication topped knowledge.

If a project was sound its initial size was of little concern to Henrietta Szold. What was important were its basic principles, its educational potential, its capacity for organic growth. "I am so constituted," she wrote, "that I see no promise in any movement which is not built up slowly, bit by bit, each layer of stone and each trowelful of cement tested by every known principle of organization." Hadassah's first mission to the Holy Land consisted of two trained nurses; but their terms of reference, the charge placed upon them, and the relation of their professional services to the voluntary agency with which they worked were the same qualitatively as those of the great overseas medical unit and the mighty medical organization which later followed.

Miss Szold set up an ethical code for voluntary service. Though she adhered to the democratic process and accepted the discipline of majority rule, she did not hesitate to exercise the privileges of a minority whenever she felt it necessary to defend and propagate dissenting views. In 1921 she criticized Hadassah's decision to declare its autonomy vis-à-vis the general American Zionist Organization. She was an anti-partitionist in 1937 and a binationalist in 1941. But she allowed herself no breach of discipline in pursuance of her opinions. Democracy was a good way of life and had overriding validity and authority, in spite of its slow ways.

Miss Szold set great store on the avoidance of conflict of interest in public service; this for her was a categorical imperative. Her view was rooted in Jewish tradition. Rabbis were deemed all the truer to their charge when they refused to make of the Torah a spade with which to dig, when they chose to earn their livelihood as cobblers, carpenters, or hewers of wood —but in the vineyard of the Lord toiled as freewill laborers. The absolute separation of profit from service was no mere matter of bookkeeping. There was to be no loophole for temptation or compromise even unconsciously to cloud judgment or weaken responsibility.

Unpaid service was to have its crown of glory. Henrietta Szold enlarged the status of voluntary work, its scope and meaning. It could be no haphazard occupation or a leisurely stopgap for overflowing social ills. It was not freed of responsibility because it was freely given. Quite the contrary. Service to a cause enforced special demands upon the volunteer worker such as technical study to validate judgment, selflessness to justify authority, and dedication to merit acclaim. Miss Szold delved deeply into the basic problems in the relationship between professional and volunteer social workers. She understood that success or failure in communal activities is often determined by the association between executive and lay leadership. The volunteer can be discouraged or frustrated by a proud assumption on the part of the professional that technical knowledge is of itself wisdom, while the professional executive may impugn authoritarian attitudes to volunteer directors.

Henrietta Szold foresaw and forestalled such dangers. She prized the worth of the volunteer and repudiated the idea that he could not be effective. Simultaneously, she respected the intellectual integrity of the professional worker and was solicitous for his freedom of growth. She solved the dilemma by demanding of the volunteer serious dedication to study and knowledge, and of the professional the selflessness of the volunteer. She saw the two with mutual respect in a partnership that could build up an inspiring structure of social service. She in her own person uniquely combined competence and devotion with professional excellence and a constant pursuit of expanding goals. Withal, she yearned to be a "volunteer."

In 1916 a challenging opportunity presented itself. Under the inspiration of Federal Judge Julian W. Mack, a group of friends granted Miss Szold a modest life annuity and thus freed her from the need of earning a living. With single-minded dedication, she became the servant of the Zionist cause at a crucial moment in its history. Since a wartime blackout enveloped European Jewry, many of the tasks of the World Zionist Organization, then only twenty years old, fell to Americans. A provisional Committee for Zionist Affairs under the chairmanship of Louis D. Brandeis was called to leadership. Henrietta Szold was a member of its executive in her personal capacity and as head of Hadassah.

Organizing Medical Aid for Palestine

In 1916, pleas came to American Jewry from the temporary seat of the World Zionist Organization in neutral Denmark to send doctors, nurses, and supplies to the stricken

Yishuv. The idea of overseas medical succor was not new. The Red Cross had a notable history of medical corps operating in theaters of war and at centers of catastrophe, but it operated only with the outbreak of crises, and then departed. Missionary organizations had established individual hospitals for primitive and under-developed populations here and there, healing the body, but often in the process altering the beneficiary's own faith.

The agency of mercy that Henrietta Szold created followed a new pattern. Born in war, it was yet free of war hysteria and stopgap calculations. It was an expression of Zionism. Miss Szold believed that every Zionist act had to deepen the Jewish stakes in the ancient homeland and raise its standards. She refused to accept the low and sometimes minimal standards set by the Palestine government in its health services. In spite of carping pressures, Hadassah continued with its long-range planning and its high standards, which were to make a permanent impact on the history of Israel.

Henrietta Szold plunged with fervor into the task of assembling the American Zionist Medical Unit. A pioneer program which would have taxed any major public health organization became possible through the ready union of the Joint Distribution Committee with the Zionist forces. This frail woman and a small group of disciples undertook a project of governmental scope, involving the clearance of passport and war travel permits in America and Europe, diplomatic negotiations, and preparations for the proper functioning of a comprehensive medical unit. The organization and equipment of a professional staff and the facilities for five hospitals, clinics, public health centers, a new nurses' training school, itinerant ophthalmological and dental services, an anti-malaria campaign, epidemic control and environmental sanitation must have seemed a daring undertaking for an inexperienced volunteer. And yet Miss Szold molded into a cohesive corps the health pioneers and teachers who rallied to her call, impressing upon them their historic charge. She mastered the politics, the logistics, and the mechanics of the task; she was diplomat, quartermaster, courier, all in one. Above all, she communicated her own intensity of purpose.

Miss Szold had serious doubts about her own qualifications:

"Isn't it ridiculous that I should be directing hospitals, nurses' training schools, laboratories, clinics, school hygiene, and most services?" Hebrew texts were not available for the nurses' school and books had to be adapted, translated, and printed. Lectures had to be transcribed into Latin characters for doctors whose reading knowledge of Hebrew was scant. The preventive program had to be correlated with curative work. Palestine was rampant with cholera, typhus, malaria, favus, trachoma. "That the Unit . . . is imperfect," Miss Szold wrote, "no one knows better than I do; but . . . there remains an achievement, one of the bright spots in the history of the early reconstruction movement in Palestine. I am not very conversant with medical literature, but I have no hesitation in expressing my doubt whether any such big piece of constructive medical work has ever been done in a colony." According to Justice Brandeis, the differential in population between sixty thousand Jews in 1918 and the half million of 1939 was in no small measure due to that "constructive medical work" for which Henrietta Szold was responsible. She was the architect of its practical development from a clinic in a shack by the side of the road which opened in 1912 to a Medical School for the Hebrew University and Hadassah, the full functioning of which she did not live to see.

Miss Szold's special responsibility for a time was the development of the epidemiological work. The scientific anti-malaria unit she organized became a pilot plant recognized by the League of Nations and utilized by afflicted countries beyond Palestine. She was in close contact with the pioneers in Galilee and elsewhere, who found in her a friend and colleague. The hospital and health facilities of Hadassah made available to the *Kupat Holim* proved a vital factor in the inception and development of labor's great health organization. Over the years trachoma, tuberculosis, leprosy and other endemic diseases were rooted out. Malnutrition among children was dealt with by a school-wide system of balanced luncheons prepared by the children themselves as part of courses in domestic science. The study of nutrition influenced the school, the home, and the community.

Concern with Arab Question

Miss Szold's concerns were by no means limited to Jews. The Arab question troubled her deeply, and she supported a policy of active effort to serve the Arab community in Palestine. In consonance both with ancient Biblical teaching and modern medical principles, Hadassah hospitals and clinics were freely available to all who needed service. Over the entrance of the Nathan and Lina Straus Health Center, from which the child welfare work was directed, an inscription stated in Hebrew, Arabic, and English that it was open "for All Races and Creeds."

Some projects served the Arab population primarily. Arab mothers and children learned the fundamentals of child care from Arabic-speaking Hadassah nurses. The Mufti of Jerusalem was treated at the Hadassah Hospital and its doctors went to his home to care for him. (There they saw pieces of the Torah from synagogues which had been desecrated by Arab rioters.) During the riots of Arabs against Jews, Hadassah doctors and nurses attended the Arab wounded in first-aid stations set up in the dangerous Arab quarters. From princes to wandering Bedouins, Arabs came from all the surrounding countries for specialized treatment. When an earthquake shook the capital city of Amman in Transjordan, Hadassah was first to offer medical and relief services. When the Mandatory government established a school luncheon system in Arab schools, it was set up by the teachers of Hadassah.

Early in Miss Szold's work in Palestine she had become disturbed, perplexed, and aroused by the moral and political issues in the Arab-Jewish conflict. She had courageously denounced failures and errors on both sides. On her way to her post in Palestine in 1920, she had written: "There were scores of things I have been wondering about, especially the very serious Arab situation of which the powers that be are, it seems, not to be held wholly guiltless." A year later she wrote: "An order came from the highest quarters that no public meetings would be allowed . . . November 2, Balfour Day, the third anniversary of the opening of our hospital . . . appropriate day for the graduation of the first nurses . . . that there may

be no suspicion aroused in any Arab mind of a political demonstration. . . . My whole American make-up rebels against it.
I have found myself almost wishing that I might have the courage to act against orders, to cause some disturbance, and to
suffer death itself as the penalty of my rebellion."

Even during the most serious disturbances under the Mandatory regime, from 1936 to 1939, Miss Szold went about the
country on tours of duty. For many years she lived in an Arab
neighborhood in Jerusalem, and found there many happy relationships. At a point of critical tension, a prominent member
of the Arab Executive, himself involved in activities of violence
against Jews, sent a message through a friend to ask Miss Szold
to keep away from a particular area of the city where trouble
was expected.

Toward the Mandate's failure to use its influence and power
to effect an Arab-Jewish rapproachement, she expressed mounting indignation. "Cold neutrality, especially with an under-
developed population like the Arabs, can work great mischief.
Children must be told when they are wrong. . . . The Government. . . . sticks to cold neutrality bordering on lies," she
reported, "while lives are lost and terror reigns . . . Jewish
passers-by are suddenly held up by the police . . . while Arabs
go unmolested." But she saw England's fears: "Two hundred
million Muslims in India, Arabia, Egypt, Syria and Iraq." Yet
Miss Szold hoped England would act nobly. "If in place of
Royal Commissions Great Britain would set up a body of wise
men with the task of studying race antagonisms between Jacob
and Esau," she said, "and determine the thousand ways that
might lead from Arab heart to Jewish heart and back from
Jew to Arab, and from Arab head to Jewish head and vice-
versa, the tripartite problem might be solved."

In Henrietta Szold's view, the failure of British and Arab alike
was no release of Jewish responsibility. "I am heart-broken
because the Jews don't seem to realize that the Arab question
and the way they are going to solve it are the supreme test,"
she wrote. "We Jews should have found a way by now to meet
the race problem. The more remarkable our achievements are,
and they are remarkable, the more I long for an Isaiah to show
up our littleness . . . You see that instead of objecting to 'per-
fidious Albion,' my mind dwells on our own inadequacies . . .

Can one of us be at peace with himself so long as this appalling misunderstanding exists between us and our neighbors . . . ?"

She advocated the study of Arabic and Arab civilization in Jewish schools. She pleaded for a respectful attitude toward the bearers of that civilization, notwithstanding "agitators or the dupes of agitators." "We shall ally ourselves with the best of our Arab fellows, to cure what is diseased in us and in them— the healing of my people and the healing of the nations."

Miss Szold's search for positive action in Arab-Jewish relations led her to join *Ihud*, an organization that had the twofold program of seeking rapproachement between Jews and Arabs, and of advocating the idea of binationalism. This came in the early years of World War II, at a time when the post-war aims of the Zionist movement were almost unanimously focused upon the establishment of a Jewish commonwealth in Palestine. A few Zionists, individuals and groups, were exploring the implications of a possible binationalist state as a pattern that might find acceptance among Arabs or as preferable to a partitioning of the country. In *Ihud*, the definition of political objectives was joined to cultural and social studies. The essential for Miss Szold was the search for a basis of collaboration between Jew and Arab; the study of Arab-Jewish relations was a moral imperative. Beyond all political formulas was the supreme goal of peace.

Discussions became charged with conflict and led to one of the most difficult moments in the close relations between the National Board of Hadassah and Henrietta Szold. Two decades later Israel's Prime Minister David Ben-Gurion, referring to American Zionist leaders, declared her "eminently worthy to stand at the head of this noble band. I often had differences of opinion on political matters with Henrietta Szold," he added, "but even when I disagreed with her I could not help appreciating the moral grounds of her errors—or what I considered her errors."

Above Politics

In general, however, Henrietta Szold was considered a non-political figure. Though she was wont to quote Aristotle's dictum that politics is the highest manifestation of the human mind and declared herself a political Zionist, she eschewed "politics." Her participation invariably took the form of actual work. She rebelled at the pragmatic realities and the pressures which harassed her as a public servant, but she achieved a noteworthy career in the hierarchy of Zionism on the American scene and in its world organization.

Her physical stamina permitted her to work sixteen and at times even twenty hours out of the twenty-four. "My day extends from 4:30 in the morning until 12 at night, and I am kept busy all the hours." This was her timetable over the years. Even during the oratorical era of Zionism when speechmaking was forced upon her, her speeches concentrated upon concrete tasks and practical problems. She had a genius for details, and these she refused to consider unimportant. She attached to the means the moral measure by which the ends were judged. She was consistent in her principles. Everywhere she inspired an attitude of trust that seldom wavered and that came to her across all party lines.

Miss Szold was deeply religious and meticulous in observance. There was a wholeness and a completeness about her as a Jewess, which is not often encountered in modern life. Ritual, prayer, learning, and ethical teachings were integrated in the unity of Judaism as faith, aspiration, and practice. She clung to the Hebrew language, which she considered the key to the treasury of Israel's literature. The secularism around her did not sway her. She was a steadfast attendant at Sabbath services and made her home a center of open hospitality after synagogue services. She was one of the founders of the Yeshurun Congregation in Jerusalem, which was at the beginning called the "American" synagogue. It began in a home with adequate seating for the women in contrast to the Oriental neglect of the female section. It emphasized reverence and decorum in worship and sought without preachment to emphasize the spiritual and religious heritage.

Educational Responsibilities

In 1927, in a painful hour, the World Zionist Organization, weighed down by a cumbersome, overlarge, and inefficient machinery, abandoned the party system of electing an executive;

it substituted instead a cabinet of three, chosen on the basis of personal qualifications and with power to reorganize and go forward. Colonel (later Brigadier General) Frederick Kisch and British Zionist leader Harry Sacher were charged with the political and economic portfolios, and Henrietta Szold had the responsibility for education and health and also for social welfare, which was not yet a recognized department. Relations with the Mandatory power were strained. During the frequent visits abroad by the other two members of the triumvirate in frantic efforts to stem the tide of political deterioration, Miss Szold occasionally found herself compelled to deal with financial, agricultural, and political affairs as well—all with inadequate finances.

Education was perhaps the greatest sufferer from the general penury. There was no free compulsory education for the children even at the elementary level, and the director of the Jewish school system had resigned in despair. The Mandatory regime concentrated on aid to Arab schools. The precarious state of the budget was further aggravated by the alignment of the Jewish school system with social, political, and religious parties. Unfortunately education, like Zionism, was tripartite: schools were related to the ideologies of the Labor, Mizrahi, and General Zionists, none of which could or would mix; small classes or schools could not be consolidated even under the threat of vanishing support. It took great courage and indifference to public opinion or political preferment to take up the cudgels for a unified system of education. Miss Szold broached the question time and again, declaring from the platform of the Zionist Congress: "I am religious and Jewish myself, but I do not believe in the rule of priests. School children must not be drawn into religious strife."

Miss Szold's representative position brought her in close contact with the British administration and its officials trained in the colonial school. She confronted them with dignity and courage, and won their respect. She obtained the first sizable grant from the government for Jewish educational needs. Salaries had been irregularly paid and were generally in arrears. Teachers were struggling on the thin edge between want and constant indebtedness. Hunger stalked the classroom. Miss Szold was able to bring calm on the pedagogic front, not so much by her deeds, as by her complete identification with the teachers and their personal problems. With their cooperation and devotion, by a miracle of good husbandry and with government aid, she restored order and spirit into the department of education.

From her colleagues in the triumvirate we have an intimate picture of her tireless labors, and an appraisal of her mastery of the complicated network of duties that she quietly assumed. Her simple life became an ascetic one. Gone was the grace of the Mediterranean mid-day break which climate and custom dictated. She came to her desk at seven in the morning with her lunch in a little paper bag and did not stop till the dinner hour. In the evening, she resumed her work.

In addition to Miss Szold's public health responsibilities, she set herself the goal of making social welfare a *bona fide* portfolio. It was least understood in the *Yishuv*, and its problems were often painfully related to those of education. Urchins were earning pennies in street work and there was no legislation to stop or help them. Among the poverty-stricken Oriental groups, youngsters were enticed to missionary schools where instruction was baited with a slice of bread, and both were free. Miss Szold tried to warn an uncomprehending community of the possible development of juvenile delinquency.

Official Portfolio of Social Welfare

It took years of patient demonstration to establish the validity of competent social welfare work. In 1931, under Itzhak Ben Zvi, President of *Vaad Leumi* and later of Israel, Miss Szold was invited to join the Executive of the Jewish National Council in Palestine (*Vaad Leumi*), was elected to its cabinet, and assigned the portfolio of social welfare as a fully recognized department.

Unlike the immigrants she had welcomed to Baltimore forty years earlier, the refugees to Palestine found no land of opportunity. The plasma for life had to be created from barren hills, eroded valleys, and dried-out streams. The widely differentiated peoples came from the somber *mellahs* and slums of the Mediterranean basin, from the sophisticated centers of the Russian intelligentsia, and the mystic ghettos of Poland. They came in poignant flight from Hitlerism. And they came by any and every means of transportation across the hostile frontiers and through doors that were being slammed in their faces.

Henrietta Szold now made immigrants and immigration her daily work, from the period of defiance of the Mandatory's harsh immigration policy until the organization of illegal immigration by an heroic underground. She covered the length and breadth of the country, dealing with the whole range of human wants and problems. She introduced family case work as then practiced in the best organized Western communities. She persuaded the Mandatory to assign a Hebrew-speaking parole officer and laid out the plan of a Boy's Town, Kfar Avodah LeNearim, to offer vocational training for socially maladjusted boys. She also drew up comprehensive plans for vocational education. Working hours after midnight in the hope of enlisting the interest of the Young Women's Hebrew Association in New York, she wrote in her small fine hand a long document on the technical training of girls in Jerusalem, which though emotionally the most remembered city was the most forgotten in economic planning. Eventually her dream was realized when Hadassah initiated its vocational education program with a model high school and technical workshops.

Work for Children

Within the broad compass of Henrietta Szold's work, the primary place was ceded to children. She wanted to leave a permanent structure of child care that would answer completely "The Cry of the Children," the title of a tractate she wrote on their behalf. She thought that she had found the answer in *Lemaan Hayeled ve-Hanoar*, "For the Sake of the Child and the Youth," a coordinating center to guide and assist in every aspect of child welfare. She visited the Federal Children's Bureau in Washington and maintained a continuous exchange of information with its directors. She studied the work of the Swiss Pro Juventute and of forward-looking agencies in other countries. What governments and national organizations did elsewhere, Henrietta Szold tried single-handedly to do in establishing the counterpart of a Children's Bureau for Israel, one that had a character of its own accruing from its special status in a small and unique country. Miss Szold looked upon this as her ultimate service.

Although the direction of Youth Aliyah consumed the final decade of her life, the goal of a Children's Foundation remained uppermost in Henrietta Szold's mind. She made herself the executor of her testament and put its provisions into operation under her own watchful eyes. In the Jewish tradition of Ethical Wills, Miss Szold's will was not an excursion into abstract thoughts. It was the firm definition of the basic constitution of *Lemaan Hayeled,* a testament of action. Those whom she gathered around her for an anticipated eightieth birthday have cause to remember her words and voice as she read that will. Over the years she had been quietly setting aside gifts that had come to her on birthdays or special occasions from Hadassah and personal friends. She was often chided for her abstinence, for her travel in third class, and the tiny back rooms in small hotels she chose when on public missions. The enlarged gifts on the occasion of her eightieth birthday became her gift "for the sake of the child and the youth." She was pressed for time and feared that in the turmoil and chaos of the world, the cry of the children would be drowned out. Her goal was a national fund, a *Keren Hayeled,* an instrument for the healing of the children. After her death and in spite of her request to the contrary, the Foundation she established was named *Mosad Szold,* the Henrietta Szold Foundation for Child and Youth Welfare, which aims to serve through research and basic publications all institutions, organizations, and bodies concerned with the education, social welfare, health, recreation and guidance of children. Henrietta Szold's dream of coordination and dynamic initiative in planning child welfare may be accounted "unfinished business," a legacy of conscience still to be executed.

Youth Aliyah

Had her career terminated with her thrust into the future of social service in Israel, Henrietta Szold would yet be preeminent in Jewish womanhood. But she was destined to be a still greater instrument of service to her people. During the spring of 1933, she travelled through Palestine with her sister Bertha, on a "farewell" tour before returning to her family in the United States. It was during that beautiful serene spring that Hitler came to power.

By summer the Jews of Palestine had organized themselves as a committee of the whole to welcome Jews who could or would escape from Germany. At an historic meeting in Haifa, Chaim Weizmann was appointed the head of German immigration into Palestine, and Henrietta Szold was asked to take charge of the children. Some two years earlier Jewish youth in Germany had organized itself with Zionist fervor for an *Aliyah* or ascent to *Eretz Yisrael*. The year before Hitler's accession Recha Freier, an inspired German Jewess, spearheaded a youth pioneer movement. Seeing no hope for Jewish children in Germany she pleaded that Henrietta Szold undertake direction of the movement to transfer them to a children's village in Palestine. Miss Szold refused. *Halutzim* (pioneers) or immigrants she would welcome, one and all. Yet to the request that she organize an *Aliyah* of children, her answer was "no." She was not willing to take a child from his living parents or to make a youth a pioneer before he could use the option of a free man.

Then Hitler came to power, In her seventy-fourth year, Miss Szold sat pondering on the future in a little room with packed trunks, ready to return to America, when the call came from Palestine Jewry for her to lead the youth out of Hitler's Germany. Calmly and without a word Henrietta Szold unpacked her trunks. She turned her back on retirement and freedom and faced the urgent tasks.

Thus began the movement known as Youth Aliyah. It is a hybrid term in any language—Jugend-Aliyah, Aliyah des Jeunes, Youth Aliyah. Youth has many faces, *Aliyah* has one, directed always to *Eretz Yisrael*. Its motion is always upward, for it is etymologically an "ascent."

Its charting demanded precision, psychological acumen, and the spirit that could lift a generation from the lowest depths of despair to life renewed. "My new job, the organization of the transfer of the children from Germany to Palestine," Miss Szold wrote, "is growing under my hands from day to day. It deals with children—it is not child's play. The responsibility is great. . . ."

When the first group arrived in February, 1934, Henrietta Szold was ready for them. "Day after tomorrow, 'my' children arrive from Germany. I go to Haifa to meet them, have them examined medically, and get their possessions out of the customs. Then I accompany them to Ain Harod, to see them installed there. I want to see them tucked away in their beds." While awaiting their arrival, she had been making the rounds on behalf of social welfare work. "After four days spent in Haifa, Ain Harod, and Kfar Giladi, it took me two hours and a half," she wrote, "to remove the mud from my shoes, my overshoes, my coat, my dress, my unders. It rained and hailed and blew and stormed. Such depths of mud as I trudged through: I was dragging with me a mountain of earth . . . The first group of boys and girls arrived from Germany at Haifa . . . I went up to meet them, and then traveled to Ain Harod with them and stayed with them there for two days. It was a great experience for me . . ."

Henceforth the day of a group's arrival in the settlement was declared a festival. At the entrance a broad wreath proclaimed the ancient Hebrew greeting: "Blessed Be Those Who Come." A band met them with song and dance. In the evening, all dressed in Sabbath clothes, gathered around a banquet table festooned with flowers, and there were speeches of welcome.

Henrietta Szold allowed nothing to interfere with her awaiting and greeting personally each group of children at the point of their arrival. Youth Aliyah called into play all the attributes of dedication in her nature, all her power as a creative educator. Forgetful of her years and with a mental and emotional drive of a young mother with an imperiled child, she gave herself completely to the children snatched out of the gigantic gas chamber that was "Greater Germany."

The blueprinting of daily activity that followed the Festival of Welcome was as exacting as an engineer's plan for a bridge over dangerous shoals. Henrietta Szold kept in touch with each individual child through his period of training. At the end of the first six months he would write to her what he had learned and what he wanted to do. "All the lessons of the previous lives

I have lived—all the experience I have gathered—do not suffice to furnish me with the wisdom required for the nation-building purpose or education of the young children," she confessed. Youth Aliyah integrated work and study. The child found that he was fulfilling an important function in his social group. There was a real need of him. He was ploughing the waste fields, producing food, working in freedom. And he was also wanted for himself. He was a human being preparing the way for others. The Youth Aliyah graduates became "nation-builders" in the conquest of the soil, in the fight for a free world, in the struggle for independence. They sought danger, welcomed hardship, and learned joyful service to others.

Miss Szold encouraged close ties of the children with surviving parents. She urged them not to forget German, reminding them that Goethe was a German and that many non-Jews had also suffered under Hitler. She sought out examples of humanitarianism that would dispel from among the children the feeling that all Christians were their enemies. She hailed the Children to Palestine movement in America, through which Christian friends of Youth Aliyah showed their solidarity with suffering Jewish children.

Miss Szold was deeply involved in every aspect of the work of Youth Aliyah as a world movement. In connection with marshalling of the children in Germany and their preparation for life in Palestine, she paid three visits to Germany, in 1933, in 1935, and in 1937. During the last journey, by special permit of the Gestapo, she went to Germany for a week end during the business of the Zionist Congress in Zurich. Those who saw her off at the railroad station said goodbye to a sprightly, quick-stepping figure, but when she returned her friends were shocked to see the bent and shrunken figure of Miss Szold looking her seventy-seven years. There was no need of words to tell the harrowing experience—the meeting in the synagogue with the Gestapo on watch; desperate parents hanging on her words, some pleading for rescue of their children, some wanting a living word of little ones they were never to see again. When she had finished speaking and answering all the questions, a congregation emotionally all but spent rose and sang, under the eyes of the Gestapo, "*Hatikvah*," hymn of the Zionist movement and now Israel's national anthem. Miss Szold spoke little of that experience, but she wrote to her sisters: ". . . those three days will be unforgettable for their misery. What I saw in Germany two years ago was a gruelling experience; what I saw this time cannot be described in language at my command."

In 1935, Miss Szold gave her first formal report to the Zionist Congress on her Youth Aliyah work. Young people from Germany decorated the podium with roses, strewed petal leaves on the aisle to the platform, and announced the establishment of a colony in her name as the expression of the gratitude of German Jewry. "Your indefatigability," the young settlers said to her, "your devotion to the work and your power to build new Jewish lives will inspire us in the performance of our own duties." She was introduced by Dr. Weizmann with the words: "This is the first time that a Zionist leader's path is strewn with roses." Miss Szold's reply to the encomium with which her report was greeted was simple: "Were I not close to seventy-five, I would yet dare to make promises, and say that I shall do everything to make your words true. Now I can only thank God that . . . I was privileged to help to some extent. . . . The dear God has dealt well with me."

Between the sessions of the Congress and early in the morning Miss Szold was constantly in conference with her aides from all parts of the world in seeking ways and means to raise funds, without which the children could not be saved. It was a grim battle for money, with human lives at stake. Henrietta Szold suffered for what she considered dereliction on the part of her people in failing to raise sufficient sums for the rescue of the children. When Hadassah offered to enter into partnership with Youth Aliyah, the news came to her like a transfusion.

The struggle with inadequate funds and the mounting heartbreaks took their toll of that woman of valor. Henrietta Szold was a partner in agony of concentration camp, gas chamber, and of the devastation of war. All this anguish was deepened by vexing internal difficulties and tribulations that attended the operations of rescue. Though Henrietta Szold's will to act was not paralyzed or weakened, her heart grew "tired," and she was finally forced to move from her office to the Hadassah Hospital. There, as each boatload arrived, she was given an immediate report about the children individually. There were always some who needed special attention—the tuberculosis sufferers, the disoriented, and also the talented creative youth.

Henrietta Szold's last conscious service was a fulfillment of a long and ardent wish: she joined in her hands the hands of Chaim Weizmann and Judah Magnes. On December 27, 1944, Dr. Weizmann had come to the sickroom accompanied by Dr. Magnes, according to Miss Szold's report: "Dr. Weizmann was very gentle with me. He did not want me to talk . . . but I said I must tell him two things. First among the many great and fine things he had done for Zionism none was so fine and so great as his coming to Palestine at this time on account of his attitude toward the English people. He expressed pleasure at that . . . The second fine thing you have done today is to visit me together with Dr. Magnes." From Dr. Magnes it was learned that when they left her room, Dr. Weizmann turned to him and said: "We will never quarrel again."

Legacy of Henrietta Szold

To evaluate the place within the framework of history of one who is remembered as a contemporary is a difficult task. In the case of one whose greatness lies in personality, moral stature, and social service, the ultimate test is in the hands of her successors, her pupils, her disciples, who must reflect the measure of that greatness. Yet acclaim for Henrietta Szold did not wait. In her lifetime and in the years since her death, she has been universally recognized as the greatest Jewish woman of her time.

Wherein lay her greatness? She herself rejected the word, acknowledging only an unusually compelling sense of duty and the physical stamina that permitted her to work even twenty hours a day. She was certain that many another could do as well as she. Yet there was a qualitative distinction, more important than the amazing extent of her total achievements. She created a harmonious unity between goal and method. She inspired disciples without seeking them. What she achieved as an individual grew in geometric proportion with the seeding of a host of spirits. The rich fruitage of her life came from her own reverent approach to others which may be summarized in the word "education" taken in its broadest sense. She made of her pupils and disciples her partners.

Henrietta Szold was also essentially a pioneer. In international social service she anticipated some of the most productive ideas which were to enter American foreign policy half a century later. She anticipated also the program of specialized social and educational agencies in the United Nations of today. She was a trail blazer in the fields of public health, child care, social service in all its ramifications, and the elevation of woman's function in the modern world. She represented a perfect combination of Americanism and Hebraism. The United States and the Land of Israel were not a hyphenated juxtaposition but represented in Henrietta Szold's life two mighty streams of history which met. She was not an American in Jerusalem. She was the bearer of Americanism, and her life and work in the ancient homeland carried the hallmark of the conceptual philosophy of the young American democracy. Reciprocally she invested her Americanism with the rich heritage of Jewish ethics, its moral fervor, its Messianic dedication to a greater humanity.

No encomium was spoken about her when she was laid to rest on the Mount of Olives. On her tombstone these words were carved: "Here rests Henrietta Szold, daughter of Rabbi Benjamin, 5 *Tevet*, 5621—1 *Adar*, 5705." All Jerusalem marched in solid procession up the mountain behind her bier. A Youth Aliyah child recited the *kaddish*.

Thirty days later, at a memorial service for Henrietta Szold in Carnegie Hall in New York City, many American leaders paid their tribute. Of all the eulogies, perhaps the best description of her life was a passage read from the Book of Job:

> I delivered the poor who cried, and the fatherless who had none to help him. He who was about to perish, blessed me. I caused the widow's heart to sing for joy. Righteousness was my garment and justice my robe. I was eyes to the blind, feet to the lame, a father to those in need. I searched out the cause of those whom I did not know. I dared reach out to the fangs of the wicked and pluck the victims from his grasp. . . .

FOR FURTHER READING
Books about Henrietta Szold

DECTER, Midge, "The Legacy of Henrietta Szold," *Commentary*, Volume 30, December, 1960, pp. 480-88. A wonderful essay full of rich insight into Szold and her work.

LOWENTHAL, Marvin, *Henrietta Szold, Life and Letters* (New York: Viking, 1942). Still an indispensable source for a study of Henrietta Szold.

DASH, Joan, *Summoned To Jerusalem: The Life of Henrietta Szold* (New York: Harper and Row, 1979). The definitive biography, it is well written and thorough.

LEVIN, Marlin, *Balm In Gilead: The Story of Hadassah* (New York: Schocken, 1973). A popular account of the growth and achievements of a great organization.

Beginnings of Jewish Enlightenment

1. Isaac Eisenstein-Barzilay, "The Background of the Berlin Haskalah" in *Essays on Jewish Life and Thought in Honor of Salo W. Baron* edited by Joseph L. Blau, Arthur Hertzberg, Philip Friedman, and Isaac Mendelsohn, p. 183.
2. See Don Patinkin, "Mercantilism and the Readmission of Jews to England" in *Jewish Social Studies*, 1946, for a different interpretation. Patinkin emphasizes the personal character and particular circumstances confronting Cromwell as the major influences leading to the readmission of the Jews.
3. Selma Stern, *The Court Jew*, Chapters 14-15. See also F. L. Carsten, "The Court Jews, a Prelude to Emancipation," in *Yearbook III*, pp. 140-156.
4. Cecil Roth, *History of the Jews of Italy*, Chapter 5. See also his more recent volume *The Jews in the Renaissance*.
5. Salo Baron, *A Social and Religious History of the Jews*, Volume II, p. 208.
6. Cecil Roth, *A Life of Menasseh Ben Israel*, Chapters 6 and 8.
7. For Spinoza's views on Biblical criticism see Solomon Goldman, *Book of Books*, pp. 44-46. His views on freedom of thought and speech will be found in his *Tractatus Theologicus Politicus*, Chapter 20. For Spinoza's general views on Judaism see Jacob Agus, *The Evolution of Modern Jewish Thought*, pp. 299-314.
8. *Essays on Jewish Life and Thought, op. cit.*, p. 188. I am indebted for many details about early Jewish enlightenment in Germany to Dr. Eisenstein-Barzilay's excellent essay.
9. Solomon Maimon, *An Autobiography*, p. 106.
10. *Ibid.*, p. 100.

The Struggle for Jewish Emancipation

1. Howard M. Sachar, *The Course of Modern Jewish History*, Chapter 3. See also H. Graetz, *History of the Jews*, Volume V, pp. 432-434.
2. Robert Anchel, *Les Juifs de France*, pp. 236-7. See also his *Napoleon et les Juifs*, Chapter 1.
3. Cecil Roth, *History of the Jews of Italy*, pp. 445-463.

4. For the life and achievements of Crémieux, see S. Posener, *Adolph Crémieux.*
5. Sol Liptzin, *Germany's Stepchildren,* Chapters 1 and 2.
6. The best account of the struggle for Jewish emancipation in Russia is Louis Greenberg, *The Jews in Russia,* Volume I. See also Sachar, *op. cit.,* Chapter 4.

Emergence of Modern Orthodoxy

1. The most detailed and comprehensive account of the origins and development of Reform Judaism is David Philipson, *The Reform Movement in Judaism.* See Chapters 1 and 2.
2. Mordecai M. Kaplan, *The Greater Judaism in the Making,* p. 226.
3. Bernard Heller, *Odyssey of a Faith,* pp. 177-184.
4. See *Leopold and Adelheid Zunz, An Account in Letters,* edited with an introduction by Nahum N. Glatzer, Chapters 11-26.
5. Solomon Schechter, *Studies in Judaism,* Third Series, pp. 47-83. See also Meyer Waxman, *A History of Jewish Literature,* Volume III, pp. 366-370.
6. Kaplan, *op. cit.,* pp. 227-231.
7. Philipson, *op. cit.,* Chapter 7.
8. Schechter, *op. cit.,* Volume I, Introduction.
9. Waxman, *op. cit.,* pp. 377-383. See also Louis Ginzberg, *Students, Scholars and Saints,* Chapter 6.

Samson Raphael Hirsch

1. The term "Orthodoxy" is of ecclesiastic origin. An Orthodox Christian was a man who rigidly adhered to the creed and who, notwithstanding criticism, believed in its infallible truth. Within the Jewish community, the designation "Orthodox Jew" was first employed in 1807 by the president of the Paris Sanhedrin, Abraham Furtado. Several decades later, it made its appearance in Germany, but the odium of backwardness and excessive piety was now attached to it.
2. After Heinrich Heine, who at that time was still interested in Judaism, heard Bernays' sermon, he declared: "I have heard Bernays preach . . . None of the Jews understand him; he desires nothing for himself and will never play any other part. But he is a man of mind . . ." Quoted by Graetz, *History of the Jews,* Volume V, p. 577.
3. *Ibid.,* p. 574.
4. Ludwig Geiger, ed., *Abraham Geiger: Leben und Lebenswerk.*
5. Quoted in *Samson Raphael Hirsch, ein Lebensbild,* Jubilauems-Nummer des "Israelit," Frankfurt, 1908.
6. Translated into English by Rabbi Bernard Drachman in 1899 and published by Funk & Wagnalls, New York.
7. *Shabb.,* 118 a, b.
8. I. *Macc.* 1:30.
9. Joseph Wohlgemuth, *S. R. Hirsch und das gesetzentreue Judentum,* in the monthly *Jeshurun,* Volume XIV, nos. 1-2.
10. Herman Schwab, *The History of Orthodox Jewry in Germany.*
11. Cf. Geiger, *Wissenschaftliche Zeitschrift fuer juedische Theologie,* Volume II, pp. 352 ff.
12. Drachman, *op. cit.,* p. 219.
13. Philip Bloch, *Memoir of Heinrich Graetz,* prefatory to the index volume (VI) of the American edition, p. 18.

14. Graetz obtained his Ph.D. degree in 1845 from the University of Jena.
15. In this letter, dated July 19, 1846, declining Geiger's invitation to attend this rabbinical conference, Mannheimer wrote: "Out of my innermost conviction I must express the very gravest doubts that the meeting to which you had the kindness to invite me will bear rich fruit. The Rabbinical Assembly has become the platform of a party and has consequently begun to adopt an attitude of compromise towards the fundamental principles of the day . . . Do you really suppose that a few trite remarks will dispose of the problem of the 'mixed marriage,' the 'personal Messiah,' the 'celebration' or 'rest' interpretation of the Sabbath Law? Have you not considered that if I am to allow one thing, I must have the corresponding power to prohibit the other? And can you really believe that I will participate in this work of destruction? No, I am of no use to you and you must thank me if I withdraw and stay where I am, when I would anyhow be one of a minority, if not altogether alone."
16. "Samson Raphael Hirsch—The Man and His Thought," *Conservative Judaism*, Volume XIII, Winter, 1959, p. 36.
17. S. R. Hirsch, *Die Religion im Bunde mit dem Fortschritt. Von einem Schwarzen.*
18. *Tradition*, Spring 1960, Volume I, no. 2, p. 299.
19. According to Jakob Rosenheim, *Samson Raphael Hirsch's Cultural Ideal and Our Times*, pp. 19 ff., a scrutiny in 1890 of the school lists, which were accurately kept and published by the Pupils' Association, indicated that complete success in the religious sense was achieved with 60 per cent of the boys, and even a higher percentage among the girls.
20. This view was called in Germany "Denkglaeubigkeit," which may be translated "intellectual or enlightened Orthodoxy," although Hirsch himself used the term "Torah" as the all-embracing name for Judaism.
21. Dayan Dr. I. Grunfeld, *Judaism Eternal*, Volume I, p. 37.
22. *Erste Mitteilungen aus Naftali's Briefwechsel*, and *Zweite Mitteilungen aus einem Briefwechsel ueber die neueste juedische Literatur.*
23. Wohlgemuth, *op. cit.*, p. 37.
24. Salo W. Baron, *A Social and Religious History of the Jews*, Volume II, p. 254.
25. The introduction of confirmation is attributed to Israel Jacobson, a man of wealth and influence, an official of the Duke of Brunswick's Treasure and president of the Berlin "Temple."
26. The "Verein der Reformfreunde" published in the *Frankfurter Zeitung* of July 15, 1843, and in *Der Israelit des Neunzehnten Jahrhunderts* of the same year, articles in which the abolition of circumcision and the renunciation of historical Judaism in its entirety were declared necessary, and a sort of Jewish church, based on Mosaic monotheism, was recommended.
27. S. A. Hirsch, "Jewish Philosophy of Religion and Samson Raphael Hirsch," *The Jewish Quarterly Review*, 1890, Volume II, p. 124.
28. *Ethics of the Fathers*, 2:2.
29. E.g., Eduard Gans, Moses Moser, Eleazar Liberman and others. Cf. Heinrich Graetz, *op. cit.*, Volume V., p. 587.
30. This appeared in a work which Hirsch left in manuscript form at the time of his death—a translation and explanation of the prayer book which was published posthumously under the title *Uebersetzung und Erklaerung zu Israels Gebeten* (Translation and Explanation of Israel's Prayers).
31. About that time, the Jewish press gradually became an important factor as

a medium of intellectual communication. Under Ludwig Philippson's editorship, the *Allgemeine Zeitung des Judentums* (1837-1921) strove to represent all interests of all strata, educated and uneducated alike. In 1937 its successor, the *CV Zeitung* in Berlin, published a special issue to commemorate the centenary of this first successful Jewish weekly. It was followed in 1840 by the *Archives Israélites de France* and in 1844 by the *Univers Israélite* in Paris. In London, *The Jewish Chronicle* was started in 1841, and in Mainz the *Israelit* in 1860.

32. S. R. Hirsch, *Gesemmelte Schriften,* edited by N. Hirsch, 6 vols. Frankfurt a/Main, 1902-1912. At present a Hebrew edition is contemplated, in addition to the classic Hebrew version of the *Nineteen Letters* by M. S. Aronsohn in Vilna.

Beginnings of American Judaism

1. Moshe Davis, "Jewish Religious Life and Institutions in America" in *The Jews, Their History, Culture and Religion* edited by Louis Finkelstein, pp. 364-5. See also Joseph Blau, *American Jewish Yearbook*, 1956.
2. For a full-length sketch of Gershon Mendes Seixas see David De Sola Pool, *Portraits Etched in Stone*, pp. 344-375.
3. Nathan Glazer, *American Judaism*, p. 23.
4. For a fascinating account of some of these Western communities see Jacob Rader Marcus, *Memoirs of American Jews*, 1775-1865, pp. 58-87. See also Morris U. Schappes, *Documentary History of the Jews in the United States*, p. 223.
5. Hyman Grinstein, *The Rise of the Jewish Community of New York*.
6. Blau, *op. cit.*
7. Davis, *op. cit.*, p. 366. See also article by Emily Solis-Cohen in *The Universal Jewish Encyclopedia*, Volume VI, p. 588.

Isaac Mayer Wise

1. *Selected Writings of Isaac M. Wise*, p. 59.
2. *Ibid.,* p. 77.
3. *The Reform Movement in Judaism*, p. 477.
4. *The Occident*, Volume VIII, nos. 5, 10, 12 (August 1850-March 1851).
5. *Asmonean*, Volume IX, nos. 22, 23 (March 17, 24, 1854).
6. *Reminiscences*, p. 149.
7. See *Occident*, Volume XII, nos. 1-9 (April-December, 1854); *Asmonean*, January-March, 1854.
8. *Israelite*, Volume II, no. 18 (November 9, 1855).
9. *Ibid.,* Volume XI, no. 17.
10. *Sinai to Cincinnati*, p. 175.
11. *Ibid.,* p. 178.
12. *Ibid.,* p. 300.
13. *Essence of Judaism*, p. 8.
14. *Sinai to Cincinnati*, p. 30.
15. *Judaism—Its Doctrines and Duties*, pp. 3 and 4.
16. *Occident*, Volume I, no. 12 (March, 1849).
17. *Jewish Theology*, p. 18.
18. *Ibid.,* p. 17.

Forerunners of Conservative Judaism

1. Sabato Morais, "Can We Change Jewish Ritual?" in *Tradition and Change*, edited by Mordecai Waxman, p. 64.

2. Moshe Davis, *Yahadut Amerika Be-hitpathutah.* I am indebted to Dr. Davis' pioneer work for much of the material in this introductory essay. See also his chapter "Jewish Religious Life and Institutions in America," in *The Jews,* edited by Louis Finkelstein, pp. 365-397.
3. Bertram Wallace Korn, *Eventful Years and Experiences,* Chapter 7.
4. Philip Cowen, *Memoirs of an American Jew.* For biographical sketches of Solomon Solis-Cohen and Meir Sulzberger see Davis, *op. cit.,* pp. 71-83.
5. David Philipson, *My Life as an American and a Jew,* p. 23.
6. Moshe Davis, *Yahadut Amerika Be-hitpathutah,* pp. 71-83.
7. Bernard Drachman, *The Unfailing Light,* Chapter 20.
8. Abraham Karp, "New York Chooses a Chief Rabbi," *Publication of the American Jewish Historical Society,* March, 1955, pp. 129-198.
9. Davis, *op. cit.,* pp. 277-285.
10. Cyrus Adler, *I Have Considered The Days,* pp. 242-244.

Rise of Modern Hebrew Literature

1. Simon Halkin, *Modern Hebrew Literature,* Chapter 2.
2. See Meyer Waxman, *A History of Hebrew Literature.* I have found the detailed summaries of the great works in Hebrew and Yiddish literature in Volumes III and IV particularly helpful. See also Hillel Bavli, "The Modern Renaissance of Hebrew Literature" in *The Jews,* Chapter 12.
3. Solomon Schechter, *Studies in Judaism,* Chapter 2. See also Shalom Spiegel *Hebrew Reborn,* Chapter 5.
4. Nachman Krochmal, *Moreh Nebuche Hazman,* edited by Ravidowitz, Chapter 1.
5. Morris R. Cohen, *Reflections of a Wondering Jew,* pp. 66-68.
6. Waxman, *op. cit.,* Volume III, pp. 489-500.
7. *Ibid.,* Chapter 5.
8. Sol Liptzin, *Jewish Book Annual,* 1952-53.
9. Spiegel, *op. cit.,* pp. 192-196. See also Louis Greenberg, *The Jews in Russia,* p. 124, and the lengthy introduction to Dimitry Pisarev, *Selected Philosophical, Social and Political Essays.*
10. Waxman, *op. cit.,* pp. 234-255. See also Spiegel, *op. cit.,* pp. 174-187, and Ahron Opher in *Universal Jewish Encyclopedia,* Volume V, pp. 63-65.
11. Spiegel, *op. cit.,* pp. 199-205.
12. Waxman, *op. cit.,* Volume III, pp. 278-298; 345-346; Volume IV, pp. 341-350. See also Joseph Klausner, *Historia Shel Ha-safrut Ha-Ivrit Ha-hadaskah,* Volume V, pp. 14-231.
13. Waxman, *op. cit.,* Volume IV, pp. 44-54.

Development of Yiddish Literature

1. A. A. Roback, *The Story of Yiddish Literature,* pp. 51-56. See also Yudel Mark, "Yiddish Literature," in *The Jews,* edited by Louis Finkelstein, Volume II, pp. 859-862; and Meyer Waxman, *op. cit.,* Volume II, Chapter 12.
2. Nahum Minkoff, "Old Yiddish Literature," in *Past and Present,* Volume III, pp. 145 ff.
3. *Ibid.,* pp. 146-147. See also Waxman, *op. cit.,* pp. 631-632.
4. Hasye Cooperman, "The Bube Maaseh," in *Jewish Heritage,* Volume I, No. I. See also article on "Elias Levita" by Joshua Bloch in *Universal Jewish Encyclopedia,* Volume VI, pp. 639-640.

5. Naomi Ben-Asher, "Literature of a Vanished World," in *Midcentury: An Anthology of Jewish Life and Culture in Our Times* edited by Harold Ribalow, pp. 295-304.

6. On the relation of Ḥasidism to the development of Yiddish literature, see Samuel Niger, "Yiddish Literature in the Past Two Hundred Years," in *Past and Present*, pp. 166-168; and his article *"Vegn dem Onhoib fun der Neier Yiddische Literature,"* in *Jewish Book Annual*, 1944-45, p. 37.

7. See *The Golden Mountain, Marvelous Tales of Rabbi Israel Baal Shem and of His Great Grandson, Rabbi Nachman retold from Hebrew, Yiddish, and German Sources* by Meyer Levin.

8. Sketches of the life and work of Israel Axenfeld and Solomon Ettinger can be found in Niger, *Past and Present*, pp. 176 ff., and of Axenfeld, Ettinger, and Isaac Meir Dick in Waxman, Volume IV, pp. 479-485.

9. Shalom Spiegel, *Hebrew Reborn*, Chapter 11. Works of Mendele available in English include *Fishke the Lame*, translated by Angelo S. Rappoport (London, 1928); *The Nag*, translated by Moshe Spiegel (Beechhurst Press, New York, 1955); *The Parasite*, translated by Gerald Stillman (Thomas Yoseloff, New York, 1956); *The Travels and Adventure of Benjamin the Third*, translated by Moshe Spiegel (Schocken, New York, 1949).

10. A. A. Roback, *I. L. Peretz, Psychologist of Literature*. See also *Stories and Pictures*, translated by H. Frank; Maurice Samuel, *Prince of the Ghetto; Peretz*, translated and edited by Sol Liptzin; and Philip Goodman in *Jewish Book Annual*, 1952-3.

11. For the details of Peretz's early background in Zamosc, see *Yivo Annual*.

12. On the Czernowitz Conference, see "Peretz und Yiddish," in *Jewish Book Annual*, 1951-52.

Sholom Aleichem

1. Maurice Samuel, *The World of Sholom Aleichem*, p. 22.

2. Letter written by Sholom Aleichem to Israel Cohen in 1908, quoted by Joseph Leftwich in *The Jewish Advocate*, March 12, 1959.

3. *The Day* (Yiddish), April 12, 1959, from an article by B. Z. Goldberg.

4. Samuel, *op. cit.*, pp. 11 and 12.

5. Sol Liptzin, *Congress Bi-Weekly*, March 16, 1959.

Rise of Jewish Nationalism

1. *The Zionist Idea* edited by Arthur Hertzberg. See also Mordecai M. Kaplan, *The Greater Judaism in the Making*.

2. For Hess' concept of Jewish nationalism see *Rome and Jerusalem: A Study in Jewish Nationalism* by Moses Hess, translated with notes by Meyer Waxman, and *Life and Opinions of Moses Hess* by Isaiah Berlin.

3. Salo W. Baron, *Modern Nationalism and Religion*, Chapter 7. See also Baron, "The Modern Age" in *Great Ages and Ideas of the Jewish People* edited by Leo Schwarz, pp. 315-484.

4. *Road to Freedom: Writings and Addresses by Leon Pinsker*, with an introduction by B. Netanyahu, contains the full text of *Auto-Emancipation* as well as a selection of Pinsker's correspondence. See also Mordecai Kaplan, *op. cit.*, and Martin Buber, *Israel and Palestine*, pp. 123-142.

5. Alex Bein, "The Origin of the Term and Concept 'Zionism'," in *Herzl Year Book*, Volume II, pp. 1-28.

6. Chaim Weizmann, *Trial and Error*, pp. 34-38.

7. Josef Fraenkel, "Colonel Albert E. W. Goldsmid and Theodor Herzl" in *Herzl Year Book*, Volume I, pp. 145-153.

8. *Rabbi Samuel Mohliver*, compiled by M. Ben-Zvi. This pamphlet includes an essay on his life and work by Rabbi J. L. Fishman, and extracts from his Zionist writings. See also Hertzberg, *op. cit.*

9. The story of the *Bilu* movement is told in detail in Maurice Samuel, *Harvest in the Desert*.

10. For the life and thought of Ahad Ha-am, see Leon Simon, *Ahad Ha'am* (1960); *Essays, Letters, Memoirs* by Ahad Ha-am, translated and edited by Leon Simon; and *Selected Essays of Ahad Ha-am*, translated by L. Simon.

Glossary

Aggadah:
  The part of the Talmud which includes stories, chronicles, proverbs and epigrams. Complements the *Halakhah* of the Talmud, which is completely devoted to law.
Ahad Ha-am (Hebrew, "one of the people," pen name of Asher Ginzberg; 1856-1927):
  Hebrew essayist and philosopher of cultural or spiritual Zionism. Born in the Ukraine, he lived and exerted influence in Odessa (1896-1908), London (1908-1922), and finally in Tel Aviv, where he spent the last five years of his life. He opposed Herzl's political Zionism, holding that the revival of a Jewish nation must be based on the revitalization of Judaism.
Alliance Israélite Universelle:
  A French Jewish organization organized in 1860 to protect Jewish civil and religious liberties. Still extant, it maintains a network of Jewish schools in the Middle East and North Africa.
Ashkenazim (Hebrew, "Germans"):
  Term used to describe Jews who settled in Central and Eastern Europe. They have their own characteristic rituals and pronunciation of Hebrew, which differs from that of the Sephardim, or Jews who settled around the Mediterranean basin.
Balfour Declaration (November 2, 1917):
  Official document issued by British Foreign Secretary Lord Arthur Balfour (1848-1930), which gave international recognition to Zionist aims. It declared that the British government favored "the establishment in Palestine of a national home for the Jewish people," and was issued with the support of the

Allied Powers and the backing of President Woodrow Wilson.

bet hamidrash (Hebrew, "house of study"):
School or synagogue where students gathered for study, discussion, and prayer.

Bilu (plural, *Biluim:* from initials of *Bet Yaakov lekhu ve-nelkhah,* "O house of Jacob, come ye and let us go"):
Name given to first Zionist pioneers to emigrate to Palestine (1882) in flight from pogroms in Russia.

Buber, Martin B. (1878-   ):
Religious philosopher, interpreter of *Hasidism* to Western world, and particularly noted for "I-thou" philosophy of religion as dialogue between man and God. Since 1938, professor at the Hebrew University in Jerusalem and now Professor Emeritus.

Conservative Judaism:
The middle-of-the-road religious trend in American Jewish life which seeks to preserve the best aspects of Jewish tradition while permitting changes in customs and ceremonies in consonance with the changing social, economic, religious, and moral needs of the Jewish people. Pioneers of this school of thought in the United States were Sabato Morais, Solomon Schechter, and Cyrus Adler.

Diaspora (Greek, "dispersion"):
Term applied since Biblical time to Jewish settlements outside of Palestine.

din (Hebrew, "judgment"):
Term applied to a law, legal decision, or lawsuit. Hence, *bet din* ("house of law") for rabbinical court.

Emancipation:
Term used to describe the great social and cultural changes that began in Western Europe in the eighteenth century. As new concepts of freedom, religious tolerance, and human equality took hold, the disabilities imposed on Jews were gradually removed. Emancipated from the ghettos to which they were formerly confined, Jews now began to enjoy the civil and political liberties granted all citizens of England, France, and other Western countries.

Enlightenment (see *Haskalah*).

Galut (Hebrew, *Golah,* "exile"):
Lands where Jews lived outside of Palestine. Usually referred to a forced exile, while living in Diaspora was voluntary.

Geiger, Abraham (1810-1874):
One of the founders of the Reform movement in Germany.

His principal scholarly works dealt with the Bible and its translations, the Sadducees and Pharisees, and other aspects of Jewish history.

Gemarah:

A detailed commentary by later scholars on the Mishnah. The Talmud is composed of the Mishnah, which is mainly the interpretation of the Biblical law, and the later Gemarah.

ghetto:

Originally, quarters set up by law to be inhabited only by Jews. Used today to describe any area inhabited exclusively by Jews, though it has lost its legal connotation.

Graetz, Heinrich (1817-1891):

German historian, noted for his eleven-volume *History of the Jews*, which was the first scientific Jewish history to be based on thousands of source documents.

hakham:

Title given officiating rabbi in Sephardi communities.

Halakhah (Hebrew, "law"):

The legal part of Talmudic and later Jewish literature, as contrasted with *Aggadah*, the non-legal and narrative portions.

Hasidism:

Religious and social movement founded in the eighteenth century by Israel Baal Shem Tov. In contrast with the stress on scholarship and Talmud study, *Hasidism* emphasized emotion and love of God. It appealed to the Jewish masses by teaching that even the ignorant person is beloved by God, and can serve Him with joy and prayer. There were many *tzaddikim* or *Hasidic* teachers, including Dov Ber of Mezhirich, Levi Yitzhak of Berdichev, and Shneour Zalman of Ladi.

Haskalah (Hebrew, "enlightenment"):

The movement, which began in Berlin, to spread modern European culture among Jews (c. 1750-1880). With the breakdown of the ghettos, the *maskilim* (those advocating and practicing Enlightenment) held that complete emancipation would come to Jews only as they absorbed Western civilization and modernized and Westernized their religious customs and practices.

Hess, Moses (1812-1875):

First articulate Jewish nationalist in modern Europe, and one of the first exponents of political Zionism. His *Rome and Jerusalem* (1862), an early Zionist classic, asserted that "the Jews are a nation, destined to be resurrected with all other civilized nations."

Hirsch, Baron Maurice de (1831-1896):

German railroad magnate and philanthropist, who contributed generously to many Jewish causes, including the Alliance Israélite Universelle. Hirsch set up the Jewish Colonization Association (I.C.A.), which settled Jews on the land in Argentina and Brazil, and subsidized vocational training and cooperative credit institutions in Russia, Austria, and elsewhere. He also supported colonies in Palestine.

Jabotinsky, Vladimir (1880-1940):
Writer and founder of Revisionist Zionism. He parted company with official Zionism in 1921, calling for immediate creation of a Jewish state on both sides of the Jordan.

Kabbalists:
Followers of *Kabbalah*, the mystical religious stream in Judaism, which went through many stages. The *Zohar* (thirteenth century) is one of its most important books, and Isaac Luria (1534-1572) of the Safed Brotherhood one of its major teachers.

Klausner, Joseph (1874-1958):
Lithuanian-born scholar and from 1919 professor at the Hebrew University in Jerusalem. Author of many important studies on modern Hebrew literature, Messianism, Jesus and Christianity.

Levin, Shemaryahu (1867-1935):
Writer, orator, and Zionist leader. A member of the World Zionist Executive from 1911 to 1918, he promoted Zionism in the U. S., England, and Canada during and after World War I.

Liberal Judaism (see Reform)

Lovers of Zion (Hebrew, *Hovevei Zion*):
Pre-Zionist societies organized in the late nineteenth century in Russia, Poland, Rumania, and England to purchase land and encourage Jewish settlement in Palestine. These groups were finally superseded by the World Zionist Organization.

Magnes, Judah L. (1877-1948):
American rabbi and first president of the Hebrew University (1925-1948). Active in *Ihud* movement, which advocated Arab-Jewish understanding and a binationalist Jewish and Arab commonwealth in Palestine.

maskil (plural, *maskilim*):
Those engaged in the *Haskalah*, who sought to educate themselves in Western culture.

Mendele Mocher Sephorim (pen name of Sholom Jacob Abramowitsch, c. 1836-1917):
His early writing was in Hebrew, but he later adopted Yiddish

as his principal medium of literary expression. His realistic portraits of ghetto dwellers established him as a writer of first rank
of a new and promising Yiddish literature.

Midrash:

A specific kind of textual interpretation used by the ancient
rabbis to teach the people the meaning of certain Biblical passages. Illustrative parables, stories, and poetic interpretations
are used. Over a hundred collections of Midrashim exist.

Mitnagdim:

Orthodox Jews opposed to the *Hasidic* movement.

mitzvot (singular, *mitzvah*, "commandment"):

The 613 obligations or duties listed in the Torah, which are
traditionally regarded as representing an opportunity to fulfill
one's duty to God and man. A person is said to have "earned a
mitzvah" by performing a good deed.

Motzkin, Leo (1867-1938):

Zionist leader and follower of Herzl. Served as chairman of the
Zionist Executive from 1925 to 1933.

Nordau, Max (1849-1923):

Hungarian-born Zionist leader, who spent most of his active
years in France. In the early days of Zionism, he was the most
dominant figure next to Herzl. He had an important role in
drafting the Basel program at the first Zionist Congress, and
delivered major addresses at the first nine Congresses.

Orthodox Judaism:

Adherence to accepted traditional Judaism. Has come to mean
today strict adherence to Jewish laws and practices.

Pale of Settlement:

Certain districts of Czarist Russia (in Poland, Lithuania, White
Russia, Ukraine, Bessarabia, and Crimea) where Jews were
given permission to reside. Abolished only after the overthrow
of the Czar in 1917.

Peretz, Isaac Leib (1852-1915):

One of the founding fathers of modern Hebrew and Yiddish
literature. Especially famed for his Yiddish short stories, his
tales of *Hasidism* and of the common people.

Pharisaic Judaism:

Judaism taught by the Pharisees, a Jewish religious and political
party during the Second Temple period, who believed that the
written law had to be supplemented by the oral law. The
Pharisees are misrepresented in Christian literature as hypocrites who adhere to the letter rather than the spirit of the law.
Actually they were not hypocrites but liberals who felt that

ethical and ritual law while binding was subject to the interpretations of the religious authorities of the age.

Pinsker, Leon (1821-1891):

Physician and communal worker in Odessa, and active in
Lovers of Zion movement. After pogroms of 1881, wrote *Auto-*
Emancipation, a pamphlet advocating the re-establishment of a
Jewish state.

pogrom (Russian, "destruction"):

Term used to describe any organized massacre or attempt to
annihilate a specific group of people. Applied particularly to
attacks against Jews in Russia, and has since been used to describe all such acts of violence.

Reconstructionism:

A religious movement founded by Mordecai M. Kaplan and his
disciples in 1934, which interprets Judaism as an evolving religious civilization, emphasizing a non-supernaturalistic approach
to Jewish religious belief and practice.

Reform Judaism:

The liberal religious movement originating in Germany, which
seeks to adapt Judaism to meet contemporary conditions. Emphasis is on prophetic ideals and the universal values of Judaism
as against its legalistic and ritualistic aspects.

Revisionism:

A militant Zionist party founded by Vladimir Jabotinsky
which advocated resistance to the British Mandate and the
establishment of a Jewish state on both sides of the Jordan.

Rothschild, Baron Edmond de (1845-1934):

Head of Rothschild banking house in France. Established and
supported some forty agricultural settlements in Palestine
which were eventually supervised by P.I.C.A. under the direction of his son James de Rothschild.

Samuel, Herbert L. (1870-   ):

British statesman and philosopher. His memorandum to the
British Cabinet in 1914 paved the way for Balfour Declaration.
Served as first High Commissioner for Palestine (1920-1925).

Sanhedrin:

Greek term applied to the higher courts of rabbinic law, which
legislated in the latter period of the Second Temple in Palestine. The Great Sanhedrin had seventy-one members, while
several lesser ones had twenty-three each. The president was
called *nasi* and his deputy *ab bet din*.

Sephardim (Hebrew, "Spanish"):

Jews of Spanish and Portuguese origin, whose customs, rituals,
synagogue services, and pronunciation of Hebrew differ in

some ways from those of the Ashkenazim or Jews of Germany
and Eastern Europe.

Shneour, Zalman (1887-   ):
One of the foremost modern Hebrew poets and novelists,
especially known for his works on Jewish life in the Pale of
Settlement, his cycle of tales *People of Shklov*, and his novel
Noah Pandre.

Sokolow, Nahum (1860-1936):
Zionist leader and Hebrew journalist. Was General Secretary
of the World Zionist Organization from 1905-1919, played a
key role in negotiations leading to Balfour Declaration, and
acted as chairman of Zionist Executive from 1921-1931. He
succeeded Weizmann briefly as president of the World Zionist
Organization between 1931-1935.

Syrkin, Nahman (1867-1924):
One of the founders of Poale Zion, Labor Zionist party.

Talmud:
Encyclopedic work containing the discussions and interpretations of Jewish law as found in Bible and Mishnah by generations of scholars and jurists in the academies of Palestine and
Babylonia. The purely legal sections are referred to as *Halakhah*, the non-legal as *Aggadah*. Both the Palestinian and Baby-
lonian Talmuds furnish much information on the religious,
communal, and social life of Jews between the second century
B.C.E. and the fifth century C.E.

Torah (Hebrew, "teaching):
In its restricted sense the term is used to cover the Five Books
of the Pentateuch. In its broader meaning Torah refers to all
basic Jewish teaching.

yeshiva:
Traditional Jewish school devoted primarily to study of the
Talmud and rabbinic literature.

Yishuv:
The Jewish community in Palestine.

Zangwill, Israel (1864-1926):
Anglo-Jewish author, most famed for his *Children of the
Ghetto, The Melting Pot,* and *The King of the Schnorrers.*

Zionism:
Movement to secure Jewish return to *Eretz Yisrael,* the ancestral homeland. *Political* Zionism, led by Theodor Herzl, sought
to achieve this by international negotiations; *cultural* Zionism,
fathered by Ahad Ha-am, concerned itself with the revitalization of Palestine as a cultural center for Jewish life and
thought.

*About the Contributors

NORMAN BENTWICH is the author of *Solomon Schechter, Philo, Josephus, Hellenism, The Religious Foundations of Internationalism,* and other works.

LOUIS FALSTEIN is an Anglo-Jewish writer whose works include *Face of a Hero* and *Sole Survivor.*

M. Z. FRANK is the author of *Sound the Great Trumpet,* and a frequent contributor to the Anglo-Jewish press.

EDWARD W. JELENKO is on the staff of the American Friends of the Hebrew University. From 1942 to 1956 he served as Director of European Intelligence Research and Analysis of the United States Department of State.

ALFRED JOSPE is National Director of Program and Resources for the B'nai B'rith Hillel Foundations. He is the author of *Religion and Myth in Jewish Philosophy, Handbook for Student Leaders,* and co-author of *A College Guide for Jewish Youth.*

ISRAEL KNOX, Associate Professor of Philosophy at New York University, is author of *The Aesthetic Theories of Kant, Hegel, and Schopenhauer,* and *Rabbi in America: The Story of Isaac Mayer Wise.*

MILTON R. KONVITZ is Professor of Industrial and Labor Relations and Law at Cornell University, and author of *Fundamental Liberties of a Free People, The Constitution and Civil Rights,* and articles on these topics in the *Encyclopedia Brittanica.*

MARVIN LOWENTHAL is Professor of Literature at Brandeis University, and author of *A World Passed By, The Jews of Germany,* etc. He is the editor of *Diaries of Theodor Herzl* and *Life and Letters of Henrietta Szold.*

*The contributors are identified by their occupations at the time of the writing of the essays

SIMON NOVECK, formerly Rabbi of the Park Avenue Synagogue in New York, and former Director of the B'nai B'rith Department of Adult Jewish Education, is author of *Adult Education in the Modern Synagogue* and editor of *Judaism and Psychiatry* and of the B'nai B'rith Great Books Series.

TAMAR DE SOLA POOL has long been active in national and international Zionist affairs, especially in Hadassah, of which she was President.

CECIL ROTH is Reader in Jewish Studies at Oxford University, and author of over twenty-five books, including *A Short History of the Jewish People, The Marranos, The Jewish Contribution to Civilization*, and others.

Index

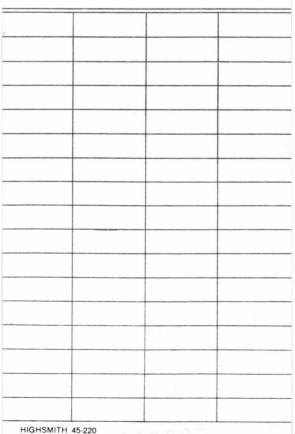

DATE DUE